A Textbook of Body Measurement For Sports and Health Education

ANTHROPOMETRICA

Edited by

Kevin Norton & Tim Olds

CBS

CBS PUI **BUTORS**

CBS Publishers   ISBN : 81-239-1350-8 Hard Cover
CBS Publishers   ISBN : 81-239-1310-9 Paper Back
UNSW Press   ISBN : 0-86840-223-0

First Indian reprint : 2006

First published : 1996
Reprint : 2000

This edition has been published in India by arrangement with
University of New South Wales Press, Australia

Sales Territory : India, Bhutan and Nepal

Publishing Director : Vinod K. Jain

Published by :
Satish Kumar Jain for CBS Publishers & Distributors,
4596/1-A, 11 Darya Ganj, New Delhi - 110 002 (India)
E-mail: cbspubs@vsnl.com • Website: www.cbspd.com

Branch Office :
2975, 17th Cross, K.R. Road, Bansankari 2nd Stage, Bangalore-70
Fax : 080-26771680 • E-mail : cbsbng@vsnl.net

Printed at :
S.D.R. Printers, Delhi - 110 094, India

CONTENTS

Section 2 Tools for analysis

Chapter 8

Two, Three and Four-compartment Chemical Models of

Robert Withers, Joe Laforgia, Steven Heysfield, Ai-Mian Wang and Robyn Pillans

Section 3 Applications for Anthropometry

Chapter 9

Shelley Kay

Chapter 10

Kamal Kothiyal

Preface

Anthropometry is a very old science, and, like many old sciences, has followed a variety of paths. The diversity of anthropometric paths is both its richness and its bane. While preparing this book, we have been struck by the fact that armies of anthropometrists working in different areas have been marching in parallel without ever meeting. These groups include nutritionists, ergonomists, psychologists and exercise scientists, among others. Ergonomics, for example, has developed a detailed repertory of sites and techniques which resemble those used in exercise science, although relying more heavily on soft tissue areas. Most ergonomists would, however, be unaware of the anthropometry work done in other sciences, just as many other scientists would, for the most part, be unfamiliar with ergonomic anthropometry.

One consequence of multiple anthropometric traditions has been a lack of standardisation in the identification of measurement sites, and in measurement techniques. For example, there are over fourteen different definitions in the literature of how to measure the waist-to-hip ratio, which is nonetheless considered a major index of cardiovascular risk. The locations and names of the skinfold sites have been of great concern, particularly those in the iliac and abdominal regions. Stature, the most basic of all anthropometric measurements, has been determined using free standing, semi-stretch and stretch techniques, and with a variety of measuring instruments. This lack of standardisation makes comparisons across time and space frustratingly difficult. One of the major aims of this book has been to develop a basic anthropometric profile which constitutes a consensus, a profile which can be used throughout the world. In an age where anywhere in the world is only an email away, this will make possible the establishment of on-line electronic national and international anthropometric databases. An Australian anthropometric database, with facilities for electronic downloading, has been functional for two years now, and continues to grow.

A second aim has been to create a textbook containing core topics for students of anthropometry, and to allow them to be assessed and accredited. Australia's first national accreditation scheme was set up in 1994 by the Australian Sports Commission. This important quality control dimension of anthropometry is reinforced by a meticulous description of techniques, target error tolerances and analytical methods. These guidelines have been adopted by sports institutes and universities, and endorsed by supporting professional organisations.

Finally, we want to emphasis the diversity of applications of anthropometry – in nutrition, health, psychology, ergonomics and sport. There are other chapters which we would have liked to include – on the application of anthropometry to children and the elderly, medical aspects of growth and development, the secular trend, biomechanics, the representation of the body in art and cinema throughout history, and on economic aspects of height and mass. These will have to wait for a second edition.

There are many people whom we should thank for their help in preparing this book. We would like to especially thank our graphic designers Sophia Arab and Andrew Medhurst, and the students who have tirelessly helped us in collating information and checking manuscripts: Anthony Gillespie, Eric Hunter and Rod Russell. Thanks also to Sen Van Ly and Doanh Dang for their invaluable technical assistance.

Kevin Norton, PhD
Tim Olds, PhD

Contributors

Peter J. Abernethy
Lecturer
Department of Human Movement Studies
The University of Queensland
St Lucia QLD 4072
Australia

Linda Baines
Department of Human Movement Studies
The University of Queensland
St Lucia QLD 4072
Australia

Kim Birchall
Human Bioenergetics Laboratory
The University of New South Wales
PO Box 88 Oatley NSW 2223
Australia

Robert W. Bryant
Professional Officer
Department of Human Movement Studies
The University of Queensland
St Lucia QLD 4072
Australia

Robert G. Carlyon
Professional Officer
Department of Human Movement Studies
The University of Queensland
St Lucia QLD 4072
Australia

J. E. Lindsay Carter
Emeritus Professor
Department of Exercise and Nutritional Sciences
San Diego State University
San Diego CA 92182
USA

Melissa Clough
Human Bioenergetics Laboratory
The University of New South Wales
PO Box 88 Oatley NSW 2223
Australia

Neil P. Craig
Senior Sports Scientist
The South Australian Sports Institute
PO Box 219 Brooklyn Park SA 5032
Australia

Briony Dickerson
Human Bioenergetics Laboratory
The University of New South Wales
PO Box 88 Oatley NSW 2223
Australia

Loretta Downie
Human Bioenergetics Laboratory
The University of New South Wales
PO BOx 88 Oatley NSW 2223
Australia

Barbara Eden
Lecturer
School of Sport and Leisure Studies
The University of New South Wales
PO Box 88 Oatley NSW 2223
Australia

Christopher J. Gore
Co-ordinator
Laboratory Standards Assistance Scheme
Australian Institute of Sport
PO Box 21 Henley Beach SA 5022
Australia

Steven B. Heymsfield
Professor of Medicine
Weight Control Unit
Obesity Research Centre
St Luke's–Roosevelt Hospital
Columbia University College of Physicians and Surgeons
1090 Amsterdam Ave, New York NY 10025
USA

Shelley J. Kay
Lecturer
Human Bioenergetics Laboratory
The University of New South Wales
PO Box 88 Oatley NSW 2223
Australia

Deborah A. Kerr
Post-doctoral Fellow
Department of Medicine
The University of Western Australia
4th floor, G Block
QEII Medical Centre
Nedlands WA 6009
Australia

Kamal Kothiyal
Lecturer
Department of Safety Science
The University of New South Wales
PO Box 1 Kensington NSW 2033
Australia

Joe LaForgia
Lecturer
School of Pharmacy and Medical Sciences
University of South Australia
Holbrooks Rd Underdale SA 5032
Australia

Elizabeth L.A. Lowe
Lecturer
Human Bioenergetics Laboratory
The University of New South Wales
PO Box 88 Oatley NSW 2223
Australia

Sen Van Ly
Professional Officer
Human Bioenergetics Laboratory
The University of New South Wales
PO Box 88 Oatley NSW 2223
Australia

Michael J. Marfell-Jones
Dean
Faculty of Science and Health Sciences
Central Institute of Technology
Private Bag 39 807
Wellington Mail Centre
New Zealand

Michelle Neill
Department of Human Movement Studies
The University of Queensland
St Lucia QLD 4072
Australia

Kevin I. Norton
Associate Professor
School of Physical Education, Exercise and
Sports Studies
University of South Australia
Holbrooks Rd Underdale SA 5032
Australia

Timothy S. Olds
Lecturer
Human Bioenergetics Laboratory
The University of New South Wales
PO Box 88 Oatley NSW 2223
Australia

Scott C. Olive
Lecturer
Human Bioenergetics Laboratory
The University of New South Wales
PO Box 88 Oatley NSW 2223
Australia

David G. Pederson
Senior Lecturer
Faculty of Information Sciences and Engineering
The University of Canberra
PO Box 1 Belconnen ACT 2616
Australia

Robyn K. Pillans
Head
Chemistry Department
Annesley College
89 Greenhill Rd
Wayville SA 5034
Australia

Zi-Mian Wang
Research Associate
Weight Control Unit
Obesity Research Centre
St Luke's–Roosevelt Hospital
Columbia University College of Physicians and
Surgeons
1090 Amsterdam Ave, New York NY 10025
USA

Nancy O. Whittingham
Senior Lecturer
School of Physical Education, Exercise and
Sports Studies
University of South Australia
Holbrooks Rd, Underdale SA 5032
Australia

Robert T. Withers
Reader in Exercise Physiology
School of Education
The Flinders University of South Australia
PO Box 2100
Adelaide SA 5001
Australia

The South Australian Sports Institute
PO Box 219
Brooklyn Park SA 5032
Australia

Sarah M. Woolford
Sports Scientist

measurement

&

measurement

t
e
c
h
n
i
q
u
e
s

Chapter 1
Essential Anatomy for Anthropometrists

Michael Marfell-Jones

1 Introduction

To become a competent anthropometrist, one needs to be conversant with the basic anatomy of the human body. The most obvious reason for this need is that the majority of anthropometric terms are derived from anatomical landmarks, but more importantly, a knowledge of anatomy is essential in facilitating the anthropometrist's search for landmarks and providing the theoretical support for the subjective decisions necessary in locating them.

This chapter is designed to introduce the reader to the human skeleton and to extend that knowledge into the realm of gross muscle structure so that the reader has a sound basic grasp of the two systems which contribute most to the natural gross shape or morphology of the body.

2 Terminology

An extremely attractive feature of studying anatomy is that the basic information does not alter with the advance of science. Certainly, small amounts of new knowledge come to light from time to time, but the bulk of what one learns won't change in the next 100 years, so only needs to be learnt once. The challenge is that anatomy has a language of its own and to gain any benefit from its study one has to learn the building blocks of the language – the anatomical terms. Once those terms are learnt, however, and their meaning understood, the human body becomes not only structurally familiar, but also functionally obvious. To facilitate this process, anatomical terms which need to be memorised are printed in **bold type**.

Modern anatomical terms are nearly all derived from Latin and Greek (since those were the languages of some of the most noted early anatomists). Those readers without the benefit of a classical education, however, will not be too disadvantaged and continual correct usage of any new terminology will rapidly make it familiar.

As well as learning the anatomical names of the basic individual skeletal and muscular structures of the body, the reader will also need to become familiar with the terms used to describe the position of one structure, or part of a structure, relative to another structure or part. This is essential in order to fully comprehend the three-dimensional nature of the human body and in order to pinpoint the very specific locations on the body referred to by anatomists and anthropometrists alike.

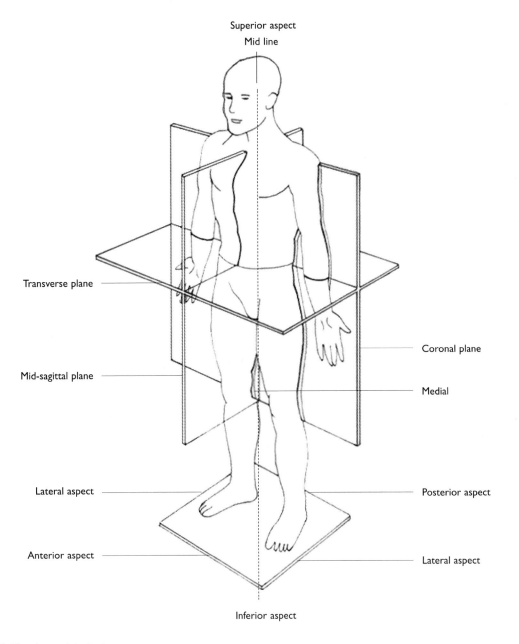

Superior aspect
Mid line

Transverse plane

Coronal plane

Mid-sagittal plane

Medial

Lateral aspect

Posterior aspect

Anterior aspect

Lateral aspect

Inferior aspect

Figure I The planes of the body

Figure 1 shows a human body in what is termed the "anatomical position". This is defined as the position of the living body standing erect with the arms by the sides and the palms facing forwards (Basmajian, 1982).

[All anatomical relational descriptions of body parts refer to this position irrespective of the position the body may be in at a given moment. For example, the knee is always anatomically inferior to (below) the hip, even though during the full extension phase of a handstand, the knee is functionally above the hip.]

The body can be divided along many planes, the three standard ones being

- the **sagittal** plane, which divides the body into right and left parts (when these are equal, the plane is a **mid-sagittal** one);
- the **coronal**, or **frontal** plane, which divides the body into front and back parts; and
- the **transverse** or **horizontal** plane, which divides the body into upper and lower parts.

These planes are shown in Figure 1. Many of the anatomical terms used to describe relative position are also shown in Figure 1, where their meanings are, in the main, obvious. These meanings are confirmed in Table 1, where their definitions are given. As can be seen, these terms come in reciprocal pairs.

Table 1 Anatomical terms and their definitions.

Term	Definition
superior	above
inferior	below
lateral	further from the centre line
medial	nearer the centre line
anterior (or ventral)	towards or at the front
posterior (or dorsal)	towards or at the back
proximal*	nearer the point of attachment to the trunk
distal*	further from the point of attachment to the trunk
superficial	nearer the surface
deep	further from the surface
ipsilateral	on the same side
contralateral	on the opposite side

* Note: "proximal" and "distal" are only used in relation to the limbs.

3 The skeleton

The skeleton can be considered as having two regions. Those bones that make up the central column of the body are said to be part of the **axial skeleton**. This is made up of:

- the bones of the **skull** and **lower jaw**
- the **vertebræ**
- the **ribs** and **sternum**

The bones of the skull and lower jaw, together with the first seven (**cervical**) vertebræ constitute the **head** and **neck** region of the body. The next twelve (**thoracic**) vertebræ, together with the ribs and the sternum, constitute the **thorax**. Below this region is the **abdomen**, whose bony components are the five **lumbar** vertebræ. The remaining vertebræ are fused together in two groups, the five **sacral** vertebræ making up the **sacrum** and the four **coccygeal** vertebræ making up the **coccyx**.

The lay terms for the four major appendages of the body are "arms" and "legs". Anatomically, however, these overall structures are referred to as **limbs**, "arm" and "leg" having more specific anatomical meanings which will be referred to later.

Each **upper limb** consists of:

- a **clavicle** and **scapula** which form almost half of the **pectoral girdle**
- an arm bone - the **humerus**
- two forearm bones - the **radius** and the **ulna**
- eight wrist or **carpal** bones
- five bones which make up the palm of the hand - the **metacarpals**
- fourteen finger bones or **phalanges**

Each **lower limb** consists of:

- an **innominate** or **hip bone**, forming half the **pelvic girdle**
- a thigh bone - the **femur**
- a knee cap - the **patella**
- two leg bones - the **tibia** and the **fibula**
- seven rear-foot or **tarsal** bones
- five **metatarsals** (corresponding to the metacarpals in the hand)
- fourteen **phalanges**

These bones are all depicted in Figures 2 and 3. The anthropometrist needs to learn their names by heart in preparation for learning the next level of detail - the bony landmarks. [There are other smaller bones in the body, for example the **ossicles**, found in the inner ear, and very small **sesamoid** bones, found in certain tendons, but these are not of major concern to the anthropometrist (except when measuring the foot width of someone with a bunion).]

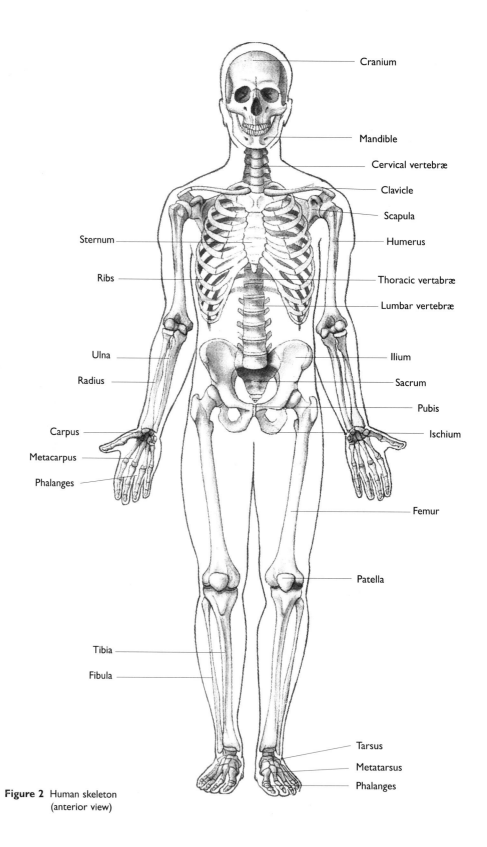

Cranium

Mandible

Cervical vertebræ

Clavicle

Scapula

Sternum

Humerus

Ribs

Thoracic vertæbræ

Lumbar vertebræ

Ulna

Ilium

Radius

Sacrum

Pubis

Carpus

Ischium

Metacarpus

Phalanges

Femur

Patella

Tibia

Fibula

Tarsus

Metatarsus

Phalanges

Figure 2 Human skeleton
(anterior view)

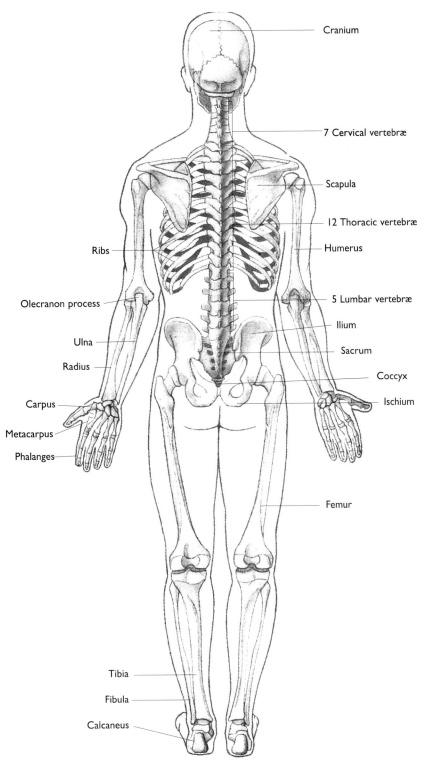

Cranium

7 Cervical vertebræ

Scapula

12 Thoracic vertebræ

Humerus

Ribs

5 Lumbar vertebræ

Olecranon process

Ilium

Ulna

Sacrum

Radius

Coccyx

Carpus

Ischium

Metacarpus

Phalanges

Femur

Tibia

Fibula

Calcaneus

Figure 3 Human skeleton
(posterior view)

3.1   The head and neck

The **skull** is made up of over 20 individual bones, the names of the majority of which are not crucial to the anthropometrist. It is sufficient to recognise that there are two distinct areas to the skull – the **cranium** and the bones of the face and beneath the facial part of the skull, the moveable lower jaw, or **mandible**.

Two landmarks of the skull are of significance to the anthropometrist. The lower bony margin of the eye socket, known as the **orbitale** (Figure 4), is one of the landmarks used to ensure that the head is in the Frankfort plane prior to measuring stature. [The other landmark used for this purpose, the **tragion**, is not a bony landmark.]

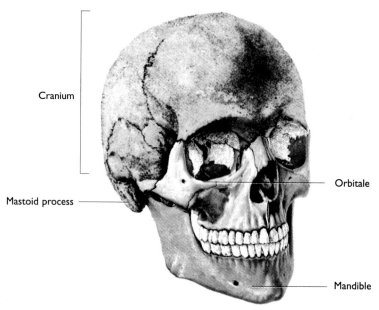

Cranium

Orbitale

Mastoid process

Mandible

Figure 4 Skull

The easily-palpated bumps protruding vertically downward behind the bottom of each ear are called the **mastoid processes** (Figure 4). These landmarks are used to ensure that the upwards pressure exerted on the skull during the measurement of "stretch stature" is directed through the correct points. The skull is balanced on the top of the **vertebral column**, the first seven vertebræ of which, the **cervical vertebræ**, constitute the neck. The first and second of these, the **atlas** and the **axis** respectively, are specially modified to provide a small platform (the atlas) for the head and a pivot (the axis) on which that platform can rotate.

3.2 The pectoral girdle

Consisting mainly of the **clavicle** (Latin for "little key") and **scapula** (Latin for "shoulder blade") on each side of the body, the pectoral girdle is not a complete bony circle. Although the medial ends of the two clavicles are joined to the sternum anteriorly, the medial borders of the scapulæ are joined to the vertebral column posteriorly by muscles (the **rhomboids**) rather than bone.

The clavicle provides a brace for the shoulder joint which not only holds the shoulder clear of the rib cage when desired, but also absorbs shock from the upper limb by transmitting it to the trunk via the sternum. The lateral end of the clavicle joins the antero-medial aspect of the **acromion process** of the scapula at the **acromio-clavicular** joint. The joint capsule of this joint can easily be palpated beneath the skin by keeping the fingers in contact with the superior surface of the clavicle and moving them laterally. Inexperienced anthropometrists sometimes identify this bump as the outer edge of the acromion process itself, resulting in a misidentification of the **acromiale** and a consequent mismeasurement of the length of the arm.

The scapula forms the outer major bony component of the pectoral girdle. This bone, which lies against the back of the upper chest wall, is basically triangular, with an upper outer corner which is significantly modified to provide attachment for muscles and a shallow socket with which the arm bone, the **humerus**, articulates (Figure 5). Its most inferior point, the **inferior angle**, can be palpated by running the thumb up the lateral aspect of the back until the bony angle of the scapula is located. This palpation can be made easier, if necessary, by having the subject put the ipsilateral arm behind their back.

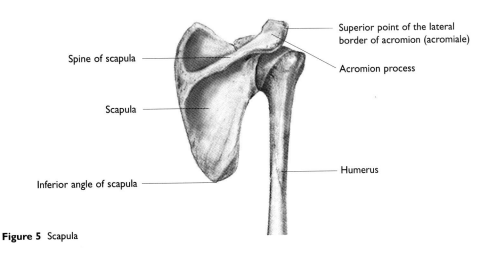

Figure 5 Scapula

11

The **spine of the scapula** is far more prominent laterally than medially, with its most lateral part elongating forwards to form the **acromion process**. The most superior part of the lateral border of this process is the defined location of the acromiale. The acromiale is not necessarily easy to locate, particularly when the subject is very muscular or has a thick subcutaneous fat layer. However, if you run your thumb gently, but firmly, up the lateral aspect of the deltoid muscle, the first bony point you come to should be the lateral border of the acromion process.

3.3   The arm

The part of the upper limb between the shoulder joint and the elbow joint is known as the **anatomical arm**. It contains a single long bone, the **humerus**, the head of which articulates proximally at the shoulder joint with the scapula. The distal end of the humerus is of greater interest to the anthropometrist than the proximal end, given its greater palpability (Figure 6). This end of the bone is specially shaped to facilitate its articulation at the elbow with the proximal ends of the two forearm bones, the **radius** and the **ulna**. Laterally, this end of the humerus is ball-shaped. This part, which articulates with the concavity in the **head of the radius**, is called the **capitulum** (Latin for "little head"). Medial to the capitulum, the end of the humerus is shaped like a pulley. This part , the **trochlea** (Latin for "pulley") fits into the **trochlear notch of the ulna**. Two prominences project from either side of the distal end of the humerus. Projecting medially proximal to the trochlea is the **medial epicondyle**. Projecting laterally proximal to the capitulum is the **lateral epicondyle**.

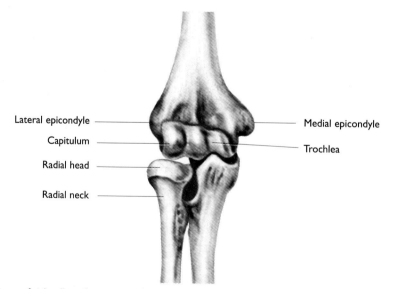

Figure 6 Bones of right elbow (anterior view)

3.4 The forearm

The part of the upper limb between the elbow joint and the wrist joint is the
anatomical forearm. It contains two long bones, the **radius**, laterally, and the **ulna**,
medially. The proximal ends of the radius and the ulna are shaped so that they are
complementary to the capitulum and trochlea respectively of the humerus (Figure 6).
The ball shape of the capitulum permits the head of the radius not only to slide
backwards and forwards on it as the elbow extends and flexes, but also to rotate on it
when the radius rotates on its long axis during **pronation** and **supination** (Figure 7).
The very prominent most proximal part of the ulna is the **olecranon process** (Figure 3).
The distal ends of the radius and ulna have distinctive processes projecting distally on
their lateral and medial sides respectively (Figure 8). These processes both have the
same name – **styloid process** – so reference to them also needs to specify which bone
is meant by using the process's complete title, for example, "ulnar styloid process".

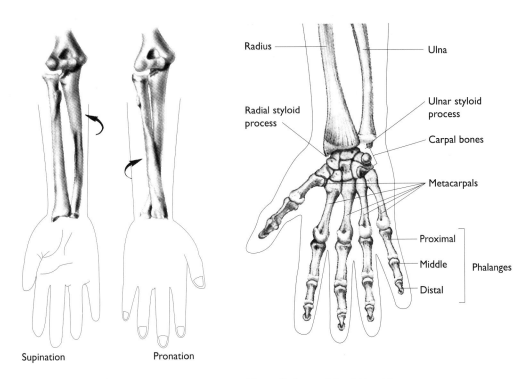

Supination   Pronation

Figure 7 Supination and pronation
of the right forearm

Figure 8 Bones of the right wrist
and hand (anterier view)

3.5 The wrist and hand

There are eight small (**carpal**) bones in the **wrist**, arranged in two irregular rows of four. Though each has a name, it is not necessary for the beginning anthropometrist to know them. The proximal row lies partly outside the hand (in the area the lay person refers to as the "wrist"). The distal row lies completely within (and forms) the base of the hand. The bony palm consists of five **metacarpal** bones.

Each of the four fingers contains three **phalanges**, a **proximal**, **middle** and **distal** (or **terminal**) **phalanx**. The thumb only has two phalanges (proximal and distal).

3.6 The ribs and sternum

There are twelve **ribs** on each side of the thorax, corresponding to the twelve thoracic vertebræ. Each curves laterally and slightly downward from the vertebræ, continuing forward, then medially to join the sternum. The bony part of each rib does not reach the sternum, but is connected to it by **costal cartilage** (the Latin word for rib is "costa").

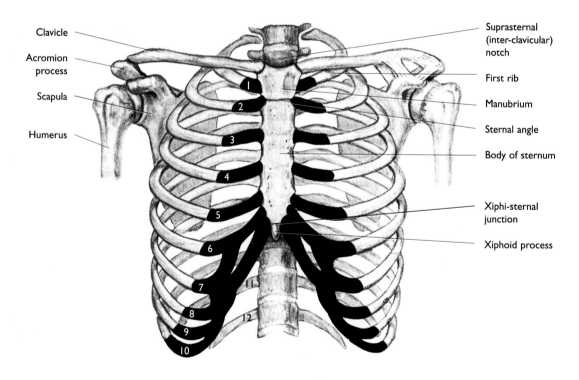

Figure 9 Rib cage and sternum

Ribs one to seven have their own costal cartilage connecting them directly to the sternum (Figure 9). For this reason, they are designated as "true" ribs. The costal cartilages of ribs eight, nine and ten connect to the sternum only indirectly through the cartilage above. Hence these three ribs are designated "false" ribs. Ribs eleven and twelve do not connect at all with the sternum and are therefore known as "floating" ribs.

The sternum consists of three parts. The superior part is named the **manubrium** (Latin for "handle"), the middle part is the **body**, and the small inferior part is the **xiphoid process** (Greek for "sword-like"). The supero-lateral surfaces of the manubrium make the very important connection with the medial ends of the clavicles. Consequently the shallow notch on the top of the manubrium is known as the **inter-clavicular**, as well as the **suprasternal notch**. The manubrium and body connect at the **sternal angle** (also known as the Angle of Louis) via a moveable joint which permits the body to move forwards and backwards slightly in relation to the manubrium during the movements of breathing. The angle is usually easily palpable as a small horizontal ridge a little way below the suprasternal notch, and its level is useful to be able to identify as it is here that the costal cartilage of the second rib joins the sternum.

3.7   Lumbar vertebræ, sacrum and coccyx

Below the thoracic vertebræ, the vertebral column continues with five lumbar vertebræ. These vertebræ are progressively larger and stronger than the thoracic ones, and do not have any adjoining ribs.

The five vertebræ immediately below the lumbar section of the vertebral column are fused together into a solid triangular mass, the **sacrum** (Latin for "sacred"), and the final four vertebræ of the column are also fused together as a group, forming the vestigial tail (or **coccyx**).

3.8   The pelvic girdle

The **innominate** ("unnamed") or **hip** bone on each side of the body consists of three bones fused together. The large fan-shaped plate of bone at the top is the **ilium**. The bulge of bone to the lower rear is the **ischium**, and the smaller bone protruding into the centre of the lower front is the **pubis** (Figure 10). The pubic bone joins its contralateral equivalent in the midline, and the two iliac bones are joined together posteriorly by the sacrum to form the pelvic girdle.

The three component bones are fused together in the region of the **acetabulum**, the bony socket into which the head of the femur fits. Three bony landmarks of the pelvic girdle, all on the ilium, should be noted. These are:

- the **iliac crest**
- the **iliac tubercle**
- the **anterior superior iliac spine** (Figure 10)

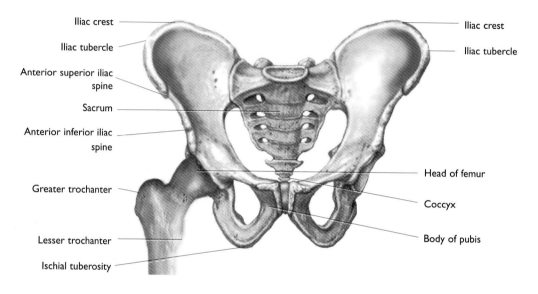

Figure 10 Bones of the hip region

3.9 The thigh

The part of the lower limb between the hip joint and the knee joint is designated the **anatomical thigh**. The single long bone in this region is the **femur**, the head of which articulates with the acetabulum of the hip bone. Inferior (and lateral) to the **head of the femur** is the **neck** and lateral to the neck is a large collar of bone. The large protuberance that this makes on the supero-lateral aspect of the shaft is called the **greater trochanter** (Figure 10).

At its distal end, the shaft of the femur broadens out to form two large bulges, or **condyles** (Greek for "knuckles") which articulate with the corresponding condyles of the larger of the two leg bones, the tibia. These condyles are most easily seen from the rear. The most lateral aspects of each condyle form smaller bulges of their own, known as **epicondyles** (Figure 11).

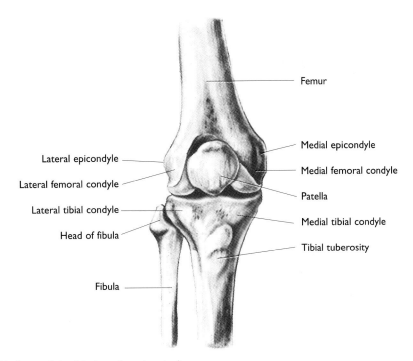

Lateral epicondyle

Lateral femoral condyle

Lateral tibial condyle

Head of fibula

Fibula

Femur

Medial epicondyle

Medial femoral condyle

Patella

Medial tibial condyle

Tibial tuberosity

Figure 11 Bones of the right knee (anterior view)

3.10   The leg

The part of the lower limb between the knee and the ankle is called the **anatomical leg**. It contains two long bones, of disparate size. The larger, medial one is the **tibia**, and the smaller, lateral one is the **fibula** (Figures 2 and 3). The proximal end of the tibia is expanded (from the shaft) into two **tibial condyles** (Figure 11). These articulate with and support the condyles of the femur. Below the condyles, on the anterior aspect of the tibia, is a distinctive bump, the **tibial tuberosity**, which is the point of attachment of the large tendon of the **Quadriceps Femoris** muscle.

The fibula does not participate in the knee joint itself, other than to provide an attachment for one of its supporting ligaments, the **lateral collateral ligament**.

There is one other significant bone in this region – the **patella** (Latin for "little plate"). This bone is found embedded in the quadriceps tendon, just above the level of the knee joint space. Like other bones which develop in tendons, the patella is classified as a **sesamoid bone**. Its role is both to provide protection for the quadriceps tendon as it slides backwards and forward over the front of the knee joint, and to substantially increase (by approximately twofold) the amount of force the muscle can exert in extending the leg.

3.11   The ankle and foot

At the distal end of the leg, the tibia extends on its medial side and the fibula extends on its lateral side, to form a combined stirrup of bone. This sits on and articulates with the **talus**, the most superior of the seven **tarsal** bones, to form the **ankle joint**. This medial protrusion of the tibia is called the **medial malleolus**. The corresponding protrusion of the fibula is called the **lateral malleolus** (Figure 12).

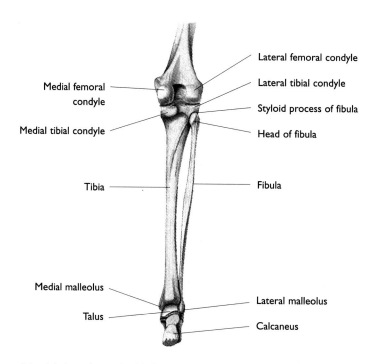

Figure 12 Bones of the right knee, leg and ankle (posterior view)

The foot is the crucial platform for the entire body during standing and locomotion. The rear half of the foot consists of seven distinct bones, the **tarsals**. The individual names of the rear two tarsals should be noted, since they are by far the largest and play the greatest role in weight-bearing. These two bones are the **talus**, which sits on top of the **calcaneus** (heel-bone). The talus articulates with the calcaneus below, and with the tibia and fibula above. These two bones are shown in Figures 12 and 13. Distal (and anterior) to the seven tarsal bones are the five **metatarsals**, and distal to these are the fourteen **phalanges** (three for each digit except the big toe).

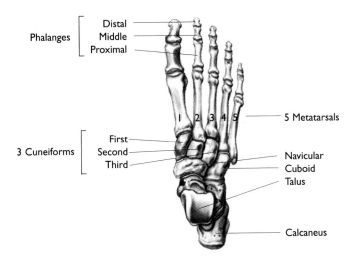

Figure 13 Bones of the foot (superior view)

4 The muscles

As well as knowing all the necessary bony landmarks of the body, the anthropometrist should be very familiar with the names and location of all the superficial major muscles and muscle groups, as these, along with the skin and subcutaneous fat, contribute just as much as the skeleton in determining size and shape.

Some muscles are sufficiently large or distinctive to warrant individual mention. Others need not be identified individually, the naming of the group to which they belong more than adequately meeting the anthropometrist's need.

Although the names may appear strange initially, muscles are named logically (albeit from Latin or Greek origins) on the basis of one or more characteristics such as position, shape or action. This can be very helpful for remembering where the muscle is and what it does. Like bones, muscles demonstrate bilateral symmetry throughout the body. The locations of the muscles or groups discussed are shown in Figures 14 and 15.

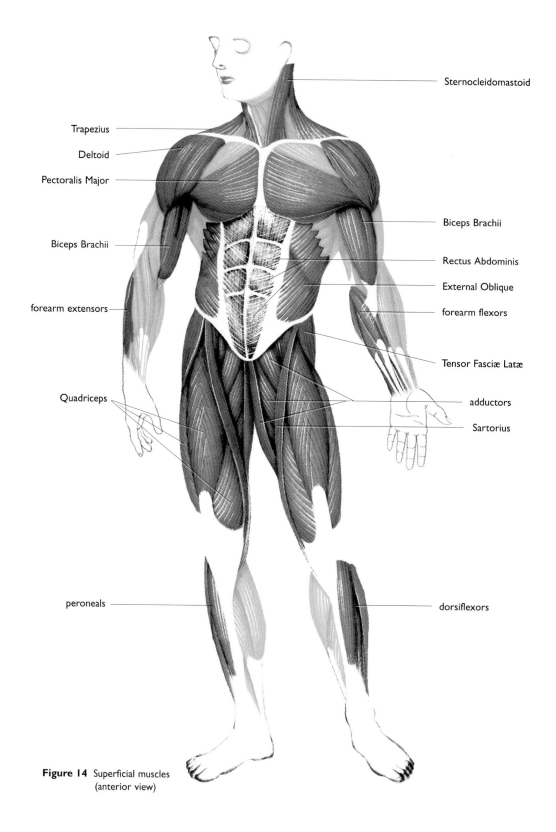

Sternocleidomastoid

Trapezius

Deltoid

Pectoralis Major

Biceps Brachii

Biceps Brachii

Rectus Abdominis

External Oblique

forearm extensors

forearm flexors

Tensor Fasciæ Latæ

Quadriceps

adductors

Sartorius

peroneals

dorsiflexors

Figure 14 Superficial muscles
(anterior view)

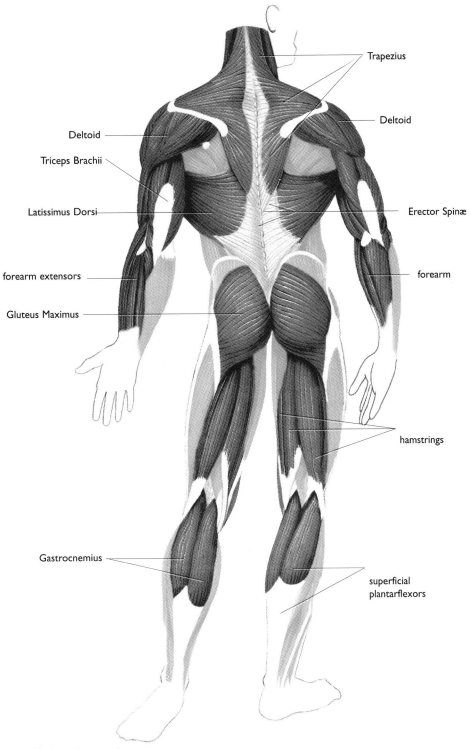

Trapezius

Deltoid

Deltoid

Triceps Brachii

Latissimus Dorsi

Erector Spinæ

forearm extensors

forearm

Gluteus Maximus

hamstrings

Gastrocnemius

superficial
plantarflexors

Figure 15 Superficial muscles
(posterior view)

21

4.1 Head and neck muscles

Although the head and neck contain many muscles, ranging from those involved with mastication to those of expression, only two muscles are of note for the anthropometrist. The first, **Trapezius**, is found at the back of the neck and superior medial back. It is named thus because together with its contralateral twin, it forms the shape of a trapezium. It is the muscle that gives the shape to the slope of the shoulder. The second, **Sternocleidomastoid** (commonly referred to as "sternomastoid") lies at the side of the neck, its size largely determining the neck's thickness. This muscle is a good example of the name describing the position, each of the three parts of the name referring to the three bones (sternum and clavicle below, and mastoid process above), that the muscle runs between.

4.2 Shoulder muscles

The very obvious superficial muscle at the shoulder is **Deltoid**. This runs from the outer aspect of the horseshoe formed by the spine of the scapula, the acromion process and the clavicle, to the lateral humerus, and inserts about half-way down the length of the humerus. It forms the bulk of the shoulder.

4.3 Arm muscles

Anteriorly on the arm, lies one of the best-known muscles of the body, **Biceps Brachii** (two-headed muscle of the arm), commonly called just "Biceps". Posteriorly, **Triceps Brachii** is located.

4.4 Forearm muscles

The muscle group constituting the bulk of the medial forearm is the **forearm flexor group**, whilst the bulk of the lateral forearm is made up of the **forearm extensor group**.

4.5 Chest muscles

The prominent (at least in most adult males) bulge of muscle each side of the upper chest is the **pectoral group**. The most superficial, and by far the larger of the two muscles in this group is **Pectoralis Major.**

4.6 Back muscles

The solid columns of muscle lying either side of the vertebral column are collectively named the **erector spinæ group** (from their combined action). The large, flat muscle spanning out from the lower back to run around the side of the thorax, just below the armpit, to the medial arm is called **Latissimus Dorsi**. The greater its development, the more noticeably V-shaped the torso becomes.

4.7 Abdominal muscles

The **abdominal group** of muscles forms the walls of the abdomen for most of its circumference. The most superficial two (of the four) muscles in the group are **External Oblique**, at the side, and **Rectus Abdominis**, running vertically either side of the mid-sagittal plane between the ribcage and the pubic bone.

4.8 Posterior hip muscles

The **gluteal group** provides the large bulk of muscle which forms the rump or bottom. The largest member of this muscle group, and the most superficial posteriorly, is **Gluteus Maximus**.

Though a member of the gluteal muscle group, **Tensor Fascia Latæ** lies more lateral to the hip than posterior to it. This muscle is often very prominent in athletes whose sport involves a great deal of running or bounding.

4.9 Thigh muscles

The thigh muscles are grouped conveniently into three groups, one situated anteriorly, one medially and one posteriorly.

The bulk of the **anterior group** is formed by **Quadriceps Femoris** (named after its four parts and commonly called the "quads"). The bulk of the **medial group** is made up of the **adductors**; and the **posterior group** is formed by the **hamstrings**.

4.10 Leg muscles

The leg has four distinct muscle groups, three of which are superficial and distinguishable. Antero-lateral to the tibia, lies the **dorsiflexor group**, which gets its name from its group action at the ankle joint. Lateral to the fibula lies the **peroneal group** (perone is Greek for "fibula" which is Latin for "a long pin or skewer"). Posteriorly to both bones lie the **deep plantarflexor group** and the **superficial plantarflexor group**, only the latter of which is palpable. The most superficial muscle of the superficial plantarflexor group is **Gastrocnemius**.

5 Reference

Basmajian, J.V. (1982)
    Primary anatomy.
    Baltimore: Williams & Wilkins.

Chapter 2
Measurement Techniques in Anthropometry

Kevin Norton, Nancy Whittingham, Lindsay Carter, Deborah Kerr, Christopher Gore and Michael Marfell-Jones

1   Introduction

Anthropometry like any other area of science depends upon adherence to the particular rules of measurement as determined by national and international standards bodies. The international anthropometric standards body adopted for the purpose of this textbook is the International Society for the Advancement of Kinanthropometry (ISAK). The anthropometric sites and descriptions in this book are based on those by Ross and Marfell-Jones (1991) and are supported by ISAK. The main reasons for using the ISAK guidelines are that this group is truly international and has worked for a number of years to develop recommendations for anthropometric assessment of athletes in particular, but with scope for broader applications to the general population. Within Australia these guidelines have been endorsed by both the Laboratory Standards Assistance Scheme (LSAS) of the Australian Sports Commission (ASC) and the Australian Association for Exercise and Sports Science (AAESS).

This chapter introduces the student to a number of techniques required to obtain a comprehensive anthropometric profile on a person. The procedure should take an experienced anthropometrist about 25 minutes, while an inexperienced person might require about 1 hour or more to complete the task. The measurement sites included are those which are routinely taken for monitoring purposes on athletes, both in the laboratory and in the field. Sites which are known to be predictive of health status in the general population are also included. Once the measurement of these anthropometric sites is complete, the practitioner can utilise a number of tools using various computations for data analyses, some of which are discussed in Section 2. These include somatotyping, fractionation of body mass into bone, muscle, fat and residual mass components, proportionality estimates, prediction of body density (and subsequently percent body fat) using a number of regression equations, and transformation of the data into age and gender specific percentile scores for individual sites, overall obesity and proportional mass rankings, as well as other indices such as waist-hip ratio, sums of skinfolds and skinfold-corrected girths.

There are many reasons why measurements of body dimensions are taken. Several of these are discussed in Section 3. Although there will always be the occasion where specific and perhaps unusual anthropometric measurement sites are required, there exists a single "core" of body sites which are most often included in an anthropometric profile of a person. Adoption of a standard profile and methodology allows comparisons to be made locally, nationally and internationally between sample groups. It is this core of measurement sites which is presented in the following chapter.

2 The subject

Subjects must be informed as to what measurements are to be taken and must complete a consent form as part of the preliminaries of the test protocol. Throughout the marking and measurement session, the subject stands relaxed, arms comfortably to the side and feet slightly apart. Some measurements require the subject to place the feet together. These have been identified in part 5 "The anthropometric profile". The measurer should be able to easily move around the subject and manipulate the equipment. This will be facilitated by setting aside adequate space for these measurement procedures. For measurements to be made as quickly and efficiently as possible the subjects should be asked to present themselves in minimal clothing. Swimming costumes (two-piece for women) are ideal for ease of access to all measurement sites and therefore the measurement room should be at a comfortable temperature for the subject.

3 Data collection

Where possible a recorder should be used to assist the measurer and enter data. Ideally the recorder will be knowledgeable in measurement techniques. The recorder will be able to verify accuracy of site location and ensure the correct sequence of measurement sites. Despite careful attention to the standards there is still the possibility that errors will occur in the recording of data. This may occur due to poor pronunciation by the measurer, inattention by the recorder or the recorder's failure to follow the steps which are designed to eliminate such errors. Ideally, data collection should involve one measurer and one recorder to minimise measurement error but in large surveys a team of anthropometrists may be used to expedite data collection.

It must be remembered that the measurer and the recorder work as a team and it is the responsibility of the recorder to help the measurer wherever necessary. The recorder repeats the value as it is being recorded thereby enabling the measurer to do an immediate check. In some cases measurements may be repeated or even taken a third time. In the first case the average value is used. In the second case the median value is used for data analysis.

4 Anthropometry equipment

The following equipment items are essential tools for the anthropometrist.

Anthropometry tapes

A flexible steel tape calibrated in centimetres with millimetre gradations is recommended for girths. The Lufkin (W606PM) is the preferred metal tape. If fibreglass tapes are used regular calibration against a steel tape is required as these non-metal tapes may stretch over time. If any other type of tape is to be used it should be non-extensible, flexible, no wider than 7 mm and have a stub (blank area) of at least 3 cm before the zero line.

Figure 1 Anthropometry tapes

In addition to assessing girth measurements an anthropometric tape is also required to accurately locate a number of skinfold sites and mark distances from bony landmarks. The tape needs to be enclosed in a case with automatic retraction.

Stadiometer

This is the instrument used for measuring stature and sitting height. It is usually attached to a wall so that the subjects can be aligned vertically in the appropriate manner. A sliding head piece is lowered to the vertex of the head. It is recommended that the head piece be constructed with a locking device.

Weighing scales

The traditional instrument of choice is a beam balance accurate to the nearest 100 g. In the field situation, spring balance scales with an accuracy to the nearest 500 g have been used. However, the use of electronic scales is becoming more general and the accuracy of some of these scales is equal to or greater than that of the beam balance provided calibration of both machines is maintained. For example, relatively inexpensive digital bathroom-type scales are now available which incorporate a load cell as the sensor (e.g. AND-Mercury

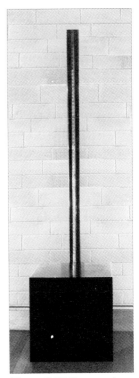

Figure 2 Wall-mounted stadiometer and anthropometry box

29

scales). They are easily transported and can therefore be used in the laboratory and the field. The accuracy of these instruments is to within 50 g. Calibration weights, certified by a government department of weights and measures and totalling at least 120 kg, are required as standard equipment.

Skinfold calipers

The Harpenden calipers have been used as the criterion instrument by ISAK. The manufacturers of these calipers report a compression of 10 g.mm^{-2} in new calipers (see Chapter 4). They are calibrated to approximately 50 mm in 0.2 mm divisions but may be accurately interpolated to the nearest 0.1 mm. As an alternative, the Slim

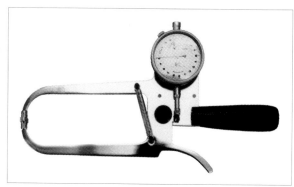

Figure 3 Harpenden skinfold calipers

Guide calipers may be used. They are highly reliable, have the same jaw compression as the Harpenden and produce almost identical readings (Anderson & Ross, 1986; Schmidt & Carter, 1990; see Chapter 4). However, they require some adaptation in positioning and handling. They are calibrated to 80 mm which may be an advantage when measuring non-athletic populations although they lack the resolution of the Harpenden calipers since measurements can be read only to the nearest 0.5 mm. It should be pointed out that the application of skinfold data to any regression equation (see Chapter 7) should be made with additional caution if calipers are used which are different to the type described in the original paper.

Anthropometer

The Siber-Hegner GPM anthropometer with foot plate is the instrument of choice although it is relatively expensive. This instrument is used to measure the vertical heights between specific anatomical landmarks on the subject and the floor or sitting surface. Estimates of segment lengths using the differences between pairs of heights are called projected segment lengths. For example, acromiale-radiale length can be obtained by subtraction: acromiale height minus radiale height. More recent techniques allow direct measurement of segment lengths using a segmometer as described below. The upper segment of the Siber-Hegner GPM anthropometer is referred to as a large sliding caliper. It is used to measure direct segment lengths (e.g. radiale-stylion), large bone breadths (e.g. biacromial) and non-bone breadths (e.g. bideltoid).

Figure 4 Siber-Hegner GPM anthropometer

Segmometer

This instrument is manufactured from a steel carpenter's tape which has attached two straight branches, each approximately 7 cm in length. It is used to measure segment lengths directly. Selected heights (e.g. iliospinale and trochanterion heights) which can be measured from landmarks on the subject to the anthropometry box (the box height is then added to this length) can also be made using a segmometer. The segmometer is designed to be used in place of the anthropometer (Carr, Balde, Rempel & Ross, 1993) although it is not appropriate for measuring large bone breadths.

Figure 5 Segmometer (photo courtesy Dr Tim Ackland)

Large sliding calipers

This instrument is usually the upper segment of the anthropometer. It comes with two straight branches that allow measurements of large bone breadths such as the biiliocristal and biacromial breadths. These branches are attached to a rigid metal scale which is important since considerable pressure must be exerted when these bony dimensions are measured. The distance between the branches should be verified to ensure it has been assembled correctly.

Figure 6 Large sliding calipers

Figure 7 Small sliding (bone) calipers

Small sliding calipers

These calipers are used for biepicondylar humerus and femur breadths. The Mitutoyo adapted calipers are an ideal instrument for these measurements. These are engineering vernier calipers to which have been added longer arms which are able to encompass the biepicondylar breadth of the femur and humerus and are highly accurate (to within 0.1 mm). Alternatives to the Mitutoyo are the Harpenden bone calipers or the large sliding caliper which is part of the Siber-Hegner anthropometer, although there is greater potential for loss of resolution using this equipment. The Harpenden bone calipers are easy to use but the measurement scale may be less reliable than the Mitutoyo, especially if the arms become loose. The Siber-Hegner caliper is more cumbersome to handle over relatively small breadths such as the biepicondylar breadths and lacks the necessary resolution for these bony measurements.

Wide-spreading calipers

The measurement of anterior-posterior chest depth requires this instrument which has two recurved branches. This allows the caliper branches to be placed over the shoulder to locate the correct anatomical landmarks for measurement of anterior-posterior chest depth. Anthropometers such as the Siber-Hegner GPM and Harpenden can be purchased with interchangeable straight and recurved branches.

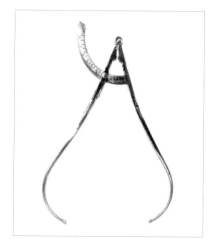

Figure 8 Wide-spreading calipers

Anthropometry box

This box (cube) should have dimensions with all side lengths of approximately 40 cm. The actual height of the box used in any laboratory should be known exactly. It is necessary to have a cut-out section on one side of the box which enables the subject's feet to be positioned under the box during measurement of the iliospinale height. The box is particularly useful for assisting in the measurement of heights such as iliospinale and trochanterion using a segmometer. In these cases the measured height from the box to the landmark is added to the height of the box.

This gives the true landmark height from the floor and saves the back of the anthropometrist who need not bend to the floor but only to the top of the box. The box is also useful when measuring other lengths and breadths where the subject is required to be seated (on the box).

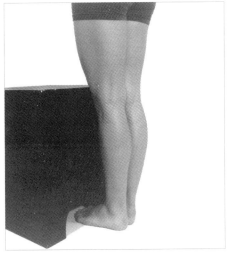

Figure 9 Anthropometry box with cut-out section

5   The anthropometric profile

There are two general "profiles" commonly used for anthropometric assessment, the so-called **restricted** and **full** profiles. Both profiles can be entered onto the same proforma (Figure 10). The top part of the proforma includes a section where demographic information can be entered. This includes a test and tester ID number, name, sport or occupation, birth and test dates, subject postcode (for future geographical analyses), gender and country of birth details. It also has a place for the anthropometry box height (if used), as well as a check box for exercise habits. The information on exercise patterns involves a summary of regular activity during the past twelve months. The first two measurements taken in the anthropometric profile, that is, mass and height, should also be entered on the top section of the proforma. Throughout this chapter the anthropometric sites are numbered in a way which correspond to the site ID on the proforma. The 16 shaded ID numbers on the proforma refer to variables included in the restricted anthropometric profile. The 22 other variables listed are required to complete a full anthropometric profile. Additional sport- or population-specific variables measured during profiling of specific individuals or groups can be added.

Restricted anthropometric profile
In addition to stature and body mass, the short or restricted profile consists of the following nine skinfolds, five girths and two breadths:

Table 1 Sites included in the restricted profile

Skinfolds		Girths	Breadths
triceps	abdominal	arm (relaxed)	humerus
subscapular	front thigh	arm (flexed)	femur
biceps	medial calf	waist (minimum)	
iliac crest	mid-axilla	gluteal (hips)	
supraspinale		calf (maximum)	

For efficient profiling these sites are identified in this chapter with an ® symbol. The anatomical landmarks required for exact location of these sites are also identified with this ® symbol. Measurement of these sites (in addition to stature and body mass) will enable computations to be made for somatotype, relative body fat (using a restricted number of prediction equations), indices of body surface area, body mass index, waist to hip ratio, fat patterning, and skinfold-corrected girths. Other comparisons such as obesity estimates and proportional mass rankings relative to other populations of interest can also be performed.

Full anthropometric profile

In addition to stature and body mass, the long or full anthropometric profile consists of the following nine skinfolds, thirteen girths, and sixteen lengths and breadths:

Table 2 Sites included in the full profile

Skinfolds	Girths	Lengths/Heights	Breadths
triceps	head	acromiale-radiale	biacromial
subscapular	neck	radiale-stylion	biiliocristal
biceps	arm (relaxed)	midstylion-dactylion	
iliac crest	arm (flexed)	iliospinale to floor	transverse chest
supraspinale	forearm (maximum)	trochanterion to floor	anterior-posterior-
abdominal	wrist (distal styloids)	trochanterion-tibiale-	chest depth
front thigh	chest (mesosternale)	laterale	
medial calf	waist (minimum)	tibiale laterale to floor	humerus
mid-axilla	gluteal (hips)	tibiale mediale-	femur
	thigh (1 cm gluteal)	sphyrion tibiale	
	thigh (mid tro-tib-lat)		
	calf (maximum)	foot length	
	ankle (minimum)	sitting height	

Measurement of these sites (in addition to stature and body mass) will enable computations to be made for somatotype, relative body fat (using a large number of prediction equations), indices of body surface area, body mass index, waist to hip ratio, fat patterning, and skinfold-corrected girths. The full profile also allows estimates of bone, muscle, fat and residual masses using the fractionation of body mass technique (Drinkwater & Ross, 1980; Kerr, 1988). Since segment lengths are included, proportionality analyses can be made. Other comparisons such as obesity estimates and proportional mass rankings relative to other populations of interest can also be performed. A number of other sport specific anthropometry sites are also described in this chapter. They are included since they are often used for comparison across specific sporting populations (e.g. arm span in swimmers).

5.1 Stature

There are three general techniques for measuring stature: free standing, stretch and recumbent. The last may be used for infants up to 2–3 years or adults unable to stand and will not be considered here. The other two methods give slightly different values. It must also be remembered that there will be diurnal variation. Generally, subjects are taller in the morning and shorter in the evening. A loss of about 1% in stature is common over the course of the day (Reilly, Tyrrell & Troup, 1984; Wilby, Linge, Reilly & Troup, 1985). Repeated measures should be taken as near as possible to the same time of day as the original measurement.

Equipment
In the laboratory a stadiometer should be mounted on a wall and used in conjunction with a right-angled head board which is at least 6 cm wide and which can be placed firmly on the subject's head while fixed to the stadiometer. The floor surface must be hard and level.

The stadiometer should have a minimum range of measurement of 60 cm to 210 cm. The accuracy of measurement required is 0.1 cm. It should be checked periodically against a standard height such as a Siber-Hegner anthropometer. In the field, when a stadiometer is not available, a girth tape fixed to a wall and checked for height and vertical positioning, may be used in conjunction with a 90° head board such as a large carpenter's set square. As a "last resort" method, a piece of paper taped to a wall may be used to identify the height, using a head board. Assessment of the height can then be completed using a steel tape. This method is not acceptable in a laboratory.

Anthropometry Proforma

Test ID

Name: ....

DOB: .... Test Date: ....

Subj. Postcode: .... Gender: M ☐ F ☐

Country of Birth: .... Box Ht: ....

Mass (kg): .... Height (cm): ....

Lab: Tester ID ☐ ☐ ☐ : ☐

Sport: ....

Intensity	Frequency	Duration
Nil	≤2	<3
Walk	≥3	3-12
Vigorous		>12

	ID	Site	Trial 1	Trial 2	Trial 3	Median
Skinfolds	1	triceps				
(mm)	2	subscapular				
	3	biceps				
	4	iliac crest				
	5	supraspinale				
	6	abdominal				
	7	front thigh				
	8	medial calf				
	9	mid-axilla				
Girths	10	head				
(cm)	11	neck				
	12	arm (relaxed)				
	13	arm (flexed and tensed)				
	14	forearm (maximum)				
	15	wrist (distal styloids)				
	16	chest (mesosternale)				
	17	waist (minimum)				
	18	gluteal (hips)				
	19	thigh (1 cm gluteal)				
	20	thigh (mid tro-tib-lat)				
	21	calf (maximum)				
	22	ankle (minimum)				
Lengths	23	acromiale-radiale				
(cm)	24	radiale-stylion				
	25	midstylion-dactylion				
	26	iliospinale b. ht				
	27	trochanterion b. ht				
	28	trochanterion-tibiale laterale				
	29	tibiale laterale to floor				
	30	tibiale mediale-sphy. tibiale				
Breadths/	31	biacromial				
Lengths	32	biiliocristal				
(cm)	33	foot length				
	34	sitting height				
	35	transverse chest				
	36	A-P chest depth				
	37	humerus				
	38	femur				
Sport	39					
Specific	40					
Sites	41					
	42					

Figure 10 Standard anthropometric proforma

Chapter 2

Method

The stretch stature method requires the subject to stand with the feet together and the heels, buttocks and upper part of the back touching the scale. The head when placed in the Frankfort plane need not be touching the scale. The Frankfort plane is achieved when the orbitale (lower edge of the eye socket) is in the same horizontal plane as the tragion (the notch superior to the tragus of the ear). When aligned the vertex is the highest point on the skull as illustrated in Figure 11.

Figure 11 The head in the Frankfort plane

The measurer places the hands along the jaw of the subject with the fingers reaching to the mastoid processes. The subject is instructed to take and hold a deep breath and while keeping the head in the Frankfort plane the measurer applies gentle upward lift through the mastoid processes. The recorder places the head board firmly down on the vertex, crushing the hair as much as possible. The recorder further assists by watching that the feet do not come off the floor and that the position of the head is maintained in the Frankfort plane. Measurement is taken at the end of a deep inward breath.

5.2 Body mass

Body mass exhibits diurnal variation of about 1 kg in children and 2 kg in adults (Sumner & Whitacre, 1931). The most stable values are those obtained routinely in the morning twelve hours after food and after voiding. Since it is not always possible to standardise the measurement time, it may be important to record the time of day when measurements are made.

Equipment

The instrument of choice is a beam balance or portable electronic scales incorporating a load cell. Both should be accurate to within 100 g.

Method

Nude mass can be measured by first weighing the clothing which is to be worn during measurement and subtracting this from the mass. Generally the mass in minimal clothing is of sufficient accuracy. Check that the scale is reading zero, then the subject stands on the centre of the scales without support and with the weight distributed evenly on both feet. The head is up and the eyes look directly ahead.

5.3   Anatomical landmarks – refer to Figure 12

Landmarks are identifiable skeletal points which generally lie close to the body's surface and are the "markers" which identify the exact location of the measurement site, or from which a soft tissue site is located, for example, subscapular skinfold and arm girth. All landmarks are found by palpation. For the comfort of the subject, the measurer's finger nails should be kept trimmed.

The landmark is identified with the thumb or index finger. The site is released to remove any distortion of the skin, then is relocated and marked using a fine tipped felt or dermographic pen. The site is marked directly over the landmark. The mark is then re-checked to ensure that there has been no displacement of skin relative to the underlying bone.

The landmarks described here are those required for the measurement sites included in this chapter. All landmarks are identified before any measurements are made. The order of their identification is as listed here. These sites represent only a small portion of the potentially infinite number of sites over the surface of the body. They are included since they are the sites typically referenced when profiling individuals and are consistent with the recommendations of the ISAK working group on standards and instrumentation and supported by the Laboratory Standards Assistance Scheme of the Australian Sports Commission. It should be pointed out however that other sites are often required for analyses in ergonomics, child growth and development and specific sporting populations. [Note: Landmarks essential for the restricted profile are identified by the symbol®.]

Acromiale®

Definition: The point at the superior and lateral border of the acromion process, midway between the anterior and posterior borders of the Deltoid muscle when viewed from the side.

Location: Standing behind and on the right hand side of the subject palpate along the spine of the scapula to the corner of the acromion. This represents the start of the lateral border which usually runs anteriorly, slightly superiorly and medially. Apply the straight edge of a pencil to the lateral aspect of the acromion to confirm the location of the border.

The landmark is a point on the most lateral and superior part of the border which is adjudged to be in the mid-deltoid position when viewed from the side.

Radiale®

Definition: The point at the proximal and lateral border of the head of the radius.

Location: Palpate downward into the lateral dimple of the right elbow. It should be possible to feel the space between the capitulum of the humerus and the head of the radius. Slight rotation of the forearm is felt as rotation of the head of the radius.

Mid-acromiale-radiale®

Definition: The point equidistant from acromiale and radiale.

Location: Measure the linear distance between acromiale and radiale with the arm relaxed and extended by the side. Place a small horizontal mark at the level of the mid-point between these two landmarks. Project this mark around to the posterior and anterior surfaces of the arm as a horizontal line. This is required for locating the triceps and biceps skinfold sites. When marking the sites for triceps and biceps skinfolds the subject must assume the anatomical position. The triceps skinfold is taken over the most posterior part of the triceps and the biceps skinfold is taken over the most anterior part of the biceps when viewed from the side (at the marked mid-acromiale-radiale level).

Stylion

Definition: The most distal point on the lateral margin of the inferior head of the radius (i.e. the styloid process of the radius).

Location: Using a thumb nail the anthropometrist palpates in the triangular space identified by the muscle tendons of the wrist immediately above the thumb. This site is also called the anatomical "snuff box". Once the snuff box has been identified, palpate in the space between the distal radius and the most proximal aspect of the first metacarpal in order to correctly identify the styloid process.

Midstylion

Definition: The midpoint, on the anterior surface of the wrist, of the horizontal line at the level of the stylion.

Location: The tape is aligned with the stylion landmark and a horizontal line is drawn close to the mid-point of the wrist. The mid-point is estimated between the medial and lateral edges of the wrist. A vertical line is drawn at this position which intersects the horizontal line.

Dactylion

Definition: The tip of the middle (third) finger when the arm is hanging down and the fingers are stretched downward.

Location: No marks are required for this site since it is the point on the end of the third finger. The other fingers are designated the second (index finger), fourth and fifth dactylia (digits). Finger nails should not be used as landmarks for the end of fingers.

Subscapulare®

Definition: The undermost tip of the inferior angle of the scapula.

Location: Palpate the inferior angle of the scapula with the left thumb. If there is difficulty locating the inferior angle of the scapula, the subject should slowly reach behind the back with the right arm. The inferior angle of the scapula should be felt continuously as the hand is again placed by the side of the body. A final check of this landmark should be made with the hand by the side in the functional position.

Mesosternale

Definition: The midpoint of the sternum at the level of the centre of the articulation of the fourth rib with the sternum (chondrosternal articulation).

Location: This landmark is located by palpation beginning from the top of the clavicles. Using the thumb the anthropometrist should roll down from the clavicle to the first costal space (i.e. between the first and second ribs). The thumb is then replaced by the index finger and the procedure is then repeated down to the second, third and fourth intercostal spaces. The fourth rib is between the last two spaces.

Xiphoidale®

Definition: The xiphoidale is found at the lower extremity of the sternum. The landmark is the inferior tip of the xiphion.

Location: It is located by palpation in the medial direction of the left or right costal arch toward the sternum. These arches (which form the infrasternal angle) articulate at the xiphi-sternal junction.

Ilio-axilla line®

Definition: The imaginary vertical line joining the observed mid-point of the armpit with the lateral superior edge of the ilium.

Location: With the subject's arm placed horizontally in a lateral position, locate the lateral superior edge of the ilium using the right hand and the mid-point of the visible armpit. The left hand is used to stabilise the body by providing resistance on the left side of the pelvis. The imaginary vertical line intersects both these landmarks.

Iliocristale®

Definition: The point on the most lateral aspect of the iliac tubercle on the ilio-axilla line.

Location: With the subject's arm placed horizontally in a lateral position, locate the most lateral superior edge of the ilium using the right hand. The left hand is used to stabilise the body by providing resistance on the left side of the pelvis. The landmark is made at the identified edge of the ilium which is intersected by the imaginary vertical line from the mid-axilla.

Iliospinale®

Definition: The most inferior or undermost tip of the anterior superior iliac spine.

Location: To locate the iliospinale, palpate the superior aspect of the ilium and follow anteriorly and inferiorly along the crest until the prominence of the ilium runs posteriorly. The landmark is the lower margin or edge where the bone can just be felt. Difficulty in appraising the landmark can be assisted by the subject lifting the heel of the right foot and rotating the femur outward. Because the sartorius muscle originates at the site of the iliospinale, this movement of the femur enables palpation of the muscle and tracing to its source.

Trochanterion

Definition: The most superior point on the greater trochanter of the femur, not the most lateral point.

Location: This site is identified by palpating the lateral aspect of the gluteal muscle while standing behind the subject. It is advisable to support the left side

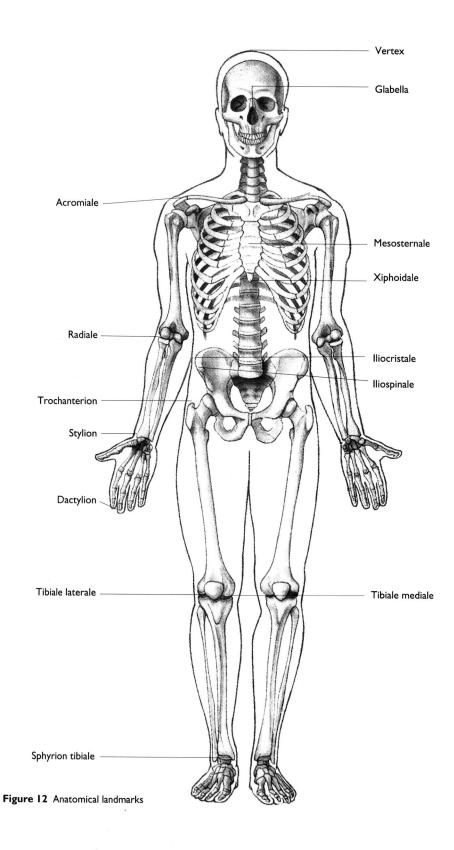

Vertex

Glabella

Acromiale

Mesosternale

Xiphoidale

Radiale

Iliocristale

Iliospinale

Trochanterion

Stylion

Dactylion

Tibiale laterale

Tibiale mediale

Sphyrion tibiale

Figure 12 Anatomical landmarks

of the subject's pelvis with the left hand while applying pressure with the right hand. Once the greater trochanter has been identified the measurer should palpate upwards to locate the most superior aspect of this bony landmark. [Note: This site is difficult to locate in persons with thick adipose tissue over the greater trochanter.]

Tibiale mediale

Definition: The most superior point on the medial border of the head of the tibia.

Location: The tibiale mediale is approximately in the same transverse plane as the tibiale laterale. It is marked with the subject seated on the box with the right leg rested over the left knee so that the medial aspect of the lower leg is able to be marked. Palpate the site bounded by the medial femoral condyle and the internal tibial tuberosity. The mark should be made at the proximal medial border while the leg is held in this position.

Sphyrion

Definition: The most distal tip of the malleolare mediale of the tibia.

Location: This landmark may be located most easily by palpation with the thumb nail from beneath and dorsally. It is the distal tip, not the outermost point, of the medial malleolus of the tibia. It is marked with the subject seated on the box with the right leg rested over the left knee so that the medial aspect of the lower leg is able to be marked.

Tibiale laterale

Definition: The most superior point on the lateral border of the head of the tibia.

Location: This is often a difficult landmark to correctly locate due to thick lateral ligaments that run across the knee joint. Palpate the site using a thumb nail using the following guidelines. Locate the area bounded by the lateral condyle of the femur and the anterolateral portion of the head of the tibia. Press inwards firmly in order to locate the superior and lateral border of the head of the tibia. It is often useful to have the subject flex and extend the knee several times to ensure that the correct position has been located. The mark should be made approximately one-third of the distance along the border moving in an anterior-posterior direction.

5.4 Skinfolds

5.4.1 Techniques for measuring skinfolds

The precise assessment of anthropometric measurements, in particular skinfold thicknesses, can be difficult and therefore extreme care is required. In general there is not enough attention paid to an accurate measurement technique and consequently reproducibility cannot be obtained. The description of the measurement procedures seems quite simple but a high degree of technical skill is essential for consistent results, especially when applied under field test conditions.

Anthropometrists wishing to become criterion measurers (i.e. those who do not make systematic errors and who can demonstrate reproducibility), must be able to routinely make accurate measurements. It is essential, therefore, that the standard protocols outlined in this chapter are strictly adhered to:

- Prior to measuring athletes or others for monitoring purposes the tester should develop the appropriate technique for taking skinfolds. This has been shown to reduce the level of error in repeated measurements and among investigators (Jackson, Pollock & Gettman, 1978; Lohman & Pollock, 1981). Repeated measures on at least twenty subjects should be made in order to establish reproducibility and an experienced anthropometrist will help to establish accuracy. A comparison of results will then expose any weaknesses in technique.

- Ensure that the skinfold calipers are accurately measuring the distance between the centre of their contact faces by using the short blades of an engineer's vernier caliper. If possible check that the tension of the jaws remains constant throughout the range of measurement (see Chapter 4). A full sweep of the needle is 20 mm and this is reflected on the small scale on the Harpenden caliper face. Before using the caliper make sure that the needle is on zero. After unlocking the small screw, rotation of the outer ring of the caliper is used to adjust the position of the caliper dial directly under the needle.

- The skinfold site should be carefully located using the correct anatomical landmarks. It is particularly important that the inexperienced measurer mark the skin with a fine tipped felt or dermographic pen for all skinfold landmarks. Skinfold thicknesses have been shown to vary by an average of 2-3 mm when the calipers were placed 2.5 cm from the correct site (Ruiz, Colley & Hamilton,

1971). Inaccurate location of skinfold sites was also found to be the greatest source of error among investigators (Ruiz et al., 1971). The right side of the body is always used for measurements irrespective of the preferred side of the subject (Ross & Marfell-Jones, 1991). It is sometimes impracticable to use the right side due to injury (swelling, casts, etc.) and at other times it is desirable to compare the two sides of the body following injury and/or rehabilitation, in which case the left side may be used. Comparisons between the left and right sides of the body have indicated that there is either no significant difference in skinfold thickness (Womersley & Durnin, 1973) or that the differences, although statistically significant, are of no practical significance (Martorell, Mendoza, Mueller & Pawson, 1988) even when the subject's musculature and bone have hypertrophied on one side such as in tennis players (Gwinup, Chelvam & Steinberg, 1971; Jokl, 1976; Montoye, Smith, Fardon & Howley, 1980). Variations from standard procedures, however, should be recorded on the proforma sheet. For example, if time permits, left-dominant subjects may be measured on their dominant side for somatotype analysis as originally described by Heath and Carter (1967).

- The skinfold is picked up at the marked line. It should be grasped so that a double fold of skin plus the underlying subcutaneous adipose tissue is held between the thumb and index finger. The near edge of the thumb and finger are in line with the marked site. The back of the hand should be facing the measurer. Care must be taken not to incorporate underlying muscle tissue in the grasp. In order to eliminate muscle, the finger and thumb roll the fold slightly thereby also ensuring that there is a sufficiently large grasp of the fold. If difficulty is encountered the subject should tense the muscle until the tester is confident that only skin and subcutaneous tissue are in the grasp. Since a double fold of skin (dermis) is also being measured, some variability may be attributed to variations in skin thicknesses at different sites over the body and among different people (Martin, Ross, Drinkwater & Clarys, 1985). Despite skin thickness decreasing with age [due to changes in collagen structure (Carter, 1980)], this should not normally be considered an important variable since it is outside of the resolution for detection with skinfold calipers.

- The nearest edge of the contact faces of the calipers are applied 1 cm lateral to the thumb and finger. If the calipers are placed too deep or too shallow incorrect values may be recorded. As a guide, calipers should be placed at a depth of approximately mid-fingernail. Practice is also necessary to ensure the same size of skinfold is grasped at the same location every time.

- The calipers are held at 90° to the surface of the skinfold site at all times. If the caliper jaws are allowed to slip or are incorrectly aligned the distance recorded may be inaccurate. Make sure the hand grasping the skin remains holding the fold while the calipers are in contact with the skin.

- Measurement is recorded two seconds after the full pressure of the calipers are applied (Kramer & Ulmer, 1981; Ross & Marfell-Jones, 1991). It is important that the measurer makes sure that fingers resting on the caliper trigger do not prevent the full caliper pressure from being exerted. In the case of large skinfolds the needle may still be moving at this point. The measurement is nevertheless recorded at this time. This standardisation is necessary since adipose tissue is compressible (Martin et al., 1985). A constant recording time enables test/retest comparisons to be made while controlling for skinfold compressibility.

- If possible 2-3 measurements should be taken at each site with the average value being used in any further calculations if two measurements are taken, and the median value used if three measurements are taken. It is especially important for the beginner to repeat measurements so that confidence and reproducibility can be established. Where possible an assistant should be used to record values and help standardise measurement techniques. The recommended levels of intra-examiner reliability (%TEM) for repeated skinfold measures are shown in Chapter 13. If these are not achieved, additional measurements should be taken.

- Skinfold sites should be measured in succession to avoid experimenter bias. That is, a complete data set is obtained before repeating the measurements for the second and then third time. This may also help to reduce the effects of skinfold compressibility. They should be measured in the same order as listed on the proforma so that the assistant is familiar with the routine and errors are minimised. [Note: If consecutive skinfold measurements become smaller, the adipose tissue is likely being compressed where the intra- and extracellular fluid content is gradually being reduced. This most often occurs in the fatter subjects. In this instance the tester should move to the next site and return to the original site after several minutes.]

- Skinfold measurements should not be taken after training or competition, sauna, swimming or showering, since exercise, warm water and heat produce hyperæmia (increased blood flow) in the skin with a concomitant increase in skinfold thickness. Additionally, dehydration has been suggested (Consolazio, Johnson & Pecora, 1963) to cause the skinfold thickness to increase due to changes in skin turgidity (tenseness).

5.4.2 Anatomical landmarks for skinfolds – refer to Figures 15 and 16.

1 Triceps®

This skinfold is raised with the left thumb and index finger on the marked posterior mid-acromiale-radiale line. The fold is vertical and parallel to the line of the upper arm. The skinfold is taken on the most posterior surface of the arm over the triceps muscle when viewed from the side. The marked skinfold site should be just visible from the side indicating that this is the most posterior point over the triceps

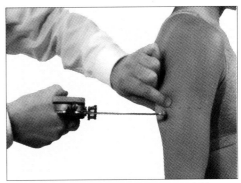

Figure 13 Measurement of the triceps skinfold

whilst held in the anatomical position (at the level of the mid-acromiale-radiale line). For measurement, the arm should be relaxed with the shoulder joint slightly externally rotated and elbow extended by the side of the body.

2 Subscapular®

The subject should be standing erect with the arms by the side. The thumb palpates the inferior angle of the scapula to determine the undermost tip. The skinfold is raised with the left thumb and index finger at the marked site 2 cm along a line running laterally and obliquely downwards from the subscapulare landmark at an angle (approximately 45°) as determined by the natural fold lines of the skin.

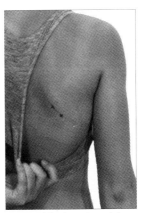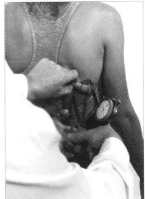

Figure 14a Location of the subscapular landmark

Figure 14b Measurement of the subscapular skinfold

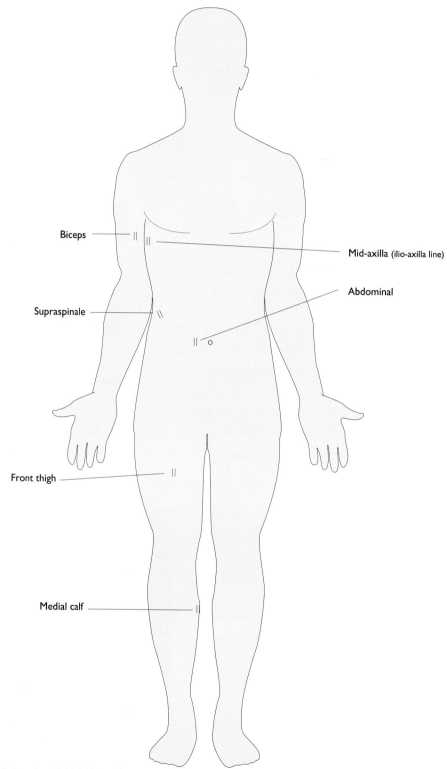

Biceps

Mid-axilla (ilio-axilla line)

Abdominal

Supraspinale

Front thigh

Medial calf

Figure 15 Location of skinfold sites (anterior view)

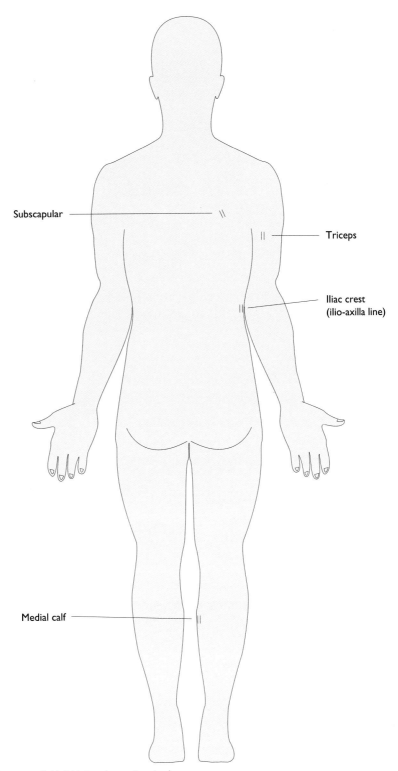

Subscapular

Triceps

Iliac crest
(ilio-axilla line)

Medial calf

Figure 16 Location of skinfold sites (posterior view)

49

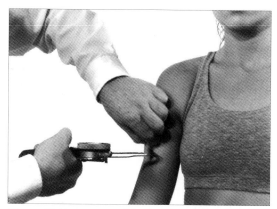

Figure 17 Measurement of the biceps skinfold

3 Biceps®

This skinfold is raised with the left thumb and index finger on the marked mid-acromiale-radiale line so that the fold runs vertically, that is, parallel to the axis of the upper arm. The subject stands with the arm relaxed, the shoulder joint slightly externally rotated and elbow extended. The fold is located on the most anterior aspect of the surface of the right arm. Check that the marked point for the biceps skinfold is on the most anterior surface over the biceps by viewing the arm from the side whilst held in the anatomical position. The marked skinfold site should be just visible from the side, indicating that this is the most anterior point over the biceps (at the level of the mid-acromiale-radiale line).

4 Iliac crest®

This skinfold is raised immediately superior to the iliocristale on the ilio-axilla line.

The subject abducts the right arm to the horizontal or places the arm across the chest to rest the right hand on the left shoulder. Align the fingers of the left hand on the iliocristale landmark and exert pressure inwards so that the fingers roll over the iliac crest. Substitute the left thumb for these fingers and relocate the index finger a sufficient distance superior to the thumb so that this grasp becomes the skinfold to be measured. The fold runs slightly downwards toward the medial aspect of the body. [Note: This skinfold is equivalent to that described by Durnin & Womersley (1974) as the suprailiac skinfold.]

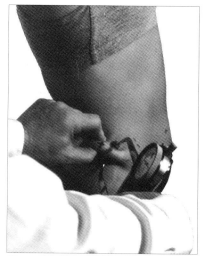

Figure 18 Measurement of the Iliac crest skinfold

5 Supraspinale®

This skinfold was originally named suprailiac by Heath and Carter (1967), but is now known as the supraspinale (Carter & Heath, 1990). It is the skinfold used when the Heath-Carter somatotype is being determined (see Chapter 6). This fold is raised at the point where the line from

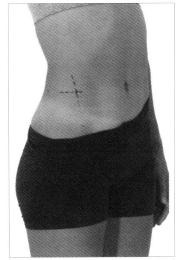

Figure 19a Location of the supraspinale landmark

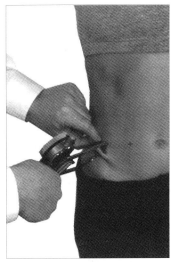

Figure 19b Measurement of the supraspinale skinfold

the iliospinale mark to the anterior axillary border intersects with the horizontal line of the superior border of the ilium at the level of the iliocristale. This is about 5-7cm above the iliospinale depending on the size of the adult subject, and may be as small as about 2cm in a young child. The fold runs medially downward at about a 45° angle.

6 Abdominal®

This is a vertical fold raised 5 cm (approximately in the midline of the belly of the Rectus Abdominis) from the right hand side of the omphalion (midpoint of the navel). It is particularly important at this site that the measurer is sure the initial grasp is firm and broad since often the underlying musculature is poorly developed. This may result in an underestimation of the thickness of the subcutaneous layer of tissue. [Note: Do not place the calipers inside the navel.]

7 Front thigh®

The measurer stands facing the right side of the subject on the lateral side of the thigh. The subject's knee is bent at right angles by placing theright foot on a box or by being seated. The site is

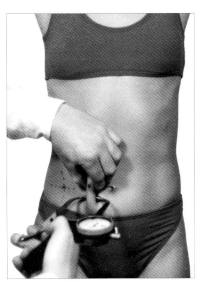

Figure 20 Measurement of the abdominal skinfold

marked parallel to the long axis of the femur at the mid-point of the distance between the inguinal fold and the superior border of the patella (while the leg is bent). The skinfold measurement can be taken while the knee is bent or with the leg straight and resting on a box. For example, if the fold is difficult to raise the subject may be asked to extend the knee joint slightly by moving the foot forward to relieve the tension of the skin. If there is still difficulty the subject may assist by lifting the underside of the thigh to relieve the tension of the skin. As a last resort for subjects with particularly tight skinfolds, a recorder (standing on the medial aspect of the subject's thigh) can assist by raising the fold using two hands so that there is about 6 cm between the fingers of the right hand raising the fold at the correct anatomical landmark and the left hand which raises a distal fold. The calipers are then located between the recorder's hands, 1 cm from the recorder's thumb and forefinger of the right hand.

Figure 21a Location of the front thigh landmark

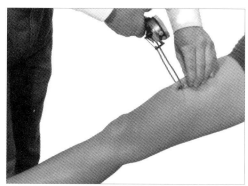

Figure 21b Measurement of the front thigh skinfold without subject assistance

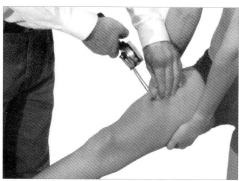

Figure 21c Measurement of the front thigh skinfold with subject assistance

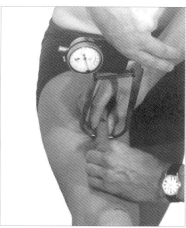

Figure 21d Measurement of the front thigh skinfold with assistance from a recorder

8 Medial calf®

With the subject either seated or with the foot on a box (knee at 90°) and with the calf relaxed, the vertical fold is raised on the medial aspect of the calf at a level where it has maximal circumference. This circumference will be determined during the measurement of girths and this level must be marked on the medial aspect of the calf during this process. View the marked site from the front to ensure that the most medial point has been correctly identified.

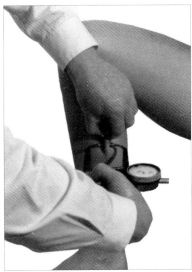

Figure 22 Measurement of the medial calf skinfold

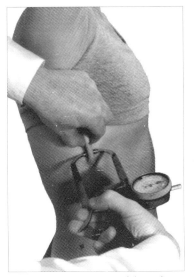

Figure 23 Measurement of the mid-axilla skinfold

9 Mid-axilla®

This is a vertical fold on the ilio-axilla line at the level of the marked xiphoidale of the sternum. It is usual practice to have the subject lift the right arm at about 90° to the body (with the subject's hand resting on their head). Elevating the arm further than this may cause the skin to become difficult to grasp.

5.5 Girths

5.5.1 Techniques for measuring girths

The cross hand technique is used for measuring all girths and the reading is taken from the tape where, for easier viewing, the zero is located more lateral than medial on the subject. In measuring girths the tape is held at right angles to the limb or body segment which is being measured and the tension of the tape must be constant. Constant tension is achieved by ensuring that there is no indentation of the skin but the tape holds its place at the designated landmark. While constant tension tapes may be available, the Lufkin tape is preferred since it allows the anthropometrist to control the tension. To position the tape, hold the case in the right hand and the stub in the left. Facing the body part to be measured, pass the stub end around the back of the limb and take hold of the stub with the right hand which then holds both the stub and the casing. At this point the left hand is free to manipulate the tape to the correct level. Apply sufficient tension to the tape with the right hand to hold it at that position while the left hand reaches underneath the casing to take hold of the stub again. The tape is now around the part to be measured. The middle fingers of both hands are free to exactly locate the tape at the landmark for measurement and to orientate the tape so that the zero is easily read. The juxtaposition of the tape ensures that there is contiguity of the two parts of the tape from which the girth is determined. When reading the tape the measurer's eyes must be at the same level as the tape to avoid any error of parallax.

5.5.2 Anatomical landmarks for girths – refer to Figure 31

10 Head

The girth of the head is obtained in the Frankfort plane at the level immediately above the glabella (mid-point between the brow ridges) while the subject is seated or standing. The tape needs to be pulled tight to compress the hair. Use of the middle fingers at the side of the head is often necessary to prevent the tape from slipping over the head. Do not include the ears and ensure that there are no hair pins, clips or similar items in the hair during the measurement.

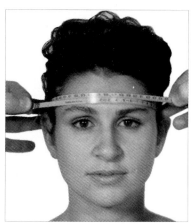

Figure 24 Measurement of the head girth

11 Neck

The girth around the neck is measured immediately superior to the thyroid cartilage (Adam's apple). The subject should maintain the head in the Frankfort plane and may be seated or standing. It is important not to pull the tape tight in this region since the tissues are compressible. The tape is held perpendicular to the long axis of the neck which may not necessarily be in the horizontal plane.

Figure 25 Measurement of the neck girth

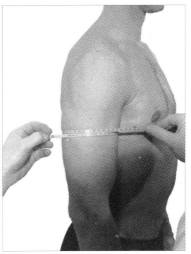

Figure 26 Measurement of the relaxed arm girth

12 Arm relaxed®

The girth of the upper arm (hanging in a relaxed position by the side of the body) is measured at the level of the mid-acromiale-radiale. The tape should be positioned perpendicular to the long axis of the humerus.

13 Arm flexed and tensed®

This is the maximum circumference of the right upper arm which is raised anteriorly to the horizontal with the forearm at about 45° to the upper arm. The measurer stands to the side of the subject and with the tape loosely in position asks the subject to partially flex the Biceps to identify the point where the girth will be maximal. Loosen the tension on the casing end, then ask the subject to "clench your fist, bring your hand toward your shoulder so your elbow's at about 45° – and fully tense the biceps and hold it" while the measurement is made.

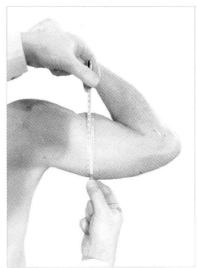

Figure 27 Measurement of the upper arm girth while flexed and tensed

14 **Forearm**

The measurement is taken at the maximum girth of the forearm with the subject holding the palm up while relaxing the muscles of the arm. Using the cross hand technique it is necessary to slide the tape measure up and down the forearm and make serial measurements in order to correctly locate the level of the maximal girth. It usually occurs just distal to the elbow.

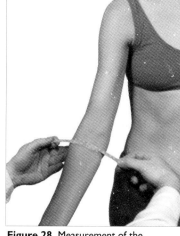

Figure 28 Measurement of the forearm girth

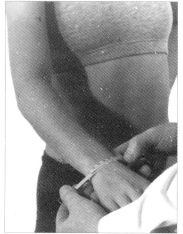

Figure 29 Measurement of the wrist girth

15 **Wrist**

This girth measurement is taken distal to the styloid processes. It is the minimum girth in this region. Manipulation of the tape measure is, therefore, required to be sure the minimal girth is obtained.

16 **Chest**

This girth is taken at the level of the mesosternale. The anthropometrist stands to the right of the subject who slightly abducts the arms allowing the tape to be passed around the chest in a near horizontal plane. The subject should breathe normally and the measurement is taken at the end of a normal expiration (end tidal) with the arms relaxed at the sides. Care is required to ensure that the tape does not deviate from the horizontal plane, particularly around the subject's back.

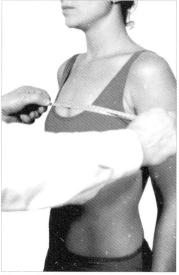

Figure 30 Measurement of the chest girth

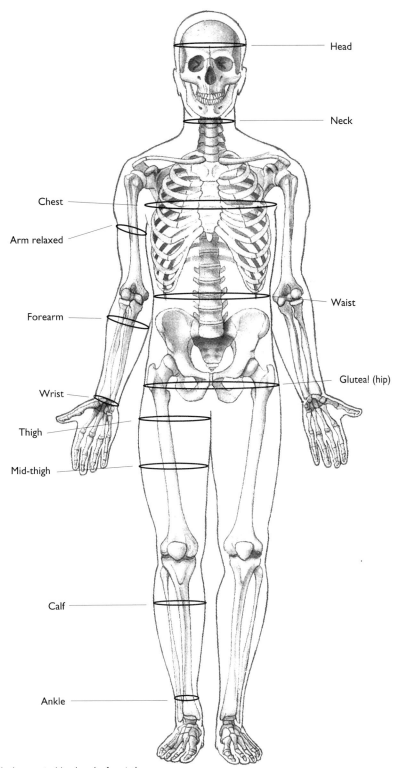

Figure 31 Anatomical landmarks for girths

17 Waist®

This measure is taken at the level of the narrowest point between the lower costal (rib) border and the iliac crest. If there is no obvious narrowing then the measurement is taken at the mid-point between these two landmarks. The measurer stands in front of the subject to correctly locate the narrowing of the waist. The measurement is taken at the end of a normal expiration with the arms relaxed at the sides.

18 Gluteal (hip)®

This is taken at the level of the greatest posterior protuberance of the buttocks which usually corresponds anteriorly to about the level of the symphysis pubis. The measurer stands at the side of the subject to ensure the tape is held in a horizontal plane when measuring this site. The subject stands with feet together and should not tense the gluteal muscles.

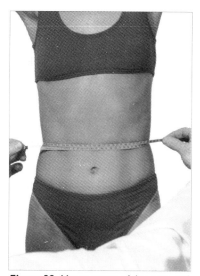

Figure 32 Measurement of the waist girth

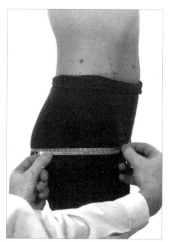

Figure 33a Measurement of the gluteal girth (side view)

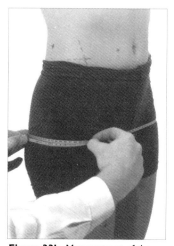

Figure 33b Measurement of the gluteal girth (front view)

19 Thigh

The girth of the thigh is taken 1 cm below the level of the gluteal fold, perpendicular to the long axis of the thigh. The subject stands erect with the feet slightly apart and mass equally distributed on both feet. It is usually helpful to have the subject stand on a box or stool for this measure. Pass the tape around the lower portion

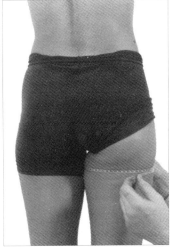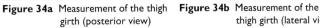

Figure 34a Measurement of the thigh girth (posterior view)

Figure 34b Measurement of the thigh girth (lateral view)

of the thigh and then slide the tape up to the correct plane.

20 Mid-thigh

This is the right thigh girth measurement taken perpendicular to the long axis of the thigh. It is taken at the level midway between the trochanterion and tibiale laterale sites. It is usually helpful to have subjects stand on a box or stool for this measure. They should assume the same position as described for thigh girth above.

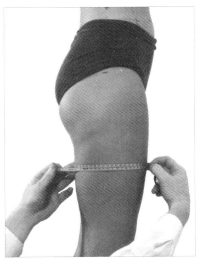

Figure 35 Measurement of the mid-thigh girth

21 Calf®

This is the maximum girth of the calf. The subject stands facing away from the measurer in an elevated position, for example, on a box or stool, with the weight equally distributed on both feet. The elevated position will make it easier for the measurer to align the eyes with the tape. The measurement is taken from the lateral aspect of the leg. Place the tape around the calf in the prescribed manner. The maximal girth is found by using the middle fingers to manipulate the position of the tape in a series of up or down measurements to identify the maximal girth. Mark this level on the medial aspect of the calf in preparation for skinfold assessment.

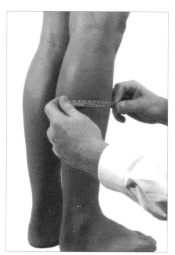

Figure 36 Measurement of the calf girth

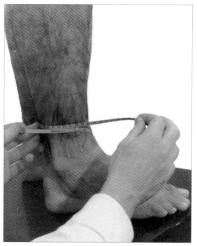

Figure 37 Measurement of the ankle girth

22 Ankle

The minimum girth of the ankle is taken at the narrowest point superior to the sphyrion tibiale. The tape needs to be manipulated up and down this region to ensure that the minimal girth is obtained.

5.6 Lengths/heights

5.6.1 Techniques for measuring lengths/heights

There are two methods for measuring body segment lengths. One involves measuring the vertical distance from the floor to a series of marked landmarks with an anthropometer. In this case the barefoot subject assumes the erect standing position with the feet together as previously described. This is the method of measuring projected segment lengths and is illustrated in Figure 42. Following these measurements it is possible (by subtraction) to determine the lengths of individual segments, for example acromiale minus radiale height, to give upper arm length (acromiale-radiale). The second method allows direct measurements of these segment lengths illustrated by Figure 43. In this case either large sliding calipers or a segmometer is the instrument used. Previous research (Day, 1986) has shown errors are more common when the projected segment lengths method is used. Therefore, it is recommended that segment lengths are measured directly. Rigid, large sliding calipers are preferable to a tape since the tape has a tendency to overestimate lengths because it is difficult to keep it straight (Day, 1986). The following guidelines are based on the use of large sliding calipers although with minimal alterations a segmometer may be substituted. Before making any measurements inspect each pointer on the caliper to make sure there has not been movement away from the landmark. It is preferable that the caliper end where measurements are to be read is located closest to the measurer's eye level.

5.6.2 Anatomical landmarks for lengths/ heights – refer to Figures 42 and 43.

23 Acromiale-radiale

This is the upper arm length where the distance is measured between these two previously marked landmarks. The subject stands erect with the palms slightly off the thighs. One arm of the caliper is held on the acromiale while the other arm is placed on the radiale. Where subjects have large deltoid muscles an anthropometer must be used to avoid curvature of the segmometer.

Figure 38 Measurement of the acromial-radiale segment length

24 Radiale-stylion

This is the length of the forearm. It is the distance between the previously marked landmarks for radiale and stylion while the subject assumes the anatomical position. One caliper arm is held against the radiale and the other arm is placed on the stylion landmark. The caliper is positioned so that it runs parallel to the long axis of the radius.

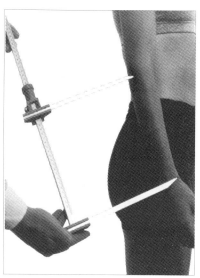

Figure 39 Measurement of the radiale-stylion segment length.

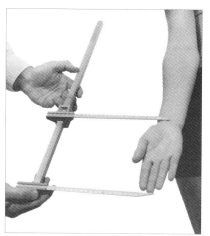

Figure 40 Measurement of the midstylion-dactylion segment length

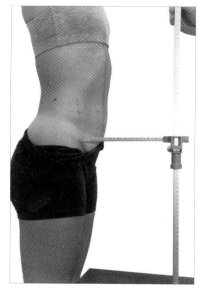

Figure 41 Measurement of the iliospinale-box height

25 Midstylion-dactylion

This is the length of the hand. The measurement is taken as the shortest distance from the marked midstylion line to the dactylion. The subject places the hand in a supinated position (palms facing up) and the fingers fully extended (not hyperextended). One end of the caliper is placed on the marked midstylion line while the other end is positioned on the most distal point of the third digit.

26 Iliospinale

The height from the top of the box to the iliospinale is measured. The subject stands with feet together facing the box so that their toes are placed in the cut-out portion of the box. The base of the caliper is placed flush on top of the box and the caliper oriented vertically upwards with the moving arm positioned at the marked iliospinale site. [Note: The height of interest is the height from the floor to the landmark iliospinale. This is obtained by adding the box height to the height recorded on the data proforma for the iliospinale-box height.]

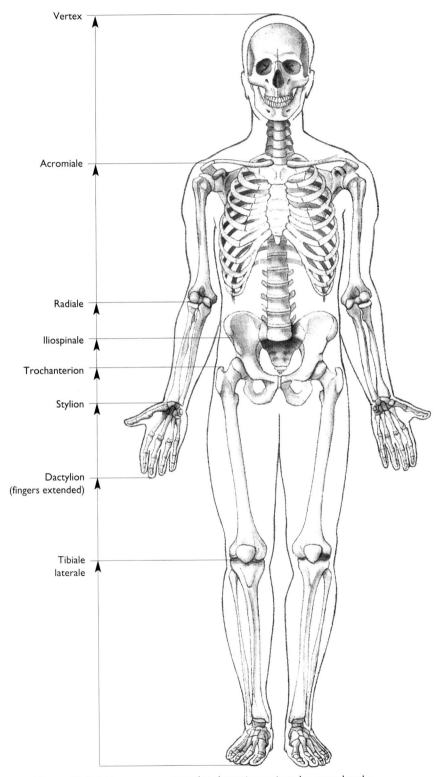

Vertex

Acromiale

Radiale

Iliospinale

Trochanterion

Stylion

Dactylion
(fingers extended)

Tibiale
laterale

Figure 42 Height measurements used to determine projected segment lengths

63

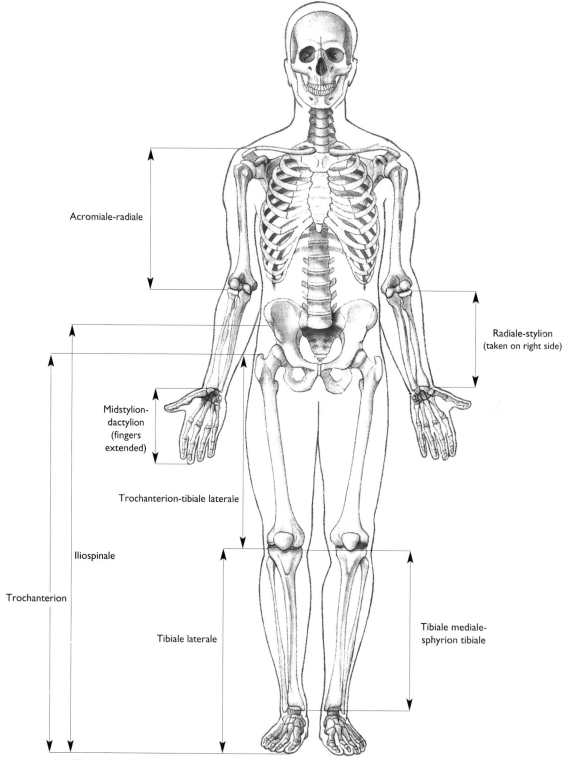

Acromiale-radiale

Radiale-stylion
(taken on right side)

Midstylion-
dactylion
(fingers
extended)

Trochanterion-tibiale laterale

Iliospinale

Trochanterion

Tibiale laterale

Tibiale mediale-
sphyrion tibiale

Figure 43 Directly measured segment lengths

27 Trochanterion

This is the height from the top of the box to the trochanterion. The subject stands with feet together and the lateral aspect of their right leg against the box. The base of the caliper is placed flush on top of the box and the caliper oriented vertically upwards with the moving arm positioned at the marked trochanterion site. [Note: The height of interest is the height from the floor to the landmark trochanterion. This is obtained by adding the box height to the height recorded on the data proforma for the trochanterion-box height.]

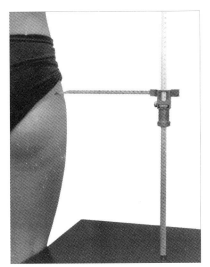

Figure 44 Measurement of the trochanterion-box height

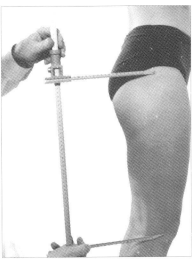

Figure 45 Measurement of the trochanterion-tibiale laterale segment length

28 Trochanterion-tibiale laterale

This is the length of the thigh. The distance from the trochanterion to the tibiale laterale is measured while the subject stands on the box with their right side facing the anthropometrist. One end of the caliper is placed on the marked trochanterion and the other end is placed to the marked tibiale laterale site.

29 Tibiale laterale

This is the length of the lower leg, that is, the distance from the floor (i.e. top of the box when the subject stands on the box) to the tibiale laterale

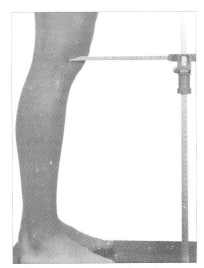

Figure 46 Measurement of the tibiale laterale height

landmark. It is usual practice to have the subject stand on the box while the base of the caliper is on the top of the box and the moving arm is placed on the marked tibiale laterale site. The caliper should be held in the vertical plane. The height from the tibiale laterale to the top of the box is then measured.

30 Tibiale mediale-sphyrion tibiale

This is the length of the tibia. It is the measured length between the tibiale mediale and the sphyrion tibiale. The subject should be seated on the box for this measurement with the right ankle crossed over and resting on the left knee. This should present the medial aspect of the leg in a near horizontal plane. One end of the caliper is placed on the marked tibiale mediale site and the other end positioned on the marked sphyrion site.

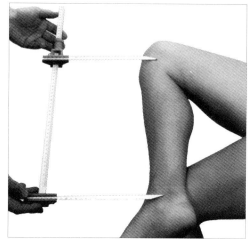

Figure 47 Measurement of the tibiale mediale-sphyrion tibiale segment length

5.7 Breadths

5.7.1 Techniques for measuring breadths (and lengths).

Both the small sliding (bone) calipers and the large sliding calipers are held in the same way. The calipers lie on the backs of the hands while the thumbs rest against the inside edge of the caliper arms, and the extended index fingers lie along the outside edges of the arms. In this position the fingers are able to exert considerable pressure to reduce the thickness of any underlying soft tissue and the middle fingers are free to palpate the bony landmarks on which the caliper faces are to be placed.

The measurements are made when the calipers are in place, with the pressure maintained along the index fingers.

5.7.2 Anatomical landmarks for breadths (and lengths) – refer to Figure 53.

31 Biacromial

This is the distance between the most lateral points on the acromion processes. This site is measured with the arms of the large sliding calipers placed on the most lateral points of the acromion processes. This usually does not correspond to the previously marked acromiale landmarks, which are typically superior, medial and anterior to these lateral points. The subject stands with the arms hanging at the sides, and the measurer,

Figure 48 Measurement of the biacromial breadth

standing behind the subject, should bring the anthropometer blades in to the acromion processes at an angle of about 45° pointing upwards. Firm pressure should be applied to compress the overlying tissues.

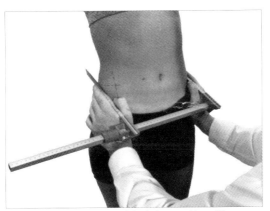

Figure 49 Measurement of the biiliocristal breadth

32 Biiliocristal

The distance between the most lateral points (iliocristale) on the iliac tubercles is measured. The branches of the anthropometer are kept at about 45° pointing upwards and the measurer stands in front of the subject. Firm pressure is applied by the anthropometrist to reduce the effect of overlying tissues.

33 **Foot length**

This is the distance from the longest toe (which may be the first or second phalanx) to the most posterior point on the heel of the foot while the subject is standing with the weight equally distributed on both feet. The calipers should be kept parallel to the long axis of the foot and minimal pressure is

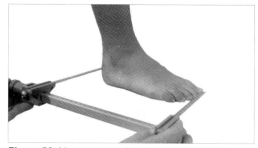

Figure 50 Measurement of the foot length

applied. It is more convenient for the measurer if the subject stands on the box during this measurement.

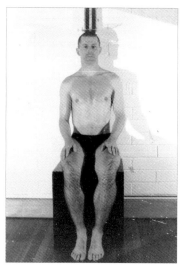

Figure 51 Measurement of the sitting height

34 **Sitting height**

The height from the table or box (where the subject sits) to the vertex when the head is held in the Frankfort plane. The measurer places the hands along the jaw of the subject with the fingers reaching to the mastoid processes. The subject is instructed to take and hold a deep breath, and while keeping the head in the Frankfort plane the measurer applies gentle upward lift through the mastoid processes.

[Note: sitting height should be taken with the same technique as was used for stature.]

35 **Transverse chest**

The distance is measured between the most lateral aspect of the thorax when the superior aspect of the caliper scale is positioned at the level of the mesosternale (at the front) and the blades are positioned at an angle of 30° downward from the horizontal. This will prevent the calipers from slipping between the ribs. The measurer stands in front of the subject who may be either seated or standing. Care must be taken to avoid inclusion of the pectoral or

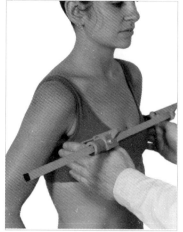

Figure 52 Measurement of the transverse chest

Latissimus Dorsi muscles. The measurement is taken at the end of a tidal expiration.

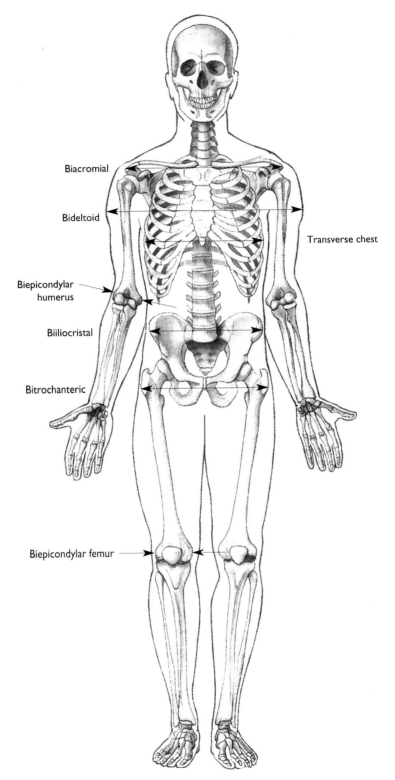

Biacromial

Bideltoid

Transverse chest

Biepicondylar
humerus

Biiliocristal

Bitrochanteric

Biepicondylar femur

Figure 53 Location of breadth measurements

36 Anterior-posterior chest depth

This is the distance measured between the recurved branches of the wide-spreading calipers when positioned at the level of the mesosternale. The measurer applies the calipers over the right shoulder of the subject who is seated in an erect position and is instructed to breathe normally. The rear branch of the caliper should be positioned on the spinous process of the vertebra at the level of the mesosternale. Measurement is taken at the end of a normal breath out (end tidal).

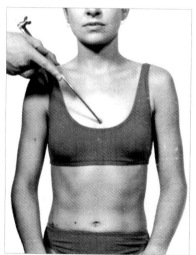 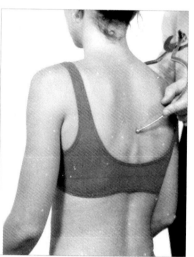

Figure 54a Measurement of the anterior-posterior chest depth (anterior view)

Figure 54b Measurement of the anterior-posterior chest depth (posterior view)

37 Biepicondylar humerus®

The distance is measured between the medial and lateral epicondyles of the humerus when the arm is raised anteriorly to the horizontal and the forearm is flexed at right angles to the upper arm. With the small sliding calipers gripped correctly, use the middle fingers to palpate the epicondyles of the humerus, starting proximal to the sites. The bony points first felt are the epicondyles. The calipers are placed directly on the epicondyles so that the arms of the calipers point upward at about a 45° angle to the horizontal plane. Maintain firm pressure with the index fingers as the value is read. Because the medial epicondyle is lower than the lateral epicondyle the measured distance may be somewhat oblique.

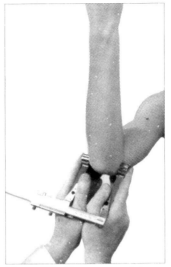

Figure 55a Locating the humeral epicondyles by palpation

Figure 55b Measurement of the biepicondylar humerus breadth

38 Biepicondylar femur®

The distance is measured between the medial and lateral epicondyles of the femur when the subject is seated and the leg flexed at the knee to form a right angle with the thigh. With the subject seated and the calipers in place use the middle fingers to palpate the epicondyles of the femur beginning proximal to the sites. The bony points first felt are the epicondyles. Place the caliper faces on the epicondyles so that the arms of the calipers point downward at about a 45° angle to the horizontal. Maintain firm pressure with the index fingers until the value is read.

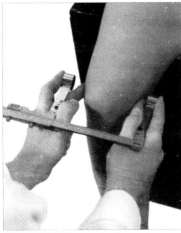

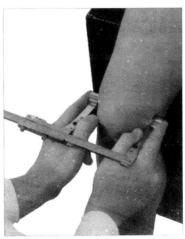

Figure 56a Locating the femoral epicondyles by palpation

Figure 56b Measurement of the biepicondylar breadth

5.7.3 Sport specific sites

The following sites have been included as a guide for anthropometrists who may require these measurements for specific groups of athletes. For example, arm span has been a routine measurement for swimmers and volleyballers in sports institutes. Bideltoid and bitrochanteric breadths are useful predictors of projected frontal surface area in sports such as cycling, running and skating.

Arm span

This is the distance between the dactylia of the left and right hands when standing against a wall. To prevent potential errors due to a large chest, the subject stands with his or her back to the wall. The outstretched arms should be in the horizontal position. It is often useful to use a corner of a room for one end of the measurement, thus only one mark needs to be made on the wall/board. An anthropometric tape is used to measure the arm span.

Figure 57 Measurement of the maximum arm span

Bideltoid breadth

This is the distance between the most lateral aspect of the deltoid muscles and is measured using the large sliding caliper. The subject stands relaxed with arms hanging by the sides and palms resting against the thighs. Minimal pressure (no indentation of the skin should occur) must be applied to the site by the measurer. The blades of the anthropometer should be angled pointing slightly upwards.

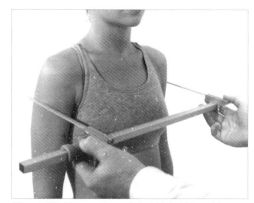

Figure 58 Measurement of the bideltoid breadth

Bitrochanteric breadth

The distance between the most lateral aspects of the trochanteria. This is not at the same level as the previously marked trochanterion landmark. The anthropometrist should stand in front of the subject and the blades of the anthropometer should be angled pointing slightly upwards.

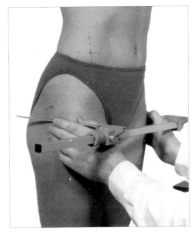

Figure 59 Measurement of the bitrochanteric breadth

6　References

Anderson, N.R., & Ross, W.D. (1986).
　　Reliability and objectivity in skinfold caliper and ultrasound measurements of skin and adipose tissue thickness at six sites.
　　In T. Reilly, J. Watkins, & J. Borms (Eds.), **Kinanthropometry III** (pp. 15-20).
　　Champaign, Illinois: Human Kinetics.

Carr, R., Balde, L., Rempel, R., & Ross, W.D. (1993).
　　Technical note: on the measurement of direct vs. projected anthropometric lengths.
　　American Journal of Physical Anthropology, 90, 515-517.

Carter, J.E.L. (1980).
　　The Heath-Carter somatotype method.
　　San Diego: San Diego State University Syllabus Service.

Carter, J.E.L., & Heath, B. (1990).
　　Somatotyping – development and applications.
　　Cambridge: Cambridge University Press.

Consolazio, C.F., Johnson, R.E., & Pecora, L. J. (1963).
　　Physiological measurements of metabolic function in man (p. 303).
　　London: McGraw-Hill.

Day, J.A.P. (1986).
　　Bilateral symmetry and reliability of upper limb measurements.
　　In J.A.P. Day (Ed.), **Perspectives in kinanthropometry** (pp. 257-261).
　　Champaign, Illinois: Human Kinetics.

Drinkwater, D.T., & Ross, W.D. (1980).
　　The anthropometric fractionation of body mass.
　　In G. Ostyn, G. Beunen, & J. Simons (Eds.), **Kinanthropometry II** (pp. 178-189).
　　Baltimore: University Park Press.

Durnin, J.V.G.A., & Womersley, J. (1974).
Body fat assessed from total body density and its estimation from skinfold thickness: measurements on 481 men and women aged 16 to 72 years.
British Journal of Nutrition, 32, 77-97.

Gwinup, G., Chelvam, R., & Steinberg, T. (1971).
Thickness of subcutaneous fat and activity of underlying muscles.
Annals of Internal Medicine, 74, 408-411.

Heath, B.H., & Carter, J.E.L. (1967).
A modified somatotype method.
American Journal of Physical Anthropology, 27, 57-74.

Jackson, A.S., Pollock, M.L., & Gettman, L.R. (1978).
Intertester reliability of selected skinfold and circumference measurements and percent fat estimates.
Research Quarterly, 49, 546-551.

Jokl, E. (1976).
Record physiology.
In E. Jokl, & R.L. Anand (Eds.),
Advances in Exercise Physiology, Medicine and Sport 9 (pp. 3-22).
Basel: Karger.

Kerr, D. (1992).
An anthropometric method of fractionation of skin, adipose, bone, muscle and residual tissue masses in males and females aged 6 to 77 years.
Unpublished Master's thesis, Simon Fraser University, Burnaby, BC, Canada.

Kramer, H.J., & Ulmer, H.V. (1981).
Two second standardization of the Harpenden caliper.
European Journal of Applied Physiology, 46, 103-104.

Lohman, T.G., & Pollock, M.L. (1981).
Which caliper — How much training?
Journal of Physical Education and Recreation, 52, 27-29.

Martin, A.D., Ross, W.D., Drinkwater, D.T., & Clarys, J.P. (1985).
Prediction of body fat by skinfold caliper: assumptions and cadaver evidence.
International Journal of Obesity, 9, 31-39.

Martorell, R., Mendoza, F., Mueller, W.H., & Pawson, I.G. (1988).
Which side to measure: right or left?
In T.G. Lohman, A.F. Roche, & R. Martorell (Eds.),
Anthropometric standardization reference manual (pp. 87-91).
Champaign Illinois: Human Kinetics.

Montoye, H.J., Smith, E.L., Fardon, D.F., & Howley, E.T. (1980).
Bone mineral in senior tennis players.
Scandinavian Journal of Sports Science, 2, 26-32.

Reilly, T., Tyrrell, A., & Troup, T.D.G. (1984).
Circadian variation in human stature.
Chronobiol. Int., 1, 121-126.

Ross, W.D., & Marfell-Jones, M.T. (1991).
Kinanthropometry. In J.D. MacDougall, H.A. Wenger, & H.J. Green (Eds.),
Physiological testing of the high-performance athlete (2nd ed.) (pp. 223-308).
Champaign, Illinois: Human Kinetics.

Ruiz, L., Colley, J.R.T., & Hamilton, P.J.S. (1971).
Measurement of triceps skinfold thickness. An investigation of sources of variation.
British Journal of Preventive and Social Medicine, 25, 165-167.

Schmidt, P.K., & Carter, J.E.L. (1990).
Static and dynamic differences among five types of skinfold calipers.
Human Biology, 62, 369-388.

Sumner, E.E., & Whitacre, J. (1931).
Some factors affecting accuracy in the collection of data on the growth of weight in school children.
Journal of Nutrition, 4, 15-33.

Wilby, J., Linge, K., Reilly, T., & Troup, J.D.G. (1985).
Circadian variation in effects of circuit weight training.
British Journal of Sports Medicine, 19, 236.

Womersley, J., & Durnin, J.V.G.A. (1973).
An experimental study on variability of measurements of skinfold thickness on young adults.
Human Biology, 45, 281-292.

Chapter 3
Anthropometry Measurement Error

David Pederson and Christopher Gore

I Introduction

If an anthropometrist measures a subject's skinfolds repeatedly, for example on several successive days, the measurements will usually vary. While a small part of the variability may be due to biological changes in the subject, the major part will probably be due to inconsistency in the technique of the anthropometrist. For example, when skinfolds are being measured the locations of sites on the body may vary slightly from measurement to measurement or the equipment being used may be calibrated to a different level each time. Clearly, it is advantageous for an anthropometrist to minimise technical variability in measurements. In the literature on measurement error, four topics predominate – **precision, reliability, accuracy** and **validity**.

The observed variability in repeated measurements taken on the same subject determines the level of **precision**. Measures of precision usually have the same units as the units of the variable under consideration. High precision corresponds to low variability in successive measurements and is the aim of a competent anthropometrist, since there will then be a high probability that a single measurement will be close to its true value, the value of interest to the measurer.

An anthropometrist does not have a single value for their precision, but has a separate value for each combination of a variable and a measurement procedure. For most anthropometric variables there are acceptable standards of precision which allow anthropometrists to evaluate their own performance. A discussion of desirable and reasonably achievable levels of precision can be found in Chapter 13.

Precision is the most basic indicator of an anthropometrist's expertise. However, if levels of precision are quoted in a technical report then readers need to know both the units and the acceptable standards in order to assess the precision of each variable. An alternative is to quote levels of **reliability**, which are often correlation coefficients and therefore have no units. The measure of reliability which will be presented in this chapter is the **intraclass correlation coefficient** (ICC), for which the values range from 0 (zero reliability) to 1 (perfect reliability).

Thus, measures of precision and reliability differ in their units and in the constraints on their possible values. There are two other differences. Firstly, precision is a characteristic of a particular measurer using a particular measurement technique on a particular variable. Reliability has the same features plus the additional feature of being dependent on the variability of subjects. In general, a measure of reliability for a particular variable will be closer to 1 for a group of subjects who are very different from each other than for a group of subjects who are all relatively alike. Secondly, a measure of precision may be used in subsequent calculations of, for example, confidence intervals, or of the sample size neede to satisfy certain criteria. Measures of reliability, on the other hand, are simply indicators of technique and are not useful for further calculations.

It is important that the measurement obtained by an anthropometrist on a particular subject should be close to the real value. The extent to which a measured value corresponds to the real value is the **accuracy** of the measurement. But what is the "real value"? There is no machine which measures skinfolds, for example, with absolute accuracy. When the accuracy of a measurement is to be determined, it is usually compared with the value obtained by a highly-skilled and experienced anthropometrist (for example, a Level 3 or Level 4 anthropometrist). The values obtained by such a person (called a "criterion" measurer) are assumed to be the real values for variables, on average.

The fourth aspect of measurement error is **validity**, which is the extent to which a measurement actually measures a characteristic. For example, the variable under study may be the general characteristic of "physical fitness" of subjects. A variable or combination of variables which proved to be poor indicators of physical fitness, according to some specified criteria, would be said to have low validity. However, validity is rarely of concern for anthropometric measurements since the variables which are measured are usually well-defined, rather than being abstract concepts.

Because of the different factors influencing precision, reliability and accuracy the correspondence between them is never certain. For example, a high level of reliability is usually an indication of a high level of precision but a high level of precision is not always accompanied by a high level of reliability. It is quite possible (and, in fact, quite common) for a measurer to demonstrate high precision and yet have low accuracy. That would be the situation when the measurer was measuring with a constant bias, but in a consistent way. However, the aim of an anthropometrist should be to achieve high levels of precision, reliability and accuracy, using a valid measuring technique.

For some anthropometric variables the measurements on subjects fall into classes. For example, the body mass of a rower may be classified as being "heavyweight" or "lightweight". Variables of that type are referred to as **qualitative**. However, the techniques discussed in this chapter are appropriate only for **quantitative** variables, for which the values are numbers. The techniques are most appropriate for quantitative variables which have many possible values or which can assume any value within a specified range.

2   Measures of precision and reliability – TEM and ICC

The measure of precision which will be used in this chapter is the technical error of **measurement** (TEM), defined as the standard deviation of repeated measurements taken independently of one another on the same subject. The units of the TEM are the same as the units of the variable measured.

It will be assumed that the same anthropometrist makes all of the measurements and the TEM is therefore intra-examiner (or intra-tester) TEM. The standard deviation of measurements taken independently on the same subject by two or more anthropometrists is inter-examiner (or inter-tester) TEM, which would be expected to exceed intra-examiner TEM if there were consistent differences between anthropometrists. If one of the two measurements on each subject is made by a criterion measurer, the inter-tester TEM may be used to investigate the accuracy of the anthropometrist who made the second measurement on each subject.

The size of the TEM will often be associated with the mean of the variable. For example, for skinfold data it is common to observe a low TEM when the sample mean is low and a high TEM when the sample mean is high. To facilitate the comparison of TEMs collected on different variables or different populations, the following formula may be used to convert the **absolute TEM** to a **relative TEM** (*%TEM*):

$$\%TEM = \frac{TEM}{Mean} \times 100$$

where Mean is the overall mean of the variable which has been measured. The relative TEM gives the error as a percentage of the overall mean and has no units. In other contexts, the %TEM may be referred to as the coefficient of variation of the variable.

The measure of reliability which will be used in this chapter is the intraclass correlation coefficient, which is most easily calculated from the results of an **analysis of variance**

(ANOVA). The mean squares from the ANOVA are combined in a ratio formula to give an ICC. There is not just one ICC for a given set of data. If a different formula is used, a different ICC is obtained. Two interpretations of the ICC presented in this chapter are:

- The ICC indicates the correlation between successive measurements on the same subject.
- The ICC indicates the ability of a measurement procedure to discriminate between subjects.

An ICC is always positive and has no units. Values range from 0 to 1, with a value close to 1 indicating high reliability since successive measurements are then in relatively close agreement.

Further information about the ICC has been given by Denegar and Ball (1993). They present numerical examples which demonstrate that intraclass correlation coefficients are more appropriate measures of reliability than interclass correlation coefficients, such as the Pearson product-moment correlation. The main reason is that interclass coefficients are insensitive to shifts in the sample mean of subjects from one time to the next, whereas intraclass coefficients may be influenced by such shifts.

3   Obtaining reliability data

One issue for reliability data is the definition of a measurement, the value that comes from a single measuring session. For some anthropometric variables, for example stature or mass, a measurement is usually a single reading. For other variables, for example skinfold thicknesses or girths, the usual practice is to take two or more readings and then to use their mean or median as the measurement. The advantage of taking multiple readings is that random errors will tend to cancel out when the mean or median is used. The methodology for a particular variable constitutes the measurement procedure and any TEM or ICC will relate to a well-defined procedure. For example, the TEM and ICC for the sum of 7 skinfolds would be specific to that variable and would almost certainly be quite different from the TEM and ICC for head girth. If the procedure is changed then new data must be obtained and the TEM and the ICC must be recalculated. For instance, if an anthropometrist changed from using Lafayette skinfold calipers to Harpenden skinfold calipers, new reliability data should be obtained for the Harpenden calipers.

The subjects measured to establish the TEM and ICC must be from the population which will be tested in the future or, at least, from a similar population. For example, if future testing is to be on a group of mature weight-lifters then reliability data should not be established on a group of pre-pubescent gymnasts. The number of subjects required to establish the TEM and ICC is determined by the resources available but would be normally at least twenty. Each subject should be measured repeatedly by the same measurer. Two measurements are sufficient and for ease of analysis the number of measurements should be the same for each subject.

A more informative analysis of reliability is possible if all of the first series of measurements are made at the same time and all of the second series of measurements are made at the same time, and so on. However, it is difficult to give a precise definition of "at the same time". For some anthropometric procedures "at the same time" will mean within the space of one morning or of one whole day. Thus, if an anthropometrist measured triceps skinfolds on 20 subjects during one morning and then repeated the measurements on the afternoon of the same day, both the first and second series of triceps skinfold thicknesses could be regarded as having been made "at the same time". Even if the 20 subjects were measured within a two day period and then three days later were measured again within a two day period, both the first and second series of skinfold measurements could be regarded as having been made "at the same time". However, if an anthropometrist measured the triceps skinfold of each subject twice, with a three day period between the two measures, but took three months to accumulate data on 20 subjects, it would not be reasonable to assume that either the first or the second series of triceps skinfold measurements were made "at the same time".

For some measurement procedures the values of subjects at one time may be consistently different from the values at another time, for example because of a change in the base reading of the apparatus being used. For instance, the zero point on Harpenden calipers may be inadvertently altered after a series of skinfold measurements so that 1 mm is added to all readings on the second occasion. The advantage of measuring all subjects at the same time for the first series and then at some time later re-measuring all subjects at the same time for the second series is that the analysis can be used to investigate whether changes have occurred between the first and second series of measures. If it is found that they have changed, ways of improving the measurement procedure can be investigated.

4 One-way and two-way tables of data

The reliability data may be placed in a table for which the columns are the subjects and the rows are the repeated measurements (see Table 1). However, the method of calculation of the TEM and ICC will depend on the nature of the data and, in particular, whether the data form a one-way table or a two-way table. The following question should be asked: Were the measurements made at separate, well-defined times, with all of the subjects being measured on one occasion at the same time and then later re-measured on a second occasion at the same time, and so on? Or, in other words, is there reason to expect that there may be a time-related difference between the sets of measures which is approximately the same for all subjects?

- If the answer is "no", the data constitute a one-way table.
- If the answer is "yes", the data constitute a two-way table.

Table 1 Hypothetical dataset: triceps skinfold measures (mm) on 10 subjects taken twice.

				Subject					
1	2	3	4	5	6	7	8	9	10
9.9	8.6	11.6	10.3	11.7	9.9	10.8	9.4	7.6	8.8
9.3	8.7	10.6	10.5	11.4	9.6	11.0	9.1	7.4	8.2

The term "one-way" is used because in that situation the data only consist of columns of numbers and the rows have no meaning. The numbers in each column may be re-arranged with no loss of information. In a "two-way" table both the rows (= time) and columns (= subjects) have meaning and a rearrangement within a column would destroy the pattern of the data. When the data form a one-way table then the ANOVA is known as a one-way ANOVA and when the data form a two-way table then the ANOVA is known as a two-way ANOVA.

A two-way ANOVA is most easily carried out on a complete table of data with no missing values. If values are missing in a two-way table the choices are:
- delete subjects until a complete table remains and then carry out a two-way ANOVA;
- carry out a one-way ANOVA;
- seek statistical advice on how to carry out a two-way ANOVA with missing values, and then how to obtain estimates of the ICC and TEM.

5 Calculation of TEM and ICC with two measurements per subject

Many authors have presented a simple formula for calculating TEM from a one-way table of data (Dahlberg, 1940) which uses the differences between the two measurements. In this section the TEM and the ICC will be calculated from a one-way table of data by first carrying out a one-way ANOVA but the TEM will also be calculated by the difference method to demonstrate that the two methods of calculation give the same answer. The TEM and ICC will also be calculated from a two-way table of data by first carrying out a two-way ANOVA. In the general formulæ, the number of subjects will be denoted by n and the number of measurements per subject will be denoted by k (for the case of equal numbers) or by $k_1, k_2, \dots, k_n$ for subjects 1 to n (for the case of unequal numbers).

The data which will be used as an example are triceps skinfold measurements (mm) on ten subjects (see Table 1), although it should be noted that a larger number of subjects would be desirable, in practice.

5.1 One-way table of data

In this section it will be assumed that the first measurements were not all made at the same time, nor were the second measurements, so that the data form a one-way table with subjects as columns. It will be common for data to be of that type, particularly in situations where the anthropometrist does not have access to all subjects as a group but must accumulate data over several months, as subjects become available. A one-way ANOVA, either using the standard formulæ given in text-books on statistics or using a statistical computer package, gives Table 2.

Table 2 One-way ANOVA table for the dataset shown in Table 1.

Source of variation	degrees of freedom	sum of squares	mean square
between subjects	9	29.812	3.312
error	10	1.060	0.1060
total	19	30.872	

Then

$$TEM = \sqrt{MS_e} = \sqrt{0.1060} = 0.33 \text{ mm}$$

where MS_e = error mean square. Since the mean of the 20 observations is 9.72,

$$\%TEM = \frac{TEM}{Mean} \times 100 = \frac{0.33}{9.72} \times 100 = 3.4\%$$

The ICC is given by

$$ICC = \frac{MS_s - MS_e}{MS_s + (k-1)MS_e}$$

where MS_s = between subjects mean square, and

$$k = \frac{\Sigma k_i - \dfrac{\Sigma k_i^2}{\Sigma k_i}}{n-1}$$

(unequal numbers case). Since k = 2, in this example,

$$ICC = \frac{MS_s - MS_e}{MS_s + MS_e} = \frac{3.312 - 0.106}{3.312 + 0.106} = 0.94$$

When the TEM is calculated by the *difference method*, the differences (d_i) between the first and second measurements are determined first. For these data the differences are as follows:

$$0.6, -0.1, 1.0, -0.2, 0.3, 0.3, -0.2, 0.3, 0.2, 0.6$$

The sum of the differences (Σd_i) is 2.8 and the sum of squares of the differences (Σd_i^2) is 2.12. Hence

$$TEM = \sqrt{\frac{\Sigma d_i^2}{2n}} = \sqrt{\frac{2.12}{20}} = 0.33 \text{ mm}$$

This is the same answer as was obtained from the ANOVA.

5.2 Two-way table of data

The data will now be re-analysed on the assumption that they form a two-way table. In anthropometry, this corresponds to the situation where, for instance, the triceps skinfold thickness was measured for 20 subjects on one day and 3 days later all 20 subjects were remeasured within one day. That is, there was a distinct time interval between the first and second series of measures, but each series was taken at the same time. A two-way ANOVA, either using the standard formulae given in text-books on statistics or using a statistical computer package, gives Table 3. The mean of time 1 is 9.86 mm and the mean of time 2 is 9.58 mm. The significance of the difference in the means can be tested with an F-test,

$$F = \frac{MS_t}{MS_e} = \frac{0.392}{0.0742} = 5.28$$

where MS_t = between times mean square.

Table 3 Two-way ANOVA table for the dataset shown in Table 1.

Source of variation	degrees of freedom	sum of squares	mean square
between subjects	9	29.812	3.312
between times	1	0.392	0.392
error	9	0.668	0.0742
total	19	30.872	

Since the between times mean square and the error mean square have 1 and 9 degrees of freedom, respectively, the F-ratio also has 1 and 9 degrees of freedom. A table of the F-distribution shows that 5% of F with 1 and 9 degrees of freedom exceeds 5.12 and it is therefore concluded that the means for times 1 and 2 are significantly different at the 5% level of significance, since 5.28 exceeds 5.12.

At this point, in practice, consideration would now be given to why the means were significantly different. If it were found that the difference was due to a change in the measurement procedure which could be identified and avoided in the future, then new data would be collected using the modified procedure and the analysis would be repeated from the beginning. For example, if an investigation revealed that the first series of triceps skinfold measures was taken with careful landmarking of acromiale, radiale and the mid-acromiale-radiale distance but the second series was taken by "eyeballing" the skinfold site, the anthropometrist would need to repeat the second series of measures using careful landmarking. However, if careful investigation of the results and technique revealed no identifiable cause for the difference in the means, then the analysis would proceed with the calculation of TEM and ICC. The latter procedure will be followed in the present case, to illustrate the methods of calculation. Firstly,

$$TEM = \sqrt{\frac{(n-1)MS_e + MS_t}{n}} = \sqrt{0.1060} = 0.33 \text{ mm}$$

Note that the same answer was obtained when the calculation was based on the one-way ANOVA. It follows that the method of differences could also have been used to obtain the TEM from the two-way table of data. The %TEM is also the same for the two analyses, namely 3.4%. In practical terms, the relative TEM is quite small, and is acceptable for skinfold measurements. It would be concluded that the measurer had produced precise measurements of the triceps skinfold.

The ICC is given by

$$ICC = \frac{n(MS_s - MS_e)}{n\,MS_s + k\,MS_t + (nk - n - k)MS_e}$$

Since k = 2, in this example,

$$ICC = \frac{n(MS_s - MS_e)}{n\,MS_s + 2MS_t + (n-2)MS_e}$$

$$= \frac{10(3.312 - 0.0742)}{10(3.312) + 2(0.392) + 8(0.0742)} = 0.94$$

Note that this is close, but not quite identical, to the ICC based on the one-way ANOVA.

6 Calculation of TEM and ICC with three measurements per subject

When three or more measurements of the same variable are available for each subject the difference method for calculating TEM described under heading 5 is inapplicable. However, the general formulae for TEM and ICC which were given under heading 5 may be used and this section contains examples of the calculations.

The data will be the same as for the two measurement example but with the addition of a third measurement of triceps skinfold thickness on each subject (Table 4).

Table 4 Hypothetical dataset: triceps skinfold measures (mm) on 10 subjects taken three times.

1	2	3	4	5	6	7	8	9	10
9.9	8.6	11.6	10.3	11.7	9.9	10.8	9.4	7.6	8.8
9.3	8.7	10.6	10.5	11.4	9.6	11.0	9.1	7.4	8.2
9.7	8.3	11.2	10.6	12.3	9.9	11.4	9.0	7.8	8.3

6.1 One-way table of data

Assuming that the data form a one-way table, a one-way ANOVA gives the results shown in Table 5.

Table 5 One-way ANOVA table for the dataset shown in Table 4.

Source of variation	degrees of freedom	sum of squares	mean square
between subjects	9	49.6630	5.518
error	20	1.8667	0.09333
total	29	51.5297	

$$TEM = \sqrt{\overline{MS_e}} = \sqrt{0.09333} = 0.31 \text{ mm}$$

Since the mean of the thirty observations is 9.76 mm,

$$\%TEM = \frac{TEM}{Mean} \times 100 = \frac{0.31}{9.76} \times 100 = 3.2\%$$

Since k = 3, in this example, the ICC is given by

$$ICC = \frac{MS_s - MS_e}{MS_s + 2(MS_e)} = \frac{5.518 - 0.09333}{5.518 + 2(0.09333)} = 0.95$$

6.2 Two-way table of data

Assuming that the data form a two-way table, a two-way ANOVA gives the results shown in Table 6. The means of the triceps skinfolds for times 1, 2 and 3 are 9.86 mm, 9.58 mm and 9.85 mm, respectively. To test whether the means are significantly different, F is calculated,

$$F = \frac{MS_t}{MS_e} = \frac{0.2523}{0.07567} = 3.33$$

Table 6 Two-way ANOVA table for the dataset shown in Table 4.

Source of variation	degrees of freedom	sum of squares	mean square
between subjects	9	49.6630	5.518
between times	2	0.5047	0.2523
error	18	1.3620	0.07567
total	29	51.5297	

Since the 95th percentile of F with 2 and 18 degrees of freedom is 3.55, it would be concluded that the means are not significantly different at the 5% level of significance. However, 3.33 is close to 3.55 and so some consideration should be given to possible reasons for the second mean of triceps skinfold being below the other two means. If no reasons were forthcoming then the measurement procedure would be accepted in its current form and the analysis would proceed.

$$TEM = \sqrt{\frac{(n-1)MS_e + MS_t}{n}} = \sqrt{\frac{9(0.07567) + 0.2523}{10}} = 0.31 \text{ mm}$$

Again, the same answer was obtained when the calculation was based on the one-way ANOVA and the %TEM is the same for the two analyses, namely 3.2%.

Since k = 3, in this example,

$$ICC = \frac{n(MS_s - MS_e)}{nMS_s + 3MS_t + (2n-3)MS_e}$$

$$= \frac{10(5.518 - 0.07567)}{10(5.518) + 3(0.2523) + 17(0.07567)} = 0.95$$

Again, this is very close, but not identical, to the ICC based on the one-way ANOVA.

7   Interpretation and application of ICC and TEM

7.1   ICC

The one-way ANOVA of the data with two measurements of triceps skinfold per subject (see heading 5.1) gave an ICC of 0.94 and an interpretation of that value is given in the following paragraph.

Suppose that the anthropometrist plans to use the same measurement procedure on a group of subjects from the same or a similar population to that which gave the 10 subjects in the test sample. Then an estimate of the correlation between successive measurements on a single subject is 0.94. Since 0.94 is close to the maximum possible ICC of 1, a high level of agreement will be expected between successive measurements. The measurement procedure will have a high level of reliability. The value of 0.94 obtained from the two-way ANOVA of the same data would be interpreted similarly.

7.2   TEM

The TEM could be used in a variety of ways. Four examples will be given, the first two using the TEM of 0.33 mm obtained from the data with two measurements of triceps skinfold per subject (see heading 5.1). All of these examples assume that the measurement procedure is unchanged since the TEM was calculated. Ideally, the subjects tested in the future should belong to the group (or population) used to obtain the TEM. Note also that a value of the TEM is unique to the anthropometrist who obtained the data, although the values for different anthropometrists who are highly experienced will usually be very close to one another.

Example 1

An athlete is measured and is found to have a triceps skinfold of 9.3 mm. What are the confidence limits of the true value for that athlete?

The standard error of the measurement will be 0.33 mm, and an approximate 68% confidence interval for the true value will be from

$$[9.3 - 0.33] \text{ to } [9.3 + 0.33] \text{ i.e. from 9.0 mm to 9.6 mm.}$$

Alternatively, an approximate 95% confidence interval for the true value will be from

$$[9.3 - 2(0.33)] \text{ to } [9.3 + 2(0.33)] \text{ i.e. from 8.6 mm to 10.0 mm.}$$

In general, the TEM is the standard error of a single measurement. (The measurement ± TEM) gives the approximate 68% confidence interval for the true value of the subject. (The measurement ± 2 × TEM) gives the approximate 95% confidence interval for the true value of the subject.

Although the TEM is the standard deviation of repeated measurements, the term standard error has been used since that is the convention when the problem being considered is one of sampling and subsequent estimation. In this case, the estimation is of the true value of the subject.

Example 2

An athlete is measured twice, one month apart, with the intention of testing whether the athlete's true value has changed between the successive measurements as a result of diet or training, for example. The values are 9.3 mm followed by 8.5 mm.

Each measurement will have a standard error of 0.33 mm. The difference between the measurements is 8.5 − 9.3 = −0.8 mm and the standard error of the difference is $0.33 \times \sqrt{2} = 0.47$ mm. An approximate 68% confidence interval for the true change will be from

$$[-0.8 - 0.47] \text{ to } [-0.8 + 0.47] \text{ i.e. from } -1.3 \text{ mm to } -0.3 \text{ mm.}$$

Since the interval does not include zero, it would be concluded that the subject did change. Effectively, a test has been carried out of the null hypothesis that the true value did not change, and that hypothesis has been rejected at the 32% (the complement of

68%) level of significance. Alternatively, an approximate 95% confidence interval for the true change will be from

$$[-0.8 - 2(0.47)] \text{ to } [-0.8 + 2(0.47)] \text{ i.e. from } -1.7 \text{ mm to } 0.1 \text{ mm.}$$

Since the interval includes zero, it would be concluded (at the 5% level of significance) that the true value of the subject did not change between the two successive measurements. In general, the TEM $\times \sqrt{2}$ gives the standard error of the difference between 2 successive measurements. (The difference $\pm$ standard error) gives the approximate 68% confidence interval for the true change. (The difference $\pm$ 2 standard errors) gives the approximate 95% confidence interval for the true change.

Example 3

The sum of seven skinfolds ($\Sigma 7$) is measured twice on an élite female gymnast, two weeks apart, to monitor her body composition. The gymnast's coach wants to know if her subcutaneous fat is being maintained at a constant level. The $\Sigma 7$ values were 38 mm at the first measure and 41 mm two weeks later. Before conducting these measures the anthropometrist had obtained a TEM of 2.9 mm for $\Sigma 7$ on a sample of 30 élite female gymnasts.

The difference between week 0 and week 2 is $38 - 41 = -3$ mm, and the standard error of the difference is $2.9 \times \sqrt{2} = 4.1$ mm. An approximate 68% confidence interval for the true change is $[-3 - 4.1]$ to $[-3 + 4.1]$ i.e. -7.1 mm to 1.1 mm. Since the interval includes zero, it would be concluded (at the 32% level of significance) that the gymnast's true value did not change. Alternatively, an approximate 95% confidence interval for the true change is $[-3 - 2(4.1)]$ to $[-3 + 2(4.1)]$, i.e. -11.2 mm to 5.2 mm. Again, since the interval includes zero, it would be concluded (at the 5% level of significance) that the athlete's true value did not change.

Example 4

Suppose that, for the situation considered in Example 3, the coach is keen for $\Sigma 7$ to be no greater than 40 mm. Having observed 41 mm at the second time of measurement, can the coach conclude that the true value of $\Sigma 7$ exceeded 40 mm at the time of measurement?

An approximate 68% confidence interval for the true value will be from

$$[41 - 2.9] \text{ to } [41 + 2.9] \text{ i.e. from } 38 \text{ mm to } 44 \text{ mm.}$$

Since 40 is within the interval, it would be concluded (at the 16% level of significance) that the gymnast's true value did not exceed 40 mm. The difference between the observed value of 41 mm and the upper limit of 40 mm is well within the range attributable to random error. The level of significance is 16% rather than 32%, which may be expected since the interval was a 68% confidence interval, because the test being carried out is one-sided. The interest is in whether the true value exceeds 40 mm rather than in whether the true value is not equal to 40 mm.

Alternatively, an approximate 95% confidence interval for the true value will be from

$$[41 - 2(2.9)] \text{ to } [41 + 2(2.9)] \text{ i.e., from 35 mm to 47 mm.}$$

Since 40 is within the interval, it would be concluded (at the 2.5% level of significance) that the gymnast's true value did not exceed 40 mm.

8   Theoretical background

Consider the triceps skinfold measurement of 9.9 mm on the first subject in Table 1. It may have been the case that the subject's true value at that time, taken in the long term, was 9.6 mm but there was an error of 0.3 mm attributable to, say, measurement error or to the subject's biological variability over time. An equation could be written as follows:

$$9.9 = 9.6 + 0.3.$$

Generally, the following model (Model 1) can be written:

measurement on the subject = true value of the subject + error

This is an appropriate model if the data are considered to form a one-way table. It is the model which forms the basis for the one-way ANOVA. The average error is assumed to be zero so that the measurement is equal to the true value, on average. The variance of error effects may be written as $\sigma_e^2(1)$ and if it can be assumed that the subjects are a random sample from a population of subjects then the variance of the subjects' true values can be written as $\sigma_s^2(1)$.

For Model 1 the TEM is the square root of an estimate of $\sigma_e^2(1)$ and the ICC is an estimate of

$$\frac{\sigma_s^2(1)}{\sigma_s^2(1) + \sigma_e^2(1)}$$

Thus the ICC is an estimate of the proportion of the combined variability for subjects and error that may be attributed to variability between subjects.

Now consider the case when the data form a two-way table (e.g. as discussed by Denegar & Ball, 1993; Guilford, 1965; Verducci, 1980). Again, it may have been the case that the true value of the subject, taken in the long term, was 9.6 mm, but there was an increment (applicable to all subjects) of 0.5 mm associated with the first time of measurement and an error (unique to the subject) of −0.2 mm. The following equation could therefore be written:

$$9.9 = 9.6 + 0.5 - 0.2$$

Generally, this model (Model 2) can be written:

measurement on the subject = true value of the subject + time effect + error

This is an appropriate model if the data are considered to form a two-way table. Every subject has the same time effect included in their measurement at time 1 and every subject has the same time effect (probably different from the time 1 effect) included in their measurement at time 2. This model forms the basis for the two-way ANOVA. The time effect is not present in Model 1 and the variance of time effects may be written as σ_t^2. The variance of subject effects is $\sigma_s^2(2)$ and the variance of error effects is $\sigma_e^2(2)$.

Under headings 5.2 and 6.2, which dealt with the two-way ANOVA, it was suggested that an F-test should be used to determine whether time effects differed from one another. If they were found to differ, the measurement procedure was investigated to see whether an improved procedure (such as the rigorous landmarking of subjects) would eliminate or, at least, minimise the time differences. If this were done and there were still time differences then the approach used has been to regard the persistent between-time variability as a component of unavoidable, random error.

For Model 2 the TEM is the square root of an estimate of $[\sigma_e^2(2) + \sigma_t^2]$. If a two-way table of data is analysed with a one-way ANOVA and then with a two-way ANOVA, the TEMs from the two analyses will be equal since $\sigma_e^2(1) = \sigma_e^2(2) + \sigma_t^2$.

For Model 2 the ICC is an estimate of

$$\frac{\sigma_s^2(2)}{\sigma_s^2(2) + \sigma_t^2 + \sigma_e^2(2)}$$

Thus the ICC is an estimate of the proportion of the combined variability for subjects, time and error that may be attributed to variability between subjects. If a two-way table of data is analysed with a one-way ANOVA and then with a two-way ANOVA, the ICCs from the two analyses will be close to one another if the between-time variability is small.

In general, ICC will be close to 1 if there is high variability between subjects [$\sigma_s^2(1)$ or $\sigma_s^2(2)$ is large] or if there is low variability between repeated measurements on the same subject [$\sigma_e^2(1)$ or $\sigma_e^2(2)$ is small] or if both of those conditions exist. For Model 1, a value of 1 for the ICC would indicate a perfect ability to discriminate between subjects [$\sigma_e^2(1) = 0$; repeated measurements on the same subject are identical] and a value of 0 would indicate no discriminative ability [$\sigma_s^2(1) = 0$; all subjects are identical in their effect]. A similar statement could be made about ICC for Model 2 if between-time variability was negligible. From the viewpoint of the ability of measurements to discriminate between subjects, a value of the ICC close to 1 is therefore desirable.

If two different measurement procedures were being compared for a single group of subjects then the ICC could be used to make the comparison since both σ_s^2 and σ_e^2 could be conceived to depend on the measurement procedure. If two laboratories were being compared, each using the same measurement procedure, the ICC could be used but a fair comparison would require the assumption that the subjects used by each laboratory came from the same population. Otherwise, one laboratory may have a lower ICC than the other because the subjects it employed were inherently less variable (i.e. σ_s^2 was lower), not because of a deficiency in the test procedure which resulted in a high σ_e^2.

Target TEMs for different levels of accreditation are discussed in Chapter 13.

9 References

Dahlberg, G. (1940).
Statistical methods for medical and biological students.
London: George Allen & Unwin.

Denegar, C.R., & Ball, D.W. (1993).
Assessing reliability and precision of measurement: an introduction to intraclass correlation and standard error of measurement.
Journal of Sports Rehabilitation, 2, 35-42.

Guilford, J.P. (1965).
Fundamental statistics in psychology and education.
New York: McGraw-Hill.

Verducci, F.M. (1980).
Measurement concepts in physical education.
London: C.V. Mosby.

Chapter 4
Calibrating Harpenden Skinfold Calipers

Robert Carlyon, Christopher Gore, Sarah Woolford and Robert Bryant

1   Introduction

Skinfold calipers are a relatively inexpensive and expedient method to monitor changes in skinfold patterns and total skinfold thickness by measuring subcutaneous body fat. An anthropometrist can conduct duplicate measures on a group of 20 or 30 subjects to establish their own technical error of measurement (TEM – see Chapter 3) but it should be appreciated that the TEM is specific to the measurer, their sample population and to the caliper used. However, TEMs assume constant equipment characteristics over time. If the equipment characteristics are variable; for example, if skinfold caliper jaw pressure (force per unit surface area = $N.mm^{-2}$) is not calibrated, then TEMs are of limited use.

Edwards, Hammond, Healy, Tanner and Whitehouse (1955) studied caliper performance using upscale (i.e. jaw opening) calibration and also investigated the effects of jaw pressure on the accuracy of measuring subcutaneous tissue thickness. They found that the pressure exerted by the caliper had a significant effect on both the thickness of the skinfold measurement and the consistency with which the measurement was repeated. If the jaw pressure was too light, skinfold measures were not only larger but also less reproducible. They found that skinfolds were very reproducible for jaw pressures between 9 and 20 $g.mm^{-2}$ (equivalent to 0.088–0.196 $N.mm^{-2}$). They also recommend that calipers should not vary in jaw pressure by more that 2.0 $g.mm^{-2}$ (0.020 $N.mm^{-2}$) over a jaw gap range of 2–40 mm and that a standard jaw pressure should be 10 $g.mm^{-2}$ (0.098 $N.mm^{-2}$). Other studies (Behnke & Wilmore, 1984; Keys, 1956) have also recommended an upscale caliper jaw pressure of 10 $g.mm^{-2}$. In contrast, Schmidt and Carter (1990) used downscale (i.e. jaw closing) determination of jaw pressure and found a mean of 8.25 $g.mm^{-2}$ (0.081 $N.mm^{-2}$) for ten new Harpenden calipers. They also assessed Lange, Slim Guide, Skyndex and Lafayette calipers and none had downscale jaw pressure of greater than 8.67 $g.mm^{-2}$ (0.085 $N.mm^{-2}$).

Despite the recommendation of Edwards and associates (1955) of a standard jaw surface of 6 mm x 15 mm, the differences between various brands of calipers found by Schmidt and Carter (1990) are a consequence of the fact that there is still no standard for either jaw surface area or spring tension. Accordingly, the recommended jaw pressure of 10.0 $g.mm^{-2}$ (0.098 $N.mm^{-2}$) can be obtained with small surface area jaws and light springs, or with large surface area jaws and strong springs. Using foam rubber blocks to provide a dynamic downscale calibration of five common brands of calipers, Schmidt and Carter (1990) demonstrated that calipers with light springs tend to produce higher readings, that is, not compress the foam rubber as much as calipers with strong springs. Two recent studies have verified that these differences for dynamic foam block calibrations translate into different skinfold thicknesses. Gruber, Pollock, Graves, Colvin and Braith (1990) showed that Harpenden calipers yielded consistently lower skinfold values than Lange calipers, while Zillikens and Conway (1990) found that Holtain calipers gave systematically lower readings than did Lange calipers.

This chapter describes four methods of calibrating skinfold caliper jaw pressure and also how to calibrate jaw gap. British Indicators Ltd recommend that Harpenden calipers should be returned to them for calibration, but the information contained in this chapter offers an alternative for anthropometrists concerned about maintaining their own more frequent checks on calipers. The data presented in this chapter also challenge the recommendations of Edwards et al. (1955) for absolute jaw pressure of 10.0 ± 2.0 g.mm^{-2} (0.098 ± 0.020 N.mm^{-2}). The results presented suggest that differences of only 1.0 g.mm^{-2} (0.0098 N.mm^{-2}) over a jaw gap range of 2–40 mm may lead to errors in skinfold totals. We also propose that both upscale and downscale calibration may be required to adequately characterise skinfold calipers. While yet unable to propose more stringent absolute calibration pressure tolerances due to inadequate data, we do suggest an expedient method of checking the relative calibration jaw pressure (with foam rubber blocks) which is useful within an anthropometry laboratory.

2   Caliper description

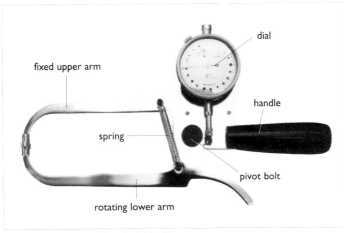

Figure 1   The Harpenden skinfold caliper

The Harpenden calipers are a precision instrument using two springs to apply a closing force to the caliper jaws and each jaw has a surface area of 90 mm2 (6 mm x 15 mm). The upper jaw is the "fixed" jaw which supports the pivot about which the lower

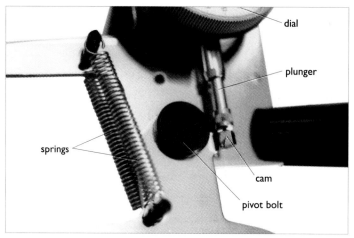

Figure 2 Close-up view of the pivot of the Harpenden caliper

jaw is rotated, the handle, and the indicating dial (Figure 1). Hooke's Law on elasticity states that the strain in a spring is directly proportional to the stress acting on the spring. That is, the increase in a spring's length is directly proportional to the force acting on the spring. If Hooke's Law was not taken into account during the design phase, skinfold calipers would have a jaw pressure which would vary proportionally with the jaw gap. Under these circumstances, it may be difficult to adhere to the recommendation by Edwards et al. (1955) that the jaw pressure should not vary by more than 2.0 g.mm^{-2} (0.020 N.mm^{-2}) over the operating range.

The design of the Harpenden calipers appears to cater for Hooke's Law because the springs have been placed between the jaws in such a position that, as the jaw gap increases, the point at which the springs apply the force is effectively moved along the jaw "levers" closer to the pivot position. Provided that the characteristics of the springs are unchanged from their design specification, the result of the action is that the force applied to the jaws remains relatively constant as the jaw gap increases. This constant force translates to a relatively constant jaw pressure over the normal operating range for the calipers.

The springs are installed on the "jaw" side of the pivot. The design of the lower moving jaw includes a small cam on the side of the pivot opposite to the springs and the jaws. This cam interacts with the plunger of the indicator gauge to determine the distance between the two jaws (Figure 2).

The characteristics of the springs may alter with age and contamination from the environment in which they are used. In addition, the pivot's lubricant tends to degrade with time and contamination, while the contact surfaces at the interface between the cam and the indicator gauge plunger tend to wear. These factors, along with any physical damage to the jaws or their alignment, should be the major concerns of any calibration procedure.

3 Jaw pressure calibration methods

There are four possible methods of calibrating jaw force [grams (g) or more correctly Newtons (N)] and jaw pressure (e.g. force per unit surface area in $g.mm^{-2}$ or $N.mm^{-2}$) of skinfold calipers. Calibration can be either static (jaws stationary) or dynamic (jaws moving), and it can be either upscale (jaws opening) or downscale (jaws closing).

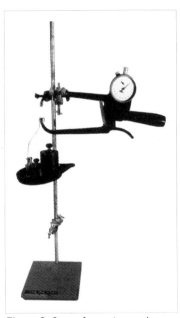

Figure 3 Set-up for static upscale calibration.

a Static upscale (Figure 3)

One of the first references to caliper calibration is that of Edwards et al. (1955, p.142) which used static upscale (i.e. jaw opening) calibration. This can be done by fixing one arm horizontally in a clamp and suspending a pan with weights from the other. The jaw opening at a series of weights from 900 g upwards in 10 g intervals can then be recorded. However, the major shortcomings of this calibration method are that it is not dynamic (the jaw opens and then stays open) and that it is directly opposite to the downscale (i.e. jaw closing) mode in which calipers are used to measure skinfold thicknesses.

b Dynamic upscale

No research is available that describes the pressure of calipers when the jaws are opening slowly. However, this method may be useful to assess hysteresis compared with dynamic downscale calibration and whether there is excessive opening resistance associated with the caliper pivot. ("Hysteresis" refers to different stress-strain characteristics when something is stretched, as opposed to when the stretch is released. In this case, it is the extent to which the strain on the caliper springs during calibration reflects the stress to which the springs have been subjected during the past as well as the present stress. Thus, if upscale calibration affects the spring characteristics, "altered" jaw pressures may be measured during the subsequent downscale calibration).

c Static downscale (Figure 4)

Schmidt and Carter (1990) clearly described how to use static downscale (i.e. compression) determination of jaw pressure. They used a calibrated spring scale to measure the pressure exerted by calipers at jaw openings of 10, 20, 30, 40 and 50 mm.

They were careful to ensure that the angle of pressure exerted on the caliper jaw face was held at 90°. This method is well controlled but fails to mimic the dynamic mode in which calipers are used.

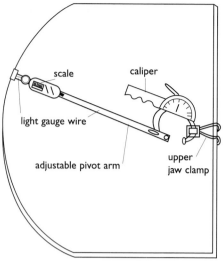

Figure 4 Set up for static downscale calibration. Redrawn with permission of Paul Schmidt and Lindsay Carter.

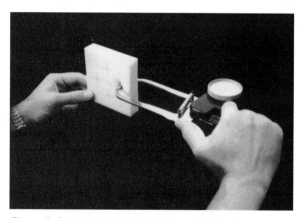

Figure 5 Engineer using foam blocks for calibration.

d Dynamic downscale (Figure 5)

Schmidt and Carter (1990) were the first to describe how several thicknesses of closed-cell foam rubber blocks could be used to simulate the characteristics of human skin and adipose tissue to provide a dynamic calibration of skinfold calipers. The essential characteristic of this procedure is that the caliper jaws are closing slowly, which replicates the true mode of use. Using foam blocks for this technique has a number of limitations. First, the foam blocks are relatively easy to damage and, as described by Carter and Schmidt (1990), will deteriorate unless stored out of direct light and without compression. Also, due to the manufacturing process, the density of closed cell foam is not identical at all locations which means that measurement sites must be carefully marked on the foam to allow reproducible results. Finally, foam blocks only allow a relative calibration and do not allow an absolute, quantified jaw-closing pressure.

Chapter 4

3.1   Absolute calibration

3.1.1   Load cell calibration of jaw pressure

Figure 6 illustrates an arrangement which can measure the absolute jaw force of skinfold calipers in any of the four possible combinations described above. Although developed independently of the system described by Schmidt and Carter (1990), this system incorporates many of the principles used in the earlier apparatus. While the system described by Schmidt and Carter (1990) used a spring balance to measure the force being applied by the springs, the system shown in Figure 6 used a 2 kg load cell (Scale Components, Brisbane, Australia) mounted on a lever arm which was free to rotate about a pivot attached to a back-board. An "S" style load cell was used to minimise side movements. The load cell was positioned on the lever arm so that the force required to separate the jaws was at 90° over the full jaw gap range. For this to occur, the pivot of the calipers under test was aligned vertically with the pivot of the lever arm and a clamp was used to restrain the upper jaw of the calipers. The load cell was connected to a strain gauge amplifier/indicator, the output from which was applied directly to the input of a computerised data acquisition system. A novel feature of this calibration system is the "gap controller" (Figure 6) which can be used to slowly open or close the jaws (at approximately 0.2 mm.s^{-1}) whilst the dynamic opening or closing force is recorded on the data acquisition system.

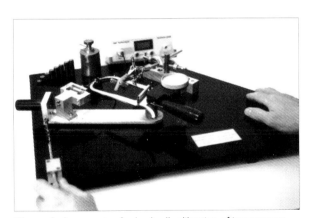

Figure 6 An apparatus for load-cell calibration of jaw pressure.

The precision of the calibration rig was expressed using the coefficient of variation (i.e. standard deviation divided by the mean, expressed as a percentage) for triplicate measures of jaw pressure at 5, 10, 15, 20, 25, 30, 35 and 40 mm. The overall mean coefficient of variation averaged across all 8 jaw gaps was 0.22% for dynamic upscale calibration and 0.80% for static downscale calibration. The major disadvantages of a load cell calibration system are that it is relatively expensive and requires some technical expertise to assemble.

3.1.2 Case studies – servicing calipers and replacing springs

The benefit of absolute calibration of skinfold calipers can be demonstrated by considering several case studies. The data in Table 1 were collected on four old and four brand new calipers and illustrate three key points for calibration of skinfold calipers.

Table 1 Dynamic upscale calibration of various Harpenden calipers. Data collected using both a calibrated spring balance* and calibrated load cell†. (Note: the resolution of the scale was 25 g while that of the load cell was 3 g.)

		jaw gap (mm)							
		5	**10**	**15**	**20**	**25**	**30**	**35**	**40**
Caliper ID	**Condition**	pressure at jaw gap (g.mm-2)							
A1*	original springs	9.52	9.82	10.12	10.42	10.71	11.01	11.31	11.61
	serviced pivot	9.82	9.82	10.12	10.12	10.42	10.42	10.42	10.59
	new springs, serviced pivot	10.12	10.12	10.12	10.12	10.12	10.12	10.12	10.12
C4†	original springs	8.96	9.08	9.14	9.21	9.24	9.30	9.32	9.39
	new springs	10.41	10.40	10.26	10.22	10.17	10.18	10.13	10.20
A2†	original springs	10.57	10.86	10.96	10.98	11.10	11.11	11.11	11.11
	new springs	9.61	9.62	9.61	9.62	9.58	9.58	9.54	9.53
A3†	original springs	11.01	11.09	11.15	11.10	11.10	11.18	11.21	11.04
	new springs	10.24	10.27	10.32	10.30	10.32	10.21	10.12	10.14
B1*	brand new	10.12	10.12	10.12	10.12	10.12	10.12	10.12	10.12
B2*	brand new	10.12	10.12	10.12	10.12	10.12	10.12	10.12	10.12
B3*	brand new	10.12	10.12	10.12	10.12	10.12	10.12	10.12	10.12
C1†	brand new	10.45	10.49	10.45	10.36	10.26	10.18	10.08	10.11

- The condition of the caliper pivot (well greased and operating smoothly) is critical to the performance of calipers. (The results for caliper A1 illustrate that servicing the pivot reduced the jaw pressure from 11.61 to 10.59 g.mm^{-2} at a gap of 40 mm.)
- The age or characteristics of different springs alter the pressure exerted by the jaws, although this varies with different calipers. (Whilst calipers A2 and A3 had jaw pressures that were greater than 10.0 g.mm^{-2}, caliper C4 was less than 9.5 g.mm^{-2} and A1 varied between 9.5 and 11.6 g.mm^{-2} for a jaw gap ranging from 5 to 40 mm.)

- Differences in new spring characteristics (for instance, type of spring steel and length of spring) may result in differences between calipers that have the pivot serviced. (While calipers B1, B2 and B3 had jaw pressures that were 10.12 g.mm^{-2} at a gap of 10.0 mm, caliper C1 was 10.49 g.mm^{-2}). Until further data have been collected on each of these points, the best approach for an anthropometrist to adopt that will enhance the likelihood of obtaining reproducible results during many years of measures is to ensure that:
  - their own calipers are well greased at the pivot,
  - the pivot bolt is not over-tightened, and
  - they buy several sets of calipers springs at one time so that the springs are likely to come from one manufacturing lot (and therefore to have similar mechanical characteristics).

3.1.3 Physiological implications of differences between springs

Edwards et al. (1955) recommend that the jaw pressure should be 10.0 ± 2.0 g.mm^{-2} (0.098 ± 0.020 N.mm^{-2}). We investigated this proposal using a highly experienced anthropometrist with a defined TEM to make repeat measures on athletes using caliper C4. The same caliper (C4) was used to measure subcutaneous skinfold thicknesses of 10 female athletes from a variety of sports, first with original springs (estimated to be approximately 4 years old and used for 30,000 measurements) and then new springs. Anatomical landmarks for seven sites (triceps, subscapular, biceps, supraspinale, abdominal, front thigh and medial calf – see Chapter 2) were marked and were measured using caliper C4. The sum of seven skinfolds ($\Sigma 7$) was then calculated for each set of springs. The TEM for the anthropometrist who conducted these measures had been established one month previously using the same calipers and 19 subjects whose $\Sigma 7$ ranged from 47.1 to 121.8 mm. The TEM and TEM% for $\Sigma 7$ was 0.96 mm and 1.12%, respectively. This TEM is of the same magnitude as reported by Lohman (1981) for repeated measures. The sum of seven skinfolds assessed with new and original springs were compared using Student's paired t-test with the significance level set at $p < 0.05$.

The $\Sigma 7$ data for the 10 athletes are presented in Table 2. The mean $\Sigma 7$ for caliper C4 was 91.4 mm with new springs and 96.9 mm with original springs. The difference between the new and original springs (5.4 mm), was statistically significant ($t = 9.38$, $p < 0.001$), which was also greater than could be accounted for by measurement error (TEM). A TEM of 0.96 mm, indicates that each measure of $\Sigma 7$ has a standard error of

0.96 mm and thus the standard error of the difference between the two measurement series is $\sqrt{2} \times 0.96 = 1.36$ mm. The 95% confidence interval for an error-free change between the two measurement series is from $[5.4 - (2 \times 1.36)]$ to $[5.4 + (2 \times 1.36)]$, i.e. from 2.7 to 8.1 mm. Since the calculated error-free range does not include zero, one rejects the null hypothesis that the change in $\Sigma 7$ is zero, and concludes that the measured change in $\Sigma 7$ is different for the new and original springs.

Table 2 The sum of seven skinfolds (mm) for 10 women athletes; a comparison between original and new springs on one set of Harpenden calipers.

subject	new springs (mm)	original springs (mm)	original minus new (mm)
S1	95.3	100.6	5.3
S2	110.3	116.6	6.3
S3	61.0	66.7	5.7
S4	65.8	67.2	1.4
S5	99.8	106.1	6.3
S6	88.7	96.9	8.2
S7	100.5	104.5	4.0
S8	103.7	108.9	5.2
S9	81.7	86.4	4.7
S10	107.4	114.0	6.6
Mean	91.4	96.8	5.4
SE	5.4	5.7	0.6

The results of this study illustrate that the difference between the dynamic upscale calibration with original springs (mean for jaw gaps of 5–40 mm = 9.20 g.mm^{-2}) and new springs (mean = 10.25 g.mm^{-2}) also translated into statistically significant and practically important physiological differences in sums of skinfolds. This suggests that fatigue of the springs in Harpenden calipers can alter skinfold measurements in excess of differences due to measurement error (TEM). However, it is also possible, since we did not calibrate the original C4 springs when they were new, that the original and new springs had different characteristics since they were manufactured approximately five years apart. In either case (fatigue with age or differences between springs), these results highlight that differences between springs can translate into different skinfold sums.

Furthermore, these data suggest that the static upscale recommendations of Edwards et al. (1955) may be too lenient. They recommend that a jaw pressure 10.0 ± 2.0 g.mm^{-2} (or 0.098 N.mm^{-2} ± 20%) is adequate for reproducible results. The data sheet that used to be supplied with Harpenden calipers specified that the calipers were designed to exert a constant pressure of 0.098 N.mm^{-2} ± 10%. However, our data suggest that difference of 1.0 g.mm^{-2} (0.0098 N.mm^{-2}) is excessive if valid comparisons are to be made between different Harpenden calipers. Therefore, a dynamic upscale calibration range of 10.0 ± 0.50 g.mm^{-2} (or 0.098 N.mm^{-2} ± 5%), may be required.

3.1.4   Upscale versus downscale calibration

It is also relevant to examine the differences between upscale and downscale absolute calibration. As noted above, Edwards et al. (1955) recommend a static upscale calibration pressure of 10.0 ± 2.0 g.mm^{-2}, but Schmidt and Carter (1990) used absolute static downscale determination of jaw pressure and found a mean of 8.25 g.mm^{-2} for ten new Harpenden calipers. The data presented in Table 3 for four calipers yield a mean upscale pressure of 10.04 g.mm^{-2} (averaged over all jaw openings) while the equivalent downscale figure is 8.14 g.mm^{-2}. These data agree with those of Schmidt and Carter (1990).

Why is the upscale (opening) jaw pressure greater than the downscale (closing) pressure and which is the most useful, given that calipers are actually used to make measures in the downscale mode? The force applied by the operator to open the jaws must not only be sufficient to lengthen the springs, but it must also overcome the frictional resistance associated with the springs, the pivot, and the indicator gauge. When the operator releases the jaws, some of the energy stored in the springs will be lost in overcoming the frictional forces. The remaining energy in the springs will then generate the closing force applied to the jaws. Abnormally high frictional resistance will result in an abnormally high force being required to open the jaws. In addition, abnormally high frictional resistance will result in an abnormally low force being applied when the jaws close. Therefore, the downscale calibration indicates the operating qualities of the calipers when they are being used to measure skinfold thickness while the upscale calibration is an assessment of the total mechanical qualities of the calipers. Further mechanical assessment can be made by examination of the difference between the upscale and downscale measurements which, according to data collected to date, will be in the order of 1.5 to 2.0 g.mm^{-2} (0.0147 to 0.0196 N.mm^{-2}) for mechanically sound calipers. Therefore, both upscale and downscale calibration should be conducted to adequately characterise a caliper.

Table 3 Dynamic upscale and static downscale calibration of various Harpenden calipers. Data were collected using a calibrated load cell.

Caliper ID	Calibration mode	Condition	jaw gap (mm)							
			5	10	15	20	25	30	35	40
			pressure at jaw gap (g.mm^{-2})							
	upscale	new springs	10.44	10.40	10.26	10.22	10.17	10.18	10.13	10.20
C_4	downscale		8.41	8.40	8.41	8.36	8.29	8.24	8.12	8.06
	upscale	new springs	9.61	9.62	9.61	9.62	9.58	9.58	9.54	9.53
A_2	downscale		8.29	8.27	8.21	8.05	7.98	7.95	7.85	7.75
	upscale	new springs	10.24	10.27	10.32	10.30	10.32	10.21	10.12	10.14
A_3	downscale		8.63	8.56	8.49	8.40	8.30	8.20	8.15	8.20
	upscale	brand new calipers	10.45	10.49	10.45	10.36	10.26	10.18	10.08	10.11
C_1	downscale		8.17	8.11	8.02	7.93	7.81	7.70	7.61	7.60

Using the data presented above (Table 3) combined with those of Schmidt and Carter (1990), as well as refining the recommendations of Edwards et al (1955), we propose the following guidelines for calibration of Harpenden skinfold calipers:

- Both upscale and downscale absolute calibration should be performed at jaw gaps spanning the range of 5 to 40 mm.
- Mean upscale dynamic pressure (i.e. mean pressure for the range of jaw gaps) should be in the range of 10.0 ± 0.50 g.mm^{-2} (0.098 ± 0.005 N.mm^{-2}).
- Mean downscale static pressure should be in the range of 8.25 ± 0.50 g.mm^{-2} (0.081 ± 0.005 N.mm^{-2}).
- At any jaw gap in the range 5 to 40 mm, the difference between upscale and downscale pressure should be less than 2.0 g.mm^{-2} (0.020 N.mm^{-2}).

3.2 Relative calibration

3.2.1 Dynamic downscale calibration with foam blocks

In order to monitor the calibration of a single set of calipers (or a batch of springs ordered at the same time) the following procedure using foam blocks is recommended as a useful, but inferior, alternative to absolute load-cell calibration of jaw pressure.

While the foam block method is a serviceable technique for monitoring the downscale characteristics of calipers, it is unable to assess the upscale characteristics of calipers.

Obtain five foam blocks with uncompressed thicknesses of 15.0, 25.0, 35.0, 45.0 and 55.0 mm (each block being 10 cm by 10 cm). The ED200 foam rubber (Dunlop Flexible Foams, Australia) matches the characteristics of the HD40 foam rubber used by Schmidt and Carter (1990). It is important to check the characteristics of the foam because foam rubber that is either too low or too high in density neither adequately simulates skinfold compressibility, nor gives sufficiently discriminating values to be useful. The thicknesses of the uncompressed foam blocks were chosen to yield compressed values that spanned the range of Harpenden calipers, that is, 0 to 40 mm.

Due to the manufacturing process, the density of closed cell foam is not identical at all locations. Furthermore, if repeat measures are taken at a single site within a short time (for example, every 20 seconds) the foam rubber will retain some minor distortion which will cause consecutive values to decrease (for example, on 45 mm uncompressed foam measure 1 = 22.5 mm, measure 10 = 22.0 mm, measure 30 = 21.7 mm and measure 50 = 21.7 mm). Thus, in order to obtain reproducible data and avoid these distortion problems, the following procedure should be used.

- A line is marked on two opposite faces of each foam block 2 cm from the edge.
- A mark is made at the midpoint of each line.
- The caliper jaws are placed exactly on the marked sites.
- The foam rubber is held vertically and the caliper jaws applied at right angles to the foam (Figure 5).
- The caliper dial is read 2 seconds after application of full jaw pressure.
- The blocks are measured in the following order: 15 mm, 25 mm, 35 mm, 45 mm, and then 55 mm, each measured once. This test order should be repeated a total of 10 times with each set of 5 measures taking approximately 1.0 min.
- The environmental conditions under which the foam is measured should be standardised using an air-conditioned laboratory.

3.2.1.1 The "calibration range" of foam blocks

Use data for a single set of calipers (such as that presented in Table 4) to establish a calibration range, which is defined as the mean ± 3 SDs from 10 replicate measurements on a set of five uncompressed foam blocks, with each block measured at a specific marked site. Statistically, this means that 99.7% of the observations will lie within this calibration range. When any future calibration data using the same calipers and foam blocks fall outside the calibration range it is likely that the caliper requires the springs to be replaced, a service and lubrication of the caliper pivot, or both.

Table 4 The calibration range (mean ± 3 SDs) of 10 measurements on each foam block for one Harpenden caliper.

	uncompressed thickness (mm)				
	15.0	25.0	35.0	45.0	55.0
Caliper ID	compressed thickness (mm)				
C1	2.4 ± 0.20	5.7 ± 0.44	11.6 ± 0.62	21.7 ± 0.41	30.7 ± 0.22

3.2.2 Discriminating between original and new springs

Five Harpenden skinfold calipers were used in a small study to investigate this issue: one brand new caliper (C1), two nearly new calipers (C2 and C3) which had limited use (approximately 800 jaw movements; where one movement equals one skinfold measured on one occasion), one extensively-used caliper (C4; approximately 30,000 jaw movements over four years) and finally caliper C4 with two new springs (C5). Calipers C1 and C4 were also used in absolute calibration (heading 3.1) and in Table 1. Ten replicate measurements on a set of five ED200 foam blocks were taken with each of the five calipers as described under heading 3.2.1, above.

There was a trend for the newest calipers, C1 and C5, to have much lower standard deviations (and thus lower variances) than the older calipers, C2, C3 and C4, for each of the foam blocks (Table 5). This may indicate that older calipers have greater variability than newer calipers. The unequal variances may also confound the repeated measures analysis of variance which showed that there was a significant interaction between the caliper used and the compressed thickness of the five foam blocks [$F_{(16,225)} = 43.0$, $p < 0.001$]. A post-hoc comparison of means (Table 5) is most meaningful using the two calipers with brand new springs, C5 and C1. There were no differences between any of the five calipers when applied to the 15 mm uncompressed foam block, but when using caliper C5 as the criterion, C4 yielded significantly higher values for the 25, 35, 45 and 55 mm uncompressed foam blocks. There were no differences between any of the four calipers with new or near new springs (C1, C2, C3 and C5) for the 25, and 35 mm foam blocks, but calipers C2 and C3 were significantly different from C5 on the 55 mm foam block.

Table 5 Compressed foam thicknesses (mean ± SD, mm) using 5 sets of Harpenden skinfold calipers. C1 is a brand new set of calipers. C2 and C3 are calipers with limited use. C4 is an extensively used set of calipers. C5 is identical to C4 except that two new springs have been inserted. Values in parentheses are 3 SDs.

	uncompressed thickness (mm)				
	15.0	25.0	35.0	45.0	55.0
Caliper ID	compressed thickness (mm)				
C1	2.4 ± 0.07	5.7 ± 0.15	11.6± 0.21	21.7 ± 0.14	30.7 ± 0.07
	(± 0.20)	(± 0.44)	(± 0.62)	(± 0.41)	(± 0.22)
C2	2.5 ± 0.05	5.9 ± 0.07	11.8 ± 0.26	21.8 ± 0.22	31.1± 0.20[a]
	(± 0.15)	(± 0.20)	(± 0.79)	(± 0.66)	(± 0.60)
C3	2.4 ± 0.07	5.6 ± 0.08	11.3 ± 0.22	21.2 ± 0.21[b]	30.1 ± 0.20[ab]
	(± 0.21)	(± 0.25)	(± 0.66)	(± 0.63)	(± 0.60)
C4	2.6 ± 0.05	6.8 ± 0.15[ab]	13.5 ± 0.27[ab]	23.4 ± 0.35[ab]	32.6 ± 0.29[ab]
	(± 0.15)	(± 0.45)	(± 0.81)	(± 1.04)	(± 0.87)
C5	2.4 ± 0.03	5.7 ± 0.07	11.6 ± 0.09	21.7 ± 0.12	30.7 ± 0.12
	(± 0.09)	(± 0.22)	(± 0.28)	(± 0.37)	(± 0.35)

a = significant difference from C5
b = significant difference from C1

This small study demonstrated that replacing the extensively-used springs in a set of Harpenden calipers by a pair of new springs produced significantly lower compressed thicknesses for four of the five foam blocks. However, it is also possible, since we did not calibrate the C4 springs when they were new, that the springs used in C4 and C5 had different characteristics since they were manufactured approximately five years apart. In order to verify that the new springs were similar for several Harpenden calipers, three other new, or barely used, calipers were used to measure the foam blocks. The four best calipers, C1, C2, C3 and C5, generally produced compressed thicknesses of foam that were not significantly different from each other. This finding is in accord with Schmidt and Carter (1990) who also contend that the variability between new Harpenden calipers is small.

Whether the old springs had fatigued or the new springs had different characteristics is uncertain, but this study does verify that the absolute calibration results described under heading 3.1.3 can also be discriminated using foam block downscale calibration.

3.2.3 Interpreting the calibration range of foam blocks

If one applies the calibration range criterion (mean ± 3 SDs as described under heading 3.2.1.1) to the foam block data for C5, measures taken by C4 lie outside the calibration range for all five blocks, while C1, C2 and C3 all lie within the calibration range. If the calibration range is set using C1 as the criterion, C4 falls outside the range for all but the 15 mm uncompressed block. However, C3 also falls outside the calibration for the 45 and 55 mm foam blocks, but by only 0.1 and 0.2 mm, respectively. This suggests that this calibration range method for a single caliper is useful within a laboratory to indicate when calipers are producing reliable data. Both the foam block calibration method and the absolute calibration of the calipers were able to discriminate between a caliper with original and new springs. This difference, which is discussed under heading 3.1.3, was sufficient to translate into a significant difference for subcutaneous skinfolds (Σ7). However, the foam block method should be used as an adjunct to, rather than a replacement for, absolute static downscale calibration.

Regardless of using absolute or relative downscale calibration, fatigue with age or differences between springs can translate into different skinfold sums and therefore an anthropometrist would be wise to buy several sets of caliper springs at one time so that the springs are likely to come from one manufacturing lot (and therefore to have similar mechanical characteristics).

4 Jaw gap calibration

4.1 Vernier calipers

The simplest method of calibrating jaw gap is to use the small blades of an engineer's vernier calipers placed at the exact centre of the caliper jaw faces (Figure 7). However, locating and holding the vernier calipers at the centre of the jaw faces is relatively imprecise.

4.2 Calibration rods – theory

A more accurate method of checking the caliper jaw gap is to insert a thin spacer of known diameter between the jaws and to record the dial reading. However, there are a number of potential pitfalls with this approach. Because the jaw faces angle away from being parallel as the jaws are opened, the dial reading will be greater if the spacer is

Figure 7 Engineer using Vernier caliper for jaw gap calibration.

placed near the inside edge of the jaw than if the spacer is placed near the outside edge of the jaw (Figure 8). The best spacer to use should be made from solid metal rod approximately one centimetre in diameter (Figure 9).

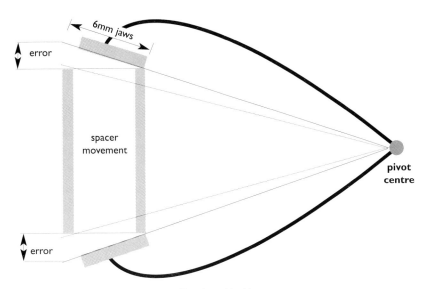

Figure 8 Diagram showing the errors in jaw gap calibration with thin spacers.

A rod of this dimension solves the problem of the jaw angle provided that the inside edge of the caliper jaw faces are placed on the ends of a calibrated rod. Since the distance from the centre of the Harpenden caliper pivot to the centre of the jaw surface is 152.4 mm, this length can be used as the hypotenuse of a right angled triangle subtending the angle A from the centre of the pivot (Figure 10). This same angle (A) is subtended from the inner edge of the jaw surface with its complementary angle subtending from the outer jaw edge. The correction to be applied to the dial reading of caliper gap for a metal rod is twice the sine of angle A using a 3 mm (half of the jaw width) hypotenuse. This correction is subtracted from the dial reading recorded for the particular length of calibration rod.

113

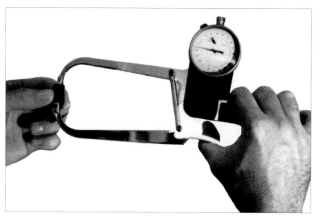

Figure 9 Engineer using calibration rods for jaw gap calibration.

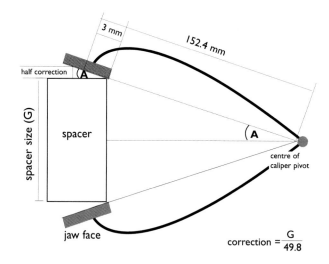

Figure 10 Diagram showing the derivation of the correction factor to be used when calibrating the jaw gap using calibration rods.

$$\sin A = \frac{half\ spacer\ length\,(G)}{jaw\ arm\ length - half\ jaw\ face\ length}$$

$$= \frac{G\!\big/\!2}{152.4 - 3}$$

$$= \frac{G}{298.8}$$

$$Correction = half\ jaw\ face\ width \times \sin A \times 2\ \mathrm{mm}$$

$$= \frac{3 \times G \times 2}{298.8} = \frac{G}{49.8} \text{ mm}$$

Therefore, the actual jaw gap $= G + G/49.8$, which should be indicated on the dial. Table 6 shows the size of the correction for jaw openings in the range of 5 to 40 mm.

Table 6 Calculated corrections for jaw gaps of Harpenden calipers.

calibration rod length (mm)	correction (mm)
5	−0.1
10	−0.2
15	−0.3
20	−0.4
25	−0.5
30	−0.6
35	−0.7
40	−0.8

4.2.1 Calibration rods – procedure

The procedure to calibrate the jaw gaps of Harpenden calipers at 5 mm steps in the range of 5 to 40 mm is described below. Calibration rods were made from accurately machined sections of 10 mm brass rod. The procedure is as follows:
(1) Allow the caliper jaws to close and reset the dial to zero.
(2) Insert the 5 mm calibrated rod between the caliper jaw faces and record the dial reading. Note that the inside edge of the jaw faces should be resting on the rod.
(3) Remove the calibrated rod and check that the caliper dial has returned to zero.
(4) Repeat steps 2 and 3 twice more.
(5) Repeat steps 2, 3 and 4 using calibrated rods of length 10, 15, 20, 25, 30, 35 and 40 mm.

The results of calibrating seven Harpenden calipers are shown in Table 7. These results show that the three oldest instruments (#1, 2 and 3 – approximately 20 years old) were within 0.1 mm of the calibrated rod measurements. This error is within the error of the calibration rod procedure because the dial of Harpenden calipers can only be read to the nearest 0.1 mm. The greatest error measured was 0.4 mm recorded for Harpenden caliper #7 which had 5 years of use. The results for the three newest

Table 7 Calculated Harpenden caliper jaw face gaps (that is, corrected for the error associated with non-parallel jaw faces as the jaw gap increases).

	calibration rod length (mm)							
	5	10	15	20	25	30	35	40
Caliper ID	calculated jaw face gap (g.mm-2)							
#1	5.1	10.2	15.1	20.2	25.2	30.1	35.1	40.0
#2	4.9	10.0	15.1	20.1	25.0	29.9	34.9	39.8
#3	5.0	10.1	15.1	20.1	25.1	30.0	35.0	39.9
#4	4.9	10.0	15.0	20.0	25.0	30.0	35.0	40.0
#5	4.9	10.0	14.9	20.0	24.9	30.0	35.1	40.0
#6	4.9	9.9	14.9	20.0	24.9	29.9	34.9	39.9
#7	4.9	10.0	15.0	20.1	25.1	30.1	35.3	40.4

instruments (# 4, 5 and 6) were within 0.2 mm of the calibration standards. The slightly greater error may be a function of the different cam and different plunger design on the latest instruments compared with those of 20 years ago.

The error from the standard calibration rods indicates the amount of caliper wear or damage which is most likely to be at the pivot or to the cam which the dial gauge uses to measure jaw gap. The cam is located only 15 cm behind the pivot (while the jaws are 152.4 cm long) and therefore has a 10 to 1 mechanical disadvantage to the jaws. That is, any wear on the cam surface will be reflected at the jaws where it will appear 10 times greater. Therefore, an error in jaw gap of 0.4 mm may be the result of 0.04 mm cam wear.

Given the limitations in the skinfold measurement technique, the errors in jaw gap are quite small. An error of 0.4 mm at a 40 mm jaw gap constitutes a one percent error which is much less than the measurement error obtained with the technique. However, regular measurement of the jaw gap is considered essential to ensure that the cam surface has not been damaged or contaminated with small pieces of extraneous substances which will produce an even greater error.

5 Conclusions and recommendations

Foam blocks can provide a cheap and expedient method to track longitudinally the reliability of jaw pressure for one pair of Harpenden calipers and to indicate when springs need replacing. On the other hand, comparison of data collected between laboratories demands that absolute calibration of jaw pressure be performed. However, the data presented in this chapter suggest that the commonly accepted recommendations of Edwards et al. (1955) of a static upscale pressure of 10.0 ± 2.0 g.mm^{-2}, and even those of British Indicators Ltd (10.0 ± 1.0 g.mm^{-2}), are too lenient. If valid comparisons are to be made between different Harpenden calipers for a sum of skinfolds, a calibration range of 10.0 ± 0.5 g.mm^{-2}, may be required. Finally, more research needs to be conducted to characterise the absolute downscale dynamic characteristics of Harpenden calipers.

Recommendations

(i)   The caliper pivot should be serviced at 12 month intervals to ensure that it is well-greased and operating smoothly, without the pivot bolt being over-tightened.

(ii) Ideally, both absolute upscale and downscale calibration should be conducted on calipers at least every 12 months (or if they are accidentally damaged) at jaw gaps spanning the range of 5 to 40 mm. Upscale calibration is an assessment of the total mechanical qualities of the calipers while downscale calibration indicates the qualities of the calipers when they are being used to measure skinfold thicknesses. Both upscale and downscale calibration should be conducted to adequately characterise a caliper.

- Mean upscale dynamic pressure (i.e. mean pressure for the range of jaw gaps) should be in the range of 10.0 ± 0.50 g.mm^{-2} (0.098 ± 0.005 N.mm^{-2}).
- Mean downscale static pressure should be in the range of 8.25 ± 0.50 g.mm^{-2} (0.081 ± 0.005 N.mm^{-2}).
- At any jaw gap in the range 5 to 40 mm, the difference between upscale and downscale pressure should be less than 2.0 g.mm^{-2} (0.020 N.mm^{-2}).

(iii) As an expedient alternative, a calibration range using foam blocks can be used to monitor the downscale dynamic pressure of a single pair of calipers within a laboratory. This method may be more expedient to check calipers more frequently than absolute calibration, for instance, to check calipers that have been accidentally dropped or have been loaned to a colleague.

(iv) Anthropometrists should be aware that Harpenden caliper springs may fatigue with age or vary their mechanical characteristics between manufacturing batches. Differences can be detected with absolute calibration or with foam block calibration. Consequently, we advise that two or 3 sets of replacement springs should be purchased with each new caliper and the caliper should be calibrated with all sets of springs when new, to ensure that all springs have similar calibration characteristics.

(v) The accuracy of caliper jaw gaps should be checked at least every 6 months using calibration rods ranging from 5 to 40 mm.

6 References

Behnke, A.R., & Wilmore, J.H. (1984).
Evaluation and regulation of body build and composition. Englewood Cliffs, NJ: Prentice Hall.

Carter, J.E.L., & Schmidt, P.K. (1990).
A simple method for calibrating skinfold calipers. Proceedings of the **Commonwealth and International Conference on Physical Education, Sport, Health, Dance, Recreation and Leisure**. Volume 3 Part 1, pp.49-53. Auckland, New Zealand.

Edwards, D.A.W., Hammond, W.H., Healy, J.M., Tanner, J.M. & Whitehouse, R.H. (1955).
Design and accuracy of calipers for measuring subcutaneous tissue thickness.
British Journal of Nutrition, 9, 133-143.

Gruber, J.J., Pollock, M.L., Graves, J.E., Colvin, A.B., & Braith, R.W. (1990).
Comparison of Harpenden and Lange calipers in predicting body composition.
Research Quarterly, 61, 184-190.

Keys, A.. (1956).
Recommendations concerning body measurements for the characterization of nutritional status.
Human Biology, 28, 111-123.

Lohman, T.G. (1981).
Skinfolds and body density and their relationship to body fatness: a review.
Human Biology, 53, 181-225.

Schmidt, P.K., & Carter, J.E.L. (1990).
Static and dynamic differences among five types of skinfold calipers.
Human Biology, 62, 369-388.

Zillikens, M.C., & Conway, J.M. (1990).
Anthropometry in blacks : applicability of generalised skinfold equations and differences in fat patterning between blacks and whites.
American Journal of Clinical Nutrition, 52, 45-51.

tools

for

analysis

Chapter 5
Similarity Systems in Anthropometry

Tim Olds, Kevin Norton, Sen Van Ly and Liz Lowe

1   Introduction

Anthropometrists often want to compare the size of two body parts (such as the upper arm and lower arm), or to compare the size of one body part to some general measure of body size (such as mass or height), or to relate some function (such as strength) to overall body size. The study of comparative sizes is called **allometry**. We are interested in these relationships not only within the one individual, but in human beings and animals in general. These relationships are not only important in theory, but have many practical implications.

2   Theoretical models for relating anthropometric variables

In some way, we want to relate an independent variable x, which is related to size or shape (examples of the x-variable are mass, height or body surface area), to a dependent variable y, which may also be size- or shape-related, or may be a functional variable (examples of the y-variable would be skinfold thickness, basal metabolic rate or speed of locomotion). When we determine the relationship between any two variables, we are faced with the task of specifying a theoretical model. Our choice of which model to use will depend on theoretical considerations and/or on statistical procedures which tell us how well x predicts y. There is no mechanical procedure for deciding which model fits best, and since the potential number of models is infinite, we cannot consider all possible models. In anthropometry, three models have commonly been used – ratio models, regression models and the general allometric equation. Each of these will be discussed.

2.1   Ratio models

The simple **ratio model** is of the form

$$y = kx$$

where k is some constant. For example, limb lengths are considered to be more or less constant fractions of body height (within ethnic subpopulations, and once bone growth has stopped).

2.2 Regression models

A slightly more complex and more general model is the (linear) **regression model**, of the form

$$y = bx + a$$

where a and b are constants. For example, Tanner (1949) uses the equation

$$SV = 0.32 \, Mass + 79.5$$

to describe the relationship between stroke volume (*SV*, ml) and body mass (*Mass*, kg). Another example of where the regression model might be more appropriate than the ratio model is the scaling of skinfold thicknesses to height. A skinfold includes a double layer of skin, the thickness of which is more or less independent of height. This would mean that there is a certain minimum value, a "floor", below which skinfolds cannot fall (Figure 1). Consequently, a plot of skinfold thicknesses as a function of height should show a positive intercept. This is clearly important when we want to compare skinfold thicknesses of people of different body size (heading 4.1.2 below).

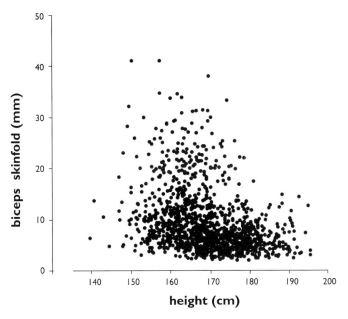

Figure 1 Scatterplot of measured biceps skinfold thicknesses (mm) against body height (cm) for subjects in the survey of Australian adults conducted by the Department of the Arts, Sport, the Environment and Territories (1992). Note that the biceps skinfold appears to have a "floor" value (about 2 mm) regardless of the height of the individual.

A good example of the difference between ratio and regression models is provided by Bogardus and Ravussin (1989). It is known that one of the primary determinants of resting metabolic rate (RMR) is fat-free mass (FFM). These authors point out that when a ratio model is used (Figure 2), people with a large absolute fat-free mass (such as the obese) often appear to have lower than "normal" RMRs. We might interpret this to mean that obese individuals have a metabolic defect which causes them to use less energy at rest, and from there to speculate that this defect might have caused their obesity (or alternatively that obesity leads to a depressed RMR). However, when a regression model is used, individuals with a higher FFM will fall close to the predicted value (Figure 2). The choice of a ratio as opposed to a regression model will therefore affect our diagnoses and data interpretation.

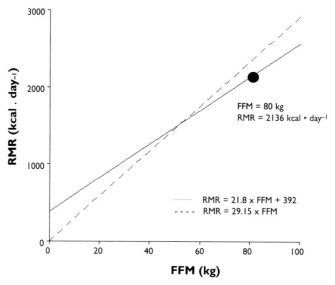

Figure 2 An individual with a fat–free mass (FFM) of 80 kg has a resting metabolic rate (RMR) of 2136 kcal.day⁻¹. While this value falls directly on the regression scaling line (solid line) with equation RMR = 21.8 x FFM + 392, it falls well below the ratio scaling line with equation RMR = 29.15 x FFM (adapted from Bogardus and Ravussin, 1989).

2.3 The general allometric equation

A third model, which is more general still, is the **power model**, or the **general allometric equation**. In the 1930s, Huxley (1932) and Teissier (1931) developed a simple and ingenious method for describing the relative size of two body parts (proportionality). They suggested that proportional relationships could be best described by a single versatile equation:

$$y = bx^a$$

or, taking logs of both sides,

$$\ln y = \ln b + a \ln x$$

where x is the size of some body part or a general measure of body size (usually height or mass), and y is the size of another body part or a body function. This equation is known as the general allometric equation.

When $a = 0$, y equals b. This would be the case, for example, when the size of some body part is not dependent on the size of the animal. For example, the size of red blood cells (RBCs) is much the same in all mammals, no matter how large the animal is. The RBC varies in size between 4 and 9.4 μm in diameter for body masses ranging from 2 g to over 4000 kg. In other words, RBC size is independent of body size. In fact, mice and horses have similarly sized RBCs (Weibel, 1984).

When $a = 1$, the size of the two body parts (or the size of the body part and the whole body) are linearly related. For example, leg length usually increases *pari passu* as body height increases. Another example is blood volume in mammals, which increases in proportion to body mass (i.e. in proportion to the cube of height). The larger the animal, the more blood it will have. If we were to plot blood volume (on the y-axis) as a function of body mass (on the x-axis), the graph would be a straight line.

When $a = 2$, the body part size increases with the square of body size. The cross-sectional area of muscle and body surface area are examples of body characteristics which increase approximately with the square of height.

When $a = 3$, the body characteristic increases with the cube of body size. For example, volume would be expected to increase approximately with the cube of height.

When $a = -1$, y decreases inversely as x increases. It has been suggested (Ford, 1984) that acceleration decreases as height (i.e. limb length) increases. For example, the mean height of sprinters increases as the sprint distance increases from 50 m to 400 m. Over longer distances, acceleration is much less important than in short sprints.

The general allometric equation has proved useful because it is flexible (by varying a and b we can describe a lot of different relationships), and because it is easy to manipulate mathematically. The equation has not been without its critics over the years (Tanner, 1949; Smith, 1980). However, it has proved to be a very powerful analytical and conceptual tool.

2.4 Why are relational models important?

An uncritical use of absolute physiological values, or values expressed per unit body mass, may lead to spurious correlations and proposed theoretical relationships which are physiologically untenable and logically incorrect (Katch, 1973). Norms which are used to diagnose pathologies are often based on allometric relationships (Tanner, 1949), and inappropriate allometry may lead to individuals being classified as pathological when in fact they are not.

Strong allometric relationships have been found between body mass and a number of functional variables. In particular, attention has been directed towards the scaling of variables related to oxygen transport. One of the strongest relationships is "Kleiber's Rule", which states that metabolic rate is proportional to body mass raised to the power 0.75. This has been found to be true for both resting and maximal metabolic rate across a very wide range of animals. Graphs which plot metabolic rate against body mass on a log-log scale show nearly all the points lying close to a line of best fit with a gradient not significantly different from 0.75 (these graphs are called "mouse-to-elephant" curves; Figure 3).

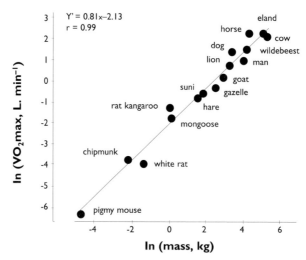

Figure 3 Regression of $\ln(VO_{2max}, L.min^{-1})$ on $\ln$(body mass, kg) for a variety of mammals (from Weibel, 1984, p. 39). The slope of the regression line (0.81) is the estimated exponent (a) of the general allometric equation.

Another interesting relationship is the association between strength and body mass. In 1956, Lietzke analysed world-record performances in different weightlifting classes. He found that the weight lifted varied with the lifter's mass raised to the power 0.67. We would also expect muscle cross-sectional area to increase with mass raised to the power 0.67 (see below). Since the force a muscle can exert is proportional to the number of active cross-bridges, which depends on the physiological cross-sectional area of the muscle, Lietzke's results reflect the expected relationship.

One fascinating use of the general allometric equation was Jerison's (1973) analysis of brain size in animals. Absolute brain size may not be the best index of intelligence. Elephants, for example, have larger brains than humans. Jerison calculated the log of brain mass in a variety of animals (in extinct animals, he estimated brain mass from skull cavity size), and regressed it against the log of body mass. He calculated a separate regression for each major animal group (e.g. mammals, fish, birds). From these regressions, he calculated an "encephalization quotient" (EQ), which was the ratio of actual brain mass to brain mass predicted from the group-specific regression. An EQ of 1.0 would indicate that the relative brain size of the animal was average (i.e. exactly as expected). Higher EQs indicated relative brain "hypergrowth". A hippopotamus has an EQ of 0.3, squirrels score 1.5, primates in general score 2.1, while *Homo sapiens* has an EQ of 7.6, indicating a quantum leap in brain development. Dolphins and porpoises score as high as humans, while eels, ostriches and alligators may be considered the dolts of the animal world.

3   Types of similarity systems

3.1   Geometric similarity

One of the striking things about humans is that they are all basically the same shape. Dwarfs are recognisably reduced versions of people of normal stature, and giants blown-up versions. This similarity of shape makes comparative anthropometry much simpler.

Of course there are exceptions to the rule. Children are not precisely scaled-down versions of adults, nor are achondroplastic dwarfs exactly diminished versions of people of normal stature. Their heads are relatively larger, for example. However, if we ignore these subtleties, we can make comparisons of individuals of different size.

It turns out that for a large number of body characteristics, different-sized humans are much like different-sized cubes (Figure 4). If the length (L) of the side of a cube doubles, its surface area (L²) quadruples, and its volume (L³) increases eight times. In a similar way, human lengths, girths and breadths generally increase linearly with height, surface areas increase with the square of height, and masses and volumes increase with the cube of height.

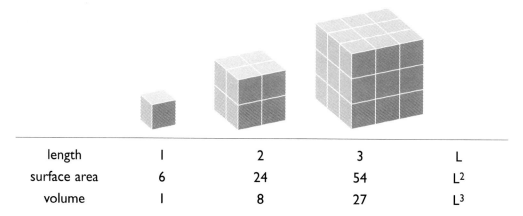

length	1	2	3	L
surface area	6	24	54	L²
volume	1	8	27	L³

Figure 4 Illustration of the principle of geometric similarity. Surface area increases proportionally to the square of length, and volume increases proportionally to the cube of length.

This process can't go on forever. From an engineering viewpoint, machines (including animals) must change form as they get bigger if they are to remain functional. Galileo speculated about how large land animals could be. He reasoned that since the strength of the bones and muscles increases with cross-sectional area (L²), and the body mass of the animals increases with volume (L³), a point will eventually be reached where the bones and muscles can no longer support the huge mass of the animals. Since the largest ever land animals, the Argentinosaurus, may have weighed 100 tonnes or more, this particular problem is unlikely to arise with humans. Moreover, bone mass increases at a relatively greater rate than body mass. This represents a structural response to functional demands which "breaks the allometric rule".

There is an interesting parallelism between allometric relationships in animals, and corresponding allometric changes in man-made objects. McMahon and Bonner (1983) have shown that steel nails, for example, show a systematic relationship between length and diameter. This relationship has not been planned by nail manufacturers, but has evolved, presumably by trial and error, over several thousand years. The nature of this relationship could be predicted from the way cylindrical objects (nails or bones) buckle under compressive forces.

3.2 Elastic similarity

Geometric similarity is not the only similarity system which has been proposed. Thomas McMahon (1983) has proposed a system of **elastic** similarity. This is based on the reasonable premise that the size and shape of animals are determined by the forces they are subjected to. The main forces largish animals are subject to are inertia and gravity. McMahon concluded that the lengths of the limbs and bones of animals measured in the direction of muscle forces increase at a relatively slower rate than the diameters or breadths of those limbs and bones (measured perpendicular to the muscle force). Specifically, he suggests that bone diameters increase proportionally to lengths raised to the power 1.5. His analysis is well supported by empirical evidence. Table 1 contrasts geometric and elastic similarity systems.

Table 1 Relationships between height and mass, and various anthropometric dimensions, as predicted by geometric and elastic similarity systems.

dimension	geometric similarity	elastic similarity
heights	$mass^{0.33}$ or $height^1$	$mass^{0.25}$ or $height^1$
breadths	$mass^{0.33}$ or $height^1$	$mass^{0.38}$ or $height^{1.5}$
girths	$mass^{0.33}$ or $height^1$	$mass^{0.38}$ or $height^{1.5}$
cross–sections	$mass^{0.67}$ or $height^2$	$mass^{0.75}$ or $height^3$
surface areas	$mass^{0.67}$ or $height^2$	$mass^{0.63}$ or $height^{2.5}$
volumes	$mass^1$ or $height^3$	$mass^1$ or $height^4$

4 Applications of similarity systems in anthropometry

Similarity systems are models of reality. They describe actual size measures only to the extent that the fundamental assumptions or axioms underlying the models apply to the real world. Both geometric and elastic similarity systems are interesting because their assumptions do seem to apply to the real world over a broad range of size variables.

However, there are many cases where the real world does not live up to the expectations of these similarity systems. Clearly, competing similarity systems cannot **all** always be true. For example, geometric similarity predicts that mass will be proportional to the cube of height. McMahon and Bonner (1983) report that life insurance tables show that the actual exponent is 2.9. Ross, Grand, Marshall and Martin (1982) report that the exponent was 2.8 for a group of Saskatchewan adolescents.

Nonetheless, departures from expected relationships are often as interesting as strict compliance with the model. When size variables do not follow the patterns suggested by the models, it is often very fruitful to ask ourselves why. This may lead to further opportunities for research and investigation.

4.1   Scaling anthropometric variables

In order to make inter-individual comparisons, and intra-individual comparisons across periods of growth, it is useful to be able to scale anthropometric variables to a common stature. Imagine two individuals. One is 180 cm tall with a triceps skinfold of 15 mm. Another is 160 cm tall with a triceps skinfold of 12 mm. Is it reasonable to compare the absolute value of the skinfolds? Wouldn't we expect the larger individual to have larger skinfolds? To get around this problem, we scale both measures to a common height (for historical reasons, variables are scaled to a common height of 170.18 cm or 5' 7").

We must assume a similarity system. Most frequently, geometric similarity is used, although it is clear that other similarity systems could also be used. In geometric similarity systems, skinfolds would be proportional to height. Therefore we "shrink down" the taller individual to the "baseline" height (170.18 cm). Their adjusted skinfold is now 15 × 170.18/180 or 14.2 mm. Similarly, we must "blow up" the shorter individual to the baseline height. Their adjusted skinfold is 12 × 170.18/160 or 12.8 mm.

Similar operations can be performed with girths, breadths, lengths, masses, volumes, surfaces and cross-sectional areas. Imagine that the 180 cm individual has a fat mass of 10 kg, while the shorter individual has a fat mass of 7.5 kg. To rescale these masses, we multiply by $(170.18/180)^3$ for the taller individual, and $(170.18/160)^3$ for the shorter individual – the exponent 3 being used because geometric similarity asserts that masses are proportional to the cube of height. The resulting values are 8.5 kg for the taller individual and 9.0 kg for the shorter individual. The general scaling procedure is as follows:

- Determine a raw score (V) for the individual.
- Adjust V for height to yield V_{adj}. V_{adj} is obtained by multiplying V by $(170.18/Ht)^d$, where Ht is the height of the individual, and d is the appropriate exponent for the similarity system being used. For geometric similarity, $d = 1$ for girths, skinfolds, lengths and breadths; $d = 2$ for surface areas and cross-sectional areas; $d = 3$ for masses and volumes.

4.1.1 The O-scale

The O-scale (Ross & Ward, 1985) is a scaling system using geometric similarity which arrives at estimates of adiposity (based on skinfolds) and proportional weight (based on mass). By comparing adiposity and proportional weight ratings, judgments can be made about the nature of body composition in the individual (i.e. the relative contributions of fat and non-fat mass)

In its simplest form, the O-scale adiposity rating uses six skinfold measures (triceps, subscapular, supraspinale, abdominal, front thigh and medial calf). The sum of these skinfolds (Σ6SF) is calculated, and corrected for height. The height-corrected values are compared to age- and gender-specific norms based on extensive North American data. The height-adjusted sum of skinfolds is then assigned a "stanine" rating (a stanine or "standard nine" category is a percentile band based on the normal distribution). Proportional weight is simply height-corrected mass. The calculated value is again compared to tables of age- and gender-specific norms, and a stanine rating determined.

A more detailed version of the O-scale is available in computerised form (Whittingham, Ward & Ross, 1992).

4.1.2 The OzScale

The OzScale is a method based on the O-scale, with the following differences:
- Australian population data have been used (Department of the Arts, Sport, the Environment and Territories, 1992);
- Some scaling procedures differ slightly. Corrected arm girth, for example, accounts for the average of the biceps and triceps skinfolds (rather than just the triceps, as in the O-scale). Also, skinfolds are corrected for minimal skin thickness.
- Results are expressed as age- and gender-specific percentiles.

Currently, data on the following variables are available in the OzScale: triceps, subscapular, biceps, supraspinale, abdominal and calf skinfolds, sum of 6 skinfolds, height, mass, relaxed arm girth, hip girth, waist girth, skinfold-corrected relaxed arm girth and skinfold-corrected waist girth.

Raw values for height, BMI and WHR are used in the OzScale (since the WHR is unitless, and BMI has its own allometric logic). Mass and girths are height-adjusted as described above. Skinfolds are adjusted and scaled to a common height using the following procedure. A skinfold includes a double thickness of skin and a double fold of fat. It is assumed that the skin thickness would be independent of the height of the subject. This thickness would represent the minimum possible value for skinfolds for any individual. These thicknesses for various sites have been obtained from cadaver analysis (Clarys, Martin, Drinkwater & Marfell-Jones, 1987). It is assumed, on the other hand, that fatfolds would vary with the linear dimensions of the subject (as do girths). Therefore the site-specific thickness of two folds of skin (τskin) in mm is subtracted from the raw skinfold measurement (T). These skin thicknesses are shown in Table 2. The resulting value is scaled to the standard height of 170.18 cm by multiplying it by 170.18/height (cm). In this way taller subjects are not disadvantaged. Then the skin thickness is added back on. The adjusted value (T_{adj}) is therefore calculated as:

$$T_{adj} = \left(T - \tau_{skin}\right)\frac{170.18}{Ht} + \tau_{skin}$$

Table 2 Minimal skin thicknesses (mm) used in correcting skinfolds for use in the OzScale. These measurements are derived from cadaver analysis (Clarys, Martin, Drinkwater & Marfell-Jones, 1987).

site	male	females
triceps	1.28	1.10
biceps	0.77	0.49
subscapular	2.07	1.74
supraspinale	1.27	0.92
calf	0.89	0.79
abdominal	1.49	1.04

While any model at all (even a cardboard box) could have been used as a metaphorical model, Ross and Wilson actually based the Phantom's anthropometric characteristics on large population surveys. Girths were taken from the data of Wilmore and Behnke (1969, 1970), skinfold thicknesses from unpublished data of Yuhasz, and other measures from Garrett and Kennedy (1971). It was assumed that in the population of Phantom models each of these characteristics was normally distributed about the Phantom value (p) with a standard deviation (s) which was constructed as the average coefficient of variation of male and female values. A full list of Phantom means and standard deviations can be found in Ross and Marfell-Jones (1991).

4.3.1.1   Phantom z–scores

The originators of the Phantom do not claim that anthropometric data are normally distributed in the population. They imagine a population of Phantoms whose characteristics are normally distributed about the mean values. This allows us to describe an individual's anthropometric characteristics as belonging to a Phantom so many z–scores from the mean Phantom. To calculate the z–score associated with an individual measure, we use the usual z–score formula

$$z = \frac{V_{adj} - p}{s}$$

where p is the Phantom mean value, and s is the Phantom standard deviation.

The Phantom value (p) for subscapular skinfold thickness is 17.2 mm, with a standard deviation (s) of 5.07 mm. If a particular individual of height 180 cm has a measured subscapular skinfold thickness (V) of 12 mm, we calculate the z–score as follows.

- First, calculate V_{adj}:

$$V_{adj} = V \times (170.18/Ht) = 11.35 \text{ mm}$$

- Then, calculate the z–score:

$$z = \frac{V_{adj} - p}{s} = \frac{11.35 - 17.2}{5.07} = -1.15$$

This individual therefore has a subscapular skinfold thickness 1.15 Phantom standard deviations below the Phantom mean.

137

people. We can see this by looking at world weightlifting records. On a kilogram for kilogram basis, small lifters easily outperform larger lifters.

It is usually assumed that the oxygen cost of running increases in proportion to body mass. With other things being equal, it is assumed that both lighter and heavier runners will have the same VO_2 (ml.kg^{-1}.min^{-1}) at the same running speed. However, an analysis of some 30 studies (n = 906 measurements), combined with data from our laboratory, showed that when the natural log of the oxygen cost of running (calculated as measured VO_2 in ml O_2.min^{-1} minus estimated resting VO_2, divided by running speed in m.min^{-1}) was plotted against the natural log of mass (kg), the slope was 0.88 (95% confidence limits: 0.84-0.91; see Figure 6).

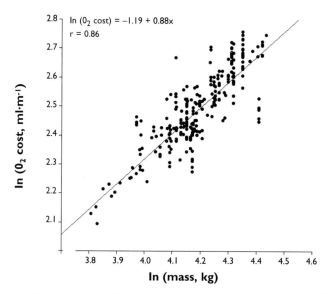

Figure 6 Regression of the natural log of VO_2 per unit speed (ml.m^{-1}) on the natural log of body mass (kg). VO_2 per unit speed is calculated as measured VO_2 (ml.min^{-1}) minus estimated resting metabolic rate (3.5 ml.kg^{-1} body mass.min^{-1}.), divided by running speed (m.min^{-1}). The data are weighted means from over 30 studies combined with individual measures from our laboratory (total n = 906).

This confirms the recent findings of Bergh, Sjödin, Forsberg and Svedenhag (1991), who, using slightly different methods, found an exponent of 0.76 (95% confidence limits: 0.64-0.88). This means that the oxygen cost of running (ml.kg^{-1}.min^{-1}) is less for heavier runners than for lighter ones.

A similar problem arises when we consider VO_{2max} values. If we express VO_{2max} in $L.min^{-1}$, larger people will obviously have greater values. Are they therefore "fitter" in the ways in which we consider fitness to be important? If we express VO_{2max} in $ml.kg^{-1}.min^{-1}$, then it turns out that larger people are disadvantaged (Nevill, Ramsbottom & Williams, 1992).

Using geometric similarity, we can say that we expect both strength and VO_{2max} $(L.min^{-1})$ to be proportional to height squared or to mass raised to the power 0.67. Should we therefore express strength and maximal ærobic power in kg lifted.$kg^{-0.67}$ body mass, and $L.min^{-1}.kg^{-0.67}$ respectively? In general terms, this would be a reasonable procedure. For example, Secher (1990) found that maximal oxygen uptake in oarsmen scaled closely to body mass raised to the power 0.67. However, the expression of functional variables is always task-specific. In many cases, we are interested just in the absolute amount of weight someone can lift. It is not helpful to know that a frail elderly person is quite strong for their size if they cannot lift the shopping out of the shopping trolley, or that a male rower has a high relative VO_{2max} if he only weighs 50 kg.

Functional scaling has been used to determine the relationship between sports performance and energy requirements in a number of sports. Klentrou and Montpetit (1992), for example, determined that oxygen uptake during backstroke swimming is a function of body mass raised to the power 0.55, while oxygen uptake during front crawl swimming is a function of mass raised to the power 0.75. Table 3 shows the relationship between aspects of performance and height as predicted by geometric similarity.

Table 3 Expected relationships between various aspects of performance as predicted by a geometric similarity system (from Åstrand & Rodahl, 1977).

performance aspect	proportional to ...
running	$height^0$ or $mass^0$
jumping	$height^0$ or $mass^0$
strength	$height^2$ or $mass^{0.67}$
work	$height^3$ or $mass^1$
power (absolute)	$height^2$ or $mass^{0.67}$
power (relative)	$height^{0.67}$ or $mass^{0.22}$

Table 4 Example of the calculation of fractional masses for a subject with a body mass (M_b) of 72.2 kg and a height (Ht) of 180.1 cm.

subset	measurement site	raw value	adj. value	Phantom mean	Phantom sd	z-score
fat mass	triceps skinfold	5.65	5.34	15.4	4.47	-2.25
	subscapular skinfold	7.35	6.95	17.2	5.07	-2.02
	supraspinale skinfold	3.60	3.40	15.4	4.47	-2.68
	abdominal skinfold	4.40	4.16	25.4	7.78	-2.73
	front thigh skinfold	7.30	6.90	27.0	8.33	-2.41
	medial calf skinfold	5.15	4.87	16.0	4.67	-2.38
mean						**-2.41**
residual mass	biacromial breadth	42.05	39.73	38.04	1.92	+0.88
	biiliocristal breadth	29.60	27.97	28.84	1.75	-0.50
	transverse chest breadth	27.60	26.08	27.92	1.74	-1.06
	AP chest depth	18.52	17.50	17.50	1.38	0.00
mean						**-0.17**
bone	bi-epicondylar femur	10.87	10.27	9.52	0.48	+1.56
	bi-epicondylar humerus	7.42	7.01	6.48	0.35	+1.51
	wrist girth	17.65	16.68	16.35	0.72	+0.46
	ankle girth	23.15	21.87	21.71	1.33	+0.12
mean						**+0.91**
muscle mass	corr. relaxed arm girth*	30.68	28.99	22.05	1.91	+3.63
	forearm girth	28.90	27.30	25.13	1.41	+1.55
	corr. chest girth*	93.79	88.62	82.46	4.86	+1.27
	corr. thigh girth*	53.86	50.89	47.34	3.59	+0.99
	corr. calf girth*	39.38	37.21	30.22	1.97	+3.55
mean						**+2.20**

s = standard deviation; adj. value = raw score adjusted for height (i.e. multiplied by 170.18/Ht).

* corr. girths are girths corrected for skinfolds. This is done by subtracting the appropriate skinfold (in cm) multiplied by π. Corrected relaxed arm girth = relaxed arm girth – π•triceps skinfold; corrected chest girth = chest girth – π•subscapular skinfold; corrected thigh girth = thigh girth – π•front thigh skinfold; corrected calf girth = calf-medial calf skinfold. The forearm girth is not corrected.

Fat mass

Phantom mean = 12.13 kg; Phantom s = 3.25 kg

$$M_{adj} = \bar{z} \times s + p \quad = -2.41 \times 3.25 + 12.13 = 4.3$$

$$M = M_{adj}\left(\frac{Ht}{170.18}\right)^3 = 4.3 \times (180.1/170.18)^3 = 5.1 \text{ kg}$$

Figure 5 shows sample print-outs from the computer programme **LifeSize** (Olds, Ly & Norton, 1994) which uses the OzScale. These show the age- and gender-specific percentile bands for a female subject measured in 1981 as a recreational athlete, and again in 1994 as a moderately active mother. There has been a drift in percentile bands over this period, even allowing for the increase in age of the subject. Since the OzScale database is cross-sectional, no allowance is made here for changes in the mean values for different age-groups over time.

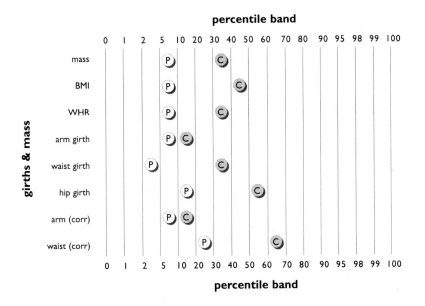

Figure 5 OzScale print-outs from the computer programme **LifeSize.** These show the age- and gender-specific percentile bands for a female subject measured in 1981 as a recreational athlete (white spheres, labelled "P") and again in 1994 when engaging in only occasional exercise (grey spheres, labelled "C").

4.2 Scaling functional variables

Often we have to compare the functional capacities of individuals of different size. For example, how do we compare the strength of a small person and a larger person? If we express strength in kilograms lifted, then we "disadvantage" the smaller person. It is unreasonable to expect smaller people to be as strong as larger people. For this reason, in order to "level out the playing field", we have weight classes in sports such as weightlifting, judo, rowing and wrestling. On the other hand, if we express strength as kilograms lifted per kilogram of body mass, it turns out that we disadvantage larger

It is important to understand that the calculated z-scores do not represent deviations from a descriptive (and much less a prescriptive) population norm. We cannot necessarily conclude that the individual above has a subscapular skinfold considerably less than most people. We could only do this if the Phantom means and standard deviations were based on data collected from an appropriate reference population. However, Phantom z-scores are useful for comparisons. We can quantify the differences between individuals or within an individual in terms of differences in z-scores. The Phantom strategy has been applied to longitudinal and cross-sectional growth studies (Ross et al., 1982), comparative studies of athletes (Ross, Leahy, Drinkwater & Swenson, 1982), and in other areas such as the study of anthropometric markers of genetic abnormalities, and studies of non-human primates.

4.3.1.2 Fractionation of body mass: four-way fractionation

Fractionation refers to the partitioning of total body mass into different compartments or submasses. The simplest fractionation procedure is to divide body mass into fat and non-fat compartments. More recently, anthropometrists have used four- or five-compartment models, with the fractional masses including skeletal or bone mass, muscle mass, fat mass, residual mass (blood, organs, etc.) and skin mass.

Matiegka (1921) was among the first to employ the fractionation procedure. He arrived at an estimate of bone, muscle and fat masses by measuring representative sites (e.g. bone breadths at the wrist, ankle, knee and elbow for skeletal mass), and using simple geometric shapes (for example, considering muscle mass as a "muscular column").

In 1980, Drinkwater and Ross developed a fractionation procedure using the Phantom model. Briefly, the fractionation strategy works as follows:
- For each of the fractional masses, a subset of representative anthropometric measures is selected. Skeletal mass is represented by bone breadths, fat mass by skinfolds, muscle mass by skinfold-corrected girths, and residual mass mainly by thoracic cavity measurements. For example, it is assumed that skeletal mass would be best represented by bone breadths: bi-epicondylar femur and humerus, wrist girth and ankle girth.
- For each measure in each of the four subsets, a z–score is calculated relative to the Phantom as described above.

- The average z-score ($\bar{z}$) within each subset is calculated. This is taken to be the number of standard deviations the fractional mass is away from the Phantom's fractional mass.
- The fractional mass that the individual would have if they were the size of the Phantom can then be calculated:

$$M_{adj} = \bar{z} \times s + p$$

M_{adj} being the fractional mass (at Phantom size), s the Phantom standard deviation for the mass in question, and p the Phantom mean mass.

- The individual is then scaled back up (or down) to their original height. Since mass is proportional to the cube of height, the appropriate equation to use is:

$$M = M_{adj} \left(\frac{Ht}{170.18} \right)^3$$

where M is the fractional mass of the subject.

This procedure clearly relies on a number of assumptions. It assumes that

- the measurement sites used to calculate each fractional mass are representative of that tissue-type throughout the body. (The student should note that although certain sites are recommended, there is a degree of flexibility. For example, it is possible to include biiliocristal breadth in the calculation of bone mass, or other skinfolds in the calculation of fat mass);
- an appropriate similarity system is being used (for example, that masses really do scale as the third power of stature);
- that the Phantom mean values and standard deviations for fractional masses are accurate.

An example of the fractionation procedure is shown in Table 4 below.

4.3 "Reference" humans

The use of a model or "reference" human is not new. Normative models of the body based on supposed "ideal" proportions have been proposed since Classical Antiquity. They are embodied in Renaissance studies of anatomy, as seen in the well-known **Vitruvian Man** of Leonardo da Vinci (Figure 7). Congruence with the normative ideal was used to quantify human beauty. In this century, large population surveys began to yield descriptive models of the typical human. Perhaps the best-known are Behnke's "reference man" and "reference woman"

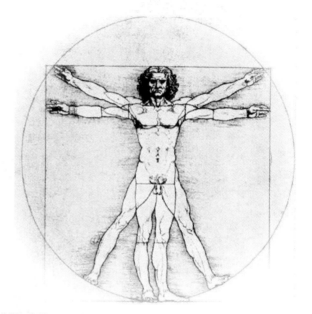

Figure 7 Leonardo da Vinci's *Vitruvian Man.*

4.3.1 The "Phantom"

The "Phantom" is a different kind of model, which its originators, Ross and Wilson, describe as a "metaphorical model". It is an arbitrary unisex reference human with specified anthropometric characteristics such as height (170.18 cm), mass (64.58 kg), percent body fat (18.87%), fat and muscle mass, girths, skinfold thicknesses and breadths. The primary use of the Phantom model is to scale anthropometric variables (refer to 4.2 above). Like the O-scale and OzScale, it uses geometric similarity and scales to a baseline height of 170.18 cm.

Smith, R.J. (1980).

Rethinking allometry.

Journal of Theoretical Biology, 87, 97-111.

Tanner, J.M. (1949).

Fallacy of per-weight and per-surface area standards, and their relation to spurious correlation.

Journal of Applied Physiology, 2(1), 1-15.

Taylor, C.R. (1987).

Structural and functional limits to oxidative metabolism: insights from scaling.

Annual Review of Physiology, 49, 135-146.

Teissier, G. (1931).

Recherches morphologiques et physiologiques sur la croissance des insectes.

Travaux de la station biologique de Roscoff, 9, 27-238.

Weibel, E. (1984).

The pathway for oxygen.

Cambridge, MS: Harvard University Press.

Whittingham, N.O., Ward, R., & Ross, W.D. (1992).

A computer based physique assessment system.

The Australian Journal of Science and Medicine in Sport, 24, 39-43.

Wilmore, J.H., & Behnke, A.R. (1969).

An anthropometric estimate of body density and lean body weight in young men.

Journal of Applied Physiology, 27, 35-31.

Wilmore, J.H., & Behnke, A.R. (1970).

An anthropometric estimate of body density and lean body weight in young women.

American Journal of Clinical Nutrition, 23, 267-274.

Withers, R.T., Craig, N.P., Ball, C.T., Norton, K.I., & Whittingham, N.O. (1991).

The Drinkwater-Ross anthropometric fractionation of body mass: comparison with measured body mass and densitometrically estimated fat and fat-free masses.

Journal of Sports Sciences, 9, 299-311.

These errors may be due to

- the assumption of geometric similarity as a scaling procedure;
- the equal weighting of each of the measures contributing to each fractional mass;
- the use of a unisex model, which disregards gender-specific distributions of fat mass amongst subcutaneous depots, and between subcutaneous and visceral depots, and
- the validity of Phantom means and standard deviations for the fractional masses.

This last point is of particular concern. Clearly, if the means and standard deviations for the fractional masses were different, we would arrive at different predicted fractional masses for individuals. How were the means and standard deviations arrived at in the first place? This has never been made clear, but they may originally have been based, at least in part, on small sample cadaver analyses.

4.3.1.2 Fractionation of body mass: five-way fractionation

Recently a revised fractionation procedure has been developed (Kerr, 1988), using a five-compartment model (i.e. skin, adipose tissue, bone, muscle and residual masses). This method also differs from the Drinkwater-Ross method in that fractional masses can be scaled according to any chosen dimension, and not just stature. When validated using data from several cadavers, adiposity was slightly underestimated for females (3–4%), and overestimated for males (6%).

5 Summary and recommendations

Similarity systems are useful tools in anthropometry when making inter- and intra-individual comparisons, establishing descriptive or prescriptive norms, and uncovering underlying mechanisms. However, they are ideal *models* which are valuable only to the extent to which they correspond to reality. Therefore competing similarity systems should be considered when scaling is required. The most commonly used similarity system is geometric similarity, and a large amount of empirical evidence suggests that it describes a range of performance and functional variables quite well. The fractionation of body mass using the Drinkwater-Ross procedure is an interesting approach, but should be treated with caution due to occasionally large and systematic errors and unclear methodological assumptions.

6 References

Åstrand, P.-O., & Rodahl, K. (1977).
Textbook of work physiology.
New York: McGraw-Hill.

Bergh, U., Sjödin, B., Forsberg, A., & Svedenhag, J. (1991).
The relationship between body mass and oxygen uptake during running in humans.
Medicine and Science in Sports and Exercise, 23, 205-211.

Bogardus, C., & Ravussin, E. (1989).
Relationship of genetics, age, and physical fitness to daily energy expenditure and fuel utilization.
American Journal of Clinical Nutrition, 49, 968-975.

Clarys, J.P., Martin, A.D., Drinkwater, D.T., & Marfell-Jones, M. J. (1987).
The skinfold: myth and reality.
Journal of Sports Science, 5, 3-33.

Department of the Arts, Sport, the Environment and Territories (1992).
Pilot survey of the fitness of Australians.
Canberra: Australian Government Publishing Service.

Drinkwater, D., & Ross, W.D. (1980).
Anthropometric fractionation of body mass.
In W. Ostyn, G. Beunen & J. Simons (Eds.), **Kinanthropometry II** (pp. 177-188). Baltimore: University Park Press.

Ford, L.E. (1984).
Some consequences of body size.
American Journal of Physiology, 247, H495-H507.

Garrett, J.W., & Kennedy, K.W. (1971).
A collation of anthropometry, Vol. 1-2.
Springield, Va: National Technical Information Service.

Huxley, J.S. (1932).
Problems in relative growth.
London: Methuen.

Jerison, H.J. (1973).
Evolution of the brain and intelligence.
New York: Academic Press.

Katch, V.L. (1973).
Use of the oxygen/body weight ratio in correlational analyses: spurious correlations and statistical considerations.
Medicine and Science in Sports, 5, 253-257.

Kerr, D. (1988).
An anthropometric method for fractionation of skin, adipose, bone, muscle and residual tissue masses in males and females aged 6 to 77 years.
Unpublished MSc thesis, Simon Fraser University, Burnaby, BC, Canada.

1   Introduction

The interest in body type or physique of individuals and populations has a long history going back to the ancient Greeks. Various systems for classifying physique have been proposed over the centuries, leading to the system called somatotyping as proposed by Sheldon (1940), and subsequently modified by others, notably Parnell (1958) and Heath and Carter (1967). Sheldon believed that somatotype was a fixed or genetic entity, but the present view is that the somatotype is phenotypical and thus amenable to change under the influence of growth, aging, exercise and nutrition (Carter & Heath, 1990).

The technique of somatotyping is used to appraise body shape and composition. The resulting somatotype gives a quantitative summary of the physique as a unified whole. It is defined as the quantification of the present shape and composition of the human body. It is expressed in a three-number rating representing endomorphy, mesomorphy and ectomorphy components respectively, always in the same order. Endomorphy is the relative fatness, mesomorphy is the relative musculo-skeletal robustness, and ectomorphy is the relative linearity or slenderness of a physique. For example, a 3–5–2 rating is recorded in this manner and is read as three, five, two. These numbers give the magnitude of each of the three components. Ratings on each component of 2 to 2½ are considered low, 3 to 5 are moderate, 5½ to 7 are high, and 7½ and above are very high (Carter & Heath, 1990). Theoretically, there is no upper limit to the ratings, and values of 12 or more occur in very rare instances. Because the components are rated relative to stature, the somatotype is independent of, or normalised for, stature.

The unique combination of three aspects of physique into a single three-number expression is the strength of the somatotype concept. The rating tells you what kind of physique you have, and how it looks. You should be able to visualise what the numbers "look like" when comparing physiques. Among many other applications, the somatotype has been used

- to describe and compare athletes at various levels of competition;
- to characterise physique changes during growth, aging and training;
- to compare the relative shape of men and women;
- as a tool in the analysis of "body image" (see Chapter 9).

It is important to recognise that the somatotype is a general descriptor of physique and does not answer more precise questions regarding specific body dimensions.
The Heath-Carter method of somatotyping is the most commonly used today.

Residual mass

Phantom mean = 16.41 kg; Phantom s = 1.90 kg

$$M_{adj} = \bar{z} \times s + p \quad = -0.17 \times 1.90 + 16.41 = 16.1 \text{ kg}$$

$$M = M_{adj}\left(\frac{Ht}{170.18}\right)^3 = 16.1 \times (180.1/170.18)3 = 19.1 \text{ kg}$$

Bone mass

Phantom mean = 10.49 kg; Phantom s = 1.57 kg

$$M_{adj} = \bar{z} \times s + p \quad = 0.91 \times 1.57 + 10.49 = 11.9$$

$$M = M_{adj}\left(\frac{Ht}{170.18}\right)^3 = 11.9 \times (180.1/170.18)3 = 14.1 \text{ kg}$$

Muscle mass

Phantom mean = 25.55 kg; Phantom s = 2.99 kg

$$M_{adj} = \bar{z} \times s + p \quad = 2.20 \times 2.99 + 25.55 = 32.1 \text{ kg}$$

$$M = M_{adj}\left(\frac{Ht}{170.18}\right)^3 = 32.1 \times (180.1/170.18)3 = 38.0 \text{ kg}$$

Estimated total mass = fat mass + residual mass + bone mass + muscle mass
= 5.1 + 19.1 + 14.1 + 38.0 = 76.3 kg

The original paper presenting the Drinkwater-Ross fractionation method (Drinkwater & Ross, 1980) found that when one added up the four masses (fat, muscle, bone and residual), the sum was nearly the same as the measured total body mass (note that total body mass is not used in calculating fractional masses). In a sample of 939 subjects, the authors reported a correlation of r = 0.97 between actual body mass and the sum of the four fractional masses, with a mean difference of only 0.3%. However, these figures conceal some large and systematic discrepancies. Withers and coworkers (1991) found mean absolute differences of 2–3% between the sum of the fractionated masses and measured body mass, but much larger absolute differences (20% for males and 30% for females) between fat mass estimated by densitometry and fat mass calculated by fractionation.

Chapter 6
Somatotyping

Lindsay Carter

Klentrou, P.P., & Montpetit, R.R. (1992).
Energetics of backstroke swimming in males and females.
Medicine and Science in Sports and Exercise, 24, 371-375.

Lietzke, M.H. (1956).
Relation between weight-lifting totals and body weight.
Science, 124, 486-487.

Matiegka, J. (1921).
The testing of physical efficiency.
American Journal of Physical Anthropology, 4, 223-230.

McMahon, T.A., & Bonner, J.T. (1983).
On size and life.
New York: Scientific American Library.

Nevill, A.M., Ramsbottom, R., & Williams, C. (1992).
Scaling physiological measurements for individuals of different body size.
European Journal of Applied Physiology, 65, 110-117.

Olds, T.S., Ly, S.V., & Norton, K.I. (1994).
LifeSize [Computer software].
Sydney: Nolds Sports Scientific.

Ross, W.D., Grand, T.I., Marshall, G.R., & Martin, A.D. (1982).
On human and animal geometry.
In M.L. Howell and B.O. Wilson (Eds.), **Proceedings of the VII Commonwealth and International Conference on Sport, Physical Education, Recreation and Dance** (pp. 77-97).
Brisbane: Department of Human Movement Studies, University of Queensland.

Ross, W.D., Leahy, R.M., Drinkwater, D.T., & Swenson, P.O. (1981).
Proportionality and body composition in male and female Olympic athletes: a kinanthropometric overview.
In J. Borms, M. Hebbelinck & A. Venerando (Eds.), **The female athlete** (pp. 74-84). Basel: Karger.

Ross, W.D., & Marfell-Jones, M. (1991).
Kinanthropometry.
In J.D. MacDougall, H.A. Wenger & H.J. Green (Eds.), **Physiological testing of the high-performance athlete** (pp. 223-308).
Champaign, IL: Human Kinetics.

Ross, W.D., & Ward, R. (1985).
The O-scale system.
Surrey, B.C: Rosscraft.

Ross, W.D., & Wilson, N.C. (1974).
A stratagem for proportional growth assessment.
Acta Pædiatrica Belgica, Suppl. 28, 169-182.

Secher , N. (1990).
Rowing.
In T. Reilly, N. Secher, P. Snell & C. Williams (Eds.), **Physiology of sports** (p. 268).
London: E. &. F.N. Spon.

Chapter 5

There are three ways of obtaining the somatotype.

(1)   The *anthropometric plus photoscopic* method, which combines anthropometry and ratings from a photograph – it is the criterion method;

(2)   the *photoscopic* method, in which ratings are made from a standardised photograph; and

(3)   the *anthropometric* method, in which anthropometry is used to estimate the criterion somatotype.

Because most people do not get the opportunity to become criterion raters using photographs, the anthropometric method has proven to be the most useful for a wide variety of applications. It can be used in the field or laboratory, requires little equipment and calculation, and measurements can be made with relative ease on subjects dressed in minimal clothing.

The purpose of this chapter is to provide a simple description of the anthropometric somatotype method, along with calculations for individual and group analyses. It is intended for students and professionals who are interested in learning "how to do it". To obtain a fuller understanding of somatotyping, its uses and limitations, the reader should consult Carter and Heath (1990).

2   The Heath-Carter anthropometric somatotype method

Anthropometric equipment includes a stadiometer or height scale and head board, weighing scale, small sliding caliper (a bone caliper), a flexible steel or fibreglass tape measure, and a skinfold caliper. Ten anthropometric dimensions are needed to calculate the anthropometric somatotype: stretch stature, body mass, four skinfolds (triceps, subscapular, supraspinale, medial calf), two bone breadths (biepicondylar humerus and femur), and two limb girths (arm flexed and tensed, calf). Descriptions of the equipment and techniques for measurement are given in Chapter 2.

Stature and girths are recorded to the nearest 1.0 mm, biepicondylar breadths to the nearest 0.5 mm, and skinfolds to the nearest 0.1 mm (Harpenden caliper) or 0.5 mm on other calipers.

Traditionally, when rating individuals using the anthropometric somatotype, the larger of the right and left breadths and girths have been used. When possible this should be done. However, in large surveys it is recommended that all measures (including skinfolds) be taken on the right side (see Chapters 2 and 3).

2.1 Calculating the Heath-Carter anthropometric somatotype

There are three ways to calculate the anthropometric somatotype:
(1)   enter the data onto a somatotype rating form;
(2)   enter the data into equations derived from the rating form; or
(3)   enter the data into computer programs such as **LifeSize**.

The use of the rating form will be described first. Figures 1 and 2 are examples of calculations using the rating form. Figure 3 is a blank rating form which the student may photocopy for use. It is assumed that the measurements have been recorded on an appropriate recording form and average or median values calculated before transfer to the rating form.

2.1.1   The Heath-Carter somatotype rating form

(i)   Record pertinent identification data in the top section of the rating form.

2.1.1.1 Endomorphy rating (steps ii-v)

(ii)   Record the measurements for each of the four skinfolds.
(iii) Sum the triceps, subscapular, and supraspinale skinfolds; record the sum in the box opposite Sum 3 Skinfolds. Correct for height by multiplying this sum by (170.18/height in cm).
(iv)   Circle the closest value in the Sum 3 Skinfolds scale to the right. The scale reads vertically from low to high in columns and horizontally from left to right in rows. "Lower limit" and "upper limit" on the rows provide exact boundaries for each column. These values are circled only when Sum 3 Skinfolds are within 1 mm of the limit. In most cases circle the value in the row "Mid-point".
(v)   In the row for endomorphy circle the value directly under the column for the value circled in number (iv) above.

2.1.1.2   Mesomorphy rating (steps vi-x)

(vi)   Record height and breadths of humerus and femur in the appropriate boxes. Make the corrections for skinfolds before recording girths of the arm (flexed and tensed) and the calf. (Skinfold correction: Convert triceps skinfold to cm by

Figure 1 Calculations of the anthropometric somatotype for subject A using the rating form.

Biceps girth in cm corrected for fat by subtracting triceps skinfold value expressed in cm.
Calf girth in cm corrected for fat by subtracting medial calf skinfold value expressed in cm.

Name __B. Roberts__
Occupation __Student__
Project __FS__

Age __21.5__ Sex M (F) No __B__
Ethnic Group __White__ Date __25 Dec 1995__
Measured by __KiN__

Sum 3 Skinfolds (mm)

Skinfolds mm

	Upper Limit																								
Triceps	10.9	14.9	18.9	22.9	26.9	31.2	35.8	40.7	46.2	52.2	58.7	65.7	73.2	81.2	89.7	98.9	108.9	119.7	131.2	143.7	157.2	171.9	187.9	204.0
Subscapular	9.0	13.0	17.0	21.0	25.0	29.0	33.5	38.0	43.5	49.0	55.5	62.0	69.5	77.0	85.5	94.0	104.0	114.0	125.5	137.0	150.5	164.0	180.0	196.0
Supraspinale	7.0	11.0	15.0	19.0	23.0	27.0	31.3	35.9	40.8	46.3	52.3	58.8	65.8	73.3	81.3	89.8	99.0	109.0	119.8	131.3	143.8	157.3	172.0	188.0

Skinfolds mm
Triceps = 15·0
Subscapular = 8·8
Supraspinale = 6·0
Sum 3 Skinfolds = 29·8 $\times \left(\dfrac{170.18}{ht = 170.7} \right) = 29.7$ (height corrected skinfolds)
Calf = 12·4

Endomorphy

	1	1½	2	2½	3	3½	4	4½	5	5½	6	6½	7	7½	8	8½	9	9½	10	10½	11	11½	12
	139.3	143.5	147.3	151.1	154.9	158.8	162.6	166.4	170.2	174.0	177.8	181.6	185.4	189.2	193.0	196.9	200.3	204.5	208.3	212.1	215.9	219.7	223.5	227.3
Height (cm) = 170·7																								
Humerus width (cm) = 6·10	5.19	5.34	5.49	5.64	5.78	5.93	6.00	6.22	6.37	6.51	6.65	6.80	6.95	7.09	7.24	7.38	7.53	7.67	7.82	7.97	8.11	8.25	8.40	8.55
Femur with (cm) = 8·65	7.41	7.62	7.83	8.04	8.24	8.45	8.66	8.87	9.08	9.28	9.49	9.70	9.91	10.12	10.33	10.53	10.74	10.95	11.16	11.36	11.57	11.78	11.99	12.21
Biceps girth (cm) = 24·9																								
-- triceps skinfolds (cm) = 1·5																								
= 23·4	24.4	25.0	25.7	26.3	27.0	27.7	28.3	29.0	29.7	30.3	31.0	31.6	32.2	33.0	33.6	34.3	35.0	35.6	36.3	37.0	37.6	38.3	39.0	
Calf girth (cm) = 33·1																								
-- calf skinfold (cm) = 1·2																								
= 31·9	27.7	28.5	29.3	30.1	30.8	31.6	32.4	33.2	33.9	34.7	35.5	36.3	37.1	37.8	38.6	39.4	40.2	41.0	41.7	42.5	43.3	44.1	44.9	45.6

Mesomorphy

	½	1	1½	2	2½	3	3½	4	4½	5	5½	6	6½	7	7½	8	8½	9
Weight (kg) = 52·6																		
Ht³/Wt = 45·56																		
Upper Limit	39.65	40.74	41.43	42.13	42.82	43.48	44.18	44.84	45.53	46.23	46.92	47.58	48.25	48.94	49.63	50.33	50.99	51.68
Mid-point and	40.20	41.09	41.79	42.48	43.14	43.84	44.50	45.19	45.89	46.32	47.24	47.94	48.60	49.29	49.99	50.68	51.34	
Lower Limit below	39.66	40.75	41.44	42.14	42.83	43.49	44.19	44.85	46.24	46.93	47.59	48.26	48.95	49.64	50.34	51.00		

Ectomorphy

½	1	1½	2	2½	3	3½	4	4½	5	5½	6	6½	7	7½	8	8½	9

	ENDOMORPHY	MESOMORPHY	ECTOMORPHY
Anthropometric Somatotype	3	2	5
Anthropometric plus Photoscopic Somatotype			

BY: __KiN__
RATER:

Figure 2 Calculations of the anthropometric somatotype for subject B using the rating form.

Biceps girth in cm corrected for fat by subtracting triceps skinfold value expressed in cm.
Calf girth in cm corrected for fat by subtracting medial calf skinfold value expressed in cm.

Name ______			Age ______	Sex M	F	No ______
Occupation ______			Ethnic Group ______			Date ______
Project ______			Measured by ______			

Skinfolds mm	
Triceps	=
Subscapular	=
Supraspinale	=
Sum 3 Skinfolds	=
Calf	=

Sum 3 Skinfolds (mm)

Upper Limit	10.9	14.9	18.9	22.9	26.9	31.2	35.8	40.7	46.2	52.2	58.7	65.7	73.2	81.2	89.7	98.9	108.9	119.7	131.2	143.7	157.2	171.9	187.9	204.0
Mid-point	9.0	13.0	17.0	21.0	25.0	29.0	33.5	38.0	43.5	49.0	55.5	62.0	69.5	77.0	85.5	94.0	104.0	114.0	125.5	137.0	150.5	164.0	180.0	196.0
Lower Limit	7.0	11.0	15.0	19.0	23.0	27.0	31.3	35.9	40.8	46.3	52.3	58.8	65.8	73.3	81.3	89.8	99.0	109.0	119.8	131.3	143.8	157.3	172.0	188.0

$\times \left(\frac{170.18}{ht = ___} \right) =$ (height corrected skinfolds)

Endomorphy	1	1½	2	2½	3	3½	4	4½	5	5½	6	6½	7	7½	8	8½	9	9½	10	10½	11	11½	12

Height (cm)	=
Humerus width (cm)	=
Femur with (cm)	=
Biceps girth (cm)	=
-- triceps skinfolds (cm)	=
Calf girth (cm)	=
-- calf skinfold (cm)	=

139.3	143.5	147.3	151.1	154.9	158.8	162.6	166.4	170.2	174.0	177.8	181.6	185.4	189.2	193.0	196.9	200.3	204.5	208.3	212.1	215.9	219.7	223.5	227.3
5.19	5.34	5.49	5.64	5.78	5.93	6.07	6.22	6.37	6.51	6.65	6.80	6.95	7.09	7.24	7.38	7.53	7.67	7.82	7.97	8.11	8.25	8.40	8.55
7.41	7.62	7.83	8.04	8.24	8.45	8.66	8.87	9.08	9.28	9.49	9.70	9.91	10.12	10.33	10.53	10.74	10.95	11.16	11.36	11.57	11.78	11.99	12.21
23.7	24.4	25.0	25.7	26.3	27.0	27.7	28.3	29.0	29.7	30.3	31.0	31.6	32.2	33.0	33.6	34.3	35.0	35.6	36.3	37.0	37.6	38.3	39.0
27.7	28.5	29.3	30.1	30.8	31.6	32.4	33.2	33.9	34.7	35.5	36.3	37.1	37.8	38.6	39.4	40.2	41.0	41.7	42.5	43.3	44.1	44.9	45.6

Mesomorphy	½	1	1½	2	2½	3	3½	4	4½	5	5½	6	6½	7	7½	8	8½	9

Weight (kg)	=
Ht/∛Wt	=

Upper Limit	39.65	40.74	41.43	42.13	42.82	43.48	44.18	44.84	45.53	46.23	46.92	47.58	48.25	48.94	49.63	50.33	50.99	51.68
Mid-point	and	40.20	41.09	41.79	42.48	43.14	43.84	44.50	45.19	45.89	46.32	47.24	47.94	48.60	49.29	49.99	50.68	51.34
Lower Limit	below	39.66	40.75	41.44	42.14	42.83	43.49	44.19	44.85	45.54	46.24	46.93	47.59	48.26	48.95	49.64	50.34	51.00

Ectomorphy	½	1	1½	2	2½	3	3½	4	4½	5	5½	6	6½	7	7½	8	8½	9

	ENDOMORPHY	MESOMORPHY	ECTOMORPHY	
Anthropometric Somatotype				BY:
Anthropometric plus Photoscopic Somatotype				RATER:

Figure 3 Blank anthropometric somatotype rating form.

Biceps girth in cm corrected for fat by subtracting triceps skinfold value expressed in cm.
Calf girth in cm corrected for fat by subtracting medial calf skinfold value expressed in cm.

dividing by 10. Subtract converted triceps skinfold from the arm girth, flexed and tensed. Convert calf skinfold to cm, subtract from calf girth).

(vii) On the height scale directly to the right of the recorded value, circle the height value nearest to the measured height of the subject. (Note: Regard the height row as a continuous scale).

(viii) For each bone breadth and girth circle the number nearest the measured value in the appropriate row. (Note: Circle the lower value if the measurement falls midway between two values. This conservative procedure is used because the largest girths and breadths are recorded).

(ix) Deal only with columns, not numerical values for the first two procedures below. Find the average deviation of the circled values for breadths and girths from the circled value in the height column as follows:

- Column deviations to the right of the height column are positive deviations. Deviations to the left are negative deviations. (Circled values directly under the height column have deviations of zero and are ignored).
- Calculate the algebraic sum of the ± deviations (D). Use this formula:

$$mesomorphy = (D/8) + 4.0$$

- Round the obtained value of mesomorphy to the nearest one-half (½) rating unit.

(x) In the row for mesomorphy circle the closest value for mesomorphy obtained in number (ix) above. (If the point is exactly midway between two rating points, circle the value closest to 4 on the scale. This conservative regression toward 4 guards against spuriously extreme ratings).

2.1.1.3 Ectomorphy rating (steps xi-xvi)

(xi) Record weight (kg).

(xii) Obtain height divided by cube root of weight (HWR). Record HWR.

(xiii) Circle the closest value in the HWR scale to the right [see note in step (iv) above].

(xiv) In the row for ectomorphy circle the ectomorphy value directly below the circled HWR.

(xv) Move to the bottom section of the rating form. In the row for Anthropometric Somatotype, record the circled ratings for endomorphy, mesomorphy and ectomorphy.

(xvi) Sign your name to the right of the recorded rating. The identification data in the upper section of the rating form are somewhat arbitrary. Investigators may change these to suit their purposes.

2.1.1.4 The mesomorphy calculation

Two principles are important in understanding the calculation of mesomorphy on the rating form:

(1) When the measurements of bone breadths and limb girths lie to the right of the circled height column, the subject has greater musculo-skeletal robustness relative to height (i.e. higher mesomorphy) than a subject whose values lie to the left of the height column. The average deviation of the circled values for breadths and girths is the best index of average musculo-skeletal development relative to height.

(2) The scale is constructed so that the subject is rated 4 in mesomorphy when the average deviation falls in the column under the subject's height, or when the four circled values fall in the subject's height column. That is, the average deviation ($\pm$) to the left or right of the height column is added to or subtracted from 4.0 in mesomorphy. For subject A, mesomorphy $= 1111/8 + 4.0 = 5.4$; for subject B, mesomorphy $= -15/8 + 4.0 = 2.1$.

2.1.1.5 Height–Weight Ratio calculation

The height-weight ratio (HWR), or height divided by the cube root of weight (stature/mass^3) as it is used in somatotyping, may be determined by using a hand calculator. A calculator with a y to the x power (y^x) key is needed. To get the cube root, enter mass, i.e. base (y), press y^x, enter .3333, and press "equals". If there is an INV y^x function, this may be used instead by entering 3 (for the cube root).

2.1.1.6 Limitations of the rating form

Although the rating form provides a simple method of calculating the anthropometric somatotype, especially in the field, it has some limitations. First, the mesomorphy scales at the low and high ends do not include some of the values for small subjects, e.g. children, or for large subjects, e.g. heavy weightlifters. Second, some rounding errors may occur in calculating the mesomorphy rating, because the subject's height often is not the same as the column height. If the anthropometric somatotype is regarded as an estimate this second limitation is not a serious problem. The following procedures described in Carter (1980) and Carter and Heath (1990) can correct these problems.

2.1.2 Equations for a decimalised anthropometric somatotype

The second method of obtaining the anthropometric somatotype is by means of equations into which the data are entered. To calculate endomorphy, use the following equation:

$$endomorphy = -0.7182 + 0.1451 \times \Sigma SF - 0.00068 \times \Sigma SF^2 + 0.0000014 \times \Sigma SF^3$$

where ΣSF = (sum of triceps, subscapular and supraspinale skinfolds) multiplied by (170.18/height in cm). This is called height-corrected endomorphy and is the preferred method for calculating endomorphy.

The equation used to calculate mesomorphy is:

$$mesomorphy = 0.858 \times humerus\ breadth + 0.601 \times femur\ breadth + 0.188 \times$$
$$corrected\ arm\ girth + 0.161 \times corrected\ calf\ girth - height \times 0.131 + 4.5$$

Three different equations are used to calculate ectomorphy according to the height-weight ratio:

If HWR is greater than or equal to 40.75 then

$$ectomorphy = 0.732 \times HWR - 28.58$$

If HWR is less than 40.75 and greater than 38.25 then

$$ectomorphy = 0.463 \times HWR - 17.63$$

If HWR is equal to or less than 38.25 then

$$ectomorphy = 0.1$$

The resulting somatotypes (using height corrected endomorphy) are 1.6–5.4–3.2, and 3.0–2.1–4.8, for subjects A and B respectively (Figures 1, 2).

2.1.3 Computer programs for calculating the somatotype

The equations in 2.1.1 above can be used in computer programs for individual or group analyses. Interactive programs can be constructed for QBASIC, other languages, and for spreadsheets.

2.2   Checking the results

Now that the anthropometric somatotype has been calculated, is the result logical? There are several ways to check your results for measurement or calculation errors.

Using the rating form examples in Figures 1 and 2, the resulting somatotypes rounded to the nearest half-unit, are 1½ –5½ –3 and 3–2–5 for subjects A and B respectively. Are these reasonable somatotypes? Certain somatotype ratings are not biologically possible, although our examples are not among them. For example, a 2–2–2 or a 7–8–7 are impossible somatotypes. Generally, somatotypes high in endomorphy and/or mesomorphy cannot also be high in ectomorphy. Conversely, those high in ectomorphy cannot be high in endomorphy and/or mesomorphy; and those low in endomorphy and mesomorphy must be high in ectomorphy.

Next, look at the pattern of circled values in the endomorphy and mesomorphy sections of the rating form. Are there inconsistencies in the data? For endomorphy, are the skinfold values reasonable? For mesomorphy, is there one measure (excluding height) that is quite far apart from the others? In Figure 1, upper limb circled values are slightly to the right of, and larger relative to height, than the lower limb measures. However, this pattern is not unusual and is quite acceptable in this case. On the other hand, if the femur width was 7.95 cm instead of 9.75 cm, or corrected calf girth was 44.9 cm instead of 37.1 cm, such large deviations would suggest errors. Check for errors in recording and remeasure the subject if possible. Also, check to see that the correct skinfolds in cm have been subtracted for the corrected girth values. In Figure 2, the small corrected arm girth (23.4 cm) looks suspiciously low, but in this subject it truly represented her small muscular development in the upper limb.

If the calculation for any component is zero or negative, a value of 0.1 is assigned as the component rating, because by definition ratings cannot be zero or negative. The photoscopic rating would be one-half. If such low values occur the raw data should be checked. Values less than 1.0 are highly unlikely to occur for endomorphy and mesomorphy, but are not unusual for ectomorphy. The component ratings should be rounded to the nearest 0.1 of a unit, or nearest half-unit depending on their subsequent use.

After the values are entered into the equations (either by calculator or computer program) rather than onto the rating form, it is impossible to check the pattern of values in either the endomorphy or mesomorphy section as in the rating form, although the raw values can be examined for errors. This is a limitation of using the equations. Further checking can be done for either method by using the HWR and by plotting the somatotype.

There is a relationship between the HWR and the likely somatotypes (see Figure 4). The somatotypes in the rows are those most likely to occur for the given HWR. For example, given a HWR of 50.25, the most likely somatotypes are 1–1–8, 1–2–9 or 2–1–9. (The hyphens are left out of the figure to conserve space). The next most likely somatotypes are those in the rows directly above and below the row for 50.25. If none of these somatotypes match or are not close when interpolating for half-unit ratings, there may be errors in the data or calculations. However, other factors such as heavy meals or dehydration can affect body weight sufficiently to alter the "normal" HWR.

For subject A, HWR = 43.4, and Figure 4 shows that in the row for a HWR of 43.64 the somatotypes 1–6–3 and 2–5–3 occur. His 1½ –5½ –3 is a combination of these two ratings, therefore his anthropometric rating agrees with that expected from the HWR table. For subject B, HWR = 45.6, her 3–2–5 somatotype appears in the row above that for her HWR. Her ectomorphy is borderline between 4½ and 5, which suggests that she

Ectomorphy ratings

HWR	½ -1	1	2	3	4	5	6	7	8	9
50.91										119
50.25									118	129,219
49.59								117	128,218	
48.93								127,217	138,318 228	
48.27							126,216	137,317 227		
47.61							136,316 226	237,327		
46.95						135,315 225	146,416 236,326			
46.28					134,314 224	145,415 235,325	246,426 336			
45.62					144,414 234,324	245,425 335				
44.96				233	154,514 244,424 334	255,525 345,435				
44.30				153,513 333	254,524 344,434					

Figure 4 Distribution of somatotypes according to the HWR (height/weight$^{1/3}$).

43.64			242,422 253,523 343,433	163,613	354,534 444
42.98			162,612 252,522	263,623 353,533 443	
42.32		341,431	172,712 262,622 352,532 442	363,633 453,543	
41.66		171,711 261,621 351,531 441	182,812 272,722 362,632 452,542		
40.99		181,811 271,721 361,631 451,541	282,822 372,732 462,642 552		
40.33		191,911 281,821 371,731 461,641 551			
39.67		291,921 381,831 471,741 561,651			
38.68	5-6½-½ 10-2-1 2-10-1 661	391,931 481,841 571,751			
37.69	10-3-1 3-10-1 10½-2½-½ 11-2-1	491,941 581,851 671,761			
36.37	6½-7½-½ 10½-3½-½ 11-3-1 771	4-10-1 10-4-1 591,951 681,861			
34.71	781,871 11½-3½-½ 12-3-1	4-11-1 11-4-1 5-10-1 10-5-1 691,961			
33.06	7½-8½-½ 11½-4½-½ 12-4-1 13-3-1 881	5-11-1 11-5-1 6-10-1 10-6-1 791,971			
31.41	12-5-1 13-4-1	7-10-1 10-7-1 891,981 11-6-1			
29.75	12-6-1 13-5-1 14-4-1	8-10-1 10-8-1 11-7-1 991			

might be a 3–2–4½, i.e. half way between the two rows. The somatotypes for both subjects appear to be reasonable.

2.3   Plotting the somatotype

One of the advantages of somatotypes is that they can be displayed on a standard chart called a somatochart, so that you have a visual representation of where each one is relative to other somatotypes. The somatotype is actually three-dimensional, and a somatoplot can be envisaged as a point in three-dimensional "somatic space" (see Carter & Heath, 1990, p. 404). Traditionally, the three-number somatotype rating is plotted on a two-dimensional somatochart using X,Y coordinates derived from the rating (see Figure 5). The coordinates are calculated as follows:

$X = ectomorphy - endomorphy$

$Y = 2 \times mesomorphy - (endomorphy + ectomorphy)$

For subject A, X = 1.5, and Y = 6.5. For subject B, X = 2.0, and Y = –4.0. These points on the somatochart are called somatoplots. If the somatoplot for the subject is far from that expected when compared to a suitable reference group, check the data and calculations. Because Figure 5 is quite crowded with all the grid lines, the somatoplots should be traced onto a somatochart without the grid. Figure 6 shows a blank somatochart which the student may photocopy.

Mean somatotypes for various Australian sports are plotted on somatocharts in Figures 7 and 8. These data were collected on a large sample of high-performance athletes from state or national levels (Withers et al. 1986, 1987).

2.4   The somatotype photograph

The somatotype photograph is a valuable record of the physique, especially when change is expected and for longitudinal growth studies. It can be used as a supplement to the anthropometric somatotype rating, in assessment of body image (see Chapter 9), and in association with the anthropometric profile. Even if you are not a qualified somatotype rater, you can look for the correspondence between the anthropometric somatotype and what you see in the photograph. In other words, the photo provides you with the visual image of what a particular 2–5–3 or 6–3–1 looks like. Details of how to rate the photographs, with examples, are described in Carter and Heath (App. I, 1990). Table 1 shows some descriptive phrases or verbal "anchor points" which are

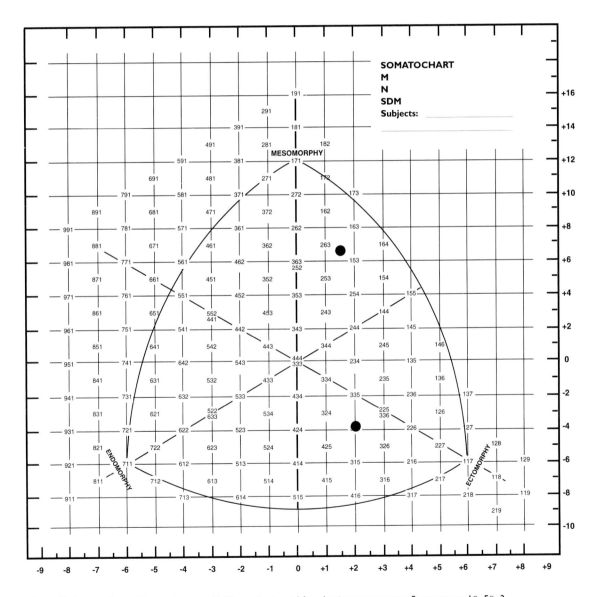

Figure 5 Somatochart with superimposed X, Y coordinate grid for plotting somatotypes. Somatotypes 12 -52 -3 (above) and 3-2-5 (below) are plotted.

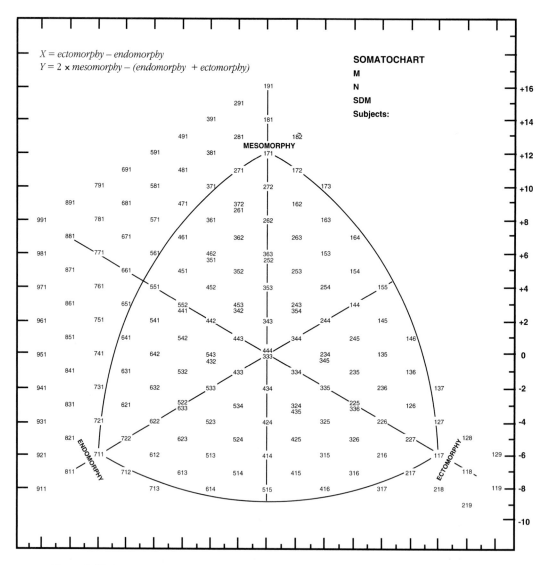

Figure 6 Blank somatochart

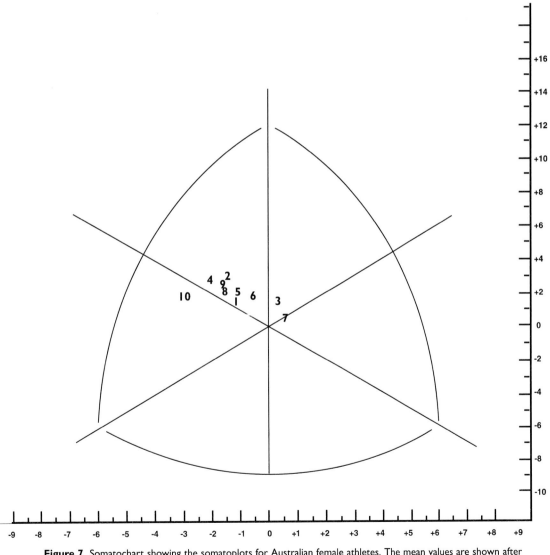

1	Basketball (3.7–4.0–2.9)	6	Squash (3.4–4.0–2.8)
2	Hockey (3.7–4.5–2.2)	7	Volleyball (3.0–3.5–3.5)
3	Netball (3.0–3.8–3.3)	8	Badminton (4.1–4.4–2.5)
4	Soccer (4.2–4.6–2.2)	9	Lacrosse (4.1–4.5–2.4)
5	Softball (3.8–4.3–2.7)	10	Cricket (4.9–4.4–2.0)

Figure 7 Somatochart showing the somatoplots for Australian female athletes. The mean values are shown after each sport. (Data from Withers, et al., 1987).

1	Australian Rules (2.1–5.7–2.5)	6	Powerlifting (2.7–7.9–0.6)
2	Basketball (2.1–4.5–3.5)	7	Heavyweight rowing (2.0–5.2–3.0)
3	Gymnastics (1.9–6.1–2.5)	8	Rugby Union (2.7–6.0–2.0)
4	Hockey (2.4–5.4–2.6)	9	Distance running (1.8–4.4–3.7)
5	Hurdles (1.8–4.1–3.9)	10	Squash (2.5–5.2–2.8)

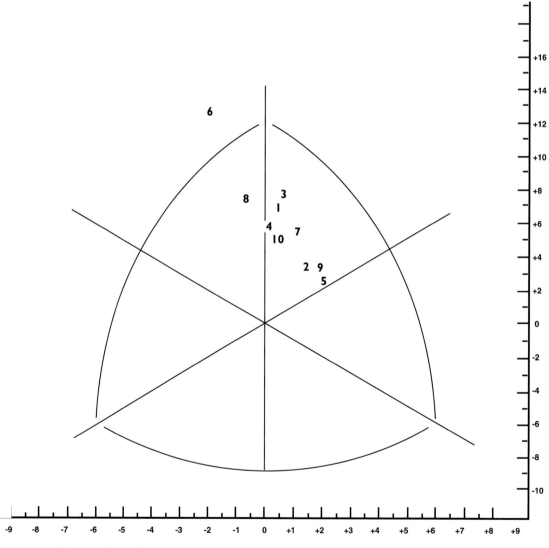

Figure 8 Somatochart showing the somatoplots for Australian male athletes. The mean values are shown after each sport. (Data mainly from Withers, et al., 1986).

associated with the component rankings. However, these are intended as broad guidelines only.

The somatotype photograph requires standardised poses of front, side and rear views of the subject (Figure 9). The recommended minimal equipment consists of a good quality 35 mm camera, with an 80 mm lens and attached flash. The camera should be mounted on a tripod, at 5.8 m from the subject and the lens at approximately mid-stature for most subjects. Commercially developed standard colour print film (ASA 200) is quite satisfactory and relatively inexpensive. The subject should be dressed in minimal clothing such as lightweight swim suits (single or two-piece), or running shorts. A more permanent somatotype station should include a data board, turntable, standard scale, white background, and flood or flash lights. (See Carter & Heath, App. I, 1990, for other options).

Table I Verbal "anchor points" used as adjuncts in the determination of somatotypes from photographs or visual inspection. (Adapted from Carter & Heath, 1990).

Endomorphy Rating Scale and Characteristics (relative fatness)

1 1½ 2 2½	3 3½ 4 4½ 5	5½ 6 6½ 7	7½ 8 8½
Low relative fatness; little subcutaneous fat; muscle and bone outlines visible.	Moderate relative fatness; subcutaneous fat covers muscle and bone outlines; softer appearance.	High relative fatness; thick subcutaneous fat; roundness of trunk and limbs; increased storage of fat in abdomen.	Extremely high relative fatness; very thick subcutaneous fat and high amounts of abdominal trunk fat; proximal concentration of fat in limbs.

Mesomorphy Rating Scale and Characteristics (musculo-skeletal robustness relative to height)

I 1½ 2 2½	3 3½ 4 4½ 5	5½ 6 6½ 7	7½ 8 8½
Low relative musculo-skeletal development; narrow skeletal diameters; narrow muscle diameters; small joints in limbs.	Moderate relative musculo-skeletal development; increased muscle bulk and thicker bones and joints.	High relative musculo-skeletal development; wide skeletal diameters; bulky muscles; large joints.	Extremely high relative musculo-skeletal development, very bulky muscles; very wide skeleton and joints.

Ectomorphy Rating Scale and Characteristics (relative linearity)

I 1½ 2 2½	3 3½ 4 4½ 5	5½ 6 6½ 7	7½ 8 8½
Low relative linearity; great bulk per unit of height; round like a ball; relatively bulky limbs.	Moderate relative linearity; less bulk per unit of height; more stretched-out.	High relative linearity; little bulk per unit of height.	Extremely high relative linearity; very stretched-out; narrow like a pencil; minimal bulk per unit of height.

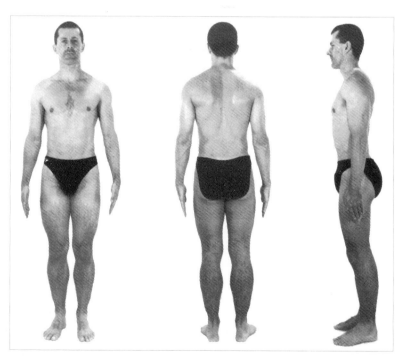

Figure 9 The three poses for the standardised somatotype photograph. The subject has a mass of 77 kg, a height of 180.4 cm. His criterion somatotype rating is 1½–6½–2½.

2.5 Somatotype categories and SAD SAMs

2.5.1 Categories

Somatotypes with similar relationships between the dominance of the components are grouped into categories named to reflect these relationships. Figure 10 shows somatotype categories as represented on the somatochart. The definitions are given in Table 2. Subject A is an ectomorphic mesomorph (or ecto-mesomorph), and subject B is an endomorphic ectomorph (or endo-ectomorph). All other somatotypes plotted within the same area are assigned the same category name. The frequencies of somatotypes within categories (or combined categories) can be used to describe the overall distribution of samples.

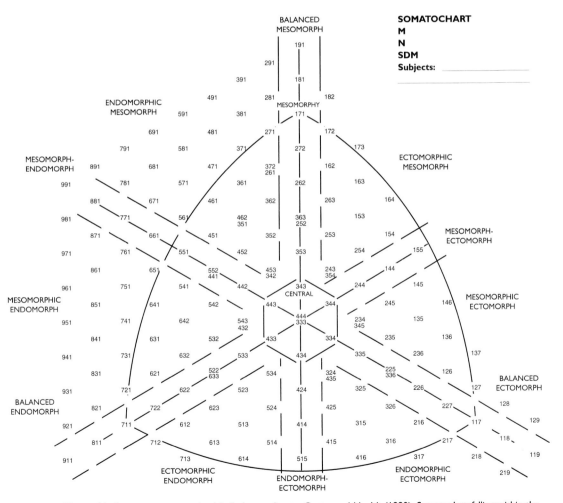

Figure 10 Somatotype categories labelled according to Carter and Health (1990). Somatoplots falling within the same area are grouped by category.

Table 2 Somatotype categories based on areas of the somatochart. (From Carter & Heath, 1990.)

central	no component differs by more than one unit from the other two, and consists of ratings of 2, 3 or 4
ectomorphic **endomorph**	**endomorphy** is dominant and ectomorphy is greater than mesomorphy
balanced **endomorph**	**endomorphy** is dominant and mesomorphy and ectomorphy are equal (do not differ by more than one-half unit)
mesomorphic **endomorph**	**endomorphy** is dominant and mesomorphy is greater than ectomorphy
mesomorph-endomorph	**endomorphy** and **mesomorphy** are equal (do not differ by more than one-half unit), and ectomorphy is smaller
endomorphic **mesomorph**	**mesomorphy** is dominant and endomorphy is greater than ectomorphy
balanced **mesomorph**	**mesomorphy** is dominant and mesomorphy and ectomorphy are equal (do not differ by more than one-half unit)
ectomorphic **mesomorph**	**mesomorphy** is dominant and ectomorphy is greater than endomorphy
mesomorph-ectomorph	**mesomorphy** and **ectomorphy** are equal (do not differ by more than one-half unit), and endomorphy is lower
mesomorphic **ectomorph**	**ectomorphy** is dominant and mesomorphy is greater than endomorphy
balanced **ectomorph**	**ectomorphy** is dominant; endomorphy and mesomorphy are equal and lower (or do not differ by more than one-half unit)
endomorphic **ectomorph**	**ectomorphy** is dominant, and endomorphy is greater than mesomorphy
endomorph-ectomorph	**endomorphy** and **ectomorphy** are equal (or do not differ by more than one-half unit), and mesomorphy is lower

The 13 categories in Table 2 can be simplified into four larger categories:

Central: no component differs by more than one unit from the other two.

Endomorph: endomorphy is dominant, mesomorphy and ectomorphy are more than one-half unit lower.

Mesomorph: mesomorphy is dominant, endomorphy and ectomorphy are more than one-half unit lower.

Ectomorph: ectomorphy is dominant, endomorphy and mesomorphy are more than one-half unit lower.

2.5.2 SAD SAMs

Somatotype data can be analysed by both traditional and non-traditional descriptive and comparative statistical methods. Often, analyses have been done using X-Y points only, rather than the three-dimensional somatotype. Because the somatotype is a three-number expression meaningful analyses can be conducted only with special techniques. Here we will describe only some of the descriptive statistics commonly used for three-dimensional analysis. For a fuller discussion, the student should consult Carter, et al. (1983), and Cressie, Withers and Craig (1986). Several definitions are essential at this point (Carter & Heath, 1990).

- **somatopoint** (S). A point in three-dimensional space determined from the somatotype which is represented by a triad of x, y and z coordinates for the three components. The scales on the coordinate axes are component units with the hypothetical somatotype 0–0–0 at the origin of the three axes.
- **somatotype attitudinal distance** (SAD). The distance in three dimensions between any two somatopoints. Calculated in component units.
- **somatotype attitudinal mean** (SAM). The average of the SADs of each somatopoint from the mean somatopoint (S) of a sample.

The SAD represents the "true" distance in three dimensional space between two somatopoints (A and B). The SAD is calculated as follows:

$$SAD_{A,B} = \sqrt{[(endomorphy_A - endomorphy_B)^2 + (mesomorphy_A - mesomorphy_B)^2 + (ectomorphy_A - ectomorphy_B)^2]}$$

The SAM is calculated by simply dividing the sum of the SADs from their mean somatopoint by the number of subjects.

Space does not permit a full treatment of the special analyses for the somatotype as a whole. These are contained in Carter, Ross, Duquet and Aubry (1983) and Carter and Heath (1990).

3 References

Carter, J.E.L. (1980).
The Heath-Carter somatotype method.
San Diego: San Diego University Press.

Carter, J.E.L., & Heath, B.H. (1990).
Somatotyping – development and applications.
Cambridge: Cambridge University Press.

Carter, J.E.L., Ross, W.D., Duquet, W., & Aubry, S.P. (1983).
Advances in somatotype methodology and analysis.
Yearbook of Physical Anthropology, 26, 193-213.

Cressie, N.A.C., Withers, R.T. & Craig, N.P. (1986).
Statistical analysis of somatotype data.
Yearbook of Physical Anthropology, 29, 197-208.

Heath, B.H., & Carter, J.E.L. (1967).
A modified somatotype method.
American Journal of Physical Anthropology, 27, 57-74.

Parnell, R.W. (1958).
Behaviour and physique.
London: Edward Arnold Ltd.

Sheldon, W.H. (with the collaboration of S.S. Stevens and W.B. Tucker) (1940).
The varieties of human physique.
New York: Harper and Brothers.

Withers, R.T., Craig, N.P., & Norton, K.I. (1986).
Somatotypes of South Australian male athletes.
Human Biology, 58, 337-356.

Withers, R.T., Whittingham, N.O., Norton, K.I. & Dutton, M. (1987).
Somatotypes of South Australian female games players.
Human Biology, 59, 575-584.

Chapter 7
Anthropometric Estimation of Body Fat

Kevin Norton

1 Introduction

Anthropometric profiles are commonly used as a basis for evaluating the level of body fat in both athletes and other members of the general community. There are a variety of ways in which people use these basic anthropometric measurements to quantify overall and regional body fat levels. However, over time, many of these methods have been applied without appreciation of the errors and assumptions associated with their use. This uncritical use of estimations of body fat is one of the most abused areas of anthropometry. This chapter will address some of the major problems associated with fat estimation using regression equations and suggest ways to minimise the inconsistencies in this application of anthropometry.

2 Body fat changes throughout life

Body fat stores change throughout life in a way which, on a population basis, is quite predictable, as shown in Figure 1. Cross-sectional data demonstrate that from relatively high levels of fatness in the first year after birth, subcutaneous fat stores slowly decrease to their lowest levels between the ages of 6 and 8 (Tanner, 1978, pp.17-19). After this, subcutaneous fat rises progressively throughout most of the developing years except for a noticeable dip at about the time of the growth spurt (about 11 to 12 for girls and 14 to 16 for boys). From this point, subcutaneous storage fat increases, reaching a peak during the fifth decade of life for men and the sixth for women, subsequently falling as age increases. This latter decline in external fatness is probably a result of selective mortality since fatness is a known risk factor for developing a number of diseases (see Chapter 12).

Since most people are concerned about their level of fatness, estimation of body fat stores is a common procedure performed in settings such as health and fitness centres and gymnasia. Similarly, the established relationship between excess fatness and decreased sports performance has resulted in fat assessment becoming an integral part of the physiological preparation of athletes. In both of these examples, the method used to determine the level of storage fat typically involves taking skinfold measurements. Often these external skinfold measurements are then used to predict total body fat using any one of a number of prediction equations available in the literature. If this method is used there are important assumptions and limitations which must be understood by the measurer in order that a balanced appraisal of the body fat level can be made. In this way, meaningful and appropriate information can be conveyed to the person on whom the measurements have been taken. It is this level of sophistication, that is an appreciation of the errors associated with conversion of skinfold measurements to total body fat estimates, which is required. It is precisely the lack of such knowledge that has been the downfall of this procedure in the past and continues to be so today.

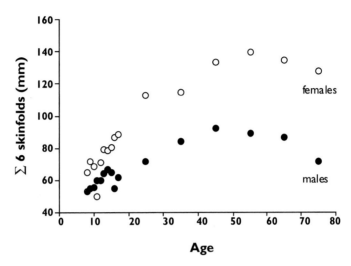

Figure 1 Changes in the sum of six skinfolds (triceps, subscapular, biceps, supraspinale, abdominal and medial calf) throughout life beyond 7 years. The data are cross-sectional and were calculated from the Australian Anthropometric Database (AADBase), 1995 (n= ~3200).

3 Using regression equations to predict body density and body fat

Accurate measurement of body fat is important, hence a variety of assessment methods have been developed (see Chapter 8). These range from visual estimation of body fat (Eckerson, Housh, & Johnson, 1992) to more high-tech methods such as using total body electrical conductivity (Malina, 1987), ultrasound (Katch, 1983) and infrared beam scanning (McLean & Skinner, 1992) among others. However, most of these methods require expensive equipment, considerable time, together with tester expertise and are generally not suitable for testing large numbers of people. On the other hand, measuring anthropometric sites such as skinfold thicknesses is safe, requires far less expense and time and can be used regularly to monitor a person's progress in a training and/or diet intervention program. Skinfold measurements also provide both a relatively accurate and direct measure of the amount of subcutaneous fat and therefore have considerable face validity. That is, they measure directly the thickness of the skin and underlying adipose tissue (predominantly fat). As a consequence of this, measurement of subcutaneous thickness has found application in a number of disciplines including anatomy, biomechanics, epidemiology, exercise science, medicine, pharmacy and pædiatrics.

Skinfolds, however, are surface measurements that, over time, have become associated with procedures to estimate whole body adiposity, including fat stored internally around organs and so forth. Since major health risks are known to be associated with body fat depots located as deep stores such as abdominal fat, the challenge has been to quantify total body fat using simple, time- and cost-efficient methods. Thus, external skinfold measurements are supposed to represent not only subcutaneous fatness but also internal fat stores. This has led to a proliferation in the number of regression equations available to make the transformation from surface anthropometry measurements to estimates of total body fat, usually expressed as percentage body fat (%BF). In the process of this transformation it is most common that estimation is made first for whole body density (BD) before finally allowing estimation of %BF. It has also led to a culture which is probably too familiar with the term "percentage body fat" without understanding the limitations of the methods used to predict it.

The methods of using either regression equations to predict BD and %BF or measuring BD directly before estimating %BF can be reviewed with regard to the assumptions (and errors) introduced at three distinct stages: (1) the errors associated with the prediction of BD from anthropometric data, (2) the measurement of BD using hydrodensitometry (underwater weighing), and (3) the errors involved in the transformation of BD to %BF scores [this is a two compartment model of body composition, i.e. fat mass (FM) and fat free mass (FFM), see Chapter 8]. This approach is illustrated in Figure 2.

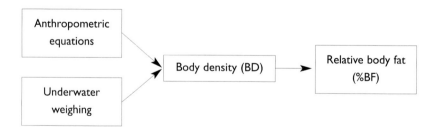

Figure 2 General procedure for estimating %BF from BD. BD can be either measured directly (using underwater weighing) or estimated using surface anthropometry.

3.1 Development of anthropometric prediction equations

There are well over 100 equations available in the scientific literature for the prediction of BD (and subsequently %BF) from anthropometric measurements. Some of the more commonly used equations, that also conform to anthropometric site descriptions outlined in Chapter 2, are included in the Appendix. Because these equations are population-specific, the user should be aware that the intended population should be similar to that on which the original equation was developed. Similarities in age, average fatness and physical activity levels of the original and intended populations (and the correct gender) are most appropriate when using these prediction equations. Furthermore, the anthropometrist should ensure absolute congruence between anatomical landmarks used in the original study and those to be used for the intended population. Where possible, the same type of skinfold caliper should be used as that described in the original report.

Most anthropometric prediction equations are developed using laboratory methods such as hydrodensitometry. The procedure involves measuring the BD of a group of subjects in the laboratory using the underwater weighing technique based on Archimedes' principle. This states that when a body is immersed in water it is buoyed up by a force which is equivalent to the weight of the volume of water displaced. Since the density of an object is defined as its mass per unit volume, then BD can be determined if the subject's mass in air is known and when it is completely submerged in water as follows:

$$BD = \frac{mass\ (g)}{volume\ (cm^3)}$$

$$BD = \frac{mass\ of\ the\ body\ in\ air\ (g)}{mass\ of\ the\ body\ (g)\ -\ mass\ of\ the\ body\ in\ water\ (g)}$$

Further adjustments are made to account for the density of the water and the residual volume of the subject so that the final equation is:

$$BD = \frac{mass\ of\ the\ body\ in\ air\ (g)}{\dfrac{mass\ of\ the\ body\ (g)\ -\ mass\ of\ the\ body\ in\ water\ (g)}{density\ of\ water} - residual\ volume}$$

The calculated BD (g. cm^{-3}) then becomes the dependent variable, y, while a series of anthropometric measurements taken on the subject immediately before the underwater weighing become the independent variables, $x_1, x_2, x_3 \ldots$ etc., used to predict y. A multiple regression equation is then developed to predict BD from the best weighted combination of the anthropometric variables (e.g. several skinfolds, and possibly other variables such as girths and bone breadths).

Several equations are then available to estimate %BF from BD. These transformations are possible because previous research (Brozek, Grande, Anderson, & Keys, 1963; Siri, 1961, pp. 108-117) has used cadavers to calculate the densities and relative proportions of the chemical components (water, protein, bone mineral and non-bone mineral) of the various body tissues. The most frequently used equation is the one proposed by Siri (1961) where:

$$\% \ BF \ = \ \frac{495}{BD} \ - \ 450$$

This equation assumes that the densities of the FFM and FM are 1.1000 and 0.9000 g.cm^{-3}, respectively. Unfortunately, the densities determined from the original cadaver studies were applied uniformly throughout the entire population without regard to the considerable individual variation in these tissue proportions and densities. Thus, there may be substantial error associated with using anthropometry-based prediction equations to estimate %BF. The error includes both the error in predicting BD from regression equations and the biological error in transforming BD to a %BF value. If BD is measured in the laboratory then the regression equation prediction error is replaced by the (typically smaller) measurement error. The assumptions and associated errors involved in these procedures are summarised below.

3.2 Prediction equation error

Since skinfolds have been shown to be the most powerful anthropometric predictors of BD and %BF, they are the key anthropometric elements used in regression equations. When these equations are used to predict BD, error is introduced due to the violation of at least three assumptions as illustrated in Figure 3.

- Firstly, it is assumed that there is both a constant compressibility of skin and subcutaneous fat, and that skin thickness at any one site is invariant throughout the population. Compressibility of the skin has been shown to vary by twofold in cadaver analysis (Martin, Ross, Drinkwater, & Clarys, 1985) and it is known that skin thickness varies among the population where it is greater in males than females and decreases with aging (Clarys, Martin, Drinkwater, & Marfell-Jones, 1987). Therefore, these factors are clearly sources of potential error (Martin et al., 1985).

- Secondly, since only a few skinfold thicknesses are measured, individual fat distribution patterns are not taken into account when predicting total body fat. Hence, selected skinfolds are assumed to be representative of the body's subcutaneous fat mass. It is, therefore, advisable to include a selection of skinfolds in the equation to predict BD and %BF from the upper and lower body, trunk and limbs.

- Thirdly, the relationship between skinfold thicknesses and total body fat is often assumed to be linear. Total body fat is, therefore, being predicted on the basis of a fixed proportion of internal and external fat where the external fat is quantified by measurement of a small, select number of skinfold sites. The relationship between subcutaneous fat mass and total body fat mass may (Martin et al., 1985), or may not be a linear one (Roche, 1987).

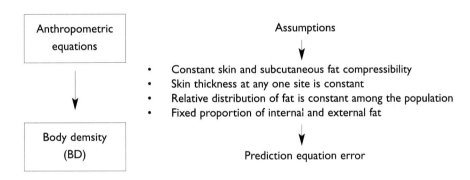

Figure 3 Assumptions associated with the anthropometric estimation of BD resulting in prediction equation error.

When cadavers are examined for body fat patterns, the subcutaneous fat to total body fat percentage ranges from 20–70% depending on such factors as age, degree of fatness, gender and measurement technique (Allen et al., 1956; Brodie, 1988a, 1988b; Brown & Jones, 1977; Chien et al., 1975; Keys & Brozek, 1953). The ratio of internal to external fat increases with age, is greater in women (Brodie, 1988a, 1988b) and may decrease (Allen et al., 1956) or stay the same (Martin et al., 1985) with the level of fatness. Jackson and Pollock (1982), for example, developed a generalised equation to predict %BF on the basis of a non-linear relationship between changes in sums of skinfolds and corresponding changes in measured BD. Their equation was a best-fit quadratic equation and may reflect the effect of a greater relative amount of externally located fat as adiposity increases (Allen et al., 1956). It could also indicate that fatter people tend to have denser FFM components (e.g. bone). However, there is a greater fat content of adipose tissue with increased total body fatness (Martin et al., 1985), which would tend to negate these effects. Whatever the cause, a given decrease in skinfold thickness results in a greater increase in BD as the sum of skinfolds becomes smaller (i.e. a leaner person). Hence, a given decrease in subcutaneous fat does not result in a constant increase in BD. This phenomenon is illustrated further in Figure 4.

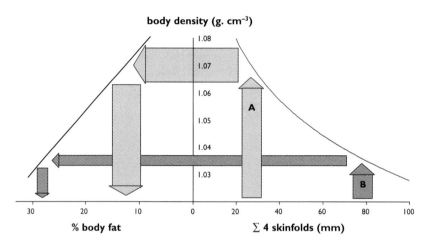

Figure 4 Example of the decrease in estimated %BF for a 10 mm decrease in skinfold thickness for two people differing in body fatness.

In this figure two people of differing adiposity both lose 10 mm from their $\Sigma 4$ skinfolds. Subject A begins at a lower level of fatness compared to subject B, hence there is a larger predicted increase in BD, and subsequent reduction in %BF. This can be most disconcerting for the overfat individual who, given the same decrease in the absolute level of $\Sigma 4$ skinfolds, is perhaps told that %BF has been altered by only 2 or 3%.

Variance in skinfold compressibility, skin thickness, fat content in adipose tissue, the ratio of internal to external fat stores, and external fat patterning among the population, have been shown to be able to cause large errors in predicting BD from skinfolds. Errors introduced when multiple regression equations are used to predict BD have been shown to vary by over twofold in extreme cases (Lohman, 1981; Lohman, Pollock, Slaughter, Brandon & Boileau, 1984; Withers, Norton, Craig, Hartland & Venables, 1987; Withers et al., 1987).

Of the more accurate estimation equations, Withers, Craig et al. (1987) and Withers, Whittingham et al. (1987), using athletes, reported BD prediction errors (standard error of estimate; SEE) of 0.00533 and 0.00508 g.cm^{-3}. These were equivalent to 2.4 and 2.3 %BF error for equations developed on these high-performance female and male athletes, respectively. Other studies on athletic groups have also indicated relatively small prediction errors, ranging from 0.0061–0.0080 g.cm^{-3} (2.7–3.6 %BF) in gymnasts and long distance runners, respectively (Lewis, Haskell, Perry, Kovacevic, & Wood, 1978; Sinning, 1978). In non-athletic groups this error is typically larger and has ranged from 0.0057–0.0125 g.cm^{-3} (2.6–5.9 %BF) depending upon factors such as measurement technique and homogeneity of the sample (Withers, Norton et al., 1987; Womersley, Durnin, Boddy, & Mahaffy, 1976). Despite the problematic nature of predicting BD from anthropometric variables, many prediction equations still enjoy widespread application (e.g. Durnin & Womersley, 1974), although they usually involve relatively large prediction errors.

3.3 Biological error

The biological error is due to inter-individual variability in the composition and density of the FFM (predominantly bone and muscle). Any violation of the following assumptions therefore contributes to this error:

- Firstly, the densities of the FM and FFM are assumed to be 0.900 and 1.100 g.cm^{-3}, respectively.
- Secondly, the proportional contributions of the components of the FFM (namely, water, protein, bone mineral and non-bone mineral) are invariant among individuals.
- Thirdly, since these relative contributions of the FFM are assumed to be constant, the densities of these individual components of the FFM must also be constant (to satisfy the first point above).

These assumptions and the resultant errors are illustrated in Figure 5.

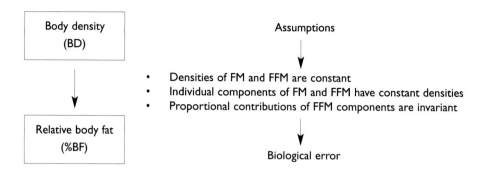

Figure 5 Assumptions associated with the estimation of %BF from BD resulting in biological error.

The assumptions underlying the derivation of the equations used to predict %BF from BD (Siri, 1956) are intended for any population irrespective of age, gender, state of training and ethnic origin. The original research used in the construction of the equation to allow transformation of BD to %BF was based upon dissection of just three cadavers (Brozek et al., 1963) with an average age of about 65 years.

The density of the FM varies little throughout human and other mammal populations (Allen, Krzywicki, & Roberts, 1959; Fidanza, Keys, & Anderson, 1953). Adipose tissue in humans has a mean density of 0.900 g.cm^{-3} and a standard deviation of 0.00103 g.cm^{-3} at 37°C. There is, however, considerable inter-individual variability in the density of FFM. More recent cadaver analysis has highlighted the degree of variation among the population with respect to the proportions of bone, muscle and residual masses that comprise the FFM (Clarys, Martin, & Drinkwater, 1984; Martin et al., 1985). On the basis of 25 cadaver dissections, Clarys et al. (1984) reported that the proportion of the adipose tissue free weight composed of muscle was between 41.9 and 59.4% whilst that for bone was between 16.3 and 25.7%. The coefficient of variation of the muscle density was only about 1%, but the density of the bone varied considerably within and among individuals (Ross et al., 1984). This led to the conclusion that the density of the FFM probably varies with a standard deviation of 0.02 g.cm^{-3} (Martin, Drinkwater, Clarys, & Ross, 1986). Clarys et al. (1984) used cadavers of similar age (mean ± SD = 76 ± 9 yr, range 55–94 yr) to those dissected by Brozek et al. (1963) which may make generalisations to younger populations inappropriate. Younger, healthy populations are likely to be much more homogeneous with respect to the densities and relative proportions of the tissues comprising the FFM, when compared to those of aged and diseased populations.

The transformation from BD to %BF therefore involves some potentially serious problems. For example, on average, athletes have denser bone and muscle (Adams, Mottola, Bagnall, & McFadden, 1982; Chilibeck, Sale, & Webber, 1995; Martin & McColloch, 1987) which will lead to an underestimation of %BF (Wilmore, 1983). This error will also result if the proportion of bone in the body is increased. These factors may help explain the extremely low values reported, including negative %BF values in professional American football players (Adams et al., 1982) and long distance runners (Behnke & Wilmore, 1974). On the other hand, older individuals who have decreased bone density through bone demineralisation or bone loss such as in osteoporosis, will have their level of body fat overestimated. These errors are highlighted in Figure 6 showing the range of FFM densities typically found in the general and specific populations and their effect on predicted body fat levels. This figure follows the logic that rather than a single line describing the relationship between BD and %BF (i.e. as described by the Siri equation), there is more likely a "family" of curves as shown (based on that presented by Martin et al., 1986). Hence, depending on factors such as training status and presence or absence of disease, a person could be placed on any one of a number of curves. If, for example, the actual relationship placed a person on the FFM density curve of 1.07, while the Siri equation assumes 1.10 g.cm^{-3}, then a measured BD of, say 1.06 g.cm^{-3}, would result in an actual 5% BF compared to Siri's estimated 17% BF. Note that a given difference between the actual and assumed FFM densities results in a larger absolute error for people with high BD (or low %BF such as athletes and lean young adults) when compared to overfat individuals with low BD.

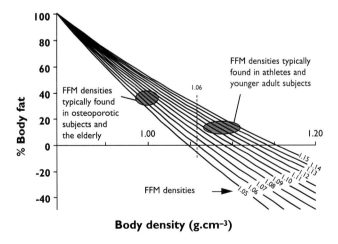

Figure 6 The effect of alterations in the fat free mass (FFM) density on subsequent estimations of %BF using the Siri (1961) equation over a range of body densities. The vertical line at BD = 1.06 g.cm^{-3} refers to the example discussed in the text.

181

It is not surprising the accuracy of the transformations from BD to %BF has been challenged (e.g. Womersley et al., 1976; Martin et al., 1986). Siri (1961) for example, estimated that the error in the transformation of BD to %BF involved a standard deviation of 0.0084 g.cm^{-3} (~3.7 % BF) in the total population. Lohman (1981) hypothesised that this might be somewhat smaller at about 0.006 g.cm^{-3} (~2.6 % BF) for relatively homogeneous samples such as highly trained athletes where inter-individual variation in FFM density is less than across the general population. The usefulness of predicting %BF has, therefore, been increased by the development of sports specific and population specific equations. Equations for various specific groups have been developed using distance runners (Pollock et al., 1977), gymnasts (Sinning, 1978), male athletes (Withers, Craig et al., 1987), female athletes (Withers, Whittingham et al., 1987) and a range of other sub-groups (see Brodie, 1988a, 1988b for review).

3.4 Measurement error in hydrodensitometry

When underwater weighing is used to measure BD the measurement or technical error is generally small. Durnin and Taylor (1960) have estimated the measurement error of this procedure to be approximately 0.0020 g.cm^{-3} (~0.9 % BF) and dependent upon several characteristics of the system used to obtain BD. The two most important of these are the measurement (or estimation) of gas in the respiratory system when weighing takes place and the mass of the athlete when submerged (Withers, 1983). A direct measurement of the athlete's lung volume during immersion using techniques such as helium dilution or nitrogen washout will result in smaller errors in BD measurement than when the lung volume is either predicted from anthropometric measurements or when a constant volume is assumed for all subjects (Withers, Borkent, & Ball, 1990). However, measurements of lung volume require specialised equipment and considerable technical expertise and so it is usually predicted from body size. Other potential contributors to the measurement error include the accuracy in obtaining the water temperature and the mass of the athlete in air (Withers, 1983).

3.5 Total error

If the error variances discussed above are assumed to be independent and additive then the SEE for estimating the %BF from either prediction equations or measured BD can be calculated. Since Siri (1961) estimated the standard deviation of the biological error to be up to 0.0084 g.cm^{-3} (~3.6 % BF) in the general population, which was later adjusted to 0.006 g.cm^{-3} (~2.6 % BF) for homogeneous samples (Lohman, 1981), then the total error (regression equation and biological error) using the best prediction equation of Withers, Craig et al. (1987) for males would be

$$total\ error\ =\ \sqrt{0.00508^2 + 0.006^2}\ g.cm^{-3}$$

or equal to approximately 3.4 % BF at the mean. Similarly, if BD is measured then the total error (technical and biological error) would be

$$total\ error\ =\ \sqrt{0.002^2 + 0.006^2}\ g.cm^{-3}$$

or approximately 2.7 % BF at the mean (Lohman, 1981). Measured BD, therefore, yields a more accurate estimation of FM when compared with using even the best anthropometric-based regression equation currently available. This error can be further reduced to about 2.6 % BF by careful technical procedures (Norton, Craig, Withers, & Whittingham, 1994; Withers, Craig et al., 1987). However, this is probably the limit of accuracy using these techniques. The error analysis is summarised in Figure 7.

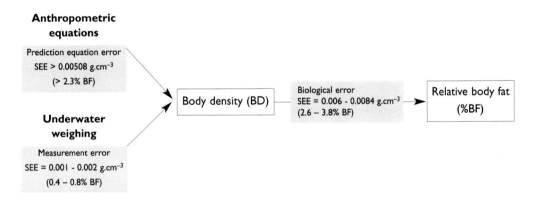

Figure 7 Errors associated with the estimation of %BF from anthropometric measurements and from underwater weighing.

4 Application of prediction equations

To illustrate the potential range of predicted BD and %BF values the following example is presented. Consider the person whose anthropometric details are shown on the anthropometry proforma.

Test ID

Name: ....**Brown, Lisa**..

DOB: ....**7/.2/.72**........ Test Date: ....**6/.5/.94**.......

Subj. Postcode: ....**2223**.............

Country of Birth: ....**Australia**..... Box Ht: ....—.............

Mass (kg): ....**58.3**............ Height (cm): ....**167.3**.........

Lab: Tester ID □ □ □: □

Sport: **Recreational running**

	Intensity	Frequency	Duration
	Nil	≤2	<3
	Walk	(≥3)	3-12
	(Vigorous)		(>12)

Gender: M □ F ☒

	ID	Site	Trial 1	Trial 2	Trial 3	Median
Skinfolds	1	triceps				13.5
(mm)	2	subscapular				10
	3	biceps				5.4
	4	iliac crest				9.8
	5	supraspinale				6.1
	6	abdominal				8.9
	7	front thigh				34.4
	8	medial calf				12.4
	9	mid-axilla				6.7
Girths	10	head				55.3
(cm)	11	neck				32.7
	12	arm (relaxed)				25.8
	13	arm (flexed and tensed)				26.9
	14	forearm (maximum)				24.9
	15	wrist (distal styloids)				15.3
	16	chest (mesosternale)				87.8
	17	waist (minimum)				73.8
	18	gluteal (hips)				99.4
	19	thigh (1 cm gluteal)				54.1
	20	thigh (mid tro-tib-lat)				49.4
	21	calf (maximum)				36.2
	22	ankle (minimum)				23.3
Lengths	23	acromiale-radiale				30.8
(cm)	24	radiale-stylion				24.5
	25	midstylion-dactylion				18.4
	26	iliospinale b. ht				91.8
	27	trochanterion b. ht				83.7
	28	trochanterion-tibiale laterale				39.8
	29	tibiale laterale to floor				45
	30	tibiale mediale-sphy. tibiale				36.1
Breadths/	31	biacromial				37.7
Lengths	32	biiliocristal				29.2
(cm)	33	foot length				23.8
	34	sitting height				90.7
	35	transverse chest				27.6
	36	A-P chest depth				18.5
	37	humerus				6.59
	38	femur				9.53
Sport	39					
Specific	40					
Sites	41					
	42					

Figure 8 Subject details for a full anthropometric profile.

Based on the measurement sites taken, and the subject's gender and other demographic information such as her age and level of physical activity, an analysis can be performed to predict BD and %BF using a number of compatible equations selected from the literature. The results of this analysis are illustrated in Figure 9. The specific equations used, along with others which have landmark descriptions essentially equivalent to those outlined in this textbook, are presented in detail at the end of this chapter.

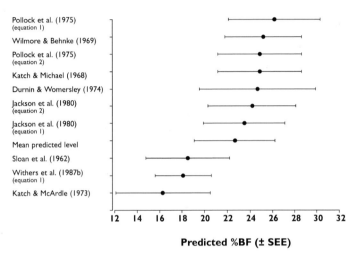

Figure 9 Results of predicting %BF of the subject whose details are shown in Figure 8. The results are mean values ± 1 standard error of estimate (SEE) as reported by the original authors (see appendix). The overall mean (± SD) predicted %BF level is also shown for reference.

This figure illustrates the range of predicted %BF scores for one subject. It was estimated that this young female had, on average, 22.7 ± 3.7% BF. The predicted levels, however, ranged among the various equations from a low of 16.3% to a high of 26.2% BF. When expressed in relative terms, this represents a range of 44% of the mean predicted value of all the equations. Note that this does not take into consideration the SEE around the individual predicted %BF levels. For example, assume that there are a number of possible equations from which to choose (e.g. as shown in Figure 9) and that any one of these equations is chosen at random. The worst case scenario (± 2 × SEE) could result in a possible range of "actual" %BF scores of between 7.9 and 34.4% BF [i.e. the lowest predicted mean value (minus 2 × SEE) to the highest predicted mean value (plus 2 × SEE)]. Therefore, if a prediction equation is used, it is advisable to report the estimated %BF level ± an error range, perhaps using 1 × SEE for the equation that has been chosen.

5 Monitoring skinfolds and other body composition indices

A reliable and relatively simple procedure for monitoring intra-individual BF levels is achieved by routinely measuring skinfold thicknesses without further transformation to %BF.

Assessment of body mass and skinfold thickness is often adequate for evaluation of an individual's BF level. This methodology has been used over a number of years for high-performance athletes at sports institutes throughout Australia (Craig et al., 1993; Telford, Tumilty, & Damm, 1984). The procedure eliminates the error in transforming skinfold thicknesses (mm) to a BD estimate (g.cm^{-3}) and finally to a %BF estimate. Recent normative tables for sums of skinfolds have been prepared on Australian athletes (e.g. Norton et al., 1994). However, since an estimate of fat mass to be lost cannot be made using this approach, it has not been the most desirable choice for the practitioner in the health and fitness profession. For those adopting this technique a number of skinfold sites are recommended so that potential problems due to individual fat patterning (unequal fat loss/gain in specific sites) during weight changes are reduced. These individual patterns of fat loss and deposition are believed to be related to regional differences in the sensitivity of adipocytes to lipolytic hormones (Smith, Hammersten, Bjorntorp, & Kral, 1979). This is probably the reason that many individuals have difficulty in reducing fat stores from specific sites.

It is recommended that health and fitness professionals and others develop their own normative database for skinfolds (and other anthropometric measurements). This information can then be used as a guide when counselling individuals interested in their level of body fat.

6 Summary

A number of options are available to the anthropometrist to quantify the level of body fat an individual possesses. For the majority of people, reporting simple sums of skinfolds is sufficient. However, transformation of skinfolds to BD and then further transformation to %BF is still often performed. This is because:
- There is no loss of information when converting skinfolds to BD and %BF
- Estimates of fat mass can only be made using this procedure
- It is often an important pedagogical tool to illustrate the relationship between

surface anthropometric measurements and total body fat stores

- Provided consistent anthropometric procedures are used, it is sensitive to change resulting from dietary and/or training interventions.

The error outlined in this chapter during transformation from anthropometric measurements to a %BF must be considered and relayed to the subject in the form of a range of predicted %BF. It is recommended that people using these procedures report a range of estimated %BF equal to the predicted mean ± 1 SD, for BD and %BF, in the same way that is suggested for accuracy of repeated skinfold measurements.

7 Appendix – Prediction equations

Following is a summary of BD prediction equations found in the scientific literature. It is not a complete list but identifies some of the more commonly used prediction equations. All of the listed equations use independent anthropometric variables whose sites are essentially equivalent with the guidelines presented in Chapter 2. In some instances the original descriptions use slightly different terminology although the landmarks are the same. For these equations the terminology used throughout this textbook has been substituted. The user should be aware that the details following may determine the appropriateness of using any one or group of prediction equations for an individual.

References

Durnin & Womersley (1974), n = 209 **males**:

Variable	Mean ± SD	Range
age (yr)	—	17.0–72.0
height (cm)	—	150.0–193.0
weight (kg)	—	49.8–121.4
BD (g.cm–3)	—	0.990–1.087
%BF (Siri, 1961)	—	5.0–50.0

Ethnicity:	Not specified.
Country:	Scotland.
Sample characteristics:	Subjects were deliberately selected to represent a variety of body types (volunteers from obesity clinics, local health clubs, sports organisations, ballet company and other sources).
Skinfold caliper used:	Harpenden.

Multiple regression equation	R	SEE
BD $= 1.1765 - 0.0744 \, (\log_{10} X_1)$	0.7–0.9	0.0103

where: X_1 (mm) = Σ 4 skinfolds (triceps, biceps, subscapular, iliac crest in mm)

Durnin & Womersley (1974), n = 272 **females**:

Variable	Mean ± SD	Range
age (yr)	–	16.0–68.0
height (cm)	–	146.0–178.0
weight (kg)	–	42.3–121.5
BD (g.cm^{-3})	–	0.968–1.078
%BF (Siri, 1961)	–	10.0–61.0

Ethnicity:	Not specified.
Country:	Scotland.
Sample characteristics:	As for males.
Skinfold caliper used:	Harpenden.

Multiple regression equation	R	SEE
BD = 1.1567 − 0.0717 (log$_{10}$ X$_1$)	0.7–0.9	0.0116

where: X$_1$ (mm) = Σ 4 skinfolds (triceps, biceps, subscapular, suprailiac in mm)

Reference

Forsyth & Sinning (1973), n = 50 **males**:

Variable	Mean ± SD	Range
age (yr)	–	19.0–22.0
height (cm)	179.0 ± 0.56	–
weight (kg)	77.20 ± 8.71	–
BD (g.cm^{-3})	1.072 ± 0.0102	–
%BF (Brozek et al., 1963)	12.2 ± 4.1	–
Ethnicity:	Not specified.	
Country:	U.S.A.	
Sample characteristics:	Varsity sports participants.	
Skinfold caliper used:	Lange.	

Multiple regression equation	R	SEE
BD = 1.10647 − 0.00162(X$_1$) − 0.00144(X$_2$) − 0.00077(X$_3$) + 0.00071(X$_4$)	0.84	0.006

where: X$_1$ = subscapular skinfold (mm), X$_2$ = abdominal skinfold (mm), X$_3$ = triceps skinfold (mm), X$_4$ = mid-axilla skinfold (mm).

Reference

Jackson, Pollock & Ward (1980), n = 249 **females**:

Variable	Mean ± SD	Range
age (yr)	31.44 ± 10.8	18.0–55.0
height (cm)	165.02 ± 6.00	146.0–181.00
weight (kg)	57.15 ± 7.59	36.0–87.0
BD (g.cm^{-3})	1.044 ± 0.016	1.002–1.091
%BF (Siri, 1961)	24.1 ± 7.2	4.0–44.0

Ethnicity:	Not specified.
Country:	U.S.A.
Sample characteristics:	Wide range of women who varied considerably in body structure.

Skinfold caliper used: Lange.

Multiple regression equation	R	SEE
(1) $BD = 1.24374 - 0.03162(\log_{10}X_1) - 0.00066(X_4)$	0.859	0.0081
(2) $BD = 1.21389 - 0.04057(\log_{10}X_2) - 0.00016(X_3)$	0.838	0.0087

where: $X_1 = \Sigma$ 4 skinfolds (triceps, abdominal, front thigh, iliac crest in mm), $X_2 = \Sigma$ 3 skinfolds (triceps, front thigh, iliac crest in mm), X_3 = age (yr), X_4 = gluteal circumference (cm).

Reference

Katch & McArdle (1973), n = 53 **males**:

Variable	Mean ± SD	Range
age (yr)	19.3 ± 1.5	–
height (cm)	176.4 ± 7.0	–
weight (kg)	71.4 ± 8.6	–
BD (g.cm^{-3})	1.0646 ± 0.0138	–
%BF (Brozek et al., 1963)	15.3 ± 5.7	–
Ethnicity:	Caucasian.	
Country:	U.S.A.	
Sample characteristics:	College physical education elective students.	
Skinfold caliper used:	Lange.	

Multiple regression equation	R	SEE
$BD = 1.09665 - 0.00103(X_1) - 0.00056(X_2) - 0.00054(X_3)$	0.86	0.0072

where: X_1 = triceps skinfold, X_2 = subscapular skinfold (mm), X_3 = abdominal skinfold (mm)

Katch & McArdle (1973), n = 69 **females**:

Variable	Mean ± SD	Range
age (yr)	20.3 ± 1.8	–
height (cm)	160.4 ± 11.3	–
weight (kg)	59.0 ± 7.8	–
BD (g.cm^{-3})	1.0394 ± 0.0152	–
%BF (Brozek et al., 1963)	25.6 ± 6.4	–
Ethnicity:	Caucasian.	
Country:	U.S.A.	
Sample characteristics:	College physical education elective students.	
Skinfold caliper used:	Lange.	

Multiple regression equation	R	SEE
$BD = 1.09246 - 0.00049(X_1) - 0.00075(X_2) + 0.00710(X_3) - 0.00121(X_4)$	0.84	0.0086

where: X_1 = subscapular skinfold (mm), X_2 = iliac crest skinfold (mm), X_3 = biepicondylar humerus breadth (cm), X_4 = thigh girth (cm).

Reference

Katch & Michael (1968), n = 64 **females**:

Variable	Mean ± SD	Range
age (yr)	–	19.0–23.0
height (cm)	165.9 ± 4.27	152.4–179.3
weight (kg)	58.38 ± 6.70	44.65–72.16
BD (g.cm^{-3})	1.049 ± 0.011	1.011–1.067
%BF (Brozek et al., 1961)	21.5 ± 5.7	3.8–37.7

Ethnicity:	Not specified.
Country:	U.S.A.
Sample characteristics:	College volunteers.
Skinfold caliper used:	Not specified.

Multiple regression equation	R	SEE
BD = 1.12569 − 0.001835(X_1) − 0.002779(X_2) + 0.005419(X_3) − 0.0007167(X_4)	0.70	0.008183

where: X_1 = triceps skinfold (mm), X_2 = gluteal girth (inches), X_3 = upper arm girth flexed (inches), X_4 = subscapular skinfold (mm).

Reference

Lewis, Haskell, Perry, Kovacevic, & Wood (1978), n = 42 **females**:

Variable	Mean ± SD	Range
age (yr)	42.3 ± 8.4	30.0–59.0
height (cm)	166.1 ± 5.6	155.0–180.0
weight (kg)	57.6 ± 6.6	46.3–77.0
BD (g.cm^{-3})	1.052 ± 0.012	1.030–1.078
%BF (Siri, 1961)	20.5 ± 5.4	9.1–30.5

Ethnicity:	Caucasian.
Country:	U.S.A.
Sample characteristics:	38 middle and long distance runners, some national and international calibre. Four subjects swam in endurance events at national level.
Skinfold caliper used:	Lange.

Multiple regression equation	R	SEE
BD = 0.97845 − 0.0002(X_1) + 0.00088(X_2) − 0.00122(X_3) − 0.00234(X_4)	0.78	0.00795

where: X_1 = triceps skinfold (mm), X_2 = stature (cm), X_3 = subscapular skinfold (mm), X_4 = arm girth relaxed (cm).

Reference

Pollock, Laughridge, Coleman, Linnerud, & Jackson (1975), n = 83 **females**:

Variable	Mean ± SD	Range
age (yr)	20.2 ± 1.2	18.0–22.0
height (cm)	166.1 ± 5.9	–
weight (kg)	57.53 ± 7.44	–
BD (g.cm^{-3})	1.0427 ± 0.0141	–
%BF (Siri, 1961)	24.8 ± 6.4	–

| | | | Country: | U.S.A. |
Ethnicity: Not specified.
Country: U.S.A.
Sample characteristics: College students.
Skinfold caliper used: Lange.

Multiple regression equation	R	SEE
(1) BD = 1.0852 − 0.0008(X_1) − 0.0011(X_2)	0.775	0.0091
(2) BD = 1.0836 − 0.0007(X_1) − 0.0007(X_2) + 0.0048(X_3) − 0.0088(X_4)	0.826	0.0082

where: X_1 = iliac crest skinfold (mm), X_2 = front thigh skinfold (mm), X_3 = wrist girth (cm), X_4 = biepicondylar femur breadth (cm).

Reference

Sloan, Burt, & Blyth (1962), n = 50 **females**:

Variable	Mean ± SD	Range
age (yr)	20.2 ± 1.7	17.0–25.0
height (cm)	165.0 ± 6.9	153.0–177.0
weight (kg)	55.5 ± 5.9	39.0–76.7
BD (g.cm^{-3})	1.0467 ± 0.0122	1.0172–1.0687
%BF (Siri, 1961)	22.9 ± 5.6	13.2–36.6

Ethnicity: Not specified.
Country: U.S.A.
Sample characteristics: University students.
Skinfold caliper used: Medical Nutrition Laboratory caliper.

Multiple regression equation	R	SEE
BD = 1.0764 − 0.00081(X_1) − 0.00088(X_2)	0.74	0.0082

where: X_1 = iliac crest skinfold (mm), X_2 = triceps skinfold (mm).

Reference

Sloan (1967), n = 50 **males**:

Variable	Mean ± SD	Range
age (yr)	−	18.0–26.0
height (cm)	177.26	163.0–191.0
weight (kg)	70.57	57.80–85.70
BD (g.cm^{-3})	1.0754 ± 0.0200	−
%BF (Brozek et al., 1963)	10.8 ± 5.14	−

Ethnicity: Not specified.
Country: South Africa.
Sample characteristics: University students.
Skinfold caliper used: Medical Nutrition Laboratory caliper.

Multiple regression equation	R	SEE
BD = 1.1043 − 0.001327(X_1) − 0.001310(X_2)	0.861	−

where: X_1 = front thigh skinfold (mm), X_2 = subscapular skinfold (mm).

Reference

Thorland, Johnson, Tharp, Housh, & Cisar, (1984), n = 141 **males**:

Variable	Mean ± SD	Range
age (yr)	17.43 ± 0.96	—
height (cm)	176.52 ± 8.60	—
weight (kg)	67.45 ± 11.30	—
BD (g.cm^{-3})	1.0798 ± 0.0096	—
%BF (Siri, 1961)	9.0 ± 3.8	—

Ethnicity:	Not specified.
Country:	U.S.A.
Sample characteristics:	Athletes of national calibre, in the events of track and field, gymnastics, diving and wrestling.
Skinfold caliper used:	Lange.

Multiple regression equation	R	SEE
BD = 1.1091 − 0.00052(X_1) + 0.00000032(X_1)^2	0.82	0.0055

where: X_1 = Σ 7 skinfolds (triceps, subscapular, mid-axilla, iliac crest, abdominal, front thigh, medial calf in mm).

Thorland, Johnson, Tharp, Housh, & Cisar, (1984), n = 133 **females**:

Variable	Mean ± SD	Range
age (yr)	16.51 ± 1.39	—
height (cm)	166.02 ± 7.26	—
weight (kg)	54.51 ± 7.93	—
BD (g.cm^{-3})	1.0661 ± 0.0105	—
%BF (Siri, 1961)	14.5 ± 4.3	—

Ethnicity:	Not specified.
Country:	U.S.A.
Sample characteristics:	Athletes of national calibre, in the events of track and field, gymnastics, diving and wrestling.
Skinfold caliper used:	Lange.

Multiple regression equation	R	SEE
BD = 1.0987 − 0.00122(X_2) + 0.00000263(X_2)^2	0.82	0.0060

where: X_2 = Σ 3 skinfolds (triceps, subscapular, iliac crest in mm).

Reference

Wilmore & Behnke (1969). n = 133 **males**:

Variable	Mean ± SD	Range
age (yr)	22.04 ± 3.10	16.80–36.80
height (cm)	177.32 ± 7.17	159.00–193.40
weight (kg)	75.60 ± 11.04	53.20–121.20
BD (g.cm^{-3})	1.0657 ± 0.0125	1.0310–1.0902
%BF (Siri, 1961)	14.6 ± 5.5	4.0–30.1

Ethnicity:	Not specified.

Country:	U.S.A.
Sample characteristics:	University students.
Skinfold caliper used:	Lange.

Multiple regression equation	R	SEE
$BD = 1.08543 - 0.000886(X_1) - 0.00040(X_2)$	0.800	0.0076

where: X_1 = abdominal skinfold (mm), X_2 = front thigh skinfold (mm).

Reference

Wilmore & Behnke (1970), n = 128 **females**:

Variable	Mean ± SD	Range
age (yr)	21.41 ± 3.76	17.80–47.80
height (cm)	164.89 ± 6.61	146.10–180.40
weight (kg)	58.58 ± 7.14	41.31–81.60
BD (g.cm^{-3})	1.0406 ± 0.0099	1.0168–1.0678
%BF (Siri, 1961)	25.7 ± 4.5	13.6–36.8

Ethnicity:	Not specified.
Country:	U.S.A.
Sample characteristics:	University students.
Skinfold caliper used	Lange.

Multiple regression equation	R	SEE
$BD = 1.06234 - 0.00068(X_1) - 0.00039(X_2) - 0.00025(X_3)$	0.676	0.0074

where: X_1 = subscapular skinfold (mm), X_2 = triceps skinfold (mm), X_3 = front thigh skinfold (mm).

Reference

Withers, Craig, Bourdon & Norton (1987a), n = 207 **males**:

Variable	Mean ± SD	Range
age (yr)	24.2 ± 4.7	15.4–39.1
height (cm)	180.0 ± 8.3	154.1–215.1
weight (kg)	74.68 ± 10.54	53.30–117.34
BD (g.cm^{-3})	1.0761 ± 0.0085	1.0465–1.0968
%BF (Siri, 1961)	10.0 ± 3.7	1.3–23.0

Ethnicity:	Not specified.
Country:	Australia.
Sample characteristics:	State representatives for badminton, basketball, cycling, field hockey, lacrosse, football, gymnastics, powerlifting, speed skating, soccer, squash, swimming, track and field, volleyball, 36% at international calibre.
Skinfold caliper used	Harpenden.

Multiple regression equation	R	SEE
[1]$BD = 1.0988 - 0.0004(X_1)$	0.749	0.0058

where: $X_1 = \Sigma$ 7 skinfolds (triceps, subscapular, biceps, supraspinale, abdominal, front thigh, medial calf in mm).
[1]This regression equation was not included in the publication of Withers et al. (1987a). It is an addition to the list of prediction equations calculated on the original data set of their study.

Reference

Withers, Norton, Craig, Hartland & Venables (1987*b*), n = 135 **females**:

Variable	Mean ± SD	Range
age (yr)	22.3 ± 3.7	17.4–35.2
height (cm)	165.6 ± 5.3	152.9–178.6
weight (kg)	58.15 ± 7.44	43.63–93.57
BD (g.cm^{-3})	1.0456 ± 0.0123	0.9916–1.0743
%BF (Siri, 1961)	23.4 ± 5.6	10.8–49.2

Ethnicity:	Not specified.
Country:	Australia.
Sample characteristics:	Sample represented a cross-section of body types and levels of habitual physical activity.
Skinfold caliper used	Harpenden.

Multiple regression equation	R	SEE
(1) BD $= 1.20953 - 0.08294(\log_{10} X_1)$	0.863	0.00625
(2) BD $= 1.16957 - 0.06447(\log_{10} X_1) - 0.000806(X_2)$ $+\ 0.00170(X_3)\ +\ 0.00606(X_4)$	0.893	0.00568

where: $X_1 = \Sigma\ 6$ skinfolds (triceps, subscapular, supraspinale, abdominal, front thigh, medial calf in mm), $X_2 =$ gluteal girth (cm), $X_3 =$ forearm girth (cm), $X_4 =$ biepicondylar humerus breadth (cm).

Reference

Withers, Whittingham, Norton, Laforgia, Ellis & Crockett (1987*c*), n = 182 **females**:

Variable	Mean ± SD	Range
age (yr)	22.5 ± 5.2	11.2–41.4
height (cm)	167.1 ± 8.2	138.4–183.8
weight (kg)	59.23 ± 8.80	26.95–87.63
BD (g.cm^{-3})	1.05665 ± 0.01162	1.01895–1.08171
%BF (Siri, 1961)	18.5 ± 5.2	7.6–35.8

Ethnicity:	Not specified.
Country:	Australia.
Sample characteristics:	State representative squads in badminton, basketball, hockey, lacrosse, squash, gymnastics, orienteering, powerlifting, rowing, track and field, netball, soccer, softball and volleyball, 27% at international calibre.
Skinfold caliper used	Harpenden.

Multiple regression equation	R	SEE
BD $= 1.17484 - 0.07229(\log_{10} X_1)$	0.834	0.00643

where: $X_1 = \Sigma\ 4$ skinfolds (triceps, subscapular, supraspinale, medial calf in mm).

8 References

Adams, J., Mottola, M., Bagnall, K.M., & McFadden, K.D. (1982).
Total body fat content in a group of professional football players.
Canadian Journal of Applied Sports Science, 7, 36-40.

Allen, T.H., Krzywicki, H.J., & Roberts, J.E. (1959).
Density, fat, water and solids in freshly isolated tissues.
Journal of Applied Physiology, 14, 1005-1008.

Allen, T.H., Peng, M.T., Chen, K.P., Huang, T.F., Chang, C., & Fang H.S. (1956).
Prediction of total adiposity from skinfolds and the curvilinear relationship between external and internal adiposity.
Metabolism, 5, 346-352.

Behnke, A.R., & Wilmore, J.H. (1974).
Evaluation and rgulation of body build and composition.
New Jersey: Prentice-Hall.

Brodie, D.A. (1988a).
Techniques for measuring body composition (Part I).
Sports Medicine, 5, 11-40.

Brodie, D.A. (1988b).
Techniques for measuring body composition (Part II).
Sports Medicine, 5, 74-98.

Brown, W.J., & Jones, P.R.M. (1977).
The distribution of fat in relation to habitual physical activity.
Annals of Human Biology, 4, 537-550.

Brozek, J., Grande, F., Anderson, J.T., & Keys A. (1963).
Densitometric analysis of body composition: revision of some quantitative assumptions.
Annals of the New York Academy of Sciences, 110, 113-140.

Chilibeck, P.D., Sale, D.G., & Webber, C.E. (1995).
Exercise and bone mineral density.
Sports Medicine, 19, 103-122.

Chien, S. Peng, M.T., Chen, K.P., Huang, T.F., Chang, C., & Fang F.S. (1975).
Longitudinal studies on adipose tissue and its distribution in human subjects.
Journal of Applied Physiology, 39, 825-830.

Clarys, J.P., Martin, A.D., & Drinkwater, D.T. (1984).
Gross tissue weights in the human body by cadaver dissection.
Human Biology, 56, 459-473.

Clarys, J.P., Martin, A.D., Drinkwater, D.T., & Marfell-Jones, M.J. (1987).
The skinfold: myth and reality.
Journal of Sports Sciences, 5, 3-33.

Craig, N.P., Norton, K.I., Bourdon, P.C., Woolford, S.M., Stanef, T, Squires, B., Olds, T.S., Conyers, R.A.J., & Walsh C.B.V. (1993).
Aerobic and anaerobic indices contributing to track endurance cycling performance.
European Journal of Applied Physiology, 67, 150-158.

Durnin, J.V.G.A., & Taylor, A. (1960).
Reproducibility of measurements of density of the human body as determined by underwater weighing.
Journal of Applied Physiology, 15, 142-144.

Durnin, J.V.G.A., & Womersley, J. (1974).
Body fat assessed from total body density and its estimation from skinfold thickness: measurements on 481 men and women aged 16 to 72 years.
British Journal of Nutrition, 32, 77-97.

Eckerson, J.M., Housh, T.J., & Johnson, G.O. (1992).
The validity of visual estimations of percent body fat in lean males.
Medicine and Science in Sports and Exercise, 24, 615-618.

Fidanza, F., Keys, A., & Anderson, J.T. (1953).
Density of body fat in man and other mammals.
Journal of Applied Physiology, 6, 252-256.

Forsyth, H.L., & Sinning, W.E. (1973).
The anthropometric estimation of body density and lean body weight of male athletes.
Medicine and Science in Sports, 5, 174-180.

Jackson, A.S., Pollock M.L., & Ward, A. (1980).
Generalized equations for predicting body density of women.
Medicine and Science in Sports and Exercise, 12, 75-182.

Katch, F.I. (1983).
Reliability and individual differences in ultrasound assessment of subcutaneous fat: effects of body position.
Human Biology, 55, 789-797.

Katch, F.I., & McArdle, W.D. (1973).
Prediction of body density from simple anthropometric measurements in college-age men and women.
Human Biology, 45, 445-454.

Katch, F.I., & Michael, E.D. (1968).
Prediction of body density from skinfold and girth measurements of college females.
Journal of Applied Physiology, 25, 92-94.

Keys, A., & Brozek, J. (1953).
Body fat in adult man.
Physiological Reviews, 33, 245-325.

Lewis, S., Haskell, W.L., Perry, C., Kovacevic, C., & Wood, P.D. (1978).
Body composition of middle-aged female endurance athletes.
In F. Landry & W.A.R. Orban (Eds.), **Biomechanics of Sports and Kinanthropometry. Book 6** (pp. 321-328).
Florida: Symposia Specialists Inc.

Lohman, T.G. (1981).
Skinfolds and body density and their relationship to body fatness: a review.
Human Biology, 53, 181-225.

Lohman, T.G., Pollock, M.L., Slaughter, M.H., Brandon, L.J., & Boileau, R.A. (1984).
Methodological factors and the prediction of body fat in female athletes.
Medicine and Science in Sports and Exercise, 16, 92-96.

Malina, R.M. (1987).
Bioelectric methods for estimating body composition: an overview and discussion.
Human Biology, 59, 329-335.

Martin, A.D., Drinkwater, D.T., Clarys, J.P., & Ross, W.D. (1986).
The inconsistency of the fat-free mass: A reappraisal with implications for densitometry.
In T. Reilly, J. Watkins, & J. Borms (Eds.), **Kinanthropometry III** (pp. 92-97). London: E. & F.N. Spon.

Martin, A.D., & McColloch, R.G. (1987).
Bone dynamics: stress, strain and fracture.
Journal of Sports Sciences, 5, 155-163.

Martin, A.D., Ross,W.D., Drinkwater, D.T., & Clarys, J.P. (1985).
Prediction of body fat by skinfold caliper: assumptions and cadaver evidence.
International Journal of Obesity, 9, 31-39.

McLean, K.P., & Skinner, J.S. (1992).
Validity of Futrex-5000 for body composition determination.
Medicine and Science in Sports and Exercise, 24, 253-258.

Norton, K.I., Craig, N.P., Withers, R.T., & Whittingham, N.O. (1994).
Assessing the body fat of athletes.
Australian Journal of Science and Medicine in Sports, 26, 6-13.

Pollock, M.L., Gettman, L.R., Jackson, A., Ayres, J., Ward, A., & Linnerup, A.C. (1977).
Body composition of elite class distance runners.
Annals of the New York Academy of Sciences, 301, 361-370.

Pollock, M.L., Laughridge, E.E., Coleman, E., Linnerud, A.C., & Jackson, A. (1975).
Prediction of body density in young and middle-aged women.
Journal of Applied Physiology, 38, 745-749.

Roche A.F. (1987).
Some aspects of the criterion methods for the measurement of body composition.
Human Biology, 59, 209-220.

Sinning, W.E. (1978).
Anthropometric estimation of body density, fat and lean body weight in women gymnasts.
Medicine and Science in Sports, 10, 243-249.

Siri ,W.E. (1961).
Body volume measurement by gas dilution.
In J. Brozek, A. Henschel, (Eds.), **Techniques for Measuring Body Composition.** Washington, DC: National Academy of Sciences, National Research Council, (pp.108-117).

Sloan, A.W., Burt, J.J., & Blyth, C.S. (1962).
Estimation of body fat in young women.
Journal of Applied Physiology, 17, 967-970.

Sloan, A.W. (1967).
Estimation of body fat in young men.
Journal of Applied Physiology, 23, 311-315.

Smith, U., Hammersten, J., Bjorntorp, P., & Kral J.G. (1979).
Regional differences and effect of weight reduction on fat cell metabolism.
European Journal of Clinical Investigation, 9, 327-332.

Tanner, J.M. (1978).
Foetus into man (pp. 17-19).
London: Open Books.

Telford, R., Tumilty, D., & Damm, G. (1984).
Skinfold measurements in well-performed Australian athletes.
Sports Science and Medicine Quarterly, 1, 13-16.

Thorland, W.G., Johnson, O.G., Tharp, G.D., Housh, T.J., & Cisar, C.J. (1984).
Estimation of body density in adolescent athletes.
Human Biology, 56, 439-448.

Wilmore, J.H. (1983).
Appetite and body composition consequent to physical activity.
Research Quarterly for Exercise and Sport, 54, 415-425.

Wilmore, J.H., & Behnke, A.R. (1969).
An anthropometric estimation of body density and lean body weight in young men.
Journal of Applied Physiology, 27, 25-31.

Wilmore, J.H., & Behnke, A.R. (1970).
An anthropometric estimation of body density and lean body weight in young women.
American Journal of Clinical Nutrition, 23, 267-74.

Withers, R.T. (1983).
The measurement of relative body fat: assumptions, limitations and measurement error.
Transactions of the Menzies Foundation, 5, 83-89.

Withers, R.T., Borkent, M., & Ball C.T. (1990).
A comparison of the effects of measured, predicted, estimated and constant residual volumes on the body density of male athletes.
International Journal of Sports Medicine, 11, 357-361.

Withers, R.T., Craig, N.P., Bourdon, P.C., & Norton, K.I. (1987).
Relative body fat and anthropometric prediction of body density of male athletes.
European Journal of Applied Physiology, 56, 191-200.

Withers, R.T., Norton, K.I., Craig, N.P., Hartland, M.C., & Venables, W. (1987).
The relative body fat and anthropometric prediction of body density of South Australian females aged 17-35 years.
European Journal of Applied Physiology, 56, 181-190.

Withers, R.T., Whittingham, N.O., Norton, K.I., Laforgia, J., Ellis, M.W., & Crockett, A. (1987).
Relative body fat and anthropometric prediction of body density of female athletes.
European Journal of Applied Physiology, 56, 169-180.

Womersley, J., Durnin, J.V.G.A., Boddy, K., & Mahaffy, M. (1976).
Influence of muscular development, obesity and age on the fat-free mass in adults.
Journal of Applied Physiology, 41, 223-229.

Chapter 8
Two, Three and Four -compartment Chemical Models of Body Composition Analysis

Robert Withers, Joe Laforgia, Steven Heymsfield, Zi-Mian Wang and Robyn Pillans

Chapter 8

1 Two-compartment models

1.1 Introduction

The three two-compartment models of body composition analysis (Table 1) involve the determination of body density (BD) by underwater weighing or hydrodensitometry, total body water (TBW) via isotopic dilution and total body potassium (TBK) by counting the gamma radiation emitted by ^{40}K which comprises 0.01181% of all naturally occurring potassium. These methods are based on the premise that the body can be divided into two chemically distinct compartments (Figure 1), namely, the fat mass (FM) and fat free mass (FFM). The FM, which is defined as ether extractable lipid, is assumed to have a density of 0.9007 g.cm^{-3} at 36°C, be anhydrous and contain no potassium whereas the FFM is regarded as having a density of 1.1000 g.cm^{-3} at 36°C, a water content of 72% and a potassium concentration of 68.1 mmol.kg^{-1}. The methodology for the two-compartment models is described and critiqued in the following text since in many cases they provide the conceptual framework on which the more sophisticated models are based.

Table 1 Two-compartment models

Models	Assumptions	Calculations
Hydrodensitometry	FFM density = 1.1000 g.cm^{-3}	%BF = 497.1/BD − 451.9
	FM density = 0.9007 g.cm^{-3}	FFM (kg) = body mass (kg) − FM (kg)
Total body water	TBW (kg)/FFM (kg) = 0.72	FFM (kg) = TBW (kg)/72 × 100
Total body potassium	TBK/FFM = 68.1 mmol.kg^{-1}	TBK (mmol) = TBK (g)/39.1 × 1000
		FFM (kg) = TBK (mmol)/68.1

FFM = fat free mass; BD = body density; %BF = percent body fat
FM = fat mass; TBK = total body potassium; TBW = total body water

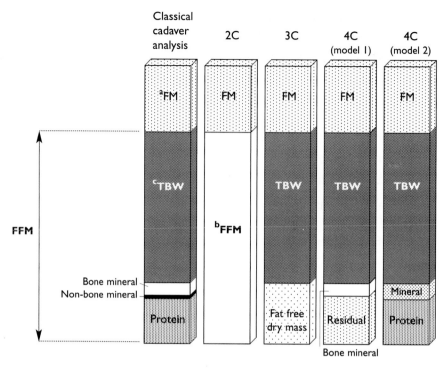

Figure 1 Schematic of classical cadaver analyses (Brozek, Grande, Anderson, & Keys, 1963) and the 2, 3 and 4 compartment (C) chemical models of body composition analysis.

[a]FM = Fat mass; [b]FFM = Fat free mass; [c]TBW = Total body water.

1.2 Description

1.2.1 Underwater weighing (UWW) or hydrodensitometry

Archimedes' Principle states that when a body is immersed in water then it is buoyed up by a force which is equivalent to the weight of the volume of water displaced. The density of an object is defined as its mass per unit volume (g.cm⁻³). Thus if we determine a subject's mass, both in air and when completely immersed in water, then his or her density may be calculated as follows:

$$density\,(g.cm^{-3}) = \frac{mass\,(g)}{volume\,(cm^3)}$$

$$= \frac{mass\,of\,body\,in\,air\,(g)}{mass\,of\,body\,in\,air\,(g) - mass\,of\,body\,in\,water\,(g)}$$

Adjustments also have to be made for water density, which depends on the temperature, and the ventilated residual volume since the underwater mass is normally measured when the subject has expired maximally. The full formula (Buskirk, 1961) is therefore:

$$BD = \frac{MB_{air}}{\left(\dfrac{MB_{air} - MB_{water}}{WD}\right) - RV}$$

where:
BD = body density (g.cm^{-3} or g.ml^{-1})
MB$_{air}$ = mass of body in air (g)
MB$_{water}$ = mass of body (g) when immersed in water
WD = water density (g.cm^{-3} or g.ml^{-1})
RV = ventilated residual lung volume (ml)

The BD is then normally converted to percentage body fat (%BF) using the equation of Brozek et al. (1963) which is derived in Figure 2:

$$\%BF = \frac{497.1}{BD} - 451.9$$

Hence, if a 75.00 kg male has an immersed mass of 3.00 kg at a water temperature of 35°C (WD = 0.9941 g.cm^{-3}) and his RV is 1300 ml then:

$$BD = \frac{75000}{\left(\dfrac{75000 - 3000}{0.9941}\right) - 1300} = 1.05445 \text{ g.cm}^{-3}$$

$$\%BF = \frac{497.1}{1.05445} - 451.9 = 19.5$$

$$\frac{1}{^cBD} = \frac{FM}{FM_{density}} + \frac{FFM}{FFM_{density}}$$

$$FM = FM_{density}\left[\frac{1}{BD} - \left(\frac{1-FM}{FFM_{density}}\right)\right]$$

$$FM = 0.9007\left[\frac{1}{BD} - \left(\frac{1-FM}{1.1000}\right)\right]$$

$$FM = \frac{0.9007}{BD} - 0.818818 + 0.818818\ FM$$

$$0.181182\ FM = \frac{0.9007}{BD} - 0.818818$$

$$FM = \frac{4.971}{BD} - 4.519$$

$$\%FM \quad or \quad \%BF = \frac{497.1}{BD} - 451.9$$

Figure 2 Derivation of the two-compartment model ([a]FM and [b]FFM) for estimating relative body fat via underwater weighing or hydrodensitometry.

Assumptions: Density of FM = 0.9007 g.cm^{-3} at 36°C (Fidanza, Keys, & Anderson, 1953)
Density of FFM = 1.1000 g.cm^{-3} at 36°C (Brozek et al., 1963)

If the body mass (kg) is equal to unity (i.e. 1) and the two compartments are represented as proportions such that FM + FFM = 1.0 then the formula can be most simply derived as shown above, where: [a]FM = fat mass; [b]FFM = fat free mass; [c]BD = body density.

The Siri equation (%BF = 495/BD − 450; Siri, 1956) can be used to convert BD to %BF. However, this equation uses a value of 0.9000 g.cm^{-3} for the density of fat at 37°C. Although core temperature approximates 37°C, the average body temperature under basal resting conditions and in a comfortable environment is likely to be 1–2°C lower than this (Burton, 1935). Moreover, the average body temperature would probably be ~36°C during underwater weighing (UWW) when the water temperature is maintained at ~35°C. Hence we have used 0.9007 g.cm^{-3} for the density of fat at 36°C. Nevertheless, the equations of Siri (1956) and Brozek et al. (1963) produce results within 1% BF over the range of 1.03 to 1.10 g.cm^{-3}.

It is important that the RV is measured when the subject is submerged in water since the net effect of the hydrostatic pressure (decreases RV), pulmonary vascular engorgement (decreases RV) and diminished compliance (increases RV) is to reduce the ventilated RV. One study (Withers & Hamdorf, 1989) found that immersion in water decreased the RV by 292 ml and this increased the predicted relative body fat from 15.2% to 17.1%.

Several reasons have contributed to making UWW the most frequently used two-compartment model for estimating body composition. Basic UWW systems can be assembled cheaply by acquiring a water container such as a wine cask, a heating system and an autopsy scale. Also, the RV can be measured by N_2 washout using CO_2 and O_2 analysers which are basic items of equipment in exercise physiology laboratories. It is also expedient compared with TBW, where the subject normally waits in the laboratory for 3–3.5 hours until the isotope equilibrates with the body fluids. Furthermore, the cost of a whole body counter for TBK would be prohibitive.

BD can be measured with great precision. Buskirk (1961) cited an average technical error, which was defined as the standard deviation of the differences between trials 1 and 2, of 0.0021 $g.cm^{-3}$ for 7 studies. Reproducibility trials in our laboratory on six 20–30 year olds yielded an intraclass correlation coefficient of 0.999 (SD of differences = 0.0011 $g.cm^{-3}$) and technical error of measurement (TEM) of 0.3% BF (Figure 3). While complete immersion may make this procedure unsuitable for some subjects such as the elderly, this can be avoided by using plethysmographic techniques (Garrow et al., 1979; Gundlach & Visscher, 1986) which have precisions that are comparable to those reported in this paragraph.

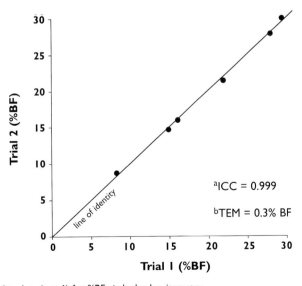

Figure 3 Reliability data (n = 6) for %BF via hydrodensitometry.

[a]ICC = Intraclass correlation coefficient, [b]TEM = Technical error of measurement.

1.2.2 Total body water (TBW) via isotopic dilution

The calculation of TBW is based on the dilution principle:

$$C_1 m_1 = C_2 m_2$$

where:

C_1 = concentration of tracer in dose solution

m_1 = mass of dose solution

C_2 = equilibrium concentration of tracer in the biological fluid of interest (plasma, urine or saliva)

m_2 = mass of TBW

This equation can be rearranged:

$$m_2 = \frac{C_1 m_1}{C_2} \qquad \text{or}$$

$$TBW(g) = \frac{concentration\ of\ tracer\ in\ dose\ solution\ \times\ dose\ solution\ (g)}{equilibrium\ concentration\ of\ tracer}$$

Therefore

$$TBW(g) = \frac{tracer\ dose\ (g)}{equilibrium\ concentration\ of\ tracer}$$

A variety of tracers (tritium, deuterium and ^{18}O) and measurement techniques (tritium: scintillation counting; deuterium and ^{18}O: infra-red absorption spectroscopy and isotope ratio mass spectroscopy) are used to determine TBW. However, deuterium has emerged as the preferred tracer because it is a stable isotope without the radiation risks of tritium and moreover it is much cheaper than $H_2{}^{18}O$. Isotope ratio mass spectroscopy is also the procedure of choice because measurements with a precision of <1.0% can be achieved. The deuterium oxide (^2H_2O) dose is normally administered orally in solution with distilled water. However, corrections need to be made for the background or pre-dose concentration in the biological fluid sampled and the fact that the TBW is overestimated by ~4% (Schoeller & Jones, 1987) because of deuterium exchange with non-aqueous hydrogen in the body. The preceding equation therefore needs to be modified:

$$rue\ TBW\ (g)\ =\ \frac{\left(\dfrac{tracer\ dose\ of\ {}^{2}H_{2}O\ (g)\ \times\ dose\ water\ enrichment\ (ppm)\ in\ excess\ of\ that\ for\ background\ saliva}{enrichment\ of\ equilibrated\ saliva\ (ppm)-\ background\ saliva\ (ppm)}\right)}{1.04}$$

Let us assume that the natural background of deuterium in the saliva of a 70 kg adult is 155 ppm and that a 103.12 g dose of $^{2}H_{2}O$ with a deuterium enrichment of 23907 ppm increases the concentration of deuterium in the saliva to 211 ppm at equilibrium. These data yield a true TBW of:

$$True\ TBW\ =\ \frac{\left(\dfrac{103.12\ \times\ (23907-155)}{211-155}\right)}{1.04}\ =\ 42055\ g\ \ or\ \ 42.055\ kg$$

Hence, the FFM is 58.41 kg (Table 1) with a relative body fat of 16.6%. The interested reader is referred to Schoeller et al. (1980) which also contains a correction factor for the molecular weight difference between H_2O (18.016) and $^{2}H_{2}O$ (20.028). Strict standardisation of our procedures for determining TBW have enabled us to attain an intraclass correlation coefficient and TEM of 0.983 and 0.5% BF, respectively, for 2 trials on 5 subjects (Figure 4).

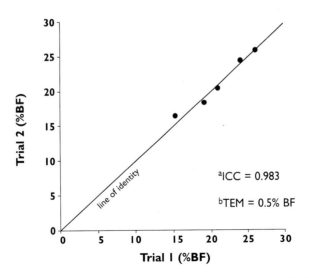

Figure 4 Reliability data (n = 5) for %BF from total body water via isotopic (deuterium) dilution.
[a]ICC = Intraclass correlation coefficient, [b]TEM = Technical error of measurement.

1.2.3 Total body potassium (TBK)

Radioactive ^{40}K is detected by very sensitive whole body counters which must be screened from background radiation since the concentration of this isotope is very low. Allowance also needs to be made for attenuation of the count by each subject's body size and shape; precision additionally depends on such factors as the type of counting system together with its design and eliminating clothing contamination. Table 1 indicates how to calculate the FFM from the TBK. Our test retest reliability trials (n = 6) using the TBK counter at the Royal Adelaide Hospital's Department of Nuclear Medicine resulted in an intraclass correlation coefficient of 0.886 and a TEM of 2.4% BF. These are inferior to our earlier reported precisions for BD and TBW.

1.3 Critique

1.3.1 Underwater weighing (UWW) or hydrodensitometry

The two-compartment hydrodensitometry model will yield incorrect values for %BF if:
- the density of ether extractable fat, which comprises the fat mass, is not 0.9007 $g.cm^{-3}$.
- the densities and relative proportions of the four FFM components [water, protein, bone mineral, non-bone (soft tissue) mineral] differ from those for the classical cadaver analyses (Table 2 and Figure 1) such that the FFM density is not 1.1000 $g.cm^{-3}$.

Table 2 Masses and volumes of the chemical components of the FFM per kilogram of body mass at average body temperature (Brozek et al., 1963).

Substance	Mass (g)	Volume at 36°C (ml)	Density at 36°C $(g.ml^{-1})$	% of FFM
Water	624.3	628.2	0.99371	73.72
Protein	164.4	122.7	1.34	19.41
Bone mineral	47.7	16.0	2.982	5.63
Non–bone mineral	10.5	3.2	3.317	1.24
Total	846.9	770.1	1.100	100.00

It is therefore appropriate to examine the validity of these constants since they are also used in multicompartment models:

(a) Fat

Fidanza et al. (1953) reported that the density of 20 ether extractable fat samples from the intra-abdominal and subcutaneous tissue of 5 subjects was 0.9007 ± 0.00068 g.cm^{-3} (mean $\pm$ SD) at 36°C with a coefficient of thermal expansion of 0.00074 g.cm^{-3}.$^{\circ}$C^{-1} over the range of 15–37°C. Hence, the small coefficient of variation of 0.08% validates the hydrodensitometric FM density assumption of 0.9007 g.cm^{-3}. However, in the interest of scientific accuracy, there is one small caveat. The preceding analyses were conducted primarily on triglyceride. While the combined cholesterol (density = 1.067 g.cm^{-3}) and phospholipid (density = 1.035 g.cm^{-3}) comprises only 1% of the ether extractable fat from rabbit adipose tissue (Méndez, Keys, Anderson & Grande, 1960), comparable figures for the fat extracted from the muscular and central nervous systems of animals may average as high as 37 and 75%, respectively (Méndez et al., 1960). Nevertheless, the lipids in the adult brain, spinal cord and nerves have been estimated to be only 200–300 g (Keys & Brozek, 1953) and Méndez et al. (1960) have proposed a similar amount for muscle lipid. Heymsfield et al. (1991) have accordingly stated that triglyceride accounts for 99% of the ether extractable lipid. The error in the FM density assumption is therefore probably negligible.

(b) FFM

The FFM density assumption of 1.1000 g.cm^{-3} (Table 2 and Figure 1) is based on the mean for the chemical analyses of only three male cadavers aged 25, 35 and 46 years (Brozek et al., 1963) but is nevertheless applied irrespective of the age, gender, genetic endowment and training of the subjects. This assumption has been challenged by many investigators (e.g. Deurenberg, Weststrate & van der Kooy, 1989; Haschke, Fomon & Ziegler, 1981; Lohman, 1981; Womersley, Durnin, Boddy & Mahaffy, 1976) since people with a FFM density less than 1.1000 g.cm^{-3} will have their %BF overestimated. Typical examples of individuals in this category are children who have a FFM hydration greater than 73.7%, those who are overhydrated or oedematous and the elderly, particularly females, whose bone mineral has been depleted by osteoporosis. The converse will apply if the FFM is greater than 1.1000 g.cm^{-3} such as in the dehydrated and those with a greater than normal proportion of bone mineral. Siri (1956; 1961) acknowledged this limitation and stated that biological variability in FFM density resulted in an error with a standard deviation of 3.8% BF ($\sim$0.0084 g.cm^{-3}) for hydrodensitometry. Lohman (1981) hypothesised that this error reduces to 2.7% BF ($\sim$0.006 g.cm^{-3}) for specific populations. Neither of the preceding estimates includes the small technical error associated with the measurement of BD. A critical appraisal now follows of the densities and relative percentages of the four FFM components (Table 2):

- **Water** – The density for water at varying temperatures, which is readily available in scientific tables (Lentner, 1981, Table 50; Weast, 1975, Table F-5), is beyond dispute.

The literature contains the following data (mean ± SD: 72.0 ± 3.7%) for the FFM hydration of five male cadavers: 67.4 and 70.4 (Forbes & Lewis, 1956); 77.56 (Mitchell, Hamilton, Steggerda & Bean, 1945); 72.1 (Shohl, 1939) and 72.62% (Widdowson, McCance & Spray, 1951). While the mean of 72.0% can be used to estimate %BF via the two-compartment isotopic dilution model (Table 1), the variability should be noted. Also, some investigators use 73.72% for FFM hydration (Table 2). Perhaps the most valid data for FFM hydration are those reported in vivo using multicompartment models of body composition analysis. The literature contains mean values in the range of 71.9-74.4% (Baumgartner, Heymsfield, Lichtman, Wang & Pierson, 1991; Friedl, deLuca, Marchitelli & Vogel, 1992; Fuller, Jebb, Laskey, Coward & Elia, 1992; Heymsfield et al., 1989a; 1990; 1991) for adult males and females but comparisons between these studies are difficult because of such factors as different values for non-aqueous hydrogen exchange and measurement of RV in air as opposed to in water.

- **Protein** – The densities of most proteins in the dry crystalline state are close to 1.27 g.cm^{-3} (Haurowitz, 1963, p. 119). However, proteins are the principal water-binding substances in humans and the resultant hydration is accompanied by a volume contraction of both the solute and the solvent. The specific volume therefore decreases until the density is 1.34 g.cm^{-3} (Haurowitz, 1963, p. 119) which appears to be the best available estimate for hydrated protein in the living cell. But proteins are known to differ in density and collagen, which is estimated to comprise 25-30% of the total body protein (mainly in bone and skin), has an average dry density of 1.36 g.cm^{-3} (Hulmes & Miller, 1979). It therefore appears that the estimate of density used for protein is far more tenuous than those used for fat and water for which the coefficients of thermal expansion are also known.

The mass of crude protein for the three cadavers (Table 2) was estimated from total body nitrogen (TBN) by assuming that all of it is incorporated into protein which comprises 16% nitrogen (protein = TBN x 6.25). Under normal circumstances > 99% TBN is incorporated into protein (Heymsfield, Wang & Withers, in press). Knight, Beddoe, Streat and Hill (1986) have reported the protein/nitrogen (P/N) ratios to be 5.80, 6.3 and 7.29 for collagen, actinomyosin and albumin, respectively. Nevertheless, their chemical analyses of two persons who died of cancer yielded whole body ratios (mean ± SD, P measured 10 times and N measured 20 times) of 6.33 ± 0.19 and 6.40 ± 0.22. They concluded that these data provided no justification to change the assumed P/N ratio of 6.25. The three cadavers summarised in Table 2 contained 16.4, 19.5 and 23.4% protein in their FFMs. This large range is probably due to differences in skeletal muscle mass which is the single largest source of protein. It is possible to compare the preceding cadaver analyses (mean = 19.8% protein in FFM) with recent *in vivo* data where total body protein has been measured by prompt gamma neutron activation analysis (P = TBN × 6.25), which has a precision of 2.7% (Heymsfield et al., 1991), and is then expressed as a percentage of the FFM determined by multicompartment analysis. Four studies (Heymsfield et al., 1989a; 1989b; 1990; 1991) have reported such information on normal adult males and females over a wide age range. While all the means (19.5–20.8%) are very close to that for the classical cadaver analyses, the individual values of 16.4–22.3% emphasise the biological variability for this FFM component.

- **Bone mineral** – The validity of the assumptions for the densities of bone mineral (BM) and non-bone mineral (NBM) can also be questioned. The former value of 2.982 $g.cm^{-3}$ is based on the mean of only four samples (Méndez et al., 1960) isolated from the long bones of animals (cow tibia at 36°C: 2.9930 and 3.0066 $g.cm^{-3}$; dog femur and tibia at 36.7°C: 2.9624 and 2.9667 $g.cm^{-3}$) but Brozek et al. (1963) further verified this value against that of the stoichiometry for the prototype mineral hydroxyapatite after allowance for water of crystallisation and CO_2. Méndez et al. (1960) also cited earlier work by Dallemagne and Melon (1945) who reported the densities of bone and dental mineral to be 2.99 and 3.01 $g.cm^{-3}$, respectively.

Table 2 indicates that the BM comprised 5.63% of the FFM for the three cadavers; however, the range was from 4.69 to 6.36% (Brozek et al., 1963). The advent of dual photon absorptiometry (DPA), and its successor dual energy x-ray absorptiometry (DEXA), facilitated the measurement of BM *in vivo*. Hence, it is now possible to compare the preceding cadaver data with that collected *in vivo* when body composition has also been determined via multicompartment methods. Higher values (mean ± SD: 6.81 ± 0.67% FFM) have been reported by Friedl et al. (1992) for 10 young soldiers whereas lower values occur (Baumgartner et al., 1991) for old males (mean ± SD: 74.1 ± 7.7 yr, n = 35, 5.00% FFM) and females (mean ± SD: 74.7 ± 5.9 yr, n = 63, 4.96% FFM). Twelve highly trained young male endurance athletes (mean ± SD: 22.2 ± 4.9 yr) registered quite homogeneous scores (mean ± SD: 5.50 ± 0.28% FFM) with a mean which approximated that for the three cadavers (Withers, Smith, Chatterton, Schultz & Gaffney, 1992). More heterogeneous data (mean ± SD: 5.42 ± 0.62% FFM) were understandably obtained for 14 males and females who spanned the age range 24–94 yr (Heymsfield et al., 1989a). The preceding investigations emphasise the biological variability for the BM fraction of the FFM.

- **Non-bone (soft tissue) mineral** – The classical cadaver analyses assumed that all the calcium was contained within bone and that it was accompanied by the same amounts of phosphorus, sodium and magnesium as in bone ash (Brozek et al., 1963). This seems a reasonable assumption since extraskeletal calcium represents less than 0.4% of total body calcium (Snyder, 1975). The overall density of the remaining extraskeletal mineral or NBM was then calculated to be 3.317 g.cm^{3} (Brozek et al., 1963).

It is possible to estimate the NBM *in vivo* by measuring: total body calcium, sodium and chloride via delayed gamma neutron activation analysis, bone calcium from dual energy X-ray absorptiometry and total body potassium by counting the gamma radiation emitted by ^{40}K. However, the published data (Heymsfield et al., 1989a; 1989b; 1990; 1991) support much smaller percentages of the FFM (0.80 – 0.90%) than the 1.24% FFM reported for the three cadavers (Brozek et al., 1963). These discrepancies are probably related to the different assumptions made for the *in vitro* and *in vivo* measurements. A standard deviation of 0.051% FFM (mean = 0.821% FFM) for 14 males and females in the age range 24–94 yr indicates the biological variability for NBM in healthy adults (Heymsfield et al., 1989a). Nevertheless, despite its high density, NBM comprises such a small fraction of the FFM that it impacts very little on the overall FFM density.

1.3.2 Total body water (TBW) via isotopic dilution

The variability in FFM hydration has already been discussed. If the FFM is more hydrated than 72% then the two-compartment TBW method will underestimate the %BF. For example, a FFM hydration of 75.7% for a 75 kg subject with a TBW of 45 kg would result in an underestimate of 4.0% BF. Interestingly, the converse applies to hydrodensitometry because the increased water decreases the FFM density.

A further consideration is that adipose tissue contains about 15% water and 2% protein. This water is included in the FFM since the FM is ether-extractable lipid which is anhydrous. The water content of the fat free adipose tissue is therefore 88% (i.e. 15/17 × 100) which is higher than the assumed FFM hydration constant of 72.0%. Hence fatter persons would logically have a FFM hydration which is greater than 72.0%.

There are also some unresolved problems associated with the measurement of TBW *in vivo*. Firstly, some investigators have compared the isotope dilution space (IDS) with the criterion of TBW measured by desiccation. This work has been summarised by Schoeller and Jones (1987) who concluded that most of these comparisons indicate that the IDS overestimates the TBW by 1–6%. This is primarily due to exchange of the isotopes with non-aqueous body constituents (Culebras & Moore, 1977; Schoeller et al., 1980). However, errors in the dilution technique can result from a loss of isotope and consequent overestimation of TBW whereas errors in the criterion desiccation method are caused by incomplete drying and subsequent underestimation of TBW. These opposite errors would therefore tend to accentuate differences between the TBW via isotopic dilution and desiccation. Nevertheless, the simultaneous use of deuterium and $H_2^{18}O$ in humans yields a 3–5% higher IDS for the former (Schoeller et al., 1980; Wong et al., 1988). Also, the IDS via $H_2^{18}O$ has been demonstrated to be 0.4–2.1% greater than the TBW via desiccation (Lifson, Gordon & McClintock, 1955; Nagy, 1980; Whyte, Bayley & Schwarcz, 1985) and theoretical calculations support an approximate 1% overestimate of TBW via $H_2^{18}O$ (Schoeller et al., 1980). Schoeller and Jones (1987) therefore concluded that the $H_2^{18}O$ and ^2H_2O dilution spaces are 1 ± 1 (mean ± SD) and 4 ± 1% larger, respectively, than the TBW. While these recommendations have been adopted by many investigators, some use a 2% correction factor for TBW via deuterium dilution (Friedl et al., 1992; Hewitt, Going, Williams & Lohman, 1993). However, if one accepts that the $H_2^{18}O$ IDS overestimates TBW by 1% then the recommendation of Schoeller and Jones (1987) for estimating the TBW from deuterium dilution was supported subsequently by Coward (1990) who indicated that the IDS ratios ($^2H_2O/H_2^{18}O$) were tightly clustered around a mean of 1.03 for 9 separate studies conducted by the Dunn Nutrition Unit at Cambridge University. Another methodological problem is that the IDS changes continually since while the isotope is equilibrating with the body's water pool it is continually being excreted from it. The routes of isotope loss and water entry have been quantified by Schoeller, Kushner, Taylor, Dietz & Bandini (1985). In practice, most investigators only make allowance for the tracer voided in the urine and ignore insensible tracer loss. Final problems concern the isotopic fractionation of samples and inter-individual variability in the time for equilibration of the tracer with the body's water pool if the plateau method is used (Wong et al., 1988).

1.3.3 Total body potassium (TBK)

Conversion of TBK to FFM is based on the assumption that the FFM contains 68.1 mmol K.kg^{-1} (Forbes, Gallup & Hursh, 1961) which is the mean for four cadaver analyses. Hence, as with the two preceding two-compartment models, this assumption ignores biological variability. The FFM of muscular subjects would obviously be overestimated because skeletal muscle contains 78–90 mmol K.kg^{-1} (Forbes, 1987, p. 39). Nevertheless, the measurement of TBK *per se* is used in other models which are discussed later in this chapter.

1.4 Summary

It may therefore be concluded that most of the error associated with these three two-compartment models lies not in the technical accuracy of the measurements but in biological or inter-individual variability which is a serious threat to the validity of the previously outlined assumptions. This latter point is highlighted in the error analyses which are contained in Table 3. It is clear that variation in the composition of the FFM can cause sizeable individual errors for the two-compartment models when the subjects are at the extremes of the adult population. However, the errors for group means will be much less than those in Table 3. For example, the two-compartment hydrodensitometry mean of 15.3% (SD = 6.7% BF) for the 29 subjects whose data are graphed later in this chapter was 2.9% BF less than that of 18.2% BF (SD = 6.3% BF) for the four-compartment criterion model (see section 3.2.1) which controls for inter-individual variability in TBW and BM. A further problem with two-compartment body composition models occurs when the FM is the variable of interest. In this case, the biological and measurement errors for the larger FFM compartment (e.g. FFM determined by isotopic dilution or TBK) are propagated to the smaller FM compartment which is calculated by subtraction. Hence, a 3% error for the FFM (assume: mass = 80 kg; FFM = 68 kg; FM = 12 kg) is translated into a 17% error for the FM.

Table 3 Errors[a] in estimated relative body fat for a male subject (15% BF) when one FFM component increases[b] or decreases[b] whilst the absolute amounts (kg) of fat and FFM stay constant[c].

change in %FFM for	95% confidence limits[b]	two-compartment models		three-compartment model[d]	four-compartment model[d]
		hydrodensitometry	total body water		
water	+3.92	+6.22	-4.52	0	0
	0	0	0	0	0
	-3.92	-6.00	+4.52	0	0
protein	+3.90	-3.22	+4.12	+0.97	+0.30
	0	0	0	0	0
	-3.90	+3.45	-4.12	-0.92	-0.26
bone mineral	+1.35	-3.36	+1.21	-0.75	0
	0	0	0	0	0
	-1.35	+3.58	-1.21	+0.80	0
non-bone mineral	+0.11	-0.17	+0.09	-0.05	-0.08
	0	0	0	0	0
	-0.11	+0.40	-0.09	+0.09	+0.12

a   A density of 1.064682 g.cm⁻³ yields 15% BF using the Brozek et al. (1963) equation. However, increasing the FFM hydration from 73.72% to 77.64% decreases the FFM and total body densities to 1.082482 and 1.050675 g.cm⁻³, respectively. Conventional hydrodensitometry yields 21.22% BF, which is 6.22% BF above the true value of 15% BF.

b   These %BF increases and decreases represent the 95% confidence limits for *in vivo* measurements on 13 males and females spanning the range of 24–94 years (Heymsfield et al.,1989a). This range presumably encloses 95% of the variability in the adult population.

c   Hence, if TBW is increased, then the three other components of the FFM decrease proportionately to maintain the FFM at 85% of body mass.

d   The three and four-compartment models are derived later in this chapter.

215

2 Three-compartment models

2.1 Introduction

Each of the three-compartment models outlined in this section controls for biological variability of one FFM component. The mass and volume of the component which is measured *in vivo* are then subtracted from the mass and volume (mass/density) of the whole body. The remainder is then partitioned into two compartments (FM and one other) of known or assumed densities.

2.2 The models

2.2.1 Siri

The FFM comprises: water, protein, BM and NBM (Figure 1). Table 2 indicates that water impacts significantly on FFM density because it has the lowest density but comprises by far the largest fraction of any of the four components. Also, the FFM hydration is acutely variable. Siri (1961) identified the variation in FFM hydration (SD = 2% of body mass) as the largest source of error in the two-compartment hydrodensitometry model. He consequently proposed a three-compartment model (FM; water; fat free dry solid) which is based on measurements of both BD and TBW. This model is depicted in Figure 1 and our modified formula is derived in Figure 5.

The original model used FM and fat free dry solid densities of 0.9000 and 1.565 g.cm^{-3}, respectively. We have used the previously justified value of 0.9007 g.cm^{-3} for FM density at 36°C and our fat free dry solid density of 1.569 g.cm^{-3} assumes a total mineral/protein ratio of 0.354 which corresponds exactly to that for the means of the three cadaver analyses summarised in Table 2. Siri (1961) argued that the total error for this model could be reduced only if the standard deviation for the total mineral/protein ratio was < 0.1. *In vivo* measurements on 31 males and females (mean ± SD: 58 ± 20 yr) by Heymsfield et al. (1990) subsequently demonstrated the total mineral/protein ratio to be 0.33 ± 0.08. The error may therefore be somewhat less than that originally thought by Siri (1961). He suggested that the standard deviation of the error for the two-compartment hydrodensitometry model of 4.0% BF, which is due to a combination of biological variability of FFM density and technical error, would be reduced to 2% BF for his three-compartment model if the error for measuring TBW was 2% of body mass. Reduction of the latter error to 1% of body mass would further decrease the standard deviation for the total error to 1.5% BF. Nevertheless, few investigators have used this

$$\frac{1}{BD} = \frac{FM}{FM_{density}} + \frac{{}^{b}W}{W_{density}} + \frac{FFDS}{FFDS_{density}}$$

$$FM = FM_{density}\left[\frac{1}{BD} - \frac{W}{W_{density}} - \left(\frac{1-FM-W}{FFDS_{density}}\right)\right]$$

$$FM = 0.9007\left[\frac{1}{BD} - \frac{W}{0.9937} - \left(\frac{1-FM-W}{1.569}\right)\right]$$

$$FM = \frac{0.9007}{BD} - 0.906410\ W - 0.574060 + 0.574060\ FM + 0.574060\ W$$

$$0.425940\ FM = \frac{0.9007}{BD} - 0.332350\ W - 0.574060$$

$$FM = \frac{2.114617}{BD} - 0.780274\ W - 1.347749$$

$$\%FM\ \ or\ \ \%BF\ = \frac{211.5}{BD} - 78.0\ {}^{f}W - 134.8$$

Figure 5 Derivation of the three-compartment model ([a]FM, [b]TBW, [c]FFDS) for estimating relative body fat[d] from measurements of [e]BD and TBW.

Assumptions: Density of FM = 0.9007 g.cm⁻³ at 36°C (Fidanza et al., 1953)
Density of water (W) = 0.9937 g.cm⁻³ at 36°C (Lentner, 1981, 50; Weast, 1975, F-5)
Density of fat free dry solid (FFDS) = 1.569 g.cm⁻³ at 36°C (Brozek et al., 1963)

If the body mass (kg) is equal to unity (i.e. 1) and the three compartments are represented as proportions such that FM + W + FFDS = 1.0 then the formula can be most simply derived as shown above, where: [a]FM = fat mass; [b]TBW or W = total body water; [c]FFDS = fat free dry solid; d: = same as Siri equation (1961) except values used for $FM_{density}$ and $FFDS_{density}$; [e]BD = body density; [f]W = W (kg)/body mass (kg).

model which is not influenced by abnormal hydration. A minor problem with this model and the two-compartment hydrodensitometry one is that they ignore the glycogen compartment, which was presumably not considered in the cadaver analyses because of its relatively small amount (~300–500 g or ~1% FFM) and rapid postmortem autolysis. While the glycogen stores can now be estimated *in vivo* using ¹³C nuclear magnetic resonance spectroscopy, their density (glucose = 1.562 g.cm⁻³; Weast, 1975, C-311) is similar to that of protein and the fat free dry solid. Furthermore, most body composition measurements are conducted in the early morning when the subject is in the post-absorptive state so that the glycogen stores would be low. Any error is therefore likely to be minimal.

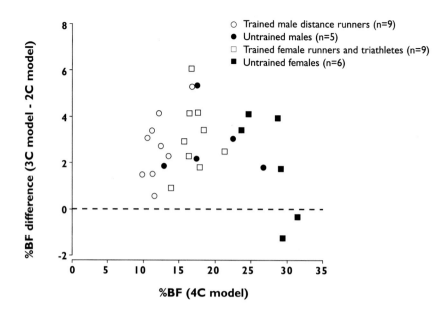

Figure 6 %BF differences between the 3 and 2 compartment (C) models graphed against the %BF via the 4 compartment model.

Data on these 18–36 year-old subjects (X̄±SD: 23±5 yr) were collected in the Exercise Physiology Laboratory at the Flinders University of South Australia and the Department of Nuclear Medicine at the Royal Adelaide Hospital.

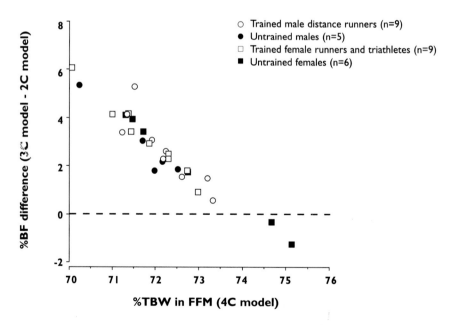

Figure 7 %BF differences between the 3 and 2 compartments (C) models graphed against the % total body water (TBW) in the FFM determined via the 4 compartment model.

Data on these 18–36-year-old subjects (X̄±SD: 23±5 yr) were collected in the Exercise Physiology Laboratory at the Flinders University of South Australia and the Department of Nuclear Medicine at the Royal Adelaide Hospital.

Chapter 8

The increase in validity achieved by combining BD and TBW (three-compartment model) as opposed to measuring just BD (two-compartment model) is highlighted in Figure 6 where %BF differences between these two models are graphed against the %BFs via the four-compartment criterion model which is described later in this chapter. The deviations from the horizontal dotted line at zero on the Y axis in Figure 6 represent the large errors (range = −1.3 to 6.1% BF) that occur when the experimenter does not control for biological variability in TBW but instead makes the two-compartment UWW assumption that the FFM hydration is 73.7% (Table 2). The variability of these errors was due to the wide range for FFM hydration which Figure 7 indicates was from 70.1 to 75.1 % (mean ± SD: 72.1 ± 1.1%). This figure also clearly demonstrates a negative linear relationship between FFM hydration and differences between the two models. This is because, all other things being equal, the FFM density increases as its hydration decreases below the two-compartment UWW assumed constant of 73.7% since water has by far the lowest density of any of the four FFM components. Hence, as the FFM density increases above the assumed constant of 1.1000 g.cm^{-3}, the greater the extent to which the two-compartment UWW model will underestimate the %BF. The converse occurs as the FFM hydration increases above 73.7%; this applies to two data points in Figure 7. Notwithstanding the lack of independence between the variables on both axes of Figures 6 and 7, the data indicate that the three-compartment model is more valid than the two-compartment one because it controls for inter-individual variability in TBW which has by far the largest fraction and lowest density of the four FFM components.

2.2.2 Lohman

Lohman (1986) used the same conceptual framework as Siri (1961; see our Figure 5) to derive the following three-compartment (fat, mineral, protein + water) model:

$$\%BF = \frac{638.6}{BD} + 396.1m - 609.0$$

where m = mineral as a fraction of body mass.

This model assumes fat, mineral and protein plus water densities of 0.9007, 3.037 and 1.0486 g.cm^{-3}, respectively (Lohman, 1992, p.19). The investigator acknowledged that, while the equation is not ideal for children and youths because of known changes in the water to protein ratio throughout growth, it may be useful for adult and aging subjects. The advantage of this model over two-compartment hydrodensitometry is that it accounts for biological variability in BM which comprises ~5.6% of the FFM with the relatively high density of 2.982 g.cm⁻³. Nevertheless, the discussion in section 3.2.1 demonstrates that for some groups little extra accuracy is achieved by measuring BM.

2.3 Summary

The three-compartment Siri equation (1961) appears to be the most logical one to use since it accounts for biological variability in TBW. The error analyses in Table 3 accordingly emphasise its superiority over two-compartment models. Nevertheless, the Lohman equation (1986) is an improvement on the two-compartment hydrodensitometry model.

3 Four-compartment models

3.1 Introduction

The two following four-compartment models are logical extensions of the previously discussed three-compartment models in that they control for inter-individual variability in more than one of the four FFM components.

3.2 The models

3.2.1 Model I

The advent of DPA, and its successor DEXA, provided an impetus to body composition research because they enabled the bone mineral mass to be measured *in vivo*. This technique is described in the literature (Mazess, Peppler & Gibbons, 1984; Mazess, Barden, Bisek & Hanson, 1990). Current technology exposes the subject to less than one fifth (0.3 μSv) of one day's background radiation (~ 2 μSv). The bone mineral content (BMC) measured by DEXA represents ashed bone (Friedl et al., 1992). Méndez et al. (1960) have reported that one gram of bone mineral yields 0.9582 g of ash because labile components such as bound H_2O and CO_2 are lost during heating at over 500°C (Heymsfield et al., 1989b). The BMC or bone ash therefore needs to be converted to BM by increasing it by 4.36% (Brozek et al., 1963; Heymsfield et al., 1989a; 1989b). Reliability trials for BM using DEXA conducted at the Royal Adelaide Hospital's Department of Nuclear Medicine on six subjects produced an intraclass correlation coefficient of 0.998 and a TEM of 25 g or 0.9% (Figure 8).

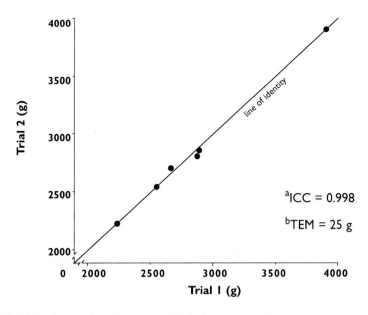

Figure 8 Reliability data (n=6) for bone mineral via dual-energy x-ray absorptiometry. [a]ICC = Intraclass correlation coefficient, [b]TEM = Technical error of measurement.

It is therefore possible to propose a four-compartment model (fat, water, BM, residual) which is based on measurements of BD, TBW and BM. In this model the masses and volumes for water and BM are subtracted from the mass and volume (mass/density) of the whole body thereby enabling the remainder to be partitioned into two compartments (FM and residual) of known or assumed densities. This model is outlined in Figure 1 and the formula is derived in Figure 9.

Similar four-compartment models have been proposed by other investigators (Baumgartner et al., 1991; Friedl et al., 1992; Fuller, Jebb, Laskey, Coward & Elia, 1992; Heymsfield et al., 1990; Lohman, 1986) who also measured BD, TBW and BM. Most of these workers estimated the NBM from the ratio of this variable to BM for the classical cadaver analyses (Table 2) to yield a value for total body mineral and they then partitioned the remainder into fat and protein compartments. However, Friedl et al. (1992) used a residual compartment (mainly protein, some non-osseous mineral, some glycogen) with a density of 1.39 g.cm^{-3} which is based on actual measurements conducted by Allen, Krzywicki and Roberts (1959) on animal and human tissue samples at 15 and 37°C. The combined density of protein and NBM for the data in Table 2 is also 1.39 g.cm^{-3}. Nevertheless, we prefer instead to base our residual density on the 364 tissue samples which were measured at 37°C (Allen et al., 1959). These data yield a residual density of 1.404 g.cm^{-3}. The slightly higher density of this dry fat-free and bone-free compartment compared with that for the combination of protein and NBM in Table 2 may be due to the small glycogen component (glucose $=1.562$ g.cm^{-3}; Weast, 1975, C-311).

$$\frac{1}{BD} = \frac{FM}{FM_{density}} + \frac{{}^{b}W}{W_{density}} + \frac{BM}{BM_{density}} + \frac{R}{R_{density}}$$

$$FM = FM_{density}\left[\frac{1}{BD} - \frac{W}{W_{density}} - \frac{BM}{BM_{density}} - \left(\frac{1-FM-W-BM}{R_{density}}\right)\right]$$

$$FM = 0.9007\left[\frac{1}{BD} - \frac{W}{0.9937} - \frac{BM}{2.982} - \left(\frac{1-FM-W-BM}{1.404}\right)\right]$$

$$FM = \frac{0.9007}{BD} - 0.906410\ W - 0.302046\ BM - 0.641524 + 0.641524\ FM$$

$$+ 0.641524\ W + 0.641524\ BM$$

$$0.358476\ FM = \frac{0.9007}{BD} - 0.264886\ W + 0.339478\ BM - 0.641524$$

$$FM = \frac{2.512581}{BD} - 0.738923\ W + 0.947003\ BM - 1.789587$$

$$\%FM\ \ \text{or}\ \ \%BF = \frac{251.3}{BD} - 73.9\ {}^{g}W + 94.7\ {}^{h}BM - 179.0$$

Figure 9 Derivation of the four-compartment model ([a]FM, [b]TBW, [c]BM, [d]R) for estimating relative body fat from measurements of [e]BD, TBW and BM.

Assumptions:

Density of FM = 0.9007 g.cm^{-3} at 36°C (Fidanza et al., 1953)
Density of water (W) = 0.9937 g.cm^{-3} at 36°C (Lentner, 1981, 50; Weast, 1975, F-5)
Density of bone mineral (BM) = 2.982 g.cm^{-3} (Méndez et al., 1960)
Density[f] of residual (R) = 1.404 g.cm^{-3} (Allen et al., 1959)

If the body mass (kg) is equal to unity (i.e. 1) and the four compartments are represented as proportions such that FM + W + BM + R = 1.0 then the formula can be most simply derived as shown above, where [a]FM = fat mass; [b]TBW or W = total body water; [c]BM = bone mineral; [d]R = residual; [e]BD = body density; [f]weighted mean calculated from Allen et al. (1959) for 37°C samples; [g]W = W (kg)/body mass (kg); [h]BM = BMC or ashed bone from DEXA printout x 1.0436 (kg)/body mass (kg).

The three and four-compartment models are theoretically more valid than the two-compartment ones because they are associated with less error when the proportions of water, protein and mineral in the FFM vary from those indicated in Table 2. However, when the %BF differences between the four-compartment and three-compartment models are graphed against the %BF from the four-compartment criterion model (Figure 10) then the individual deviations from zero on the ordinate are very small (range = −0.4 to 0.8%BF). These differences from zero represent the error remaining after control for inter-individual variability in TBW but not BM. Clearly little extra accuracy is achieved by measuring BM. The different effects for control of biological variability in TBW and BM (compare Figures 6 and 10) are primarily due to the overall BM/FFM (%) of 5.92% (SD = 0.48%) being much closer to the classical cadaver value of 5.63% than the corresponding values of 72.1 ± 1.1% and 73.72%, respectively, for FFM hydration. A secondary consideration is that the variability as a %FFM is greater for TBW (SD = 1.1% FFM) than for BM (SD = 0.48%).

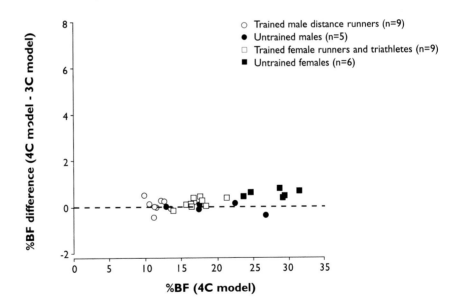

Figure 10 %BF differences between the 4 and 3 compartment (C) models graphed against the %BF via the 4 compartment model.

Data on these 18–36-year-old subjects ($\bar{X}\pm SD$: 23±5 yr) were collected in the Exercise Physiology Laboratory at the Flinders University of South Australia and the Department of Nuclear Medicine at the Royal Adelaide Hospital.

223

3.2.2 Model 2

This model is outlined in Figure 1. Cohn and coworkers (Cohn, Vaswani, Yasumura, Yuen & Ellis, 1984) at the Brookhaven National Laboratory were among the first to develop model 2 which was subsequently refined by Heymsfield et al. (1990). Three components (TBW, protein, combination of BM and NBM) of the FFM shown in the classical cadaver analysis of Figure 1 are measured and then subtracted from the body mass to yield the FM:

- TBW – determined by tritium dilution (^3H_2O) using the same principles formerly outlined for deuterium dilution (^2H_2O). This tracer exposes the subjects to a radiation dose of 120 μSv (Heymsfield et al., 1991).
- Protein – total body nitrogen is measured by prompt gamma neutron activation analysis (radiation exposure = 260 μSv; Heymsfield & Waki, 1991). As previously explained, protein is estimated by assuming a P/N ratio of 6.25.
- Total body mineral – total body calcium, sodium and chloride are determined by delayed gamma neutron activation analysis which results in a total radiation exposure of 2,500 μSv (Heymsfield & Waki, 1991). TBK is estimated using the Brookhaven whole-body counter. Various assumptions then enable the total body mineral to be estimated.

Model 2 therefore involves exposing the subject to considerably more radiation than Model 1 (2,800 μSv versus 0.3 μSv). Furthermore, it is much less available worldwide and is both more complex and expensive to implement.

3.3 Summary

Four-compartment chemical models of body composition analysis are theoretically more valid than their three- and two-compartment counterparts because of their additional control for biological variability of FFM components. This is emphasised in the theoretical error analysis of these models in Table 3. Clearly most of the increase in validity results from upgrading the two-compartment model to a three-compartment one. The additional measurement of BM provides only a small increase in accuracy. While the *in vivo* proportions of two or more FFM components may differ simultaneously from those for the classical cadavers (Table 2), a simplistic model has been adopted for Table 3 in which each component differs independently of the other three. In conclusion, there is some concern that the resultant extra control over the biological variability of the FFM may be offset somewhat by the propagation of measurement error associated with the determinations of BD, TBW and BM.

This total or propagated error can be calculated by assuming that the squared errors or error variances (standard error of estimate^2 [SEE^2] or TEM^2) are independent and additive:

$$SD \; of \; total \; error \; = \; \sqrt{SEE_a^2 + SEE_b^2 + SEE_c^2} \quad or \quad \sqrt{TEM_a^2 + TEM_b^2 + TEM_c^2}$$

where:
a = calculation of %BF from BD
b = calculation of %BF from TBW
c = the effect of bone mineral on %BF

Test retest reliability data collected in our laboratory yield standard deviations for propagated or total error of 0.9 and 0.6% BF for the SEE and TEM, respectively. The SEE includes both between- and within-subject error variance whereas the TEM, which is defined as the standard error of a single measurement (Dahlberg, 1940: pp. 122–132), considers only the latter. Hence the standard deviation for the total error via TEM < SEE. Nevertheless, these errors are much less than that due to biological variability in FFM density (SD = 3.8% BF) when body composition is estimated via the two-compartment hydrodensitometry method (Siri, 1956; 1961). Our propagated errors may well represent the technical limit of precision for the estimation of body composition via the indirect four-compartment method. However, while great confidence can be placed in the values used for the densities of water and chemically extracted fat, there will be some unaccounted error due to four-compartment model assumptions such as those for the densities of protein, BM and NBM, the validity of the BMC measurements and the use of a 4% correction factor for non-aqueous hydrogen exchange when estimating the TBW via deuterium dilution.

4   More complex models and future developments

More sophisticated five-compartment (Ryde, Birks, Morgan, Evans & Dutton, 1993) and total body carbon (TBC; Heymsfield et al., 1991) chemical models have emerged. The latter method is worthy of further comment because it currently represents state of the art for body composition analysis. This method is based on the observation that body carbon is incorporated in four compartments at the molecular level: fat, protein, glycogen and BM. The TBC method was derived from the following four simultaneous models where all units are in kilograms:

(1)   TBC = 0.77 × fat + 0.532 × protein + 0.444 × glycogen + carbon in BM

(2)   TBN = 0.16 × protein

(3)   Glycogen = 0.044 × protein

(4)   Carbon in BM = 0.05 × TBCa

The simultaneous equations can be solved:
(5)   fat = 1.30 × TBC − 4.45 × TBN − 0.06 × TBCa

In equation 5, TBC, TBCa and TBN are total body carbon, calcium and nitrogen which are measured by inelastic scattering, delayed gamma and prompt gamma neutron activation analyses, respectively. The TBC method has two intrinsic features: it is based on highly stable models that are not affected to an appreciable degree by age, gender or ethnicity and it provides fat estimates that are independent of the classical two-compartment methods. While the propagated error for the TBC method of measuring body fat is 3.4 – 4.0%, the investigators (Heymsfield et al., 1991) aim to develop the method towards a precision and accuracy which are equal or superior to direct chemical analyses of cadavers. Therefore, although the TBC method is not used widely due to the need for three neutron activation systems, it is important in the overall study of human body composition.

Powerful new technologies are also being introduced that promise to expand measurement possibilities to such hitherto unmeasured variables as skeletal muscle and glycogen. The study of body composition therefore offers vast potential for future research.

5   References

Allen, T.H., Krzywicki, H.J., & Roberts, J.E. (1959).
    Density, fat, water and solids in freshly isolated tissues.
    Journal of Applied Physiology, 14, 1005-1008.

Baumgartner, R.N., Heymsfield, S.B., Lichtman, S., Wang, J., & Pierson, R.N. (1991).
    Body composition in elderly people: effect of criterion estimates on predictive equations.
    American Journal of Clinical Nutrition, 53, 1345-1353.

Brozek, J., Grande, F., Anderson, J.T., & Keys, A. (1963).
Densitometric analysis of body composition: revision of some quantitative assumptions.
Annals of the New York Academy of Sciences, 110, 113-140.

Burton, A.C. (1935).
Human calorimetry II. The average temperature of the tissues of the body.
Journal of Nutrition, 9, 261-279.

Buskirk, E.R. (1961).
Underwater weighing and body density: a review of procedures.
In J. Brozek & A. Henschel (Eds.), **Techniques for measuring body composition** (pp. 90-106).
Washington DC: National Academy of Sciences – National Research Council.

Cohn, S.H., Vaswani, A.N., Yasumura, S., Yuen, M.S., & Ellis, K.J. (1984).
Improved models for determination of body fat by *in vivo* neutron activation.
American Journal of Clinical Nutrition, 40, 255-259.

Coward, A. (1990).
Calculation of pool sizes and flux rates.
In A.M. Prentice (Ed.), **The doubly-labelled water method for measuring energy expenditure** (pp. 48-68).
Vienna: International Atomic Energy Agency.

Culebras, J.M., & Moore, F.D. (1977).
Total body water and the exchangeable hydrogen. I. Theoretical calculation of nonaqueous exchangeable hydrogen in man.
American Journal of Physiology (Regulatory, Integrative and Comparative Physiology), 232, R54-R59.

Dahlberg, G. (1940).
Statistical methods for medical and biological students.
London: George Allen and Unwin Ltd.

Dallemagne, M.J., & Melon, J. (1945).
Le poids spécifique et l'indice de réfraction de l'os, de l'émail, de la dentine et du cément.
Bulletin de la Société de chimie biologique, 27, 85-89.

Deurenberg, P., Weststrate, J.A., & van der Kooy, K. (1989).
Is an adaptation of Siri's formula for the calculation of body fat percentage from body density in the elderly necessary?
European Journal of Clinical Nutrition, 43, 559-568.

Fidanza, F., Keys, A., & Anderson, J.T. (1953).
Density of body fat in man and other mammals.
Journal of Applied Physiology, 6, 252-256.

Forbes, G.B., & Lewis, A.M. (1956).
Total sodium, potassium and chloride in adult man.
Journal of Clinical Investigation, 35, 596-600.

Forbes, G.B., Gallup, J., & Hursh, J.B. (1961).
Estimation of total body fat from potassium-40 content.
Science, 133, 101-102.

Forbes, G.B. (1987).
Human body composition: growth, aging, nutrition, and activity (p. 39).
New York: Springer-Verlag.

Friedl, K.E., DeLuca, J.P., Marchitelli, L. J., Vogel, J.A. (1992).
Reliability of body-fat estimations from a four-component model by using density, body water, and bone mineral measurements.
American Journal of Clinical Nutrition, 55, 764-770.

Fuller, N.J., Jebb, S.A., Laskey, M.A., Coward, W.A., & Elia, M. (1992).
Four-component model for the assessment of body composition in humans: comparison with alternative methods, and evaluation of the density and hydration of fat-free mass.
Clinical Science, 82, 687-693.

Garrow, J.S., Stalley, S., Diethelm, R., Pittett, P.H., Hesp, R., & Halliday, D. (1979).
A new method for measuring the body density of obese adults.
British Journal of Nutrition, 42,173-183.

Gundlach, B.L., & Visscher, G.J.W. (1986).
The plethysmographic measurement of total body volume.
Human Biology, 58, 783-799.

Haschke, F., Fomon, S.L., & Ziegler, E.E. (1981).
Body composition of a nine-year-old reference boy.
Pediatric Research, 15, 847-849.

Haurowitz, F. (1963).
The chemistry and function of proteins (p. 119)
New York: Academic Press.

Hewitt, M.J., Going, S.B., Williams, D.P., & Lohman, T.G. (1993).
Hydration of the fat-free body mass in children and adults: implications for body composition assessment.
American Journal of Physiology (Endocrinology and Metabolism), 265, E88-E95.

Heymsfield, S.B., Wang, J., Kehayias, J., Heshka, S., Lichtman, S., & Pierson, R.N. (1989a).
Chemical determination of human body density *in vivo*: relevance to hydrodensitometry.
American Journal of Clinical Nutrition, 50, 1282-1289.

Heymsfield, S.B., Wang, J., Lichtman, S., Kamen, Y., Kehayias, J., & Pierson, R.N. (1989b).
Body composition in elderly subjects: a critical appraisal of clinical methodology.
American Journal of Clinical Nutrition, 50, 1167-1175.

Heymsfield, S.B., Lichtman, S., Baumgartner, R.N., Wang, J., Kamen, Y., Aliprantis, A., & Pierson, R.N. (1990).
Body composition of humans: comparison of two improved four-compartment models that differ in expense, technical complexity, and radiation exposure.
American Journal of Clinical Nutrition, 52, 52-58.

Heymsfield, S.B., Waki, M., Kehayias, J., Lichtman, S., Dilmanian, F.A., Kamen, Y., Wang, J., & Pierson, R.N. (1991).
Chemical and elemental analysis of humans *in vivo* using improved body composition models.
American Journal of Physiology (Endocrinology and Metabolism), 261, E190-E198.

Heymsfield, S.B., & Waki, M. (1991).
Body composition in humans: advances in the development of multicompartment chemical models.
Nutrition Reviews, 49, 97-108.

Heymsfield, S.B., Wang, Z.M., & Withers, R.T. (in press).
Multicompartment molecular-level models of body composition analysis.
In A.F. Roche, S.B. Heymsfield, & T.G. Lohman (Eds.), **Human body composition.**
Champaign, IL: Human Kinetics.

Hulmes, D.J.S., & Miller, A. (1979).
Quasi-hexagonal molecular packing in collagen fibrils.
Nature (London), 282, 878-880.

Keys, A., & Brozek, J. (1953).
Body fat in adult man.
Physiological Reviews, 33, 245-325.

Knight, G.S., Beddoe, A.H. Streat, S.J., & Hill, G.L. (1986).
Body composition of two human cadavers by neutron activation and chemical analysis.
American Journal of Physiology (Endocrinology and Metabolism), 250, E179-E185.

Lentner, C. (Ed.). (1981).
Geigy scientific tables: Vol. 1. Units of measurement, body fluids, composition of the body, nutrition.
Basle: Ciba Geigy Ltd.

Lifson, N., Gordon, G.B., & McClintock, R. (1955).
Measurement of total carbon dioxide production by means of D_2O^{18}.
Journal of Applied Physiology, 7, 704-710.

Lohman, T.G. (1981).
Skinfolds and body density and their relation to body fatness: a review.
Human Biology, 53, 181-225.

Lohman, T.G. (1986).
Applicability of body composition techniques and constants for children and youths (1986).
In K.B. Pandolf (Ed.), **Exercise and Sport Sciences Reviews, Volume 14** (pp. 325-357).
New York: Macmillan Publishing Company.

Lohman, T.G. (1992).
Advances in body composition assessment.
Champaign, Illinois: Human Kinetics Publishers.

Mazess, R.B., Peppler, W.W., & Gibbons, M. (1984).
Total body composition by dual-photon (^{153}Gd) absorptiometry.
American Journal of Clinical Nutrition, 40, 834-839.

Mazess, R.B., Barden, H.S., Bisek, J.P., & Hanson, J. (1990).
Dual-energy X-ray absorptiometry for total body and regional bone-mineral and soft-tissue composition.
American Journal of Clinical Nutrition, 51, 1106-1112.

Méndez, J., Keys, A., Anderson, J.T., & Grande, F. (1960).
Density of fat and bone mineral of the mammalian body.
Metabolism, 9, 472-477.

Mitchell, H.H., Hamilton, T.S., Steggerda, F.R., & Bean, H.W. (1945).
> The chemical composition of the adult human body and its bearing on the biochemistry of growth.
> **Journal of Biological Chemistry, 158,** 625-637.

Nagy, K.A. (1980).
> CO_2 production in animals: analysis of potential errors in the doubly labelled water method.
> **American Journal of Physiology (Regulatory, Integrative and Comparative Physiology), 238,** R466-R473.

Ryde, S.J.S., Birks, J.L., Morgan, W.D., Evans, C.J., & Dutton, J. (1993).
> A five-compartment model of body composition of healthy subjects assessed using *in vivo* neutron activation analysis.
> **European Journal of Clinical Nutrition, 47,** 863-874.

Schoeller, D.A., van Santen, E., Peterson, D., Dietz, W., Jaspan, J., & Klein, P.D. (1980).
> Total body water measurements in humans with ^{18}O and ^2H labelled water.
> **American Journal of Clinical Nutrition, 33,** 2686-2693.

Schoeller, D.A., Kushner, R.F., Taylor, P., Dietz, W.H., & Bandini, L. (1985).
> Measurement of total body water: isotope dilution techniques.
> In **Report of 6th Ross Conference on medical research: body composition assessments in youth and adults** (pp. 24-29). Columbus, OH: Ross Laboratories.

Schoeller, D.A., & Jones, P.J.H. (1987).
> Measurement of total body water by isotope dilution: a unified approach to calculations.
> In K.J. Ellis, S. Yasumura & W.D. Morgan (Eds.), **In vivo body composition studies** (pp. 131-137).
> London: Institute of Physical Sciences in Medicine.

Shohl, A.T. (1939).
> **Mineral metabolism** (pp. 13-21)
> New York: Reinhold Publishing Corporation.

Siri, W.E. (1956)
> The gross composition of the body.
> In J.H. Lawrence & C.A. Tobias (Eds.), **Advances in biological and medical physics** (pp. 239-280). New York: Academic Press Inc.

Siri, W.E. (1961).
> Body composition from fluid spaces and density: analysis of methods.
> In J. Brozek & A. Henschel (Eds.), **Techniques for measuring body composition** (pp. 223-244).
> Washington DC: National Academy of Sciences – National Research Council.

Snyder, W.S. (Chairman.) (1975).
> **Report of the Task Group on Reference Man.**
> New York: Pergamon Press.

Weast, R.C. (Ed.). (1975).
> **Handbook of chemistry and physics.**
> Cleveland: CRC Press.

Whyte, R.K., Bayley, H.S., & Schwarcz, H.P. (1985).
> The measurement of whole body water by $H_2^{18}O$ dilution in newborn pigs.
> **American Journal of Clinical Nutrition, 41,** 801-809.

Widdowson, E.M., McCance, R.A., & Spray, C.M. (1951).
>   The chemical composition of the human body.
>   **Clinical Science, 10,** 113-125.

Withers, R.T., & Hamdorf, P.A. (1989).
>   Effect of immersion on lung capacities and volumes: implications for the densitometric estimation of relative body fat.
>   **Journal of Sports Sciences, 7,** 21-30.

Withers, R.T., Smith, D.A., Chatterton, B.E., Schultz, C.G., & Gaffney, R.D. (1992).
>   A comparison of four methods of estimating the body composition of male endurance athletes.
>   **European Journal of Clinical Nutrition, 46,** 773-784.

Womersley, J., Durnin, J.V.G.A., Boddy, K., & Mahaffy, M. (1976).
>   Influence of muscular development, obesity, and age on the fat-free mass of adults.
>   **Journal of Applied Physiology, 41,** 223-229.

Wong, W.W., Cochran, W.J., Klish, W.J., Smith, E.O., Lee, L.S., & Klein, P.D. (1988).
>   In vivo isotope-fractionation factors and the measurement of deuterium- and oxygen-18-dilution spaces from plasma, urine, saliva, respiratory water vapor, and carbon dioxide.
>   **American Journal of Clinical Nutrition, 47,** 1-6.

applications for anthropometry

Chapter 9
The Psychology and Anthropometry of Body Image

Shelley Kay

1 What is "body image"?

"Body image" is a multidimensional construct broadly describing internal, subjective representations of physical appearance and bodily experience (Cash & Pruzinsky, 1990). Body image includes perceptual, cognitive and affective elements of how we internally represent our own bodies and the bodies of others. "Perceptual" here refers to visuo-spatial and other sensory judgments. "Cognitive" refers to thought processes and thinking styles, while the "affective" dimension refers to emotions and attitudes. These representations are perhaps primarily visual, but include influences from kinæsthetic, tactile and other sensory constructs. At any point in time, persons may be simultaneously monitoring such different aspects of their body as its apparent attractiveness, position in space, boundary security, relative prominence in the total perceptual field, variations in the size attributes of its different parts and so forth (Fisher, 1990).

An analysis of body image therefore involves comparing two sets of mental constructs: mental representations of our own bodies and the bodies of others. Anthropometry provides a tool to objectively quantify our own body size, shape and composition, and the size, shape and body composition of others.

Figure 1 shows the interaction of factors related to body image. Our own bodies ("self") have both an objective anthropometric representation (a set of skinfold, length, girth and breadth measures) and a perceptual, cognitive and affective representation. This mental representation is affected by influences such as gender, mass media and heredity, and also by known objective anthropometric values. Similarly, the bodies of others (by "others" we mean the general population, and specific subpopulations, such as models, sportspeople, the obese and other groups important to our body sense) have both objective and subjective representations. Once again, our subjective representations of the bodies of others are affected by gender, mass media and heredity, as well as by our knowledge of their actual size and shape. We compare the representations we have of our own bodies with the representations of the bodies of others. The congruence or incongruence of these representations is judged in relation to a number of dynamic setpoints, and trigger personal and inter-personal behaviours (exercise, diet, sex, etc). The way we compare representations and the nature of the setpoints are also affected by factors relating to gender and cultural experiences.

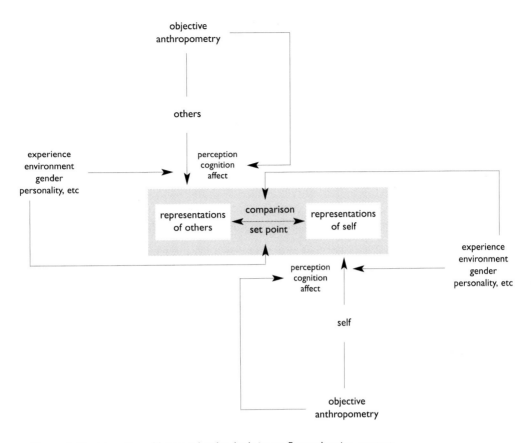

Figure 1 The interaction of factors related to body image. For explanation, see text.

2 Methodological considerations

The central areas of interest in body image research are
- the description and quantification of the internal representations we have of self and others;
- the nature of the relationship between the mental representation of self, and the mental representation of others, and
- the relationship between the mental constructs of self and others, and the objective realities.

In order to answer these questions, we need to employ some representational medium which will externalise the internal models of the bodies of self and others.

2.1 Methods of body image assessment

Instruments designed to assess body image fall into two broad classes. One group of instruments is involved with size estimation (a perceptual dimension). These instruments are usually visuo-spatial. The other group of instruments deals with subjective evaluations of attitudes and cognitions (cognitive and affective dimensions). These are usually questionnaires. The perceptual and cognitive-affective dimensions of body image may be independent. While body size estimation is the facet of body image which has the most direct links with anthropometry, it is important to distinguish *concern* about body shape and body *satisfaction* from body size estimation. One can be quite accurate in one's perception of one's own size and shape, and yet still be dissatisfied. For example, the degree to which men and women overestimate their body size is not correlated with their level of body dissatisfaction (Dolan, Birtchnell & Lacey, 1987). Equally, it is possible to be very satisfied with one's size and shape, and yet still exhibit a high degree of concern about the body (e.g. body-centred behaviour).

Among those methods which are commonly employed are:
- *the distorted image technique* which manipulates the size of a photograph (Glucksman & Hirsch, 1969), video (Alleback, Hallberg & Espmark, 1976) or mirror image (Traub & Orbach, 1964) of the subject's whole body;
- *figure drawings* representing physiques from lean to obese with reference to Body Mass Index (Stunkard & Stellar, 1990);
- *adjusting widths* to match perceived body breadths, for example by manipulating sliding calipers (Slade & Russel, 1973) or changing the width of a light beam (Thompson & Spana, 1990); and questionnaires such as
- the *Body Esteem Scale* (Franzoi & Shields, 1984);
- the *Social Physique Anxiety Scale* (Hart, Leary & Rejeski, 1989);
- the *Body Cathexis Scale* (Secord & Jourard, 1953);
- the *Body Dissatisfaction Questionnaire* (Garner & Garfinkel, 1979) and
- the *Body Shape Questionnaire* (Cooper, Taylor, Cooper & Fairburn, 1987).

Since we do not have direct access to the mental models people have of their own bodies (Are they primarily visual? Two-dimensional? Three-dimensional?), it is difficult to choose the best representational medium which allows that mental model to be translated into an external form and compared to anthropometric measurements. Relationships between actual body dimensions and body image vary according to the psychometric instruments used to assess dissatisfaction, and different anthropometric indices used to represent weight or fatness (Davis, Durnin, Dionne & Gurevich, 1994).

For body image to be analysed in a meaningful way, the choice and structure of the representational medium is critical.

2.2   Minimising the influence of the medium

Ideally, the medium should be "transparent" in the sense that the medium itself will not influence how accurately one represents one's own body image (that is, how accurately one translates one's own set of mental constructs into an external form). Early studies found that anorexics overestimated their body size, which was interpreted as a measure of body image distortion (Slade & Russel, 1973). However, these findings could equally be interpreted as a perceptual problem, namely that people may often misestimate the size of objects in general, including inanimate objects. When these same tests were administered to normal women, it became evident that both eating-disordered and non-eating disordered females misjudged their body size (Thompson, 1986). A comparison of size estimation of self, another person, food cartons and a cylinder strongly supported the notion that this technique may represent general errors in perceptual estimation rather than reflect body image distortion (Hundleby & Bourgouin, 1993).

Measurement of body image distortion by redrawing images on the computer screen also fails to discriminate between eating disordered groups and normals (Gustavson et al., 1990). This may be due to the fact that neither group misestimates the size and shape of their bodies (or both do equally). It may also be that subjects may have difficulty with estimating their body on a small screen (Probst, Van Coppenolle, Vandereycken & Goris, 1992).

2.3   The structural dimensions of body image

The representational medium must be able to reflect the major structural dimensions we use in constructing body images. It is pointless to use, say, forearm girth as an analytical dimension, if (as is likely) forearm girth is not a factor in the way we construct body images. For example, many psychometric instruments fail to discriminate between total body fatness and shape. Relatively gross anthropometric measures such as body mass or body mass index (BMI) can only approximate the proportion of fat, and may obscure the influence of specific anatomical referents, regional body parts, frame size and fat distribution on body image (Bailey, Golberg, Swap, Chomitz and Houser 1990; Davis, Durnin, Gurevich, Le Maire & Dionne 1993). Girth or breadth ratios (Furner, Hester & Weir, 1990), somatotype (Tucker, 1984) and regional fat distribution (Radke-

Sharpe, Whitney-Saltiel & Rodin, 1990) have been shown to be important dimensions of our body image.

2.4 Sensitivity: just noticeable differences

The sensitivity of the external representations must match perceptual resolution. If the differences between two representations are imperceptible, or the two representations cannot be reproducibly distinguished, then the representations will not be effective in discriminating between mental constructs. Alley (1991) found that college students could not reliably distinguish between photographs of women before and after weight loss averaging 4.7% of their initial body mass. Studies in our own laboratory have shown that most people can reliably distinguish between two figures differing in

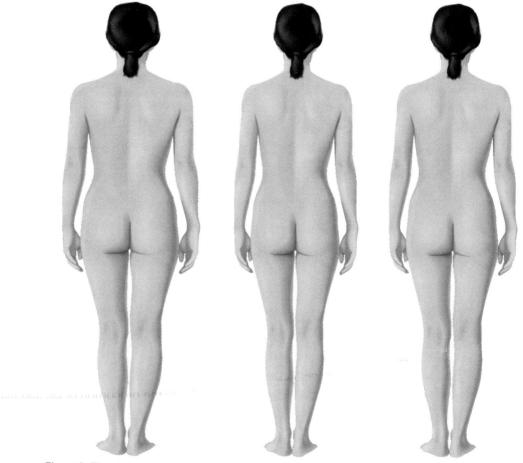

Figure 2 Three figures drawn by computer to correspond to estimated BMIs of 30, 26 and 25. Can you distinguish the figures corresponding to BMIs of 26 and 25? See end of chapter for answer.

estimated BMI by about 5%. When the difference is <2.5%, success in differentiation is no better than random (see Figure 2). For this reason, it is important to determine the just noticeable differences of the representational medium being used.

2.5 Test-retest reliability

As with all perceptual-cognitive mechanisms, body image and body satisfaction have both stable and dynamic components. There is considerable evidence that body attitudes are labile and can operate in a contextual manner with cross-situational variability (Roth & Armstrong, 1993). Satisfaction and dissatisfaction have been reported to fluctuate across situations such as being clothed, unclothed (Markee, Carey & Pedersen, 1990) or partly clothed (Haimovitz, Lansky and O'Reilly 1992), in the presence or absence of mirror feedback (Gardner, Gallegos, Martinez & Espinoza, 1989) during pre- and menstrual phase (Altabe & Thompson, 1990) and after eating foods perceived as fattening (Thompson, Coovert, Pasman & Robb, 1993). These are factors which should be controlled by rigorous assessment of test-retest reliability. Test-retest reliability varies according to the instrument used, as well as with situational contexts and subject populations. Appropriate statistical tools include the intra-class correlation coefficient, the median absolute difference and corresponding interquartile range.

2.6 Body image and anthropometric measurements

The selection of anthropometric measures must reflect body dimensions which are important in determining body image. For example, it would be pointless to use forearm girth as an analytical dimension when using line drawings if it is impossible to represent clearly differentiable forearm girths on those drawings, or if actual forearm girth cannot be validly related to a two-dimensional figure. Typically, when drawings or photos of human figures have been used, the differences between these figures have been quantified in terms of BMI (Craig & Caterson, 1990), somatotypes, mass, or girth ratios (Furner et al., 1990). However, rarely is a clear rationale given explaining how certain BMIs, somatotypes, masses or girth ratios were determined for these figures. Two-dimensional line drawings fail to represent the overall shape of the individual, the distribution of subcutaneous fat masses and other aspects of body composition which may be important in forming body image.

2.7 Anthropometric precision

A further problem is that many studies have used inexperienced anthropometrists, or have relied on self-reported data about weight and height (e.g. Gupta, Schork & Dhaliwal, 1993). Many studies have shown self-reported weight and height to be inaccurate. In one study, 34% of men and 30% of women failed to report their actual weight to within 2.3 kg. Men who misreported their mass tended to over-report it, whereas women who misreported their mass tended to under-report it (Cash, Grant, Shovlin & Lewis, 1992). An analysis of personal advertisements in an American magazine revealed a high degree of stereotypic and artificial weight and shape descriptions for both males and females seeking a companion (Anderson, Woodward, Spalder & Koss, 1993). Only 13% of white females between the ages of 34 and 44 could match the average BMI values presented as self-descriptions in these ads. In these advertisements, 97% of the females and 100% of the males described themselves as thinner than average. The application of more precise anthropometry to this area of research however, has the potential to highlight relationships with greater clarity.

3 Studies of body image

A number of external factors are known to influence the models we have of our own bodies and the bodies of others. These include age, gender, the influence of the mass media, education and genetic influences.

3.1 The influence of gender on body image

3.1.1 Body image in females

Dissatisfaction with body shape and size has become so endemic in the female population that it has been described as "normative discontent" (Rodin, Silberstein & Striegel-Moore, 1984). A large percentage of women who are of normal weight or underweight are dissatisfied with their body size (Cash, Winstead & Janda, 1986). Clothing, underwear, exercise and dieting behaviour and cosmetic surgery are often used to modify external appearance. In 1992, 350,000 cosmetic surgical operations were performed in the USA, 87% involving women. More than 150,000 Australians have had liposuction since 1983, of whom 95% are women ("The lowdown on liposuction", *She* magazine, 1994).

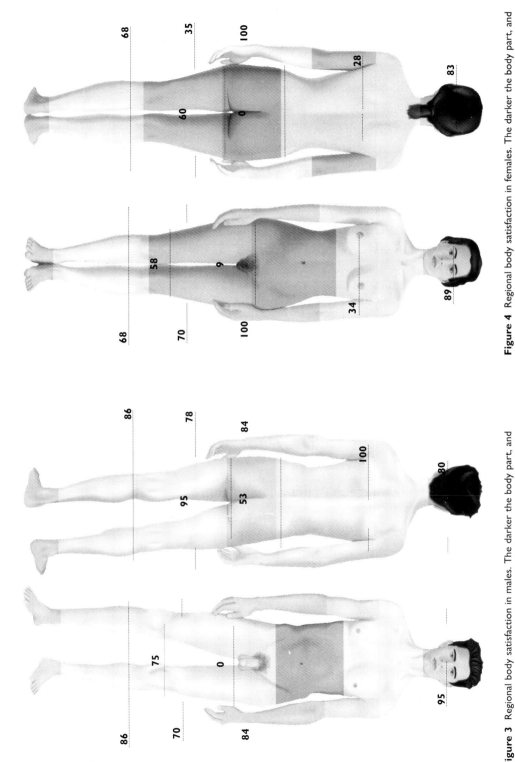

Figure 3 Regional body satisfaction in males. The darker the body part, and the lower the rating, the less satisfied subjects are with that body region.

Figure 4 Regional body satisfaction in females. The darker the body part, and the lower the rating, the less satisfied subjects are with that body region.

Women generally prefer a decidedly ectomorphic shape. The specific areas of concern for women are the waist, thighs, buttocks, legs, and stomach, with the dominant focus of concern being the hip and buttocks region. A study of adolescent girls reported slender and narrow hips as the single most desired feature (Davies & Furnham, 1986). The only girth measurement to decrease in Miss America contestants from 1959–1985 was hip size (Wiseman, Gray, Mosimann & Ahrens, 1992), despite an increase in the overall size of the general population. Researchers have measured greater body dissatisfaction in women with fat distributed in the hips and buttocks than those with more abdominal distribution (Radke-Sharpe et al., 1990). This concern, however, is not necessarily proportional to the amount of fat in these areas. Even thin subjects report dissatisfaction with their hip circumference (Bailey et al., 1990). These studies show that body dissatisfaction focuses on specific regions, and the relationship between specific regions. Girth ratios such as the chest-to-waist ratio and the waist-to-hip ratio may be useful anthropometric correlates of dissatisfaction.

Figures 3 and 4 show the results of a small survey conducted in our laboratory. Gym attendees and university students (n = 48) were asked to rate their satisfaction with various body regions on a scale of 0 (completely dissatisfied) to 10 (totally satisfied). An unrotated factor matrix was used to determine weightings for individual ratings, and mean weighted scores were adjusted to span a range of values from 0 to 100. For females, the areas of deep concern were the buttocks and the abdominal region, and also the front and rear thighs and triceps. For males, the abdominal region was the major zone of dissatisfaction.

3.1.2 Body image in males

Although dissatisfaction with body size and shape has been widely reported to be less pronounced in men than women, a large survey found that 41% of men and 53% of women were dissatisfied with their weight (Cash et al., 1986). A study of physically active men and women also demonstrated equal gender dissatisfaction with weight. While most women wanted to lose weight, men were evenly divided between those who wanted to lose and those who wanted to gain weight (Davis & Cowles, 1991). Similarly, a study of 18 year old college men showed an even split between those who desired weight loss and those who wished to gain weight (Drewnowski & Yee, 1987). The two opposite directions may cancel each other out, and lead to the mistaken interpretation that males have no dissatisfaction. Therefore, when analysing these data, absolute differences as well as directional differences between ideal and actual characteristics should be considered.

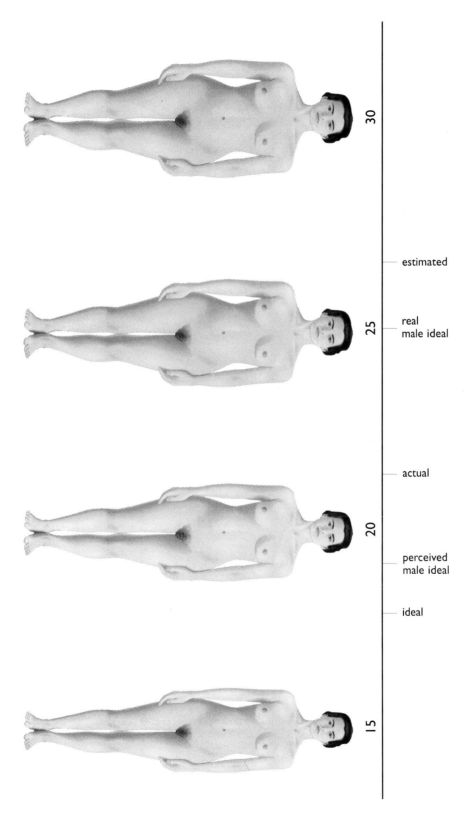

Figure 5 Female body sizes corresponding to the actual size of subjects ("actual"), the size they think they are ("estimated"), their ideal size ("ideal"), the size they believe men would consider ideal ("perceived male ideal") and the size men actually consider ideal ("real male ideal"). Body size is quantified in BMI units. Data have been collected in our laboratory.

245

246

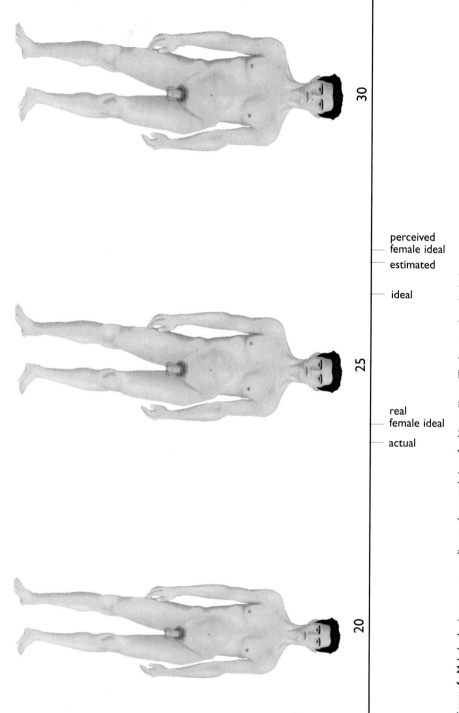

perceived
female ideal
estimated

ideal

real
female ideal

actual

30   25   20

Figure 6 Male body sizes corresponding to the actual size of subjects ("actual"), the size they think they are ("estimated"), their ideal size ("ideal"), the size they believe women would consider ideal ("perceived female ideal") and the size women actually consider ideal ("real female ideal"). Body size is quantified in BMI units. Data have been collected in our laboratory.

A consistent finding is that men desire a mesomorphic build (Tucker, 1984). Males are more concerned with gaining muscle mass, while women are mainly concerned with losing fat. Men are specifically concerned with upper body muscularity, the width of the shoulders, the arms and the chest (Franzoi & Shields, 1984).

The male homosexual subculture promotes a lean, muscular ideal, and in one study homosexual men indicated greater dissatisfaction with body build than heterosexual men (Mishkind, Rodin, Silberstein & Striegel-Moore, 1986). Homosexual men may therefore be at greater risk of eating disorders than their heterosexual counterparts (Striegel-Moore, Silberstein & Rodin, 1986).

There is a considerable misunderstanding among both genders about the kind of build the other gender actually prefers. Women believe that men prefer women with a thinner build than men actually do prefer. Men believe that women prefer men with a more muscular physique than women actually do prefer (Fallon & Rozin, 1985; see Figures 5 and 6).

3.2 The influence of age on body image

Girls as young as five years of age have expressed fears of gaining weight (Feldman, Feldman & Goodman, 1988). Concern with appearance peaks in the teens and twenties. Some studies have found that concern with appearance decreases with age (Cash et al., 1986), while others have found that the desire for a thinner shape may persist into older age (Davis & Cowles, 1991; Hallinan & Schuler, 1993). A study of parents and children showed little difference between the generations in body dissatisfaction, despite persisting gender differences (Rozin & Fallon, 1988). Gupta & Schork (1993) concluded that women, and to a lesser extent men, who were concerned about the effects of aging on appearance also tended to be preoccupied with weight loss.

3.3 The influence of the mass media on body image

Our perceptions of our own bodies are filtered through a number of normative images presented to us in the popular media. These "public" and normative body images define ideals of beauty, health and fitness. Some prescribe current ideals of sexual attractiveness. Others prescribe body shapes and sizes which are optimal for health, or describe typical or "average" humans. Objective indices of normal or healthy ranges often fail to influence how people judge their own bodies. People tend to be much more influenced by the values of extreme subgroups, such as models and sports people.

From childhood, boys and girls are exposed to representations of body stereotypes through many psychosocial influences. Dolls, movie stars, models, dancers and sporting heroes represent a glamorous association with particular body types. For example, Barbie is considered by its manufacturers as an "aspirational role model" for girls (Pedersen & Markee, 1991). Achieving the proportions of Barbie scaled using geometrical similarity to "life size" would be biologically impossible. Both Barbie and Ken's proportions deviate dramatically from adult reference groups, general population, models and anorexics, showing z scores sometimes in excess of 13 (Norton, Olds, Olive & Dank, 1994; see Figure 7). The same authors calculated that Ken (an "action figure", not a doll !) represents an ectomorphic somatotype, the difference being that the deviations from reference groups, general population and footballers are less striking but nonetheless significant (Figure 8).

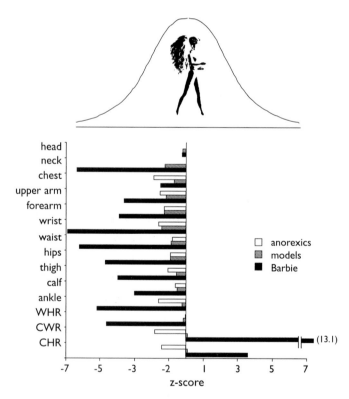

Figure 7 z-scores relative to mean values for 135 17–35 year-old South Australian females for various height-adjusted anthropometric measurements. z-scores are shown for a group of catwalk models, anorexics and the Barbie doll (Norton et al., 1994). WHR = waist-hip ratio, CWR = chest-waist ratio and CHR = chest-hip ratio

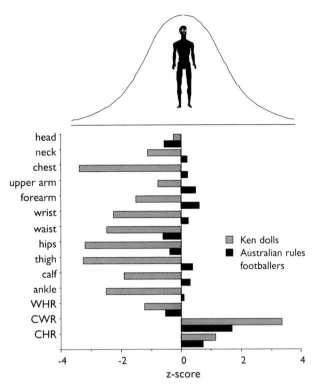

Figure 8 z-scores relative to mean values for 18–29 year old Australian males for various height-adjusted anthropometric measurements. z-scores are shown for a group of 22 Australian Rules footballers and the Ken doll (Norton et al., 1994). See Figure 7 for details.

The mass media have been accused of perpetuating different standards of attractiveness for men and women. Women portrayed in television are slimmer than men. Female movie stars and magazine models have progressively become thinner (Silverstein, Perdue, Peterson & Kelly, 1986). Investigation of television role models revealed that 69% of the females were rated as thin but only 18% of the males (Silverstein et al., 1986). Anthropometric measurements of display mannequins from the 1920s through to the 1960s determined that they have generally become thinner over time and, given the relationship between extremes in leanness and menstrual dysfunction, it was suggested that women with the same shape would be unlikely to menstruate (Rintala & Mustajoki, 1992). A significant shift to a thinner ideal has been traced through the changes in mass, hip girth and bust to waist ratio of *Playboy* centrefolds and Miss America contestants (Garner, Garfinkel, Schwartz & Thompson, 1980). By 1988, this index of women's "ideal" body image was 13–19% below that expected for age and height (Wiseman et al., 1992). This represents a weight range included as one of the criteria for anorexia nervosa recognised by the American Psychiatric Association (15% below expected weight).

Magazine articles surveyed over the same period as the centrefolds (1959–1988) indicated an overall increase in the emphasis on weight reduction. A significant rise in the proportion of diet, exercise and diet/exercise was found and from 1981, the number of exercise features surpassed the number of diet articles. Diet and exercise are disproportionately promoted to women as a means to achieving an ideal that has progressively become thinner. The ratio of diet foods ads in 48 issues of women's and men's magazines was 63:1 (Silverstein et al., 1986).

3.4 The influence of sport and education on body image

While the media are often blamed for creating unrealistic role models, sport and education may also be accused of the same. An analysis of children's educational texts from 1900 to 1980 confirms a significant trend toward depicting girls as thinner while boys have remained unchanged (Davis & Oswalt, 1992). While children's participation in sport is encouraged for both physical and psychological development, athletes and dancers who are admired for their achievements may actually present a distorted relationship between a thin and healthy body. Studies have confirmed the high risk of weight concern and eating disorders in sports such as diving, figure skating, gymnastics, ballet (Garner & Rosen, 1991) and rowing (Sykora, Grilo, Wilfley & Brownell, 1993) that emphasise leanness to enhance performance or appearance. Eating disorders in men are more common in wrestlers and jockeys than in sports that do not prescribe a certain body weight (Striegel-Moore, Silberstein & Rodin, 1986). In other sports, increased mass is an imperative and can lead to eating disorders. Bodybuilders and anorexics, for example, have comparable scores on the Eating Disorders Inventory (Pope, Katz & Hudson, 1993), and increasing abuse of anabolic steroids has been compared to behaviour characteristic of anorexics.

4 Body image and behaviour

4.1 Body image and self-esteem

From an early age, physical attractiveness is closely associated with self-esteem (Kenealy, Gleeson, Frude & Shaw, 1991). Women in particular may see themselves as being "socially defined" to a large extent by what they look like. Women are more likely than men to equate self-worth with their body image, and what they believe other people think they look like (Fallon, 1990).

Personality and character attributions are to a great extent determined by social or cultural determinants of what is physically desirable or undesirable (Lerner & Jovanovic, 1990). Endomorphy appears to be almost universally devalued in Western society. Spillman and Everington (1989) asked 234 mainly female university students to indicate the relationship between certain behavioural characteristics and different female somatotypes. In general, endomorphs were perceived as sloppy dressers, stressed, depressed and likely to have a menial job. Mesomorphs were characterised as being competent, relaxed, professional, healthy and intellectual, while ectomorphs were considered to be most concerned about their appearance, most sexually appealing and likely to exercise the most. Most respondents classified themselves as mesomorphic, but most, when asked what they would like to be, chose ectomorphy.

4.2 Eating and exercise behaviours

Body dissatisfaction has consistently been related to the degree of weight preoccupation, dieting (Davis et al., 1993) and exercise behaviour (Davis & Cowles, 1991), at least in women. Eating disorders can be viewed as one extreme of a continuum of weight concerns and dieting (Davis, Fox, Cowles, Hastings & Schwass, 1990). Body dissatisfaction motivates men and women to diet and exercise but these behaviours may not change anatomical factors that influence the degree of discontent with body region or shape. For example, bony breadths which are not dramatically altered with most exercise interventions have been shown to be associated with discontent. Davis et al. (1994) found that skeletal frame size (based on bone diameters), independent of fatness, was a significant predictor of body dissatisfaction in young women. More specifically, biiliocristal bone breadth was an important anthropometric variable predicting overall body dissatisfaction. To reinforce this, there is evidence that males decide on female sexiness based according to buttocks and hip measures rather than breasts (Mazur, 1986; Davis et al., 1993; Davies & Furnham, 1986).

Dieting is more common in girls than boys. Of Australian adolescents surveyed, a significant proportion of adolescent girls (69%) and boys (27%) had tried to lose weight (Tienboon, Rutishauser & Wahlqvist, 1994). Girls and boys in the normal range for BMI desired an average weight loss of 6.6 and 2.0 kg respectively. This difference in desirable body weight indicates that girls are more likely to want to diet.

The same degree of body dissatisfaction may lead to different behaviours in men and women. Women are much more likely to embark on exercise or diet interventions than men (Rozin & Fallon, 1988; Silberstein, Striegel-Morre, Timko & Rodin, 1988). Although women were reported more likely than men to exercise to lose weight (Davis and Cowles, 1991), the type of intervention chosen may be gender-specific. Men are more likely to choose exercise to lose weight, while women will choose hypocaloric diets (Drewnowski & Yee, 1987).

It is not clear if exercise increases or decreases body dissatisfaction. The difference between perceived current body shape and ideal body shape was greater in exercising elderly women than in non-exercising elderly women (Hallinan & Schuler, 1993). Dissatisfaction with self in relation to an ideal appears to motivate exercise behaviour but exercise may do little to improve body satisfaction. This is also evident in younger women. High frequency exercisers were reported more dissatisfied with their body shape than moderate exercisers and non-exercisers even though they weighed less and had lost more weight than the other groups (Imm & Pruitt, 1991). It would appear that having an unattainable goal could be the reason for frequent exercising. Perhaps exercising women continue imposing renewed standards upon themselves. Another proposal is that emphasis on exercise may foster an exaggerated narcissistic investment in the body (Davis et al., 1990). Perhaps false expectations of the magnitude of the effects exercise can have on body shape, size and composition serve to always disappoint those who exercise in the hope of changing their body towards an ideal. As previously suggested, individuals entering exercise or sporting environments could be exposed to new standards of a specific group's idea of an admired body.

5 Future directions: body image research and anthropometry

Previous work has focussed on global body measures. Future methods must use more sensitive and specific measures of body dimensions. Surface anthropometry, of course, would be an important tool in these analyses. To help recreate body shapes in three-dimensional space, computer simulations will be invaluable. The ability to take a comprehensive anthropometric profile and to have the computer produce this body in 3D will enable subjects to relate to a more realistic representation of body form. Identifying specific body regions, and interpreting real dimensions from these figures, must surely improve resolution compared to the relatively unsophisticated current methods.

Of particular importance is the identification of specific cues which people use in forming body images. Which body regions, and which aspects of those regions, are the dominant foci of our concerns? How much of a change needs to occur in these areas before we perceive the difference, and significantly alter our body image?

Finally, while several cross-sectional studies have been performed comparing exercising and non-exercising populations, there have been very few if any longitudinal studies of the effect of exercise, dietary interventions and changes in body composition on body image. Longitudinal data would be important to establish whether body image incongruencies precede dedication to regular exercise, and whether they are exacerbated or reduced by exercise.

[In Figure 2, the figure on the right corresponds to a BMI of 26, and the middle figure to a BMI of 25.]

6   References

Alleback, P., Hallberg, D., & Espmark, S. (1976).
> Body image – an apparatus for measuring disturbances in estimation of size and shape.
> **Journal of Psychosomatic Research, 20**, 583-589.

Alley, T. (1991).
> Visual detection of body weight change in young women.
> **Perceptual and Motor Skills, 73**, 904-906.

Altabe, M., & Thompson, J.K. (1990).
> Menstrual cycle, body image and eating disturbance.
> In T. Cash & T. Pruzinsky (Eds.), **Body images** (pp. 21-48). New York: Guilford Press.

American Psychiatric Association (1987).
> **Diagnostic and statistical manual of mental disorders** (3rd ed.).
> Washington DC.

Anderson, A., Woodward, P., Spalder, A., & Koss, M. (1993).
> Body size and shape characteristics of personal "In Search Of" ads.
> **International Journal of Eating Disorders, 14**, 111-116.

Bailey, S.M., Goldberg, J.P., Swap, W.C., Chomitz, V.R., & Houser, R.F. (1990).
> Relationships between body dissatisfaction and physical measurements.
> **International Journal of Eating disorders, 9**, 457-461.

Cash, T., & Pruzinsky, T. (Eds.) (1990).
> **Body images.**
> New York: Guilford Press.

Cash, T. F., Grant, J.R., Shovlin, J.M., & Lewis, R.J. (1992).
Are innacuracies in self-reported weight motivated distortions?
Perceptual and Motor Skills, 74, 209-210.

Cash, T., Winstead, B., & Janda, L. (1986, April).
The great American shape-up.
Psychology Today, 30-37.

Cooper, P.J., Taylor, M.J., Cooper, Z. & Fairburn, C.G. (1987).
The development and validation of the Body Shape Questionnaire.
International Journal of Eating Disorders, 6, 485-494.

Craig, P., & Caterson, I.D. (1990).
Weight and perceptions of body image in women and men in a Sydney sample.
Community Health Studies, 14, 373-383.

Davies, E. & Furnham, A. (1986).
Body satisfaction in adolescent girls.
British Journal of Medical Psychology, 59, 279-287.

Davis, C., & Cowles, M. (1991).
Body image and exercise: a study of relationships and comparisons between physically active men and women.
Sex Roles, 25, 33-44.

Davis, C., Durnin, J.V.G.A, Dionne, M., & Gurevich, M. (1994).
The influence of body fat content and bone diameter measurements on body dissatisfaction in adult women.
International Journal of Eating Disorders, 15, 257-263.

Davis, C., Durnin, J.V.G.A., Gurevich, M., Le Maire, A., & Dionne, M. (1993).
Body composition correlates of weight dissatisfaction and dietary restraint in young women.
Appetite, 20, 197-207.

Davis, C., Fox, J., Cowles, M., Hastings, P., & Schwass, K. (1990).
The functional role of exercise in the development of weight and diet concerns.
Journal of Psychosomatic Research, 34, 563-574.

Davis, J., & Oswalt, R. (1992).
Societal influences on a thinner body size in children.
Perceptual and Motor Skills, 74, 697-698.

Dolan, B., Birtchnell, S., & Lacey, J. (1987).
Body image distortion in non-eating disordered women and men.
Journal of Psychosomatic Research, 31, 513-520.

Drewnowski, A., & Yee, D. (1987).
Men and body image: are males satisfied with their body weight?
Psychosomatic Medicine, 49, 626-634.

Fallon, A. (1990).
Culture in the mirror: sociocultural determinants of body image.
In T. Cash & T. Pruzinsky (Eds.), **Body images** (pp. 80-109). New York: Guilford Press.

Fallon, A.E., & Rozin, P. (1985).
Sex differences in perceptions of desirable body shape.
Journal of Abnormal Psychology, 94, 102-105.

Feldman, W., Feldman, E., & Goodman, J.T. (1988).
Culture versus biology: children's attitudes toward thinness and fatness.
Pediatrics, 81, 190-194.

Fisher, S. (1990).
The evolution of psychological concepts about the body.
In T. Cash & T. Pruzinsky (Eds.), **Body images** (pp. 3-20). New York: Guilford Press.

Franzoi, S., & Shields, S. (1984).
The Body Esteem Scale: multidimensional structure and sex differences in a college population.
Journal of Personality Assessment, 48, 173-178.

Furner, A., Hester, C., & Weir, C. (1990).
Sex differences in the preferences for specific female body shapes.
Sex Roles, 22, 743-754.

Gardner, R.M., Gallegos, V., Martinez, R., & Espinoza, T. (1989).
Mirror feedback and judgements of body size.
Journal of Psychosomatic Research, 33, 603-607.

Garner, D., & Garfinkel, P. (1979).
The Eating Attitudes Test: an index of the symptoms of anorexia nervosa.
Psychological Medicine, 9, 273-279.

Garner, D., Garfinkel, P., Schwartz, D., & Thompson, M. (1980).
Cultural expectations of thinness in women.
Psychological Reports, 47, 483-491.

Garner, D., & Rosen, L. (1991).
Eating disorders among athletes: research and recommendations.
Journal of Applied Sport Science Research, 5, 100-107.

Glucksman, M., & Hirsch, J. (1969).
The response of obese patients to weight reduction: the perception of body size.
Psychosomatic Medicine, 31, 1-7.

Gupta, M., & Schork, N. (1993).
Aging-related concerns and body image: possible future implications for eating disorders.
International Journal of Eating Disorders, 14, 481-486.

Gupta, M., Schork, N., & Dhaliwal, J. (1993).
Stature, drive for thinness and body dissatisfaction: a study of males and females from a non-clinical sample.
Canadian Journal of Psychiatry, 38, 59-61.

Gustavson, C., Gustavson, J., Pumariega, A., Reinarz, D., Dameron, R., Gustavson, A., Pappas, T., & McCaul, K. (1990).
Body-image distortion among male and female college and high school students and eating-disordered patients.
Perceptual and Motor Skills, 71, 1003-1010.

Haimovitz, D., Lansky, L., & O'Reilly, P. (1993).
Fluctuations in body satisfaction across situations.
International Journal of Eating Disorders, 13, 77-84, 1993.

Hallinan, C., & Schuler, P. (1993).
Body shape perceptions of elderly women exercisers and non-exercisers.
Perceptual and Motor Skills, 77, 451-456.

Hart, E.A., Leary, M.R., & Rejeski, W.J. (1989).
The measurement of social physique anxiety.
Journal of Sport and Exercise Psychology, 11, 94-104.

Hundleby, J., & Bourgouin, N. (1993).
Generality in the errors of estimation of body image.
International Journal of Eating Disorders, 13, 85-92.

Imm, P., & Pruitt, J. (1991).
Body shape satisfaction in female exercisers and nonexercisers.
Women and Health, 17(4), 87-96.

Kenealy, P., Gleeson, K., Frude, N., & Shaw, N. (1991).
The importance of the individual in the "causal" relationship between attractiveness and self-esteem.
Journal of Community and Applied Social Psychology, 1, 45-56.

Lerner, R.M., & Jovanovic, J. (1990).
The role of body image in psychosocial development across the lifespan: a developmental contextual perspective.
In T. Cash & T. Pruzinsky (Eds.), **Body images** (pp. 110-127). New York: Guilford Press.

Markee, N.L., Carey, I.L., & Pedersen, E.L. (1990).
Body cathexis and clothed body cathexis: is there a difference?
Perceptual and Motor Skills, 70, 1239-1244.

Mazur, A. (1986).
US trends in feminine beauty and overadaptation.
The Journal of Sex Research, 22, 281-303.

Mishkind, M., Rodin, J., Silberstein, L., & Striegel-Moore, R. (1986).
The embodiment of masculinity.
American Behavioral Scientist, 29, 545-562.

Norton, K., Olds, T., Olive, S. & Dank, S. (1994).
Will the real Ken and Barbie please stand up?
In Procedings of the **International Conference of Science and Medicine in Sport**, 5-8 October, 1994.
Brisbane: Sports Medicine Australia.

Pedersen, E.L., & Markee, N.L. (1991).
Fashion dolls, representations of ideals of beauty.
Perceptual and Motor Skills, 73, 93-94.

Pope, H., Katz, D., & Hudson, J. (1993).
Anorexia nervosa and "reverse anorexia" among 108 male bodybuilders.
Comprehensive Psychiatry, 34, 406-409.

Probst, M., Coppenolle, H., Vandereycken, W., & Goris, M. (1992).
Body image assessment in anorexia nervosa patients and university students by means of video distortion: a reliability study.
Journal of Psychosomatic Research, 36, 89-97.

Radke-Sharpe, N., Whitney-Saltiel, D., & Rodin, J. (1990).
Fat distribution as a risk factor for weight and eating concerns.
International Journal of Eating Disorders, 9, 27-36.

Rintala, M. & Mustajoki, P. (1992).
Could mannequins menstruate?
British Medical Journal, 305, 1575-1576.

Rodin, J., Silberstein, L.R., & Striegel-Moore, R. (1984).
Women and weight: a normative discontent.
In T.B. Sonderegger (Ed.), **Nebraska Symposium on Motivation, Psychology and Gender.**
Lincoln: University of Nebraska Press.

Roth, D., & Armstrong, J. (1993).
Feelings of fatness questionnaire: a measure of the cross-situational variability of body experience.
International Journal of Eating Disorders, 14, 349-358.

Rozin, P., & Fallon, A. (1988).
Body image, attitudes to weight and misperceptions of figure preferences of the opposite sex: a comparison of men and women in two generations.
Journal of Abnormal Psychology, 97, 342-345.

Secord, P., & Jourard, S. (1953).
The appraisal of body-cathexis: body-cathexis and the self.
Journal of Consulting Psychology, 17, 343-347.

Silberstein, L.R., Striegel-Moore, R.H., Timko, C., & Rodin, J. (1988).
Behavioral and psychological implications of body dissatisfaction: do men and women differ?
Sex Roles, 19, 219-230.

Silverstein, B., Perdue, L., Peterson, B., & Kelly, E. (1986).
The role of the mass media in promoting a thin standard of bodily attractiveness for women.
Sex Roles, 14, 519-532.

Slade, P.D., & Russel, G.F. (1973).
Awareness of body dimensions in anorexia nervosa: cross-sectional and longitudinal studies.
Psychological Medicine, 3, 188-199.

Spillman, D.M., & Everington, C. (1989).
Somatotypes revisited: have the media changed our perception of the female body image?
Psychological Reports, 64, 887-890.

Striegel-Moore, R., Silberstein, L., & Rodin, J. (1986).
Toward an understanding of risk factors for bulimia.
American Psychologist, 41, 246-263.

Stunkard, A., & Stellar, E. (1990).

Eating and its disorders.

In T. Cash & T. Pruzinsky (Eds.), **Body images** (pp. 3-20). New York: Guilford Press.

Sykora, C., Grilo, C., Wilfley, D., & Brownell, K. (1993).

Eating, weight and dieting disturbances in male and female lightweight and heavyweight rowers.
International Journal of Eating Disorders, 14, 203-211.

The lowdown on liposuction. (1994, December)

She, Cosmetic Surgery, pp. 30-31.

Thompson, K. (1986, April).

Larger than life.
Psychology Today, pp. 70-76.

Thompson, J., Coovert, D., Pasman, L., & Robb, J. (1993).

Body image and food consumption: three laboratory studies of perceived calorie content.
International Journal of Eating Disorders, 14, 445-457.

Thompson, J.K., & Spana, R.E. (1990).

The adjustable light beam method for the assessment of size estimation accuracy.
In T. Cash & T. Pruzinsky (Eds.), **Body images** (pp. 21-48). New York: Guilford Press.

Tienboon, P., Rutishauser, I. & Wahlqvist, M. (1994).

Adolescents' perception of body weight and parents' weight for height status.
Journal of Adolescent Health, 15, 263-268.

Traub, A.C., & Orbach, J. (1964).

Psychophysical studies of body-image: the adjusting body-distorting mirror.
Archives of General Psychiatry, 11, 53-66.

Tucker, L.A. (1984).

Physical attractiveness, somatotype and the male personality: a dynamic interactional perspective.
Journal of Clinical Psychology, 40, 1226-1234.

Wiseman, C., Gray, J., Mosimann, J., & Ahrens, A. (1992).

Cultural expectations of thinness in women: an update.
International Journal of Eating Disorders, 11, 85-98.

Chapter 10
Ergonomics: Application of Anthropometry to Workplace Design

Kamal Kothiyal

1   Introduction

Ergonomics is the science that allows us to design work stations, processes and products that humans can use efficiently, easily and safely. Ergonomics ensures that human users are at the centre of all design activities. The human-centred approach considers information on human physical, physiological and mental capabilities and limitations for designing things for human use. It also takes into account the behavioural, social and cultural characteristics of the users. Ergonomics is, in fact, the fundamental design science.

The International Ergonomics Association defines ergonomics as:

> The study of the anatomical, physiological and psychological aspects of humans in the working environment. It is concerned with optimising the efficiency, health, safety and comfort of people at work, at home and at play. This generally requires the study of systems in which humans, machines and the environment interact, with the aim of fitting the task to the humans.

A simple model of human, machine and environment interaction is given in Figure 1. A person interacts with the machines at two points: at the controls, and at the displays. At the controls, the person passes the information to the machine and at the displays the machine passes the information to the person. An information flow loop is thus established. Environmental factors such as lighting, thermal stress, noise, etc. affect the information flow between the person and machines. Ergonomics seeks to optimise the functioning of this information flow loop.

In the literature, the term *human factors* or *human factors engineering* is often used. Ergonomics and human factors (engineering) mean essentially the same thing – that is, design for human use. However, many researchers like to make a fine distinction between the two terms – human factors emphasising the psychological (or cognitive) characteristics whereas ergonomics stresses physiological aspects of the human user.

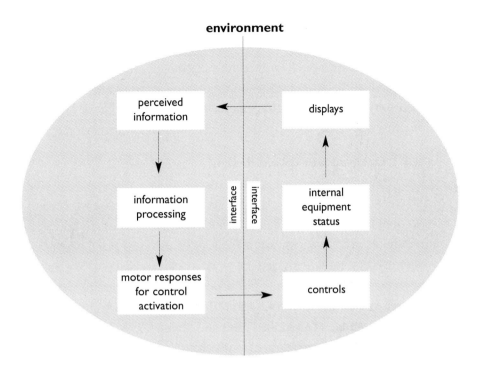

Figure 1 Human-machine-environment interaction

2 Anthropometry in ergonomics

Anthropometry – the science of human measurements – is of vital importance to ergonomics. Anthropometry discovers relationships between different body dimensions such as forearm length and stature. These relationships can be used for the design or evaluation of products. The systematic application of anthropometry can minimise the requirement for people to adapt to unfavourable working situations, which in turn will reduce musculoskeletal stress on the body. Anthropometry permits us to develop standards and specific requirements (benchmarks) against which a product, machine, tool or piece of equipment can be evaluated to ensure their suitability for the user population (Roebuck, Kroemer & Thompson, 1975).

2.1 Anthropometry and workplace design

A workplace is where we perform some job or work. The job may consist of simple tasks such as packing shampoo bottles in a box, assembling an electronic circuit for a colour TV, palpating or manipulating bones or muscles of a patient, turning a patient in the bed or making a cup of tea. Or the job may consist of complex tasks such as flying

261

an aircraft or a space shuttle, process control in a chemical or nuclear power plant, playing a piano, painting a piece of art or performing delicate brain surgery. Whatever the nature of the task or work, simple or complex, the design of the workplace should be such that the person does not, for example, have to exert more force than is necessary or adopt awkward postures which may affect his or her manipulative skills. In other words, the workplace should be optimal for the person and the task.

2.1.1 Optimal workplace design

To create an optimal workplace for the task and the person we need to take into account human anthropometric characteristics in the design process. At the same time we should not neglect environmental conditions such as lighting, noise, vibrations and thermal comfort under which the work is being carried out. Nor must we ignore the cognitive aspects of the work in the design considerations. In fact, we must consider the human-task-environment (see Figure 1) as a system in which each interacts with the others to achieve the specified goals and objectives. In this chapter our main focus is on the issues of workplace design on which anthropometry has direct bearing.

There are many questions which need to be considered in workplace design. What type of data are useful for workplace design? How should we use anthropometric data? How should we set design limits? Should the workplace be designed for the average person? The list is not exhaustive and more questions can be added to it. In this chapter, an attempt will be made to get answers to some of these questions.

2.2 Anthropometric data

Human anthropometric data can be categorised into two main types:
* static or structural data, and
* functional (dynamic) data

2.2.1 Static or structural data

Static or structural anthropometric data are closely related to the rigid structural body parts such as body limbs (upper arm, forearm, lower leg, etc.). The bony skeletal segments connected together by joints provide the firm body structure. Reference points or marks on bones are identified and measurements are made between reference points.

Static measurements are usually made in standard standing or sitting postures. A standard standing posture requires the person to stand erect with both feet together, looking straight ahead and arms hanging loosely by the sides. The head is required to be in the Frankfort plane (see Chapter 2). In the standard sitting posture, the person is required to sit on a rigid horizontal seat with the upper body straight, head in the Frankfort plane, upper arms hanging vertically downwards and forearm kept horizontal. Also, both feet must be comfortably resting on the floor. An adjustable seat may be required for this purpose.

It may be emphasised that as the measurement and collection of anthropometric data are expensive and time consuming, care must be taken to strictly follow standard measuring conditions. In this way it can be ensured that data obtained by different individual researchers and for various ethnic and occupational groups can be compared and used for design purposes.

Table I Types of measurements of interest in workplace design (from Kroemer, Kroemer & Kroemer-Elbert, 1990)

Measurement	Description
Height	A straight line, point-to-point measurement, usually measured from the floor as the subject stands, or from the horizontal surface on which the person sits.
Breadth	A straight line, point-to-point horizontal measurement in the frontal plane.
Depth	A straight line, point-to-point horizontal measurement in the sagittal plane.
Distance	A straight line, point-to-point measurement between landmarks.
Circumference	A closed measurement following a body contour.
Curvature	A point-to-point measurement following the contour, usually not circular.

Several types of static or structural dimensions can be measured. Table 1 lists some of the types of measurements which are of interest in workplace design. Some anthropometric surveys have been carried out to prepare tables of structural data which can be used by designers (NASA, 1978; Gordon et al, 1989; Pheasant, 1986). In some of these surveys several hundred body dimensions have been measured (e.g. NASA, 1978). However, most of these data are obtained not from the general population but from a variety of special population groups such as the military, air force pilots, workers in specific industries and university students. Hence the usefulness of the available data for designing workplaces and consumer products is somewhat limited. Table 2 presents some selected anthropometric data for the British population. Because ergonomists use different measures and different landmarks from other groups involved in anthropometry, Table 3 provides a description of the measurement sites for the data in Table 2.

Table 2 Anthropometric data for the adult (19–65 years) British population (from Pheasant, 1986).

Body Dimension	Male		Female	
	Mean (cm)	SD (cm)	Mean (cm)	SD (cm)
1 Stature	174.0	7.0	161.0	6.2
2 Eye height	163.0	6.9	150.5	6.1
3 Shoulder height	142.5	6.6	131.0	5.8
4 Elbow height	109.0	5.2	100.5	4.6
5 Knuckle height	75.5	4.1	72.0	3.6
6 Sitting height	91.0	3.6	85.0	3.5
7 Sitting eye height	79.0	3.5	74.0	3.3
8 Sitting shoulder height	59.5	3.2	55.5	3.1
9 Sitting elbow height	24.5	3.1	23.5	2.9
10 Thigh thickness	16.0	1.5	15.5	1.7
11 Buttock-knee length	59.5	3.1	57.0	3.0
12 Buttock-popliteal length	49.5	3.2	48.0	3.0
13 Knee height	54.5	3.2	50.0	2.7
14 Popliteal height	44.0	2.9	40.0	2.7
15 Shoulder breadth (bideltoid)	46.5	2.8	39.5	2.4
16 Hip breadth	36.0	2.9	37.0	3.8
17 Chest (bust) depth	25.0	2.2	25.0	2.7
18 Abdominal depth	27.0	3.2	25.0	3.0
19 Span	179.0	8.3	160.5	7.1
20 Head breadth	15.5	6.0	14.5	6.0
21 Hand length	19.0	1.0	17.5	9.0
22 Shoulder to elbow length	36.5	2.0	33.0	7.0
23 Elbow-fingertip length	47.5	2.1	43.0	1.9

Body dimension	Male		Female	
	Mean (cm)	SD (cm)	Mean (cm)	SD (cm)
24 Vertical grip reach (standing)	206.0	8.0	190.5	7.1
25 Vertical grip reach (sitting)	124.5	6.0	115.0	5.3
26 Forward grip reach (from the back of the shoulder blade)	78.0	3.4	70.5	3.1

Table 3 Definitions of anthropometric measures used in Table 2 (adapted from Pheasant, 1986, pp. 72-81).

Body dimension	Description
1 Stature	Floor to vertex height, usually not stretched.
2 Eye height	Floor to inner canthus (corner) of eye.
3 Shoulder height	Floor to acromiale.
4 Elbow height	Floor to radiale.
5 Knuckle height	Floor to metacarpal III.
6 Sitting height	Sitting surface to vertex.
7 Sitting eye height	Sitting surface to inner canthus (corner) of eye.
8 Sitting shoulder height	Sitting surface to acromiale.
9 Sitting elbow height	Sitting surface to underside of elbow.
10 Thigh thickness	Sitting surface to top of uncompressed soft tissue of thigh at its thickest point.
11 Buttock-knee length	Horizontal distance from top of uncompressed buttock to front of kneecap.
12 Buttock-popliteal length	Horizontal distance from the back of the uncompressed buttocks to the back of the popliteal angle (where back of the lower legs meets underside of thigh).
13 Knee height	Vertical distance from the floor to the upper surface of the knee, usually to Quadriceps muscle.
14 Popliteal height	Vertical distance from the floor to the popliteal angle.
15 Shoulder breadth	Bideltoid breadth.
16 Hip breadth	Maximum distance across the hips in the sitting position. (Note: not the biiliocristal breadth).

17 Chest (bust) depth	Maximum distance from the vertical reference plane to the front of the chest in men or breast in women. (Note: not the A-P chest depth).
18 Abdominal depth	Maximum horizontal distance from the vertical reference plane to the front of the abdomen in the sitting position.
19 Span	The maximum horizontal distance between the finger-tips when both arms are stretched out sideways.
20 Head breadth	Maximum breadth of the head above the level of the ears.
21 Head length	Distance between the glabella and occiput.
22 Shoulder to elbow length	Distance from the acromiale to the underside of the elbow in a standard sitting position.
23 Elbow-fingertip length	Distance from the back of the elbow to the tip of the little finger in the standard sitting position.
24 Vertical grip reach (standing)	Distance from the floor to the centre of a cylindrical rod fully grasped in the palm of the hand when the arm is raised vertically above the head in the standing position.
25 Vertical grip reach (sitting)	Distance from the floor to the centre of a cylindrical rod fully grasped in the palm of the hand when the arm is raised vertically above the head in the sitting position.
26 Forward grip reach (from the back of the shoulder blade)	Distance from the shoulder blade to the centre of a cylindrical rod fully grasped in the palm of the hand when the arm is raised horizontally in the sitting position.

2.2.2 Dynamic or functional data

To be able to perform a task, a worker dynamically interacts with the workplace. Depending upon the nature of work, the worker will have to constantly adopt or adjust posture so that he or she can reach a control switch, grasp a tool, apply force, make a visual contact with a person or move things around in the workplace. The dynamic nature of human interaction with the workplace has important implications for workplace design. It makes it necessary that data on the various body dimensions used for the design of workplaces be determined in the actual working conditions. This type of data, called the dynamic or functional anthropometric data, relates to the conditions in which work is done. It needs to be pointed out that these data should not be used if working conditions are changed. For example, the data on reach for a car driver strapped to the seat by the seat belt should not be used for determining the design value for a freely moving machine operator.

Functional or dynamic data depend on the interaction of the various body parts involved in the activity. The posture of the person at work is an important criterion in the dynamic data. For example, if you are trying to catch a box on a moving conveyor belt across the workbench, you may bend at the back and fully extend your upper arms to increase your arm reach. Similarly, a reader in the library may stand on toes to be able to get a book from the top shelf. Basketball players often increase their functional reach by jumping up. On the other hand, the reach of a person can be limited by restraining the body movement, for example, by the seat belt in car driving (Bullock, 1974).

Unlike static data, there are no tables of functional data readily available for designers to use. Designers will therefore have to coordinate their design process with ergonomists who can plan studies to collect the required data.

2.2.3 Sources of anthropometric variability

It needs to be pointed out that structural (and hence functional) dimensions are influenced by a variety of factors such as age, gender, occupation, environmental conditions and ethnicity.

In the process of natural growth, most human body dimensions go through a series of changes. It takes about 20 years for humans to achieve their maximum height. Various body lengths, breadths and depths are also stabilised by the time of maturity. The normal ageing process, however, continues and constantly affects biological tissues, resulting in such changes as shrinkage in stature due to flattening of vertebral discs, and a decrease in muscular strength and other capabilities.

Males and females in general differ in body dimensions. For example, the mean stature is greater in males, hip breadth is greater in females. In many dimensions no significant difference between males and females is observed. A designer should therefore not make sweeping generalisations about male and female bodies and should consider each design dimension separately.

The world today is undergoing tremendous socio-economic and political changes, resulting in ever increasing migration of people. Migration occurs not only between countries but also internally within a country. People may move from one state to another state for a variety of social, environmental and economic reasons. National populations cannot therefore be regarded as homogenous. Industrial, service and other workplaces now have mixed populations, not only in gender but also in ethnic groupings (Caucasian, Asian etc.).

Population heterogeneity is of great importance to anthropometric considerations in the design of workplaces and consumer products. For example, body proportions of people with different ethnic origins are found to be different. Black Africans have proportionally longer lower limbs than the European white population. People belonging to Chinese, Japanese, Indonesian and Vietnamese populations have proportionally shorter lower limbs than Europeans. Therefore, workplaces and facilities cannot be used easily and efficiently by all the members of the population due to these variations.

Occupation exerts considerable influence on the anthropometric characteristics of the population in that group. For example, persons in the armed forces are generally taller, bus drivers and conductors have greater girths, office workers have lower physical strength than manual workers, say in the construction industry, basketball players are taller, etc. These variations can be due either to deliberate selection criteria, prejudice or natural selection. Thus we need to be careful in selecting a data set for an application such as workplace design.

Anthropometric changes can also take place due to improvement in nutrition, diet, reduction in infectious diseases, urbanisation, physical activity, inter-community marriages, etc. The effects of these factors are normally seen over a long period of time, usually over several decades. For example, there are more older people in our populations now than at any other time of our history. Long term projects such as buildings, community facilities, etc. will need to consider these changes in their design.

Environmental factors such as high altitude, cold climate, atmospheric pressure etc. can also affect anthropometric dimensions. Exposure to low pressures can, for example, cause swelling of joints or limbs which in turn may reduce mobility and range of motion of a joint. Space or high altitude travel may also produce changes in the body dimensions, for example, spinal length may increase, in space travel, due to accelero-gravitational effects.

Though today we have more anthropometric information than we had a decade ago, still the quality of data leaves much to be desired. Currently available data are mainly two dimensional, that is, measurements made in a defined plane. There is a need to provide three dimensional coordinates of the reference points or markers on the body in a global coordinate system so that exact values of the dimension in space can be obtained (Kroemer et al, 1994). To be able to collect such data we need to have easy access to sophisticated instrumentation and techniques needed to collect the data.

2.3 Using anthropometric data

As mentioned above, there are various sources of anthropometric data available to designers. However, it is worthwhile to mention a few important features of the data, before describing a procedure for using anthropometric data.

- Anthropometric data are found to be normally distributed in most body dimensions. The important implication of this is that we can apply usual statistical procedures to manipulate and analyse data to suit the design purpose. We only need to know the mean ($\bar{x}$) and standard deviation (s) of body dimensions.
- Some dimensions are found to be more variable than others. The variability of a dimension is expressed in terms of the coefficient of variation (CV). CV, expressed as a percentage, is obtained by dividing the standard deviation (s) by the mean and multiplying by 100:

$$CV = \frac{s}{\bar{X}} \times 100$$

Body lengths such as stature, elbow height, lower leg length, etc. are found to have smaller variability (CV = 3–5%) than body breadths (hip, shoulder, etc.) or body depths (chest, abdominal depth, etc.) which have a CV in the range of 5 to 9%.

- Correlation between body dimensions varies widely. Some body dimensions (e.g. stature and eye height, stature and popliteal height) correlate very well whereas others such as weight and stature are poorly correlated.

The use of anthropometric data for design of workplaces, machines, equipment and products should proceed in a systematic manner to achieve the best results. A step-by-step procedure is outlined below:

Step 1

Select the user population. This essentially means determining the gender (male, female or both), age (children, young adult, elderly), occupation, nationality or ethnicity and cultural aspects of the user population.

Step 2

Determine what body dimensions are needed for the design. The anthropometric measures may include stature, forward reach, hip breadth, head circumference, etc. For example, the design of a computer work station may require popliteal, elbow and knee heights. For the design of a control panel, the forward reach is a required datum. Further, in this step, it should also be checked if all relevant data are available. If any data are missing, steps should be taken to get them. Missing data can be obtained in two ways. Either they can be estimated from the existing information using a statistical procedure (described later) or it should be determined experimentally by conducting measurements on a representative sample of the user population.

Step 3

Determine the design limits. The design limits depend on the design criteria. Design criteria should not be general but specific. It is no good to say that the chair should be comfortable. Criteria should be expressed in terms of specific body dimensions. For example, if all people working in the office need to be able to pick up things from the top storage shelf, the design criterion in terms of body dimension is vertical grip reach. The design limit for this case then will be set by the shortest person in the office. On the other hand, if the purpose of design is that all people coming to see an opera must be able to enter the auditorium without bending their heads, the design limit is set by the tallest person in the user population. This approach is usually referred to as *designing for the extreme* (Kantowitz & Sorkin, 1983).

It is sometime desirable to set a range of values as design limits (*design for adjustable range*). In this case the design should incorporate an adjustment in the required dimension. For example, office chairs are now designed to provide adjustable seat height. Adjustable designs are usually more costly but user acceptability is high.

A still common and popular approach with many designers is to set the design limit for the "average person" (*design for the average*). Examples of this approach can be seen in the design of public transport seats, supermarket check-out counters etc. It must however be pointed that the "average person" is an imaginary thing that exists only in the mind of the designer. In real life, it is impossible to find a person who will have all body dimension as average. Moreover, design based on "average" (50th percentile) person will put at least 50% of the user population at a disadvantage.

A percentile is a value of the dimension such that a certain percentage of people are at or below that value. For example, the 95th percentile is a value such that 95 percent of people in the population are at or below that value. To calculate the value (X) corresponding to a given percentile for a selected dimension we need to *add or subtract* to the *mean* a value obtained by multiplying *standard deviation* by a factor p which can be selected from the statistical Table 4. That is:

$$X = \overline{X} + s \times p$$

Table 4 p values for various percentiles.

percentile	p-value
2.5	− 1.96
5.0	− 1.64
10.0	− 1.28
50.0	0.00
90.0	1.28
95.0	1.64
97.5	1.96

Where p is a constant for the percentile (Table 4). For example, to calculate the 95th percentile value of stature for British males, we have (from Table 2):

$$\overline{X} \ (174.\ 0 \text{ cm}) + s \ (7.0 \text{ cm}) \times p \ (1.64) = 185.5 \text{ cm}$$

A question which is often asked by designers is how much of the user population should be accommodated in the design. In real life, not every individual in the user population can be satisfied, as the cost of such a design will be prohibitive from a commercial point of view. Technical factors such as manufacturing technique and technology can also determine the range of accommodation. In ergonomics applications an attempt is usually made to satisfy 90 to 95% of the user population.

In specific situations, however, 100% of the user population must be accommodated, no matter what the cost may be. An example of such a case is the safeguarding of machinery in workplaces. As the risk of severe injury is extremely high, all people who might directly or indirectly use the machinery must be kept away from the danger points such as rotating shafts, electric motors and cutting tools.

Step 4

Set up a full size mock-up. This is a key step in the design process and is useful for revealing design faults. Mock-ups of the equipment or facilities can be made of cheap material such as cardboard, styrofoam, timber or plastics. The construction can be temporary so that it can be altered easily if needed. Mock-up trials should involve real life conditions, that is, representative tasks, users and conditions so that when the final product or facility is manufactured, it will work as intended. If mock-up tests reveal any problems, the design process should be repeated until an acceptable match is obtained.

2.3.1 How to estimate missing data

Quite often tables of anthropometric data do not contain measurements on all body dimensions. Often anthropometric data are collected with specific applications, such as clothing or military equipment, in mind. Hence only the necessary data are collected. It is thus not surprising to find many missing data required for some other purpose. For example, Table 2 does not contain data on shoulder to finger tip length.

To get a missing value, two approaches can be taken. One is to conduct an anthropometric survey to measure the required dimension. This may not always be possible due to financial or technical constraints. The other approach is statistical in nature. The basic principle is to think of the required dimension in terms of other dimensions about which we already have data. According to statistical principles the mean values of two dimensions can be added or subtracted to get the mean value of the third dimension. For example, to estimate mean shoulder to finger tip length in males, we can add shoulder to elbow length (Dimension 22) to elbow to finger tip length (Dimension 23). That is,

$$shoulder\,to\,fingertip\,(\overline{X}) = \overline{X}_{22} + \overline{X}_{23} = 36.5 + 47.5 = 84\,cm$$

In order to calculate a percentile value from the mean value, we need to know the standard deviation of the shoulder to finger tip length. This can be calculated by using the coefficient of variation for various classes of body dimensions. In this case, the CV for short body lengths happens to be 8.8%. The standard deviation of shoulder to finger tip length would therefore be

$$s = \frac{CV \times \bar{X}}{100} = \frac{8.8 \times 84}{100} = 7.39 \, cm$$

Now, if we need the 95th percentile value of shoulder to finger tip length, we can calculate this as follows:

$$X_{95\%ile} = \bar{X} + s \times 1.64 = 84 + 7.4 \times 1.64 = 96.2 \, cm$$

2.3.2 Examples

Example 1: The maximum height of a storage shelf in a office.

The maximum height of a storage shelf should be such that all users of the office can reach for stored items without raising their arm above the shoulder level. Thus the height of a storage shelf will be determined by the person with the shortest standing shoulder height in the office. Let us assume that the office users include both males and females. As females, on average, have shorter shoulder height, we will consider the shortest female in the office. Let us also consider, for the sake of this exercise, that all users are British for whom anthropometric data are given in Table 2. Using the mean and standard deviation values for females from Table 2, and the appropriate value of p from Table 3, the 5th percentile shoulder height is

$$X_{5th\%ile} = 131 - 5.8 \times 1.64 = 121.5 \, cm$$

So the highest level of storage shelf in the office should not exceed 121. 5 cm.

Example 2: Chair seat height for office work

Chairs in office work are used by both males and females. Given the multicultural mix of Australian office employees, it is clear that chairs with fixed height are not a good idea. It is desirable to provide an adjustable chair. Thus, office chair seat height is a case of "designing for adjustability" as discussed above. To determine the range of adjustment we should consider the shortest people (say a 5th percentile Chinese female) and tallest people (say a 95th percentile British male). Chair seat height should be such that the user can place his/her feet flat on the floor. For this purpose, we should consider popliteal height as the appropriate design dimension. Popliteal height for a 5th percentile Chinese female and a 95th percentile British male can be estimated as 32.5 cm and 49.0 cm respectively . Hence the range of adjustability for chair seat height should be from 32.5 cm to 48.8 cm.

3   Workplace design

As mentioned before, the design of the workplace should consider the nature of the activity and the personal characteristics of the operator. It should also consider whether the activity will be performed in the seated or standing posture as this will influence workplace requirements. The decision whether work should be done while sitting or standing depends on a variety of factors among which the type, duration, intensity, repetitiveness and skill requirement of the activity and variability of tasks are important (Eastman Kodak, 1983). Generally, if work is to be performed over extended periods of time, requires low physiological cost (i.e. work is light) and demands fine manipulations, a seated workplace is preferred. If work is heavy, requires frequent movements and is of short duration, a standing workplace is recommended. A sit/stand workplace is preferred if tasks can be done either in standing or sitting positions.

3.1   The seated workplace

An important consideration in workplace design for the seated operator is that all items used for the task such as tools, materials, controls and supplies be placed within easy and comfortable reach of the person. The space within which a person is able to reach without stretching or leaning is limited by the functional arm reach. Figure 2 shows the normal reach surface of a seated operator. The three dimensional work space formed by arm reach is influenced by many factors such as the direction of movement, the nature of the task, working height and clothing worn by the operator. The presence of restraints such as a safety harness or seat belt, which can prevent free movement of the body, also affects the arm reach. The extent to which arm reach is affected by restraints depends on the type of restraint (Garg, Bakken & Saxena, 1982).

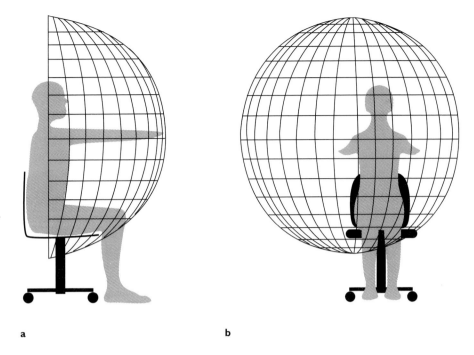

Figures 2a & 2b Normal reach surface of the left arm of a seated operator.

The normal reach envelope is also influenced by the personal characteristics (age, gender, ethnicity, disability, etc.) of the operator. To accommodate most of the user population (normally 95%) the reach envelope of the 5th %ile person in the user population should be considered for the design purpose. The logic behind this is that if the person with the shortest arm length can reach a point in the work space then all others in the user population can reach that point.

The reach capability of the seated person can be increased by leaning or stretching the body. Occasionally this can be permitted but in normal work this should be avoided as far as possible. It is important to note that frequent stretching or leaning can be damaging to the body. In addition, it may create safety problems in the workplace. For example, extreme leaning or stretching can make a person lose balance, especially if a load is supported on the hands. The forward reach capability depends on the work surface height. The reach capability will decrease at higher work surface heights as it will prevent the person from fully leaning forward.

3.2.1 Working height for the seated person

Working height is the height at which work is done. Working height generally depends on the nature of the task performed by the operator. However, individual preferences can also affect the choice of working height. Hence, both the nature of the activity and individual preference should be taken into consideration in determining the optimal working height.

As seated work mostly involves hands and arms, the working height should be such that elbow and shoulder joints are in the neutral (relaxed) positions. This implies that elbow joint angle should be at about 90° (that is, the forearm is parallel to the work surface) and the upper arm is hanging vertically downwards. In other words, work should be done at the elbow height. It should, however, be mentioned that the nature of activity will ultimately determine the actual working height. For example, research (Ayoub, 1973) indicates that precision (skilled) work is better done at working heights above (approximately 5 to 15 cm) the elbow height. Similarly, work demanding constant visual perception (e.g. inspection of parts and components) should be raised to bring it closer to the eyes. On the other hand, work involving repetitive motions such as typing should preferably be done at heights slightly below the elbow height (Bex, 1971). To be able to set appropriate working height for the task, an adjustable workplace should be designed. Table 5 summarises the recommendations regarding work surface heights for seated work.

Table 5 Work surface heights for seated work.

Type of activity	Male (cm)	Female (cm)
Precision work (Ayoub, 1973)	89–94	82–87
Fine assembly work (Ayoub, 1973)	99–105	89–95
Reading and writing (Grandjean, 1988)	74–78	70–74
Adjustable range for typing desks (Grandjean, 1988)	60–70	60–70
Work requiring force (Grandjean, 1988)	68	60

It is worth mentioning here that working height and work surface (table) height are not the same. Work surface height is merely the bench or table height whereas working height is the actual height at which work is done. In many cases work surface height and working height can be the same (for example, in writing). In the case of a computer work station, the height of the middle row of the keyboard is the average working height and is thus different from the table height on which the keyboard is kept. In industrial workplaces, various jigs and fixtures are used to hold work-pieces and thus working height is different to the bench height.

3.2 Workplace design for the standing person

The design of the workplace for the standing person follows similar design principles as are applied to seated work. The three dimensional work space for the standing operator is determined by the functional arm reach. Figures 3a and 3b show the normal reach surface for a 5th and 95th percentile female (USA). Within this work space, a person is capable of reaching any point without stretching, leaning or bending. If a standing person has freedom to change body postures, normal reach can easily be extended by stretching, leaning, stooping or bending the body (Figures 4a, 4b and 4c).

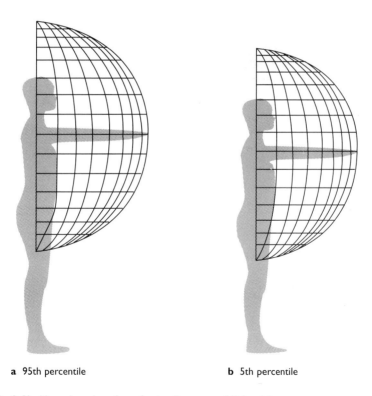

a 95th percentile   b 5th percentile

Figures 3a & 3b Normal reach surface of a standing person (US female).

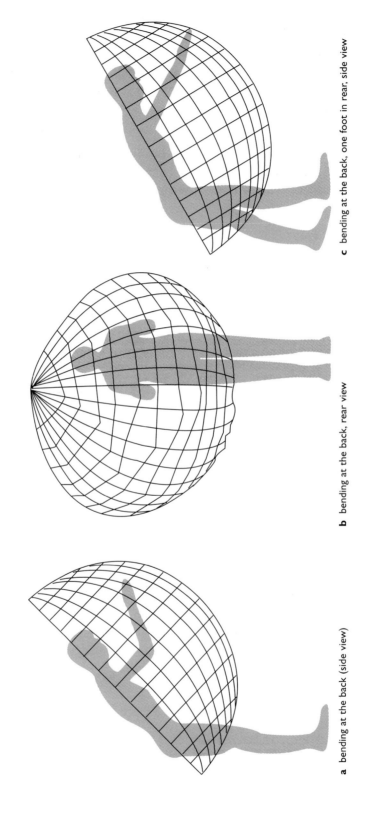

a bending at the back (side view)

b bending at the back, rear view

c bending at the back, one foot in rear, side view

Figure 4a, 4b and 4c Extended standing reach (US female, 5th percentile)

Standing reach, like the seated work space, is influenced by personal characteristics (age, gender, ethnicity, disability, etc.), the nature of the task, clothing requirements and physical restraints. Work surface height is an important factor in determining the extent of forward reach that can be achieved by bending. As the work surface height is increased, forward bending is restricted and hence forward reach is decreased. The relationship between work surface height and forward reach has been made use of in deciding the safe distance (Thompson, 1989) for keeping people away from danger points, such as rotating machine parts, robots and wild animals in zoos. The out-of-reach distance value should be determined for the 99th percentile person in the population.

3.2.1 Working height for the standing person

The optimal working height for standing work is influenced by the nature of the work and personal preferences. As a general rule, working height should be fixed at about the elbow height. But, depending on the type of work performed, the actual height can be either below or above the elbow height. For light assembly, packing and writing tasks, the optimal height is about 10 to 15 cm above the elbow height. For tasks requiring force exertion, a working height 10 to 20 cm below the elbow height is recommended. In order to accommodate individual choice of working height, an adjustable table should be provided.

3.3 Arrangement within the horizontal work area

On the workbench, materials, tools, supplies, work-pieces and other items needed for the work must be kept within the zones of convenient reach. Within the zones of convenient reach in the horizontal plane two types of work areas can be distinguished:
- maximum working area (MWA)
- normal working area (NWA)

Maximum working area is the intersection of the zone of convenient reach with the horizontal surface such as table or bench. Maximum working area is formed by the sweep of the fully outstretched arm and rotating about the shoulder. *Normal working area* is formed by the comfortable sweeping movement of the upper limb about the shoulder joint with elbow flexed at about 90 degrees. The maximum working area and normal working area are depicted in Figure 5.

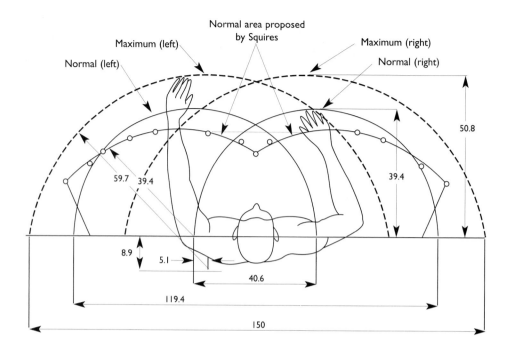

Figure 5 Normal and maximum working areas in horizontal plane. (Adapted from Sanders & McCormick, 1992, Fig. 13-11, p. 432).

The normal working area (NWA) allows hand motion to be made in a convenient zone with normal energy expenditure. Arranging all materials, tools and equipment within the normal working area allows greater productivity through maximisation of efficiency at a minimal human cost. Farley (1955) determined NWA by considering the elbow fixed during the sweep made by the extended forearm. The upper arm was assumed to hang at the side of the body in a natural position. Squires (1956) pointed out that during the sweeping movement the elbow does not stay at a fixed point but moves out and away form the body. Hence the path described by the hand would be a prolate epicycloid.

Das and Behara (1989) have extended the concept of Squires to determine the normal working area beyond the body median. They have suggested that elbow movement towards the body should be considered for determining NWA beyond the body median as the forearm-hand vector moves to the left past the median.

It is not enough to say that work should be kept within the normal work area as there are some positions which impose less stress on the body than the others. The actual layout within the NWA will depend on the activity undertaken and should be determined by experimentation. Also, the following principles should be applied before finalising workplace layout (Sanders & McCormick, 1992):

- **Importance principle** – the most important items should be in the most advantageous or accessible locations.
- **Frequency-of-use principle** – the most frequently used items should be in the most advantageous or accessible locations.
- **Function principle** – items concerned with closely related functions or actions should be grouped together.
- **Sequence-of-use principle** – items which are commonly used in sequence should be grouped together and laid out in a way which is compatible with that sequence.

4   Computerised anthropometric databases

As people become more aware that occupational health and safety problems in workplaces are not just acts of God but arise due to design deficiencies, industrial designers and manufacturers are being compelled to use ergonomics in the system design process. This will ensure that the human element is adequately considered in the design of products and workplaces. Easy availability of low cost and highly efficient computer technology has now made it possible for designers to use ergonomic information in the early stages of the design process. Several computer aided design applications have been developed and some are now available to general users (Table 6) which have the facility to use a "human form" to ergonomically evaluate a workplace or product design. The human form used in these software applications is generally based on currently available anthropometric databases for different populations and can be manipulated to select a variety of shapes, sizes and postures. The human form can be easily moved around in the workplace to evaluate reach, clearance and vision requirements or it can be manipulated to evaluate a product. Design changes, if needed, can be made and further ergonomic evaluation can quickly be carried out. The iterative process can be continued until the desired outcome is achieved.

Table 6 List of computer aided design software for ergonomic evaluation.

Software	Reference	Comments
BOEMAN	Rothwell (1985), Dooley (1982)	Developed by Boeing Corporation of America in 1969 for evaluating aircraft cockpit layout.
BUFORD	Rothwell (1985), Dooley (1982)	Developed by Rockwell International, USA for predicting reach envelope of an astronaut.
COMBIMAN	McDaniel (1976)	Developed by the University of Dayton, USA in 1973. This computerised biomechanical man model has been used in the design and evaluation of air crew stations for vision and hand reach.
CYBERMAN	Rothwell (1985), Dooley (1982)	Developed for evaluating car interiors by Chrysler Corporation.
FRANKY	Elias and Lux (1986)	Developed by Gesellschaft für Ingenieur-Technik (GIT) mbH, Germany, for the design and evaluation of human machine systems.
MANNEQUIN	HUMANCAD (1991)	This is a PC-based ergonomic drawing and design program that draws people (males/female). Provides different views. Human can walk, bend, see, reach and grasp objects. It also computes joint torques. Available to general users.
OSCAR	Lippmann (1986)	A PC-based system for evaluating simple workplaces.
SAMMIE	Porter and Freer (1987)	System for Aiding Man Machine Interaction Evaluation (SAMMIE) is used for ergonomic evaluation of a variety of workplaces and products. Highly complex and realistic models of workplaces and equipment can be developed. It is available to general users.
ERGOSHAPE	Launis and Lehtela (1990)	Developed at the Institute of Occupational Health, Finland to provide ergonomic knowledge for design of workplaces.

As discussed above, all products, processes and workplace designs must be ergonomically evaluated before proceeding to the prototype stage. The use of computer aided design software thus reduces the need for frequent expensive mock-up trials. Experimental mock-up trials can be conducted to finally decide parameters for prototype design. The use of computer software has, besides speeding up the design process, several other advantages such as reduced cost and interactive design facility. Rapid progress in the development of versatility, flexibility and lower cost is being made. It is hoped that in only a few years time, such programmes will become affordable to anyone interested in using them.

5 References

Ayoub, M. M. (1973).
Workplace design and posture.
Human Factors, 15, 265-268.

Bex, F.H.A (1971).
Desk heights.
Applied Ergonomics, 2, 138-140.

Bullock, M. I. (1974).
Determination of functional arm reach boundaries for operation of manual controls.
Ergonomics, 17, 375-388.

Das, B., & Behara, D. (1989).
A new model for the determination of the horizontal normal working area.
In A. Mital (Ed.), **Advances in industrial ergonomics and safety—I.**(pp. 195-202). London: Taylor & Francis.

Dooley, M. (1982).
Anthropometric modelling programmes – a survey.
IEEE Computer Graphics and Applications, 2, 17-25.

Eastman Kodak (1983).
Ergonomic design for people at work: Vol. 1 (pp. 12-77).
New York: Van Nostrand Reinhold.

Elias, H.J., & Lux, C. (1986).
Gestatung ergonomisch optimierter Arbeitsplätze und Produkte mit Franky und CAD. [The design of ergonomically optimised workstations and products using Franky and CAD].
REFA Nachrichten, 3, 5-12.

Farley, R. (1955).
Some principles of methods and motion study as used in development work.
General Motors Engineering Journal, 2, 20-25.

Garg, A., Bakken, G.M., & Saxena, U. (1982).
Effect of seat belts and harnesses on functional arm reach.
Human Factors, 24, 367-372.

Gordon, C.C., Churchill, T., Clauser, C. E., Bradtmiller, B., McConville, J. T., Tebbets, I., & Walker, R. (1989).
1988 Anthropometric Survey of US Army personnel: summary statistics interim report (Technical Report NATICK/TR-89-027).
Natick, MA: USA Army Natick Research, Development and Engineering Centre.

Grandjean, E. (1988).
Fitting the task to the man: A textbook of occupational ergonomics (4th ed.).
London: Taylor & Francis.

HUMANCAD (1991).
Mannequin user guide.
Melville, NY: HUMANCAD, Biomechanics Corporation of America.

Kantowitz, B.H., & Sorkin, R.D. (1983).
Human factors: Understanding people-system relationships (p. 470).
New York: John Wiley & Sons.

Kroemer, K., Kroemer, H., & Kroemer-Elbert, K. (1994).
Ergonomics: how to design for ease and efficiency (pp. 13-93).
Englewood Cliffs, NJ: Prentice Hall.

Kroemer, K., Kroemer, H., & Kroemer-Elbert, K. (1990).
Engineering physiology. (2nd ed., pp. 1-36). Englewood Cliffs, NJ: Prentice Hall.

Launis, M., & Lehtela, J. (1990).
Ergonomic design of workplaces with a two dimensional micro-CAD system.
In C. M. Haslegrave, J. Wilson, E. Corlett and I. Manenica, (Eds.) **Work design in practice** (pp. 110-118). London: Taylor and Francis.

Lippmann, R. (1986).
Arbeitsplatzgestaltung mit Hilfe von CAD [Workstation design with help from CAD].
REFA Nachrichten, 3, 13-16.

McDaniel, J. W. (1976).
Computerised biomechanical man-model.
Proceedings of the 6th Congress of the International Ergonomics Association and the 20th meeting of the Human Factors Society, pp. 384-389.

NASA (1978).
Anthropometric source book (Vol. I-III).
Publication 1024, Houston, TX: LBJ Space Centre, NASA (NTIS, Springfield, VA 22161, Order 79, 11 734).

Pheasant, S. (1986).
Bodyspace: anthropometry, ergonomics and design.
London: Taylor and Francis.

Porter, J. M., & Freer, M T. (1987).
The SAMMIE system information booklet (5th ed.).
SAMMIE CAD Ltd: Loughborough.

Roebuck, J., Kroemer, K., & W. Thompson (1975).
Engineering anthropometric methods.
New York: J. Wiley.

Rothwell, P. L. (1985).
Use of man-modelling CAD systems by the ergonomists.
In P. Johnson and S. Cook. (Eds.). **People and computers: designing the interface** (pp. 199-208). Cambridge: Cambridge University Press.

Sanders, M. S., & McCormick, E. J. (1992).
Human factors in engineering and design (7th ed.).
New York: McGraw-Hill.

Squires, P. (1956).
> **The shape of the normal work area.**
> (Report No. 275). New London, Connecticut: Navy Department, Bureau of Medicine and
> Surgery, Medical Research Laboratories.

Thompson, D.(1989).
> Reach distance and safety standards.
> **Ergonomics, 32**, 1061-1076.

Chapter 11
Anthropometry and Sports Performance

Kevin Norton, Tim Olds, Scott Olive and Neil Craig

Chapter 11

1 Concept of morphological optimisation

It is often asked "What makes a successful athlete?". The answer is obviously multifaceted and involves emphasis on a range of factors including physiological, biomechanical and skill traits within different sports. The athlete's anthropometric dimensions, reflecting body shape, proportionality and composition, are variables which play some (sometimes a major) role in determining the potential for success in a chosen sport.

It should be pointed out that to address this question it is essential to review data on the very best performers (world class) since other traits which contribute to success apart from anthropometry (for example, acquired skill level and physical fitness), will tend to be optimised and similar among elite athletes. To some extent this isolates a group of athletes who have reached the very peak of performance and who have similar training histories and physiological attributes. Therefore, if an ideal body type exists for a particular sport, only athletes with this ideal body shape will remain competitive. Thus, in developed sports, a characteristic morphology presents itself. This is particularly true for the professional levels of sport and even more so for those that excel within this competitive subset. In the process of optimising the body structures suited to sports there will always be a large number of competing "selection pressures" on the athlete. The distinctive body shapes found within sports today have come about due to both the natural selection of successful athletic body types over consecutive generations, and as an adaptation to the training demands within the present generation. The culmination of a "final" body shape and composition results from what we term **morphological optimisation**.

We can obtain a description of the physical dimensions of athletes through anthropometric profiling and then assess the relative importance of these body dimensions by comparing two things. Firstly we can look at the central tendencies (for example, the mean value) of the anthropometric variable for the athletes and compare this to other reference populations, usually the general population, but may include comparison with other groups of athletes. This analysis helps us quantify the importance of characteristic body structures and to suggest functional advantage for athletes in particular sports. The more the means of the sport resemble the population mean the larger the potential pool of athletes from which to choose.

However, we also need to consider the spread of scores within the athletic group relative to that in the general population. One way we can calculate the relative spread of values within the sample is to use the variance (or standard deviation) of scores about the mean value, provided we make some assumptions about the general distribution of scores. We usually need large numbers to work with to be confident that the variance in the sample of our athletes is close to the variance in the entire athletic population under review. Large samples make comparison between the variance of scores in the athletic population and the variance in the general population more reliable. Obtaining large athletic samples is not always possible since, by definition, we sample only the very top-level athletes and these are rare individuals. In general, the smaller the within-group variance of the athletic population, the more important the anthropometric variable is in contributing to successful performance. Small variance in the sport indicates the athletes resemble each other and strongly suggests that only a narrow range of body types will be successful in the sport. Those that deviate from this range may find it impossible to succeed at world-class level.

1.1 Quantifying selection pressures

1.1.1 Potential populations

Any group of sportspeople is drawn or selected from a wider population. This population might be considered the "catchment area" for that sporting group. We will call this wider population the **potential population** for a specific sporting group. The Australian rugby union team, for example, is drawn from the population of male citizens of Australia. Realistically, the potential population for the Australian team has age limits, say, 16 to 40 (being very generous). There are other, more diffuse, constraints on the potential population. These constraints might be geographical (a national representative is unlikely to come from outback Australia) or socio-economic (rugby union has traditionally been a sport for the upper middle class). There may also be constraints of interest: only certain sections of the population have any interest in rugby union (or, for that matter, sport or physical activity in general). Taken together, these constraints define the potential population.

It is clear that the potential population is a rather fluid and ill-defined entity. The potential population of rugby union is likely to increase dramatically following the recent announcement of a Southern Hemisphere "Super Union" accompanied by substantial financial incentives. Recently, the Australian rugby team has included many players of Micronesian and Melanesian origin. This is a result of the attractions the game offers in terms of fame and fortune. Perhaps large sections of the male population of many South Pacific nations should now be considered part of the potential population for the Australian rugby team. The potential population for North American sports, for example, is rapidly increasing with a tendency towards economic and media "globalisation". For example, the foreign contribution to NCAA male track and field championships increased from 28.1% in 1977-8 to 34.2% in 1985-6 (Bale, 1989, p. 107).

The National (USA) Basketball Association (NBA) has evolved over the past century into what is arguably the most developed of the professional sports. The potential population for the NBA is now, essentially, the entire world. Within this North American competition players come from countries such as Australia, Croatia, Germany, Lithuania, Netherlands, Nigeria, Romania, Serbia, Sudan, Venezuela and Zaire (just to name a few). Many of the tallest players come from outside the USA where they have been selectively targeted.

Anthropometric variables are distributed in some way in these potential populations. Many anthropometric variables (such as height and mass) are normally, or near normally, distributed. They can therefore be characterised by a mean (which we will call μ_{pop}) and standard deviation (σ_{pop}). Within a sporting subgroup, there is also a characteristic distribution of anthropometric variables, which might again often be characterised by a mean (μ_{sport}) and standard deviation (σ_{sport}). The following analysis of sports anthropometry will rely on a comparison of these population and subgroup parameters.

1.1.2 Selection pressures

Most sports are selective, competitive and hierarchical; only the "fittest" reach the highest level of participation. Not every physical characteristic could be expected to play a role in these selection pressures. For example, hair colour is presumably unimportant in the selection of the Australian rugby team. We would expect the distribution of hair colour in the Australian team to be much the same as the distribution in the general population. However, other physical characteristics are important. A high body mass is clearly advantageous in rugby. Lightweight individuals are simply "selected against" by being outplayed, injured or seen as lacking robustness. We would expect that body mass is a highly selected characteristic in international rugby.

Indeed, when we look at the average mass of rugby union players, we find that they are considerably greater than the general population. The mean (± SD) mass of the 1994 Australian team was 96.0 ± 11.8 kg (ARU records, 1994), while the mean mass of 18-29 year old males in Australia (DASET, 1992) is 76.2 ± 11.7 kg. The degree to which the distribution of values in the sporting population differs from the distribution of values in the potential population is a measure of the force of the selection pressure for that variable.

1.1.3 The Overlap Zone (OZ)

We would like to be able to quantify in a single index the degree of difference between the distribution of an anthropometric variable in the potential population, and the distribution in the sporting subgroup. This would allow us to:

- understand more completely the relative importance of different anthropometric indices, and formulate hypotheses on the biomechanical or physiological rationale;
- make informed judgments about talent identification criteria;
- chart the evolution of anthropometric selection pressures over time, which may be indicative of changes in the potential population or the rules or nature of the sport;
- compare selection pressures in population subgroups (such as males vs females, or state-level vs national-level teams).

Two distributions can differ from each other if the mean of one is dislocated relative to the other, and/or if the variability of one is markedly different from the other. The further apart the means are, and the greater the disparity of variances, the smaller the "overlap" between the two populations. The first panel of Figure 1 shows the distribution of heights in the general population (Australian males, 18-29 years; DASET, 1992) and the distribution of reported heights of soccer players (Reilly, 1990a; Withers, Craig, Bourdon & Norton, 1987). Because the means are not greatly different (178.6 vs 178.3 cm), and the SD of the sporting population (6.4 cm) is not greatly different from the SD of the general population (7.1 cm), there is a considerable overlap. The second panel shows the distribution of heights in the general population and the distribution of reported heights of pursuit cyclists (Foley, Bird & White, 1989; Tittel & Wutscherk, 1992; Withers, Craig et al., 1987). The sporting subpopulation here has a similar mean height (179.3 cm) to that of the general population, but a much smaller SD (3.5 cm). Therefore, the overlap is somewhat less. The third panel shows the distribution of the heights of Australian football (AFL) players (AFL records, 1994), who, with a mean height of 185.4 cm, are much taller than the general population. However, the SDs of the two populations are similar (7.1 cm for the general population, and 6.9 cm for the

AFL players). Finally, the fourth panel shows the height of discus throwers (Stepnicka, 1986). The mean height (189.9 cm) is much greater than that of the general population, and the SD (2.5 cm) is much smaller. The overlap is therefore very small.

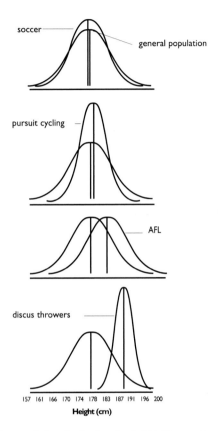

Figure 1 The potential and sporting population distributions for height. The sports are for male athletes and were derived as described in the text.

We will call this overlap the **Overlap Zone** (OZ). It can be quantified in the following way. The equation of the normal curve describing the probability distribution of some anthropometric variable V in a sporting subgroup, with mean μ_{sport} and standard deviation σ_{sport} is given by:

$$p_{sport}(V = X) = \frac{1}{\sqrt{2\pi}\sigma_{sport}} \exp\left[\frac{-\left(\dfrac{X - \mu_{sport}}{\sigma_{sport}}\right)^2}{2}\right]$$

Similarly, the equation of the normal curve describing the distribution of V in the potential population (with mean μ_{pop} and standard deviation σ_{pop}) is

$$p_{pop}(V = X) = \frac{1}{\sqrt{2\pi}\sigma_{pop}} \exp\left[-\frac{\left(\dfrac{X - \mu_{pop}}{\sigma_{pop}}\right)^2}{2}\right]$$

The intersection of these two curves can be calculated by iteration. For a wide range of values of the variable X, p_{sport} and p_{pop} are calculated. Where the sign of the difference changes, the two curves intersect.

Once the intersection point(s) have been calculated, they can be converted into z-scores on either distribution, using the familiar z-score formula:

$$z = \frac{X - \mu}{\sigma}$$

and the appropriate areas under the curves can be calculated using computer programmes or by reference to standard statistical tables.

In the upper panel of Figure 1, for example, the first crossover point occurs when X = 170.1 cm. This is equivalent to a z-score of −1.28 on the distribution of values in the sporting population. The percentage of scores falling to the left of this point on the sport distribution is 10%. This area intersects with the general population distribution. The z-score corresponding to X = 170.1 cm on the general population distribution is −1.20. The second crossover point occurs when X = 183.9 cm. This corresponds to a z-score of +0.75 on the general population distribution. The percentage of scores falling between z = −1.20 and z = +0.75 is about 66%. The z-score corresponding to X = 183.9 cm on the sport distribution is +0.87. The percentage of scores falling to the right of this point is about 19%. This area intersects with the general population distribution. The OZ value is therefore 10+66+19 = 95%.

OZ values have a theoretical range of 0 (no overlap) to 100 (perfect overlap). They are specific to one anthropometric variable only, and relate a sporting subpopulation (whose parameters must be estimated from a sample) to a potential population.

Table 1 Means, standard deviations (SD) and OZ values (%) relative to the general population (DASET, 1992) for heights (cm) of élite sportspeople. For the sources of the raw data, see Figures 4 and 5.

H/W= heavyweight; L/W= lightweight; MD= middle distance; LD= long distance.

Sport	Males			Females		
	mean	SD	OZ	mean	SD	OZ
general population	178.6	7.10		164.8	8.50	
basketball – centre	214.0	4.10	0.2	189.8	6.40	9.2
high jump	194.7	2.60	8.5	176.2	3.30	28.5
basketball – forward	196.6	4.60	11.4	185.0	7.80	21.0
discus	189.9	2.50	20.2			
rowing H/W	191.9	5.00	26.6	179.2	3.60	20.9
boxing H/W	190.2	4.60	31.1			
volleyball	190.2	9.90	42.1	177.0	6.40	40.6
gymnastics	169.4	5.40	45.4	157.0	7.40	62.0
shot put	189.1	7.35	46.7			
diving	170.9	4.30	47.3	161.2	6.00	75.7
water polo	186.8	6.30	53.9	172.1	5.90	59.2
kayak	185.3	5.40	58.1			
swimming – sprint	186.4	7.50	59.3	173.9	7.00	55.2
Australian rules football	185.4	6.90	62.7			
tennis	185.0	6.30	63.0			
marathon	172.8	5.90	64.9	164.2	4.20	67.1
basketball – guard	185.4	8.60	65.8	171.9	6.10	60.9
cycling – pursuit	179.3	3.50	66.9			
rugby union	184.9	8.70	68.1			
rowing L/W	182.7	5.50	72.7	169.3	6.20	73.0
swimming – MD	183.1	8.30	76.3	171.9	5.70	59.2
hockey – field	175.8	5.10	77.2	166.5	7.50	90.1
rugby league	181.9	6.21	79.8			
hockey – ice	179.4	4.93	82.0			
badminton	181.1	5.70	82.2	165.9	2.60	48.2
lacrosse	177.6	5.50	86.6	165.2	7.40	93.1
triathlon	177.2	7.40	92.1			
soccer	178.3	6.40	94.8			
canoeing – slalom	178.8	6.60	96.3	169.1	7.26	77.7
swimming – LD	179.6	8.60	94.8	162.6	4.60	69.1
netball – defender				174.8	4.50	40.8
long jump				169.9	3.80	54.4
netball – shooter				172.1	6.70	62.1
speed skating				165.8	3.80	62.7
ballet				163.8	4.06	65.4
pentathlon				169.2	6.00	72.5
netball – centre				165.5	5.00	74.7
softball				166.9	5.30	75.3

In general, the potential population is not the same as the age- and gender-specific general population. However, the general population parameters may serve as an operational equivalent. Table 1 shows the OZ values for height for a number of sports.

1.1.4 Caveats

The procedure outlined above should not be applied uncritically. Some important caveats should be considered.

- The method applies only to normally distributed variables. Where the distribution is not normal (for example, skinfolds), other strategies must be used. These could include performing a normalising transformation, using other distribution types (e.g. Poisson or binomial), and plotting custom distributions.
- An anthropometric variable might demonstrate a small OZ without itself being the cause of selection pressure. For example, the mass of high jumpers may be greater than that of the general population, and show only moderate overlap. However, this may be due to the covariance of mass with height. That is, it is the height which is being selected for, while the mass OZ is merely a consequence.
- Usually, the potential population can never truly be known. In most cases, general population data will serve as an operational placeholder. There are, however, special cases in which potential populations can be precisely delimited. One example is the school football team in a school where football is a compulsory sport.
- The relative numbers in the sporting and potential populations are important. If the total pool of people in a sporting group were to remain constant (as often happens, e.g. in national sporting teams) while the number in the potential population increased, the OZ values may become greater. In a population of one million, for example, 22,800 individuals fall more than 2 SDs above the mean. In a population of two million, 22,800 individuals fall more than 2.28 SDs above the mean. Potential populations can expand or shrink across time due to a change in numbers in the general population, or due to socio-economic factors.
- Although the OZ describes the range of possible values which may be found in the sporting population, in reality the most successful athletes often cluster around a narrow range. For example, despite the fact a 184 cm discus thrower could be an elite athlete and represent a nation (and would be included in the OZ value shown in Table 1), it would require exceptional ability in other areas for this person to be an international champion.

1.1.5 Applications

Gender differences

Figure 2 shows the relationship between OZ values for height for males and females in the same sports, calculated using the general population as the potential population. In sports where height is clearly important (those with very low OZ values such as basketball and high jumping), the male OZ values are in general much lower than the female values, indicating greater selectivity. This does not necessarily mean that height is more important in the male versions of the sports. More probably, it suggests that the potential population for males is much larger, since the male games offer greater financial rewards, and perhaps because males are more interested in sport in general. Interestingly, the OZ height values for many sports where height is not so critical tend to be lower for females.

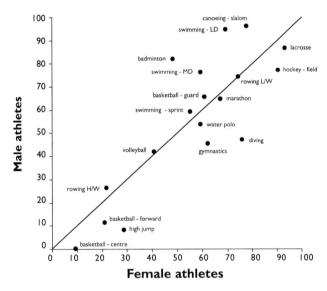

Figure 2 Height OZ values (%) for males plotted against OZ values for females in various sports. See Figures 4 and 5 for references.

Differences between competitive levels

OZ values can be used to compare the importance of anthropometric variables across different competitive levels of the same sport. Steele (1987) provides data on the heights of 15 club-level netballers. The mean height is 164.4 ± 5.2 cm, yielding an OZ value of 76.6% relative to the general population. Withers, Whittingham et al. (1987) has data on a small sample (n = 7) of state and national level netballers, mean height = 176.2 ± 3.9 cm. The corresponding OZ value is 32.1. In general, if an anthropometric variable is important for sports performance, we would expect OZ values to decrease as the level of competition increases.

Differences across time

OZ values may be used to quantify changes in the potential population meeting anthropometric specifications over time. These data are obviously more difficult to get because distributions in both the sporting and potential populations are required at corresponding time intervals. Some examples of these analyses are presented in section 3 of this chapter.

1.2 Anthropometry implications

When describing the characteristic morphological patterns within groups of athletes it is important to restrict the analysis in a number of ways.

- Firstly, underlying the study of these body patterns it is essential that where possible, anthropometrists and sports scientists relate the ways in which differences in body measurements affect performance rather than simply describe the phenotype. It is recognised, however, that even among experienced coaches and scientists this is not an easy task.

- Secondly, in addition to constraints of time, expense and athlete availability, anthropometric measurements included in any analysis should be those sites which are easily located and informative. There should be a number of sites included which are known to be under strong genetic influence (e.g. bony measurements) as well as those sites sensitive to alterations following training interventions (e.g. skinfolds and most girths).

- Thirdly, data summaries taken from the literature for comparative purposes need to have been gathered recently, unless there is a specific reason to do otherwise (see evolution of body size below). In this respect, it is suggested that the data be no more than 15 to 20 years old. This is because body shapes of athletes selected by the sports are evolving over time as well as under the influence of equipment, technological, rule and professional status changes. As a backdrop to these alterations is the continual process of evolution of body size within the general population. These factors all impact upon sport in ways which modify both the selection pressures for body types and alter the potential population of athletes from which selection is made. Even changes such as the perceived status of a sport, its prestige (for example, inclusion into the Olympic program) and the money involved in the game can impact on the players' morphology by increasing the pool of potential athletes with a predisposition to that sport. Other changes in training, diet and the use of ergogenic aids also serve to refine the body structures by increasing and decreasing particular tissue masses and these factors need to be considered.

- Fourthly, in some sports there is an important interface between the athlete and external equipment. For example, bicycle racing is one of the sports where performance is determined by the interaction between the power output of the body and a mechanical device. Therefore, in this case it would be important to consider both the bicycle and the anthropometry of the riders in biomechanical analyses of cycling performance.

- Finally, in many sports there are specialist positions or players who have specific responsibilities. In these events there must be recognition that the demands of the specialist tasks will determine the body types of those selected for the position. Examples include goal keepers in soccer, lacrosse, hockey, water polo, centres and guards in basketball and so on. In team sports such as football there are offensive and defensive specialist teams, kickers, and throwers (e.g. quarterback). Long, high and triple jumpers are often grouped together for analyses of body structure (Carter, Ross, Aubry, Hebbelinck & Borms, 1982; Withers, Craig et al., 1987) despite the specific nature of each event and the concomitant morphological optimisation within each discipline. Therefore, it is desirable, where numbers permit, to consider these and other groups of athletes independently. If we can regularly measure anatomical features of these athletes, together with aspects of physiology and performance, this will help to improve the resolution for determining the link between human structure and sports performance.

Overall, phenotypes that are successful for athletes today may be modified at another point in time under another set of rules or when equipment is improved with technological advancements. The occasion when one athlete could win Olympic gold medals in the shot put and discus, in addition to silver in both the high and long jumps is in the distant past. In fact, it is almost a century since United States athlete Robert Garrett achieved this remarkable feat in the 1896 Athens Olympics (Conners, Dupuis & Morgan, 1992).

1.3 Examples of morphological optimisation

Examples of morphological optimisation can be found in all sports at the elite level. Just a few of these are presented below.

Javelin

The first example illustrates how relatively minor changes in equipment design alter the type of athlete which is best suited to an event. World-class javelin throwers are steadily breaking new ground in terms of distances they can throw the javelin. This typically involves smallish increments in world-record distances. However in 1984, Hohn, an East German male thrower broke the world record by over 5.0 m (with a throw of 104.7 m), a large increment by any standards. In response to this (and in the interest of spectator safety!) the International Amateur Athletics Federation (in 1986) changed the rules with respect to the aerodynamics of the javelin. Specifically, the centre of mass was shifted 4 cm toward the tip and there was an increase in the diameter of the tail section. This resulted in an increased optimal release angle. Since release angle and release speed are negatively correlated (Bartlett & Best, 1988) this meant the throwers were placed on different parts of their force-velocity, and hence, power-velocity curves. The overall effect was a dramatic decline in the performances of the world's best 20 throwers by an average of 6.84 m (Watman, 1986). The performances of some athletes were affected by up to 14.34 m (the best thrower with the previous javelin), while others were affected by only 1.52 m. These modifications had resulted in a different set of physiological and morphological characteristics which were now best suited to the design of the new javelin, and, in the process, displaced the top performer.

Football codes

Although cause and effect are difficult to demonstrate, introducing interchange rules in football codes such as American and Australian football has more than likely contributed to the selection of particularly large athletes who are not suited to long duration, high intensity exercise. For example, it is not uncommon to find athletes in American football in less mobile roles (e.g. linemen), who weigh above 140 kg, of which about 20% on average is body fat (Reilly, 1990a). In Australian football games, where the distance covered by many roving players is over 10 km (Reilly, 1990a), tall players (up to 210 cm in stature) are not suited to these endurance efforts due to difficulties in general mobility together with the numerous body collisions they suffer. Prior to the last 20 years, Australian football players were not permitted to re-enter the game once they were removed. The nature of the present game allows for regular and considerable rest periods. These features, in addition to the ability to interchange fresh for fatigued players in both football codes, now more than ever means these sports not only tolerate, but demand players of extreme body size.

High jump

High jump technique underwent a dramatic change in the late 1960s. This involved changing the way in which the athlete passed over the bar. Prior to the 1968 Olympics athletes used either the Eastern cut-off, (Western) roll or straddle techniques (Dyson, 1975). Following the Mexico Olympics where the world saw for the first time the new technique called the "Fosbury flop", high jump technique was radically changed. Earlier high jumping methods required athletes to generate sufficient body rotation (total angular momentum) for the lay-out over the bar. For best results this meant straightening the free-leg as early as possible in the jump and holding it in a near horizontal position (with considerable hip extension) over the bar. This created long force arms and demanded strong extensor muscles on the part of the jumper. Thus, despite the selection pressures to minimise the height difference between the take-off centre of gravity and centre of gravity over the bar, that is, to select tall jumpers, greater emphasis was placed on strength. So the typical high jumper was not extraordinarily tall even by height standards of previous generations. The Fosbury flop enabled jumpers to complete the jump with less turning movement in the air and made fewer demands on coordination, timing and flexibility (Dyson, 1975). The result was a rather dramatic change in the anthropometry of elite level jumpers. For example, Stepnicka (1986) reported a rise in the mean height of national level jumpers of over 10 cm (183.9 versus 194.7) in only eight years following the introduction of the new technique.

Cricket

Cricket is a game where one subset of athletes has increased out of proportion with other players in the game. The fast bowlers are very tall individuals with only a few exceptions [193.6 ± 4.1 cm vs 179.1 ± 2.8 cm for other non-fast bowlers in the present Australian senior cricket squad, (Pitre Bourdon, The South Australian Sports Institute, personal communication, July, 1995; AADBase, 1995). This change has been accelerated in the last 20 years with greater emphasis on speed and angle of release. A higher release from the taller player is an advantage since the ball rises more sharply off the cricket pitch. Interestingly many of the very successful batsmen are of relatively short stature, perhaps reinforcing the importance of rapid reflexes and fine motor control.

Cycling

A further example of the intra-sport specificity of body structure is found in cycling and is illustrated in Figure 3.

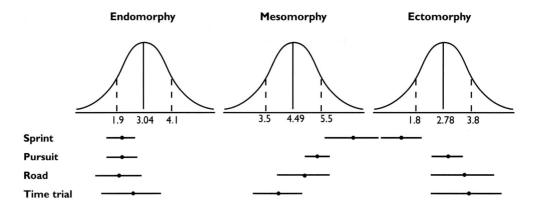

	Endomorphy	Mesomorphy	Ectomorphy
	1.9 3.04 4.1	3.5 4.49 5.5	1.8 2.78 3.8
Sprint			
Pursuit			
Road			
Time trial			

Figure 3 Characteristic somatotype ratings (representing body shapes) of elite cyclists specialising in one of four different events.

Data are mean ± SD (Foley et al., 1989) plotted in relation to somatotype distributions of a reference population. The reference group is from the Australian Anthropometric Database (AADBase, 1995; n= 70 males 18 – 29 yr).

In general, top class cyclists are reported as ectomorphic mesomorphs with little variation in fatness among the different specialties (Foley et al., 1989; McLean & Parker, 1989). However, when the different specialties within cycling are analysed more closely, distinguishing differences in body shape and composition appear. Sprint cyclists, as a group, are significantly heavier (primarily muscle mass) and shorter than the other track and road cyclists (Foley et al., 1989; McLean & Parker, 1989). The time-trialists are the tallest of the cyclists and have longer leg to height ratios compared to the other groups (Foley et al., 1989; Miller & Manfredi, 1987). This reduces aerodynamic drag of the upper body and allows time-trialists to use much higher gear ratios than any of the other cycling groups, probably because they can use longer crank arms (Foley et al., 1989).

Triathlon

Triathlon is a relatively recent sport, due to be introduced as an Olympic sport at the 2000 Olympic games. The distances for the three events comprising the Olympic triathlon have been standardised at 1.5 km swim, 40 km bike ride and 10 km run (O'Toole & Douglas, 1995). World class athletes in the individual events possess different shapes and sizes to those who excel in the triathlon. For example, Table 2 shows elite male and female triathletes relative to other top-class athletes. While the triathletes are lean and similar to high-performance cyclists and middle-distance swimmers (within sex), they are generally not as lean as the distance (10 km) runners. Some researchers have concluded that Olympic distance triathletes tend to resemble swimmers more than runners with respect to body shape or somatotype (Leake & Carter, 1991), although this tendency does not emerge from the data presented in Table 2. Male triathletes' body stature is similar to top runners while mass is intermediate between elite runners and swimmers (Leake & Carter, 1991; O'Toole & Douglas, 1995). Female triathletes appear to be similar to both the cyclists and the runners, but they are much smaller than the swimmers. These data indicate that the combination of requirements in a triathlon is selecting athletes with body proportions differing considerably from those excelling in the single sport events.

Table 2 Physical characteristics of world-class triathletes and athletes specialising in the individual sports comprising the triathlon. Data from AADBase, 1995; Burke, Faria & White, 1990; Ford, 1984; Foley et al., 1989; Leake & Carter, 1991; Mazza, Ackland, Bach & Cosolito, 1994; O'Toole & Douglas, 1995; Withers, Craig et al., 1987; Withers, Whittingham et al., 1987. MD = middle distance swimmers (200-800 m).

	Males			Females		
	Height (cm)	mass (kg)	%BF	Height (cm)	mass (kg)	%BF
triathletes	176.5 ± 7.6	69.4 ± 7.2	7 - 10	167.2 ± 4.5	57.7 ± 6.5	13 - 18
swimmers (MD)	183.1 ± 8.3	74.3 ± 9.2	7 - 10	171.9 ± 5.7	63.5 ± 6.1	16 - 19
cyclists (time-trialists)	186.3 ± 7.3	76.0 ± 6.9	6 - 9	165.0 ± 1.8	55.0 ± 2.1	12 - 15
runners (10 km)	177.9 ± 3.6	65.0 ± 7.1	6 - 8	165.4 ± 5.3	54.1 ± 5.4	12 - 14

2 Proportionality, body shape and performance

For this chapter we have focused on six morphological attributes of athletes across a broad variety of sports. These characteristics are:

- stature
- body mass
- sitting height to stature ratio
- upper limb length to stature ratio
- brachial index (defined as the ratio of the length of the forearm to the length of the upper arm)
- level of body fat assessed using the sum of skinfolds

These anthropometric variables have been selected for a number of reasons. They are relatively common measures in anthropometric profiles, there are considerable data available in the literature on high-performance athletes and they are relatively gross measures which makes it somewhat easier to link structures with physiological or biomechanical advantage. The body proportions will be dealt with individually and a discussion is presented on the selection pressures by relating them to their potential functional role in a sundry of sports. Each figure illustrating the range of mean values lists below it references from which the data were drawn. In many instances it was possible to calculate either simple weighted means or, when SDs were reported in the original papers, a combined sample distribution (mean ± SD) using techniques described by Pheasant (1988). We have restricted the data summaries to that of Olympic, World Championship and national level performers. In some cases a combination of national and state level athletes has also been used. Although this last inclusion is perhaps "diluting" the samples, at this foundation stage in the descriptive process it is important to effect a working model of morphological optimisation across an extensive array of sports. However, it should be kept in mind that:

- there is sometimes considerable variation within sport for any given anthropometric variable
- the absolute placement on the graphs for a sport may change considerably with respect to another sport given larger numbers and the incorporation of strictly world-class performers. Therefore, the figures and data contained within them are not intended to be definitive or prescriptive, nor should they be used exclusively or even necessarily for talent identification in growing children since many proportions alter at different rates and times within the population.

2.1 Stature

Although characteristic body size and shape is apparent among different sports and in specialist positions within those sports, there are many sports where height per se is a key determinant of success. In general, height among high-performance athletes is greater than the non-athletic populations although Figures 4 and 5 illustrate the range in stature for male and female athletes across a number of sports. At a glance it is obvious that the majority of sports presented are above the population norms for their respective gender.

Figures 4 and 5 illustrate extremes in tallness found for both males and females in sports such as high jump, volleyball and basketball and relative shortness in gymnastics, diving and figure skating. However, there are many other sports where the athletes don't lie at the extremes but nonetheless height has been optimised. Sports such as pursuit cycling for males and speed skating for females are two examples where there is a relatively small spread of scores around the mean.

Substantial data are available to support the fact that height is critical for success in many sports. Khosla & McBroom (1988) reviewed data from 824 female finalists in 47 different events at the 1972 and 1976 Olympics. Of these, they found that 23.3% were greater than 175 cm. In the general population (the USA was used as their reference population), there were only 2.4% of females greater than 175 cm. Finalists were also compared to the total number of women in the potential pool of athletes. This indicated that a female was 191 times more likely to make it to an Olympic final if she were $\geq$ 181 cm, than if she were $\leq$ 151 cm (Khosla & McBroom, 1988). In an earlier paper, Khosla (1968) argued that because height is so important for success at Olympic level there should be grading of events on the basis of height. One of the reasons was to increase the "fairness" of competition between nations of differing average stature. Evidence in support of this included data on the heights of 1960 and 1964 Olympic gold medallists. He showed that USA athletes won 14 gold medals in individual events in "open" competition (heavyweight boxing, athletics, throwing, swimming). By comparison, Japanese athletes won 11 gold medals in individual events, 10 of which were in "closed" competition (boxing, wrestling, judo, weightlifting where there are weight categories) and the other in gymnastics.

Tallness as well as relative shortness provide advantages in many sports and several examples are presented.

Swimming
In swimming a long body helps in starting, the kick-off in turning and obviously at the finish line. Streamlined limbs and torso will reduce drag in the water. Taller swimmers have also been shown to require less power than smaller ones to travel a given distance (Reilly, 1990b). Since a relatively high proportion of a sprint swim involves the start, turn and stretch for the finish, this is reflected in the size of the sprint swimmers (both backstroke and freestyle) compared to the longer distance swimmers. During the 1990 World Championships the male and female sprinters (50 – 100 m) averaged 186.4 ± 7.5 and 173.9 ± 7.0 cm and the long distance (25 km) swimmers 179.6 ± 8.6 and 162.6 ± 4.6 cm, respectively (Mazza et al., 1994). Moreover, when the top 18 male placegetters in the sprints were compared to the 40 non-placegetters they averaged 188.9 ± 7.9 versus 184.3 ± 6.6 cm (p=0.02). A similar pattern was found for a range of distances and swimming strokes for both males and females (Mazza et al.,1994).

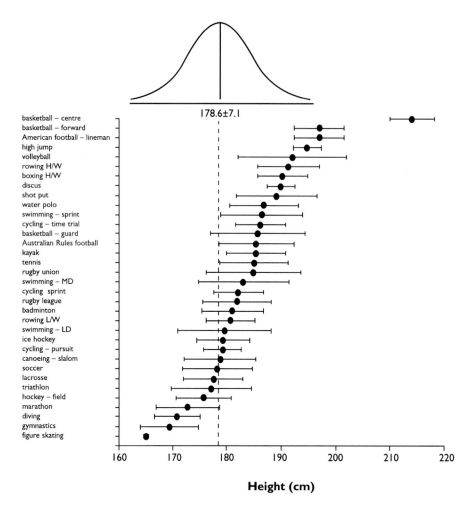

Figure 4 Plot of mean (± SD) heights for male athletes in different sports relative to a reference population of non-athletes.

Data are from: AADBase, 1995; AFL Records, 1994; ATP Tour, 1995; Burke & Read, 1987; Carlson et al., 1994; Carter et al., 1982; Claessens et al., 1991; Cox, Miles, Verde & Rhodes, 1995; Craig, 1984; DASET, 1992; Davis, Brewer & Atkin, 1992; Faulkner et al., 1989; Foley et al., 1989; Fox, 1979-1993; Hagerman, Hagerman & Meckelson, 1979; Hahn & Bourdon, 1995; Jenkins, 1995; Katch & Katch, 1984; Mazza et al., 1994; Mikkelsen, 1979; Nicholas & Baker, 1995; Niinimaa et al., 1979; O'Toole & Douglas, 1995; Parr et al., 1978; Secher, 1990; Soares, De Castro Mendes, Neto & Matsudo, 1986; Stepnicka, 1986; Wilmore & Haskell, 1972; Withers, Craig et al., 1987.

Tennis

In racquet sports height is important in serving, volleying and reaching for the ball. Consequently, both male and female professional tennis players are increasing in stature. Data from the previous 20 years report a range in mean male heights from 181 ± 5 cm for top Czech players, 180 cm for USA players and 183cm for South Africans (Reilly, 1990a). Data on current Australian male professionals (n=7) indicates an average height of 186 ± 4.1 cm (AADBase, 1995). The 1995 ATP guide lists the top 100 male players

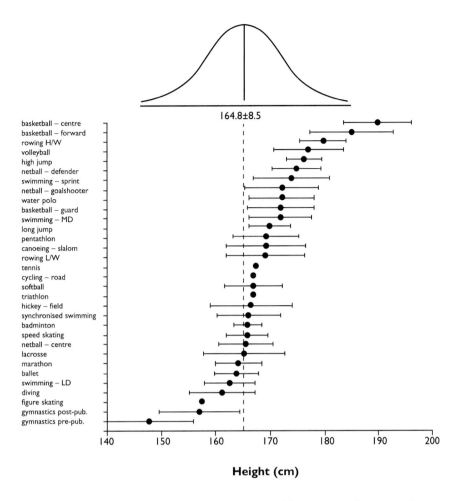

Figure 5 Plot of mean (± SD) heights for female athletes in different sports relative to a reference population of non-athletes.

Data are from: AADBase, 1995; Ackland, Schreiner & Kerr, 1994; Claessens, Hlatky, Lefeure & Holdhaus, 1994; DASET, 1992; Fleck, 1985; Faulkner et al., 1976; Fox, 1979-1993; Hahn & Bourdon, 1995; Ireland & Mitcheli, 1987; Ingen Schenau & de Groot, 1983; Khosla & McBroom, 1988; Leake & Carter, 1991; Mazza et al., 1994; Micheli, Gillespie & Walaszek, 1984; Mikkelsen, 1979; Niinimaa et al., 1979; Norton, 1984; O'Toole, Douglas & Hiller, 1989; Spence, 1980; Sovak & Hawes, 1987; Tittel & Wutscherk, 1992; Withers, Whittingham et al., 1987.

and their physical characteristics. The mean height for these players is 185 ± 6.0 cm with a mass of 76.1 ± 6.0 kg. This places the tennis players at about 1 SD above the general population for height and very nearly equal to the general population in mass. Studies on professional women players have found an average stature of between about 164 and 167 cm (Reilly, 1990c). Data on current Australian female professionals (n=5) indicates an average height of 171.3 ± 6.2 cm and mass of 60.5 ± 3.0 kg (AADBase, 1995). Thus, the more recent Australian data indicate the women deviate from the general population in height by about the same amount as the men, although they tend to be lighter than non-athletic women. Changes in equipment design and rule modifications are contributors to this evolution. The changes include modern racquets which have greater elastic recoil, a larger "sweet-spot" and which are significantly lighter than those of yesteryear (Reilly, 1990c). Because racquets are lighter, velocity upon impact is much greater and hence greater kinetic energy is imparted to the ball, placing considerably more emphasis on the service part of the game. Tall players are advantaged in this respect because they can maintain a sharper angle on the serve. Also the introduction of the tie-break to determine the winner of a set or match has reinforced the importance of a dominant serve and thus of height. In support of this a weak, but nonetheless significant, (negative) Spearman's rank order correlation coefficient (rho = -0.19; p=0.036) was found between the height of the top 100 ATP male players (in 1994) and their highest rank achieved (ATP Tour, 1995).

Volleyball

In volleyball the height of the net is fixed at 2.43 m for men and 2.24 m for women. Tall players, therefore, need to jump a lower relative percentage of their stature in order to reach above net height. Since blockers and spikers spend between 7.5 and 15 minutes in jumping activities in each game, repeated explosive jumping is a key to success (MacLaren, 1990). Although Khosla (above) argued that populations who are relatively short in stature are disadvantaged in sports requiring height, they may still be successful at international level. For example, the Japanese women's volleyball team won the gold medal at the Montreal Olympics with a team ranging in height from 169–180 cm. Based on the distribution of heights of the Japanese (mean 152 cm), less than 0.3% of women would be taller than 169 cm (MacLaren, 1990). Other volleyballers of the same competition averaged about 178 cm (Khosla, 1983).

Basketball

Basketball has always been dominated by tall players. Almost 5% of players beginning their NBA careers (USA) in the period 1990–1993 were 213.4 cm (7'0") or greater (Sachare, 1994). The two tallest players currently in the NBA stand 231.1 cm (7'7"). Interestingly, both players are from foreign countries (Romania and Sudan). Given that player size is continuing to increase (heading 3 below) there has been considerable debate in professional basketball leagues, particularly in the United States, as to the appropriateness of the current court dimensions and basket height. It is becoming increasingly difficult to fit ten players of extreme proportions, strength and agility onto the court at the same time without elevating the risk of body collisions. It has been suggested that either the court should be lengthened and widened or eventually a 4-a-side rule would be introduced to open the game up (Sachare, 1994).

Rowing

Rowing has two divisions; lightweight (less that 72.5 kg and 59.0 kg for males and females, respectively) and heavyweight (no upper limit). The heights of athletes competing in both the lightweight and open competition illustrate the size required for successful competition. Successful rowers in the open competition are larger and more mesomorphic than their non-successful counterparts (Rodriguez, 1986; Ross, Ward, Leah & Day, 1982; Secher, 1983). Since the weight of the boats (and coxswain within class) are constant, mathematical models predict the larger rower (in open competition) will be advantaged because physiological power scales to a greater degree than does the resistance of the boat in the water (Secher, 1990).

Interestingly, the OZ values for women H/W rowers have decreased dramatically over the past decade in Australia as the sport has targeted tall young athletes. For example, data collected in the early to mid-1980's show H/W women were about 167 ± 4.3cm (Withers, Whittingham et al., 1987) in stature (OZ = 65.0%). This increased to 177.2 ± 3.6 cm (OZ = 25.4%) by the late 1980's (Telford, Egerton, Hahn & Pang, 1988) and is now 179.2 ± 3.6 cm (OZ = 20.9%) (Hahn & Bourdon, 1995).

Short stature

Shortness in stature is particularly advantageous in acceleration (Ford, 1984), when changing direction (agility) and hill climbing. Perhaps the best example of the importance of the interaction of height with other physiological characteristics can be seen in the running events. In order to remove as many influences from the analysis as possible, a review of anthropometric data (Falls, 1977; Ford, 1984; Fox, 1979-1993) was performed for male world record holders specialising in a range of running distances. Figure 6 shows the relationship between the heights of these athletes relative to their specialist distances.

Figure 6 illustrates the gradual change in morphology as one moves from the shorter distances out to the marathon. The shortest athletes are those at the extremes of distance, either very short (<100 m) or long events ($\geq$ 5000 m). To investigate possible functional connections with these trends, it is useful to review aspects of performances. While the highest mean speeds are achieved in 100–200 m events, the shorter distances have a relatively longer acceleration phase and therefore a slightly lower mean speed. In these sprints (50–60 m) the athlete may be accelerating at the finish line (Radford, 1990). This will favour shorter athletes with relatively short legs. Since a leg cadence of at least 4.5 strides $\times$ s^{-1} for both males and females is a prerequisite for world-class sprinters, shorter legs will generally have a lower moment of inertia, or resistance to movement, than longer ones. Sprinters also have large power to mass ratios, reflected in the relatively high BMIs and low skinfolds.

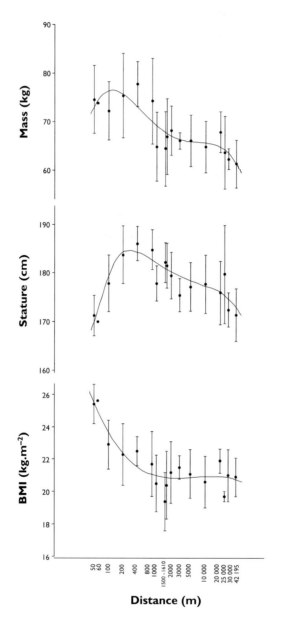

Figure 6 Relationships between male World record holders' body mass, stature and body mass index (BMI), and their specialist running distance.

Data are means (± SD) and were collated from Falls (1977), Ford (1984) and Fox (1979-1993). Lines of best fit were computer generated.

In the longer distance events excess muscle mass is an impediment, requiring considerable energy to be expended for its transportation and yet not being critical to the relatively low power production. Similarly bone, fat and residual masses are tissues which need to be minimised. This is why the athletes are typically small and lean, and have low BMIs. These athletes possess optimised amounts of muscle mass which provides adequate power to run at speeds of only slightly greater than 3 minutes for each kilometre in the marathon. The fact that they are not smaller than illustrated in Figure 6 is presumably because this would result in an imbalance between the competing pressures for body shape. For example, some pressure would be operating towards selection of bigger athletes because larger athletes are more efficient, requiring a relatively lower energy cost per unit distance travelled (see Chapter 5). At the other end of the spectrum pressures to be small would also be present since a decreased body surface area-to-mass ratio (at a constant muscle mass) is an advantage for thermoregulation and there is a lower absolute energy expenditure to move the body a set distance. Many other factors are undoubtedly involved but quantification of their influence is difficult to determine.

In the high velocity sports smaller individuals will be selected. This is because there is a relatively constant relationship between body surface area and projected frontal area (Ap). The Ap determines to a large extent the energy cost of moving, depending on factors such as velocity and equipment design. For example, Ap in speed skating is also critical. Athletes must be able to hold a low body position (trunk angle) to reduce Ap for up to 14 minutes. It has been suggested that about half the difference in performance between males and females is due to the ability of the men to hold a lower trunk angle (Ingen Schenau & de Groot, 1983). This requires great strength in hip extensors. A lower centre of gravity, short muscular legs and powerful buttocks are therefore advantageous. However, cyclists have been able to adjust to this selection pressure for smaller athletes by introducing aerodynamic changes such as aerobars and modifying body position (since they can rest on the bars). Thus, male time trialists are large athletes averaging 186.3 ± 6.7 cm (Foley et al., 1989). This gives the larger athlete a physiological advantage when cycling on the flat since VO_{2max} scales with mass to about 2/3 while VO_2 cost in cycling scales with mass to less than the 2/3 power (Swain, 1994). Nonetheless, body size and hence Ap are still critical factors in cycling. The effects of changing Ap in cycling on predicted performance times are presented in Figure 7 below.

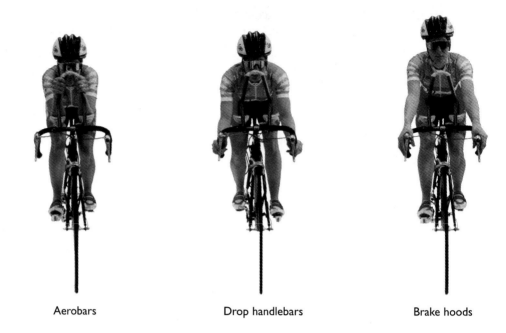

Aerobars	Drop handlebars	Brake hoods

Riding position	Distance (m)	Ap (m²)	Time (min:s)	%Δ from drop position
Aerobars	3 000	0.4234	4 : 01	-3.8
Drop handlebars	3 000	0.4796	4 : 10.6	0
Brake hoods	3 000	0.5241	4 : 17.6	+2.8
Aerobars	40 000	0.4234	56 : 51	-3.6
Drop handlebars	40 000	0.4796	58 : 59	0
Brake hoods	40 000	0.5241	60 : 44	+3.0

Figure 7 Effect of riding position on predicted performance time. Multiple simulations were performed using a computer model to quantify changes in estimated time-trial time using laboratory data for this national level female cyclist (Olds, Norton & Craig et al., 1993; Olds et al., 1995). Estimates were based on alterations in projected frontal area (Ap) of the cyclist from a standard bicycle racing position (drop handlebars).

Short stature can be found in events such as gymnastics, figure skating, ballet and diving. In these events the body is often required to move at high angular velocities. Small stature and limb lengths allow for reductions in moments of inertia which, due to conservation of angular momentum during angular motion, facilitate increased angular velocity. Thus, small athletes can spin faster and accomplish more turns than taller athletes.

In general, in sports involving high velocities or where the body's mass needs to be moved over long distances, body size is smaller. Where acceleration is important or quickness of limb movements is critical, smaller athletes will also be advantaged. Where athletes need to overcome external obstacles the larger and more powerful athletes will predominate (Ford, 1984). However, when this external object is another person who can make decisions about when and how to move, the athletes will not be as large as otherwise would be expected. This is to accommodate the decreased response time required to counteract the opponent's movements.

2.1.1 Training and heredity

Human morphology or phenotype is determined by the combination of the genetic description of the person, their genotype, the environmental conditions to which they are subjected, and the interplay between these things. That is, how the genetic make up of a person interacts with environmental influences such as exercise training. This can be described by the following simple formula (Bouchard & Lortie, 1984).

$$V_p = V_G + V_E + V_{GxE} + e$$

Where:
V_p represents the total variation seen in the anthropometric variable,
V_G represents the genetic component of the variance,
V_E represents the environmental or non-genetic component of the variance,
V_{GxE} represents the interaction effect between the genes and environment, and
e represents the random error that is included in this model of quantitative genetics.

Many studies have shown that although poor nutrition can be influential, stature is determined mainly by the genotype (Bouchard & Lortie, 1984). Final adult stature is not affected to any great extent by exercise, even in young girls with delayed menarche as a result of intense physical training (Malina, 1994; see below). Based on a number of studies, the overall heritability factor for stature (V_G/V_p) is about 0.85 (Bouchard & Lortie, 1984). This means that for success in sports requiring a specific height range, it is particularly important for potential athletes to possess the appropriate genes.

2.2 Body mass

Figures 8 and 9 illustrate the mean body mass found in male and female athletes, respectively, across a number of sports. The highest values for body mass are found in events of short duration or which have small work-to-rest ratios such as sumo wrestling, super-heavyweight lifting, linemen in American football and other strength-dependent events. Sumo wrestlers, for example, may weigh up to 263 kg (Zupp, 1994) and linemen in American football up to 143 kg (Reilly, 1990a). Two outstanding super-heavyweight lifters, Jabotinski and Alexyev were reported to weigh well in excess of 160 kg (Jokl, 1976). Other massive athletes are found in the throwing events, particularly the discus, hammer and shot put. Due to their extreme tallness, heavyweight rowers and basketball players are also heavy athletes with low levels of fatness.

Large body mass is an advantage in many sports. Khosla (1968) presented data showing the mass of male winners versus mass of other participants in open events at the 1964 Olympics. These data are shown below:

Table 3 Body mass of male Olympic winners versus the mass for all competitors in each event (data were calculated from those presented by Khosla, 1968).

Event	Mass of winner (kg)	Mean mass of heavyweight participants (kg)
Boxing	89.1	87.7
Wrestling (free-style)	106.4	102.7
Wrestling (Graeco-Roman)	135.5	115.5
Judo	120.5	104.5
Weightlifting	157.3	113.6

Clearly, mass in these open-ended events provides advantages, particularly if the additional mass is fat-free mass.

In many sports small increases in body size and mass can impact significantly on performance. Assuming constant body composition, increased body mass increases both the energy demand as well as energy supply in most sports activities. For example, a greater mass in cycling (of bike or rider) increases rolling resistance, Ap and consequently air resistance, the energy required to ride uphill, and the kinetic energy imparted to the bicycle during acceleration (Olds et al., 1995).

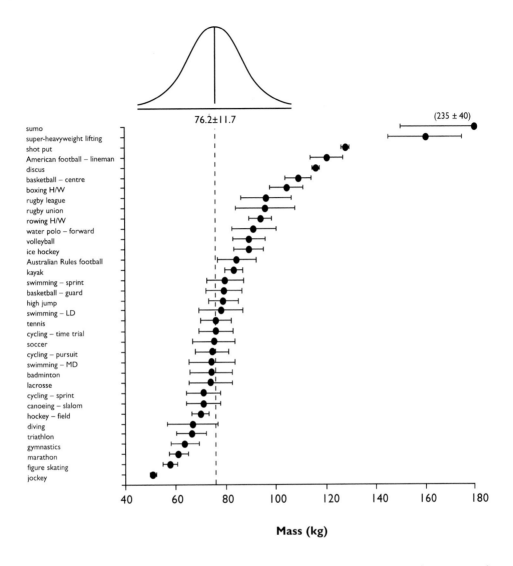

Figure 8 Body mass (mean ± SD) of male athletes in a range of sports plotted relative to a reference group of non-athletes.

Data are from: AADBase, 1995; ATP tour, 1995; Burke & Read, 1987; Carter et al., 1982; Claessens et al., 1991; Cox, 1995; Craig, 1984; DASET, 1992; Faulkner et al., 1989; Foley et al., 1989; Fox, 1979-1993; Jenkins, 1995; Katch & Katch, 1984; Mazza et al., 1994; Mikkelsen, 1979; Nicholas & Baker, 1995; Niinimaa et al., 1979; O'Toole & Douglas, 1995; Parr et al., 1978; Soares et al., 1986; Stepnicka, 1986; Secher, 1990; Wimore & Haskell, 1972; Withers, Craig et al., 1987; Zupp, 1994. See Table 1 for abbreviations.

315

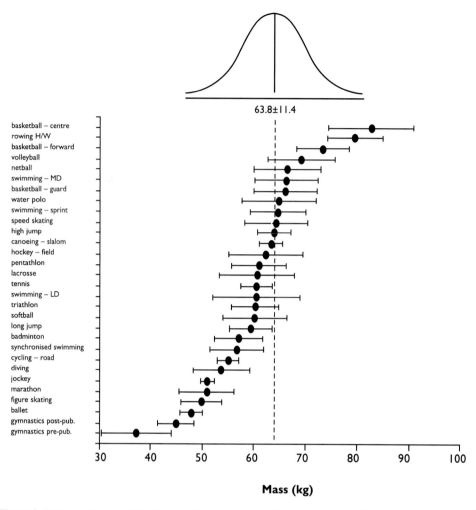

Figure 9 Body mass (mean ± SD) of female athletes in a range of sports plotted relative to a reference group of non-athletes.

Data are from: AADBase, 1995; Ackland et al., 1994; Claessens et al., 1994; DASET, 1992; Fleck, 1985; Faulkner et al., 1976; Fox,1979-1993; Jenkins, 1995; Ireland & Micheli, 1987; Ingen Schenau & de Groot, 1983; Khosla & McBroom, 1988; Leake & Carter, 1991; Mazza et al., 1994; Micheli et al., 1984; Mikkelsen, 1979; Niinimaa et al., 1979; Norton, 1984; O'Toole et al., 1989; Sovak & Hawes, 1987; Spence, 1980; Tittel & Wutscherk,1992; Withers, Whittingham et al., 1987.

The lowest mean body mass values (in sports that don't involve weight categories) are found where the body is not supported in any way by external equipment. Extremes of small body mass are found for both males and females in sports such as ultradistance running, gymnastics, figure skating and diving. Interestingly, about two-thirds of the (randomly selected) male sports fall above the mean population mass, whereas it is opposite for female athletes. Since most female competitors are taller than their non-athletic counterparts, it suggests a large difference in body fat level exists between the athletic and non-athletic groups.

2.2.1 Training and heredity

The genetic influence of body mass has often been analysed using parent-offspring assessment of BMI (Bouchard & Lortie, 1984). Although BMI (mass × height^{-2}) does not take into account aspects of body composition, it nonetheless gives some indication of relative body size. The consensus appears to be that mating of heterogeneous individuals, no matter how extreme, produces an immense range of progeny. However, a greater hereditability factor (i.e. less variation between parents and adult offspring body type) was shown for homogeneous parents, particularly when the parents had high BMI scores (Bouchard & Lortie, 1984). Similarly, estimates in the concordance between parent and sibling somatotype ratings have ranged between moderate associations using anthropometric methods [hereditability level of about 0.50 for endomorphy, 0.42 for mesomorphy and 0.35 for ectomorphy (Bouchard & Lortie, 1984)], to a relatively high 0.75 using photographic ratings (Parnell, 1958).

Textbooks indicate that approximately 14% of the body mass is bone (Goldberg, 1984). This can vary considerably depending upon both the relative proportions of the other tissue compartments and the type and amount of exercise undertaken (Chilibeck, Sale & Webber, 1995). For example, bone as a percentage of fat free mass was reported to range from 16.3–25.7% across 25 cadavers (Clarys, Martin & Drinkwater, 1984). Although it is well recognised there is a strong genetic influence on bone length, the breadth, mineralisation, cortical thickness and mass of bone are also under considerable genetic control (Bouchard & Lortie, 1984). For example, Smith, Nance, Kang, Christian & Johnston (1973) found that the intrapair variance for bone mass in monozygotic (MZ) twins was about one-fourth that of dizygotic twins (DZ), and highly significant. There was also about one-half of the variance for bone width in the MZ pairs compared to the DZ pairs. Skeletal frame size, an important contributor to body mass and in predisposing individuals to particular sports, is also dominated by genetic inheritance.

Since body mass and body height are highly correlated in population surveys, taller individuals also tend to be more massive. Therefore, sports demanding small body mass typically select shorter people, whereas high body mass is most often found in taller athletes.

2.3 Sitting height to stature ratio

The sitting height to stature ratio gives an indication of the relative length of the legs to stature. Figures 10 and 11 illustrate sitting height to stature ratio found in male and female athletes, respectively. They indicate extremes in this ratio are found for male athletes in sports requiring great upper-body strength such as weightlifters and wrestlers. Data could not be found for equivalent female athletes, but long torsos relative to stature were not common among the female athletes. This may reflect the disadvantage a relatively long torso presents in sports requiring considerable mobility and speed. In general, the figures show a high degree of parallelism, despite the upward shift in the population sitting height to stature ratio for females relative to males (see below).

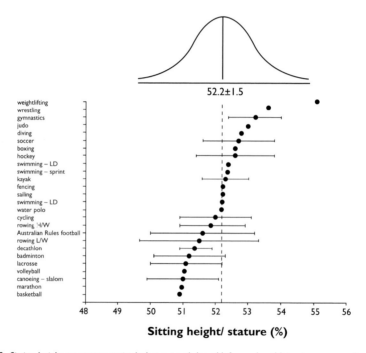

Figure 10 Sitting height to stature ratio (relative trunk length) for male athletes in a range of sports.

Data are mean (± SD) and are plotted relative to a reference population of non-athletes.
Data are from: AADBase, 1995; Ackland et al., 1994; Carter et al., 1982; Craig, 1984; Claessens et al., 1991; Hartland, 1981; LeVeau, Ward & Nelson, 1974; Mazza et al., 1994; Rodriguez, 1986.

Relatively short trunks can be found for a number of sports including basketballers, volleyballers and other sports requiring jumping such as Australian football and decathlon. Rowers also tend to have relatively short trunks. Successful heavyweight

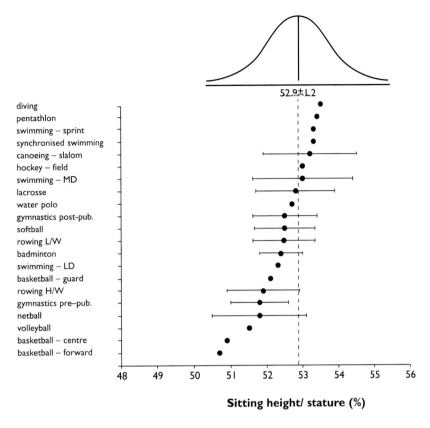

Figure 11 Sitting height to stature ratio (relative trunk length) for female athletes in a range of sports.

Data are mean (± SD) and are plotted relative to a reference population of non-athletes.
Data are from: AADBase, 1995; Ackland et al., 1994; Carter et al., 1982; Claessens et al., 1994; Mazza et al., 1994; Norton, 1984; Rodriguez, 1986; Smith, 1982.

rowers have been shown to have long limbs, both in absolute and relative (to their overall height) terms (Ross et al., 1982; Secher, 1993). When compared to a reference student population, lightweight rowers also generally have proportionally longer limbs and shorter sitting height (Rodriguez, 1986). Proportionally longer limbs may provide a mechanical advantage during competitive rowing by allowing longer stroke length. Shorter sitting height is also advantageous since it will reduce Ap, an additional source of resistance to movement, and provide increased trunk stability. Cycling time-trialists also exhibit significantly longer relative leg length when compared to cyclists in other specialties (Foley et al., 1989), although sitting height data were not presented.

2.3.1 Training and heredity

Samples from geographically diverse populations will vary in their characteristic body size and proportions. Many of the differences between groups are somewhat predictable based on evolutionary influences. For example, body mass has been shown to vary inversely with the mean annual temperature (Pheasant, 1988). Also relative lengths of limbs (as a proportion of stature) decrease as the mean annual temperature decreases, and overall body mass and fatness increase (Pheasant, 1988). Similarly, relative sitting height shows the inverse pattern where populations in colder climates have relatively shorter limbs and longer torsos.

Although men and women rarely compete against one another in athletic competition it is useful to consider structural differences and their potential effect on performance. Figure 12 illustrates age, gender and ethnic variation in sitting height. In general, women have relatively longer trunks than men. Importantly, as far as performance is concerned, there are distinct patterns of rise and fall of relative sitting height in adolescents. These trends indicate the asynchronous growth patterns of limbs and trunk during the developmental years which often impact on motor skill and coordination. This is also highlighted in Figure 11 where pre-pubertal gymnasts show a smaller relative sitting height than post-pubertal competitors. Perhaps this is one of the selection pressures resulting in progressively younger elite gymnasts (refer to heading 3 below).

The relationship between the morphology of successful athletes and their performances, suggests a link between form and function. On the basis of these patterns in body types (which are associated with particular sports), populations or, more correctly, proportions of populations may or may not be suitable for a sport, at least in terms of gross morphology. However, it may not always follow since other physiological and psychological characteristics will be important to various degrees in different events. In general, different populations of the world, and subsets within these populations, enjoy advantages in different sports. The overall advantage (within gender) is that a larger number of potential athletes with optimised morphology for specific sports will be available for selection from these genetic pools. This pattern may, in part, explain the tendency for the linear and relatively long-limbed east Africans to excel in endurance events while the short-limbed eastern Europeans and Asians have a long history of success in weightlifting and gymnastics.

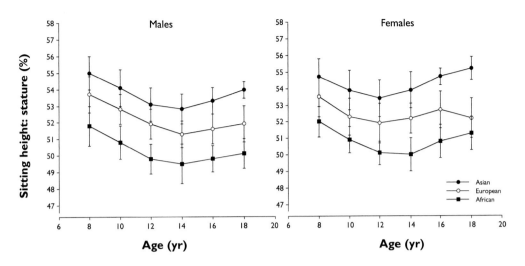

Figure 12 Sitting height to stature ratio (%) as a function of gender, age and ethnic origin.

Data are means (± SD) calculated from a number of studies listed in tables reported by Eveleth and Tanner (1976).

As with stature, the sitting height to stature ratio and other body proportions are heavily influenced by the genotype, probably more so than any other group of anthropometric measurements (Bouchard & Lortie, 1984). Heritability factors for sitting height alone is about 0.67 (Clark, 1956) to 0.71 (Bouchard & Lortie, 1984), although most other segment lengths are in excess of 0.8. This perhaps represents the influence soft tissues (lower heritability factors) have on sitting height and the subsequent ratio with stature.

2.4 Upper limb length to stature ratio

Upper limb (arm) length to stature ratio is negatively correlated with sitting height to stature ratio. That is, individuals with relatively long trunks typically have relatively short arms (and legs). Therefore, as indicated in Figures 10 and 11 and supported by Figure 13 and 14, athletes with relatively short trunks are most often associated with sports requiring long arms.

Relatively long levers are found in male and female athletes competing in diving, water polo, rowing and swimming. In swimming and rowing a long stroke length is advantageous, provided the athlete has the muscular power to support it. Long arms are also helpful to water polo players providing them with greater reach to catch the ball. Boxers have an unusual combination of long arms and trunk. Ideal proportions for boxers would be relatively long arms for greater reach, long trunks and short legs to lower the body's centre of gravity and provide stability. Although in theory divers would benefit from small stature and short limbs (to facilitate rapid body spins), male and female divers have relatively long arms relative to stature. Perhaps this relates to aspects of water entry.

Shorter limbs on the other hand are most often found in the strength athletes such as weightlifters. This is because shorter levers are required to perform less work where the mass is lifted through a smaller distance.

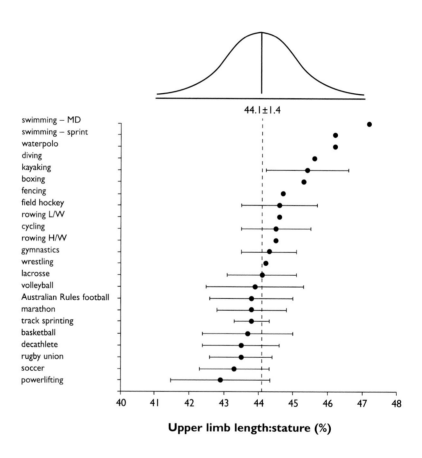

Figure 13 Upper limb length:stature ratio (mean ± SD) of male athletes in a range of sports plotted relative to a reference group of non-athletes.

Data are from AADBase, 1995; Carter et al., 1982; Craig, 1984; LeVeau et al., 1974; Mazza et al., 1994; Pavicic, 1986; Vujovic, Lozovina & Pavicic, 1986.

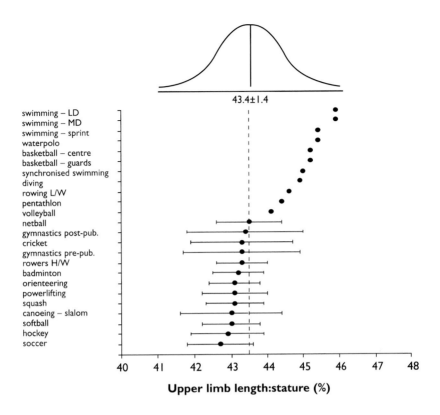

Figure 14 Upper limb length:stature ratio (mean ± SD) of female athletes in a range of sports plotted relative to a reference group of non-athletes.

Data are from AADBase, 1995; Ackland et al., 1994; Carter et al., 1982; Norton, 1984; Mazza et al., 1994; Rodriguez, 1986; Smith, 1982.

2.4.1 Training and heredity

As for sitting height to body segment ratio, arm and leg lengths are also under a high degree of genotypic control (Bouchard & Lortie, 1984). These authors refer to their earlier work showing heritability coefficients of 0.84 ± 0.10 for upper limb length.

2.5 Brachial index

Brachial index is the length of the forearm relative to the arm (upper arm). Figures 15 and 16 illustrate brachial index found in male and female athletes, respectively.

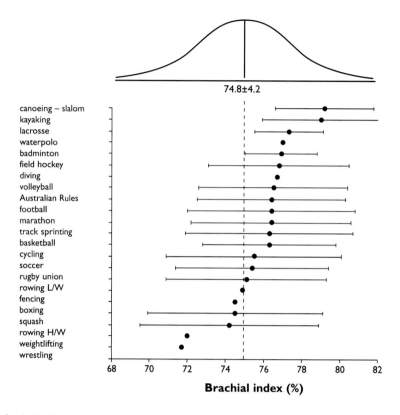

Figure 15 Brachial index (mean ± SD) of male athletes in a range of sports plotted relative to a reference group of non-athletes.

Data are from AADBase, 1995; Carter et al., 1982; Craig, 1984; Hartland, 1981; LeVeau et al., 1994; Mazza et al., 1994.

The relative lengths of the levers of the arm (and leg) are important for biomechanical reasons. Sprint swimmers, for example, have a high brachial index and large hands (Ross, Leahy, Mazza & Drinkwater, 1994) which allow a longer propulsive drive of the forearm. Slalom canoeists also possess relatively long arms for long stroke length and also a high brachial index.

On the other hand, weightlifters and wrestlers require tremendous strength and stability. This is achieved, in part, by low brachial indices and the accompanying biomechanical advantage of short force arms.

2.5.1 Training and heredity

Bouchard & Lortie, (1984) report heritability coefficients of between 0.62 ± 0.01 and 0.71 ± 0.09 for the upper arm and forearm lengths.

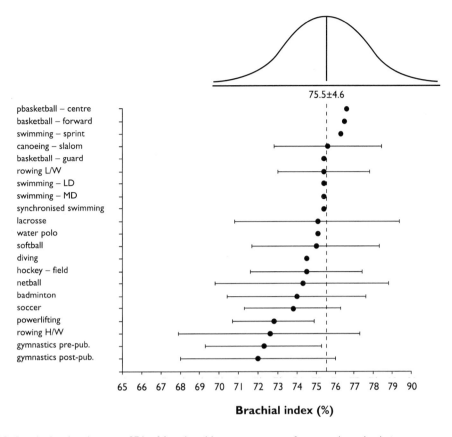

Figure 16 Brachial index (mean ± SD) of female athletes in a range of sports plotted relative to a reference group of non-athletes.

Data are from AADBase, 1995; Ackland et al., 1994; Carter et al., 1982; Norton, 1984; Smith, 1982.

2.6 Sum of skinfolds

Athletes and coaches involved at the elite level of competition recognise the importance of attaining the specific body shape, size and composition required for peak performance. One aspect of the physiological preparation of an athlete which is important and has a low hereditability factor, is an optimal level of body fat (BF). The environmental influences include interventions from the sports scientist, coach and nutritionist, level and type of training, and the timing of these factors in order to reach prime body composition. At the top level of competition it is important to accurately monitor BF levels since this body tissue compartment can change quite rapidly relative to other body dimensions and tissue masses. Hence, of particular concern to sports scientists is the measurement and quantification of BF levels. Skinfold measurements are commonly used to estimate fatness or adiposity and these measures may then be used as a basis for training and dietary interventions. The use of anthropometry for monitoring body fat levels is particularly important for the athlete involved in weight loss or weight gain programs so that specific tissue masses can be assessed. It is critical therefore, that the measurement procedures for assessing BF, and the data handling are valid. If this can be achieved then regular BF measurements will help to ensure that any change in body mass is due to a loss or gain of the appropriate component. Anthropometric assessments and the development of physiological and morphological profiles will help to describe the characteristics of elite athletes in various sports (Carter, 1984; Withers, Craig et al., 1987) and at various stages throughout the yearly training cycle. One example of how skinfold measures have been used to monitor an athlete's progress is presented below.

In this case an international level cyclist (Olympic gold medallist) was measured over a period of about seven months as he prepared for the World championships. These data provide a basis for future comparison as the athlete undergoes the usual yearly cyclic process of transition, preparatory, specific (pre-competitive) and competitive phases of training. They are also essential for determining if and where further changes are possible and to understand the link between fatness and performance.

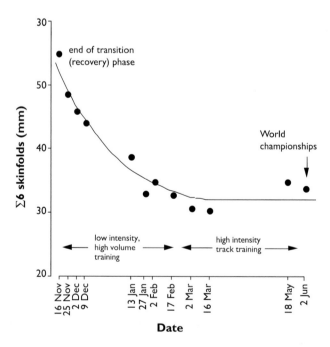

Figure 17 Sum of six skinfolds (triceps, subscapular, biceps, iliac crest, front thigh and medial calf: measurer's TEM for Σ6 skinfolds = 0.9%, ICC = 0.999) monitored over a seven month period in preparation for World Championship competition (N. Craig, unpublished data).

A high level of BF has an adverse effect on performance in many sports. This has been shown experimentally by artificially altering the body's mass (Cureton et al., 1978; Cureton & Sparling 1980; Hanson, 1973; Montgomery, 1982). For example, after loading subjects with additional weights, Cureton and Sparling (1980) found that 30% of the difference in running performance between males and females could be attributed to the differences in BF levels. Gender differences in VO_{2max}, when expressed relative to body mass, were reduced by 65% after % BF levels were matched by adding weight to the males.

The relationship between altered body mass and performance has been used for decades in the horse racing industry. Altering the "body mass" by loading horses (~1000 kg) with penalty masses (to >70 kg including jockeys) is known to handicap their performance. In fact racing bookmakers determine betting odds on the basis of an estimated decrease in performance, usually in horse body lengths for each additional kilogram allocated to the horse. For example, an estimated decrement of 1.25 horse lengths for each additional kilogram of mass is used as a basis for adjusting performance. (Mauri Aho, Chief Handicapper for the Australian Jockey Club, personal communication, July 1995).

Whether the event is primarily aerobic or anaerobic, increased fat mass (FM) will be detrimental to performance. For example, the energy requirement at any given submaximal running speed is increased with increments in body mass at the rate of about 4 kJ for each extra kg, over each km run. That is, in aerobic equivalents, VO_2 must be augmented by about $0.2 \, LO_2/kg$ for each km travelled due to a greater energy demand needed to sustain movement of a larger mass. The effect on performance is particularly obvious in sports where the aerobic and anaerobic power-to-body mass ratios are critical, such as in endurance events and field games. In sports requiring speed or explosive power, for example ball games, sprinting and jumping, excess fat will increase the body's mass and decrease acceleration (acceleration = force/mass) unless proportional increases in force are applied. This may not always be possible or even desirable particularly in events where some degree of pacing is used, for example, 4000 m cycling pursuit or middle distance running events.

Increased FM also has an impact on Ap which is important for all athletes, particularly in sports such as cycling, skating, skiing and other sports involving high velocities (Olds et al., 1995; Quinney, 1990). This is in spite of the fact that the body mass is supported in many of these activities. The extent to which changes in Ap impact on performance is illustrated above in Figure 7.

Olds et al. (1993), using a mathematical model, have estimated that an increased FM of 2 kg would increase a 4000 m pursuit cycling performance time by about 1.5 s (20 m) and a 40 km time trial by about 15 s (180 m). The energy demand of cycling will also be affected by an increased rolling resistance which increases proportionally with body mass. Furthermore, the kinetic energy imparted to the bicycle-and-rider system during acceleration at a given rate will be greater when the body mass is increased. Conversely, acceleration will be reduced if the same forces are applied by the fatter athlete. Hill climbing in cycling is particularly affected by increased body mass to the extent that each kilogram increment in body (or fat) mass will result in a decrement in performance as shown in Table 4.

Table 4 Changes in cycling performance times for a 40 km time trial as a function of both added body mass and increased slope of the course. Results are expressed as a relative (%) change compared to baseline performance (100%). Simulations were performed using mathematical models of cycling performance by Olds et al. (1993; 1995).

slope (%)	change in rider mass (kg)		
	0	+1	+5
0	100	100.2	100.9
0.5	106.4	106.7	107.7
1.0	113.6	113.9	115.4
2	130.5	131.1	133.8
5	201.7	203.6	211.2

In summary, movement at a given velocity or rate of acceleration will require overfat people to work at a greater percentage of their VO_{2max}, than they would without the added FM.

2.6.1 Physiological considerations

Work capacity decreases with increasing fatness due to the handicap of fat acting as a deadweight. The fat *per se* has no influence over the capacities of the cardiovascular and respiratory systems to deliver oxygen to the muscles during exercise.

The additional FM is usually associated with a decrease in the body surface area-to-body mass ratio (BSA/mass). Since heat generated through the increased metabolism of the working muscles must be lost via evaporation, convection and radiation, the BSA/mass ratio is of great significance in the efficiency of heat dissipation. Overfat athletes are disadvantaged in exercise of long duration as they have a lower heat tolerance than their leaner counterparts, primarily due to the differences in the BSA:mass ratio (Pyke, 1981). The higher this ratio, as evident in the lean person, the more effective is the heat loss when the ambient or environmental temperature is lower than that of the skin. Furthermore, because of differences in water content, the amount of heat energy required to raise the temperature of a given mass of adipose tissue by a set amount (specific heat) is less than that of the fat free mass (FFM). There have been a number of studies to determine the specific heat of various tissues of the body (Minard, 1970). Estimates of specific heat of the whole body have ranged from 2.68 $J.g^{-1}.°C^{-1}$ for a very obese person to 3.39 $J.g^{-1}.°C^{-1}$ for a lean person who would have a greater relative water content (Minard, 1970). A given heat load per unit of body mass will, therefore, raise the body temperature more in the overfat than in the lean individual. This is important since approximately 75% of all energy conversion within the body is eventually lost as heat energy (Åstrand & Rodahl, 1986). To highlight this fact consider the following example using these extremes. Two 70 kg people, one overfat and the other lean, perform the same work, say, consuming 4 L O_2 per minute for 2 hr of running. This would generate enough heat (1 L O_2 = 21 kJ energy × 0.75 heat load) to raise their 70 kg bodies by about an additional 40°C and 32°C, respectively. However, since they obviously regulate their temperatures to some lower value during exercise (say 40°C) this means the overfat person must dissipate about 20% more heat (and therefore 20% more sweat, assuming all is lost via evaporation) than their leaner counterpart in order to maintain the same body temperature.

Eventually there will be a decreased quality (skill deterioration) and quantity (maximum capacity of the energy systems) of performance due to elevated anaerobic metabolism and heat stress in the overfat person.

2.6.2 Patterns of body mass and fat levels

There are specific groups of athletes who demonstrate characteristic patterns of body composition and bodyweight control (Brownell, Nelson, Stern & Wilmore, 1987; Fogelholm, 1994). Considerable data are available which demonstrate that BF and other tissue masses conform to predictable patterns for specific athletes as well as for specific positions within sports (Holly, Barnard, Rosenthal, Applegate & Pritikin, 1986; Sinning, 1985; Soares et al., 1986; Telford, Tumilty & Damm, 1984; Wilmore, 1983). These BF patterns will be discussed in relation to skinfold data presented for high-performance male and female athletes in the Figures 18 and 19.

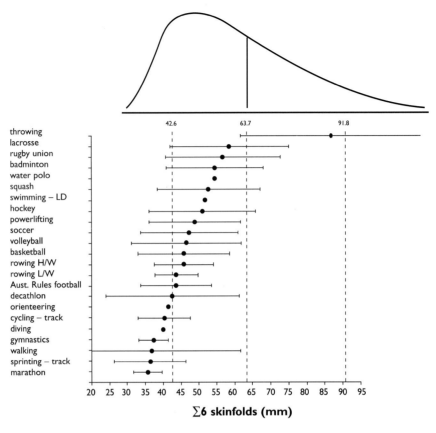

Figure 18 Sum of six skinfolds (mean ± SD) for male athletes in a range of sports plotted relative to a reference group of non-athletes.

The reference group is from data presented by DASET (1992). The skinfolds are triceps, subscapular, biceps, supraspinale, abdominal and medial calf. Note the distribution of skinfold data is positively skewed. Median and interquartile range values are shown for reference (dotted lines).

These and other groups of athletes can be broadly classified into the following categories based on their level of body fat:

Low levels of body fat

Within this group of lean athletes there are the following subdivisions based on body weight control:

- Athletes in weight-class events which require them to "make weight" prior to competition. Sports in this category include judo, horse racing (jockeys), boxing, wrestling and rowing weight divisions, and karate.

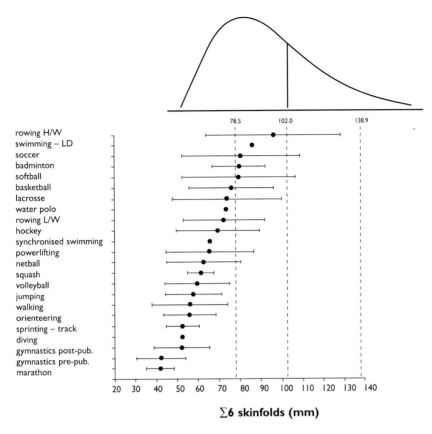

Figure 19 Sum of six skinfolds (mean ± SD) for female athletes in a range of sports plotted relative to a reference group of non-athletes.

The reference group is from data presented by DASET (1992). Note the distribution of skinfold data is positively skewed. Median and interquartile range values are shown for reference (dotted lines).

It is usual for athletes in this group to possess low levels of body fat. Consequently, this requires loss of body fluid for body weight reductions and results in the athletes undergoing severe dietary and/or dehydration regimes immediately prior to "weigh-ins". It is also usual for these athletes to compete in weight divisions well below their natural body mass. The practice of using rapid (1–6 days) dehydration regimes to reduce body mass (by up to 8%) has obvious health implications ranging from changes in whole body metabolism, metabolic activity of adipose tissue, endocrine function and the altered distribution of body fat (Brownell et al., 1987). In addition to the rapid weight changes which may be extreme (up to 9 kg in one week), some athletes may undergo these fluctuating changes in body mass and composition up to thirty times or more each season (Brownell et al., 1987). It appears that despite such adverse physiological effects with repeated bouts of rapid weight loss, peak power output in events lasting less than about 30 s may not be affected. In fact at least one study has found mass specific peak power output ($W.kg^{-1}$) increased following dehydration of up to 5% body mass (Jacobs, 1980). It should be pointed out, however, that many athletes undergo weight loss of greater than 5% body mass and that laboratory tests do not usually incorporate skills tests which may be adversely affected (Klinzing & Karpowicz, 1986; Maffulli, 1992). A number of studies have shown a reduction in performance quality and quantity in events lasting greater than about 30 s following dehydration (Horswill et al., 1990; Klinzing & Karpowicz, 1986; Webster et al., 1990). It is likely that a combination of a reduction in muscle and skin blood flow (Claremont et al., 1976; Horstman and Horvath, 1973), sweat rate (Sawka et al., 1983), and possible alterations in muscle glycogen and mineral concentrations (Horswill et al., 1990) are responsible for these decrements. It should be pointed out that although most weight-division sports allow the athletes to rehydrate following the weighing trials, not all athletes attain euhydration before competition.

- Athletes who reduce body weight and fat mass primarily for aesthetic reasons. The sports included in this category are gymnastics, competitive aerobics, figure skating, bodybuilding and diving and other sports where judging is based on appearance as well as performance. The BF reductions may also help performance.

- Athletes who compete at low levels of fat specifically to improve physical performance. This group includes athletes in sports in which low fat mass is the norm. For example, volleyball, Australian rules football, sprinting, jumping and distance events such as cycling, triathlon and running. A number of investigators have found deterioration of performance in these events as body fat levels increase (Wilmore & Costill, 1987). Often, there is also an inverse relationship between level of competition and level of body fat (Burke, Read & Gollan, 1985) or level of success at the elite level. For example, successful heavyweight rowers have been shown to have lower skinfolds measurements than less successful athletes (Hahn, 1990).

Moderate levels of body fat

These athletes are involved in sports such as badminton, tennis and other racquet sports, cricket, baseball and sailing where loss of fat may help fitness and performance but generally body fat levels tend to be higher than in many other sports. For example, male sailors in the Montreal Olympics averaged 16.4% BF (range 13 – 24% BF) across various sailing events (Shephard, 1990). First-class Australian cricketers average about 11% BF with some players above 15% BF (AADBase, 1995).

Higher than average body fat

Sports in this category include throwing events (hammer, discus, shot put) and sports such as ultra-distance swimming.

Excess fat in athletes involved in throwing events may be detrimental to performance. This is because FM will decrease acceleration, particularly when located on the limbs. Perhaps this is one area of athletics where future competitors will differ greatly from those of today. However, extremely low levels of BF are rarely found in combination with extraordinary FFM, heavyweight bodybuilders being an exception (Fry et al., 1991).

The low density of fat gives it buoyancy characteristics which are advantageous for channel or ocean swimmers provided an adequate muscle mass is present to supply the sufficient propulsive forces. Additionally, fat provides insulation against cold water (Holmer & Bergh, 1974). It has been suggested that the higher levels of body fat in female competitive swimmers improves their efficiency (O_2 uptake per unit distance) relative to males due to an elevation of the body out of the water and a corresponding reduction in hydrodynamic drag (Pendergast et al., 1977). This may be interpreted to mean that all swimmers tend toward fatness. However, perhaps the most definitive response to this interpretation is found in the descriptive anthropometric data collected on elite swimmers (Mazza et al., 1994). Data collected during the 1990 World Swimming Championships shows all groups of male swimmers have low levels of fatness with the sum of six skinfolds (triceps, subscapular, supraspinale, abdominal, front thigh, medial calf) equal to 41.8 ± 9.1 mm for the 1500 m athletes and 60.3 ± 13.6 mm for the long distance specialists. For the females the sum of six skinfolds ranged from 62.3 ± 6.7 mm for the 800 m group to 104.6 ± 29.8 mm for the long distance swimmers (Mazza et al., 1994).

In the longer swimming events fat serves to improve performance in two ways. Firstly, fat gives greater buoyancy to the swimmer and contributes to improved efficiency by decreasing hydrodynamic drag. Secondly, hypothermia is a potentially life-threatening problem in endurance swimming events. For heat to be lost from the body it must pass down two thermal gradients, from core to skin (Tc − Ts), and from skin to water (Ts − Tw). The Tc − Ts gradient is the one which is most influenced by body fat, particularly subcutaneous fat stores (Nadel et al., 1974). There is, therefore, a requirement of a thicker fat layer as thermal insulation to preserve body heat in the water, despite high rates of heat production during competition (about 6–10 times resting levels). Pugh and colleagues (1960) calculated that a 1 cm subcutaneous fat layer (about the average thickness over the body in their male channel swimmers) is able to maintain a difference of about 1.7°C between the core and surrounding water (Tw = 16°), when the skin blood flow has been significantly reduced due to strong vasoconstrictor drive. When heat production is elevated to 10 times resting levels the same 1 cm fat layer is estimated to maintain a 10-fold difference in temperature between the body core and surrounding water.

Both theoretical estimates and experimental measurements of the second thermal gradient (Ts − Tw) have been made. The convective heat transfer coefficient determines the heat flux between the body and the surrounding environment as follows:

$$H_c \;=\; \frac{\dot{E}}{\Delta T \; x \; BSA}$$

where:

H_c = *convective heat transfer coefficient* $(W \, x \, m^{-2} \, x \, °C^{-1})$

$\dot{E}$ = *energy in a given time* (W)

ΔT = *difference between mean skin and water temperature* $(°C)$

BSA = *body surface area* (m^2)

Nadel et al. (1974) have calculated that H_C in still water is over 200 times greater than still air under average water and temperature conditions. Since the body's surface area is included in the equation then athletes with smaller *BSA*/mass ratios are suited for long distance swimming events, particularly in cold water.

Subcutaneous fat provides a cushioning effect to heavy falls and body collisions in sports such as Australian rules football and rugby but would be detrimental to performance due to reasons mentioned above. Therefore, it is characteristic for high-performance athletes in these sports to have low levels of BF (Withers, Craig et al., 1987). High body mass *per se* is undoubtedly of great significance in events such as sumo wrestling and possibly in certain positions (e.g. defensive linemen) in American football, provided adequate strength is also present.

2.6.3 Training and heredity

Although the level of BF is known to have a considerable genetic basis, it still remains the tissue compartment most responsive to training and dietary interventions. Bouchard and Lortie (1984) indicated the heritability factor for body fatness, assessed via skinfold measurements, was about 0.55. More recent summaries by the same authors now suggest the heritability factor for percent body fat is about 25% for biological inheritance with an additional 30% from cultural inheritance (Bouchard & Perusse, 1994). Despite accounting for a significant proportion of the variance in fatness, training and dieting, either alone or in combination, have been shown to have profound effects on the level of fatness for some individuals (see Chapter 12).

3　Evolution of human body size

Changes in the body size of athletes need to be considered in the context of on-going modifications of body dimensions within the general population. Therefore, a discussion is presented on the relatively recent evolution of human size before concentrating on athletic data.

The observed distribution of height and body size within any population is due to a combination of both environmental and genetic factors. These represent the culmination of evolutionary influences up to that point in time, for example climatic conditions or altitude and the stability of the genetic pool. Together these factors determine the current morphological and physiological characteristics of a population.

Changes in the distributions of body dimensions over time are due mainly to environmental factors and to a lesser extent genetic influences. Environmental factors include the nutritional status of the population and the prevalence of major diseases or plagues. For example, analysis of excavated bones of adult individuals who lived during the last two millennia has given a quite clear account of fluctuations in human height since biblical times (Kunitz, 1987) as illustrated in Figure 20.

These studies suggest that our height (predominantly European) has fluctuated considerably during this period. It is because of this pattern of changing body dimensions that records of human stature are so valuable in sciences as diverse as medicine, anthropology and economics.

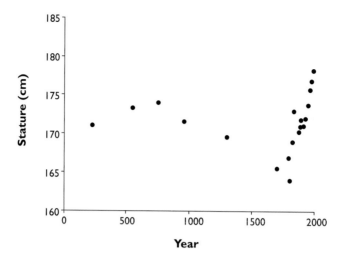

Figure 20 Changes in stature in humans measured over the past 2000 years.

The data were collected using archeological excavation and historical records. There are between 36 and 10,863 subjects used for individual data points shown. Data are from: AADBase, 1995; DASET, 1992; Kunitz, 1987; Meredith, 1976; NSW Department of Public Health, 1955; Roth & Harris, 1908).

As a species, humans have never been larger in our history (as far as we can tell). Our present stature has resulted from an unprecedented growth spurt from about the mid-19th century. Essentially, it has been known for at least a century that humans are increasing in size over successive generations. This phenomenon is called a "secular trend". Although the exact reasons for the secular trend are unknown, it may be due to better nutrition, interbreeding between previously geographically diverse populations, the large-scale process of immunisation, the end of the industrial revolution, urbanisation, and a range of other less likely possibilities including the influence of assortative and selective mating and changes in world temperature and humidity (Floud, Wachter & Gregory, 1990).

Whilst it is not known whether this is a cause or effect there has been an almost linear decrease in the age of menarche in many countries over the past 150 years. Figure 21 illustrates this phenomenon.

Although there has not been an adequate explanation for this change it is possible that girls require a certain body size to initiate the physiological and structural changes accompanying menarche. For example, using the regression equation presented in

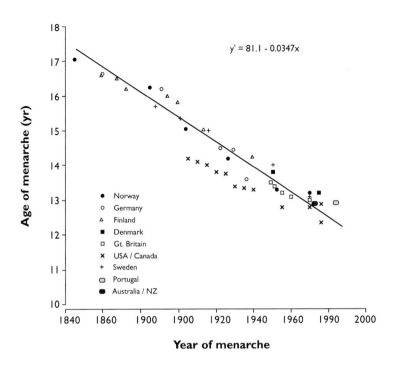

Figure 21 Age of menarche as a function of year of menarche for girls in a number of countries over the past 150 years. Data were collated from Jokl, 1976; Ross et al., 1976; Sobral et al., 1986 and Tanner, 1978.

Figure 21 and the secular trend data (below), the average size (i.e. height, reflecting maturation) of girls at the turn of the century at menarche is almost identical to the size of the now younger girls who reach menarche (on average, about 150 cm). It is also of interest to note that physical exercise seems to delay the onset of menarche (Malina, 1982; Ross et al., 1976) whereas it has reported that inactivity in young athletes (due to injury) may accelerate maturation (Ross & Marfell-Jones, 1991). Despite the postponement of menarche, current data suggest no influence of physical activity and chronic exercise training on final statural growth (Malina, 1994). Data on Australian children collected at intervals this century illustrate the secular trend for height.

It has been argued, and a considerable amount of data are available to support the contention, that the rate of change in height in the western world has slowed down in most countries (Tanner, 1978). This slowing of the secular trend was thought to have begun during the period 1960–1970. However, the data shown in Figures 22 and 23 suggest that the secular trend for height in Australia is not levelling off. The combined data show a linear increase in height (correlations ranged between 0.970 – 0.999 for the individual age and gender groups) which averages 1.23 cm per decade for females and 1.33 cm per decade for males. Thus, it appears the overall rate of height change is relatively steady, and has been from at least the early part of this century.

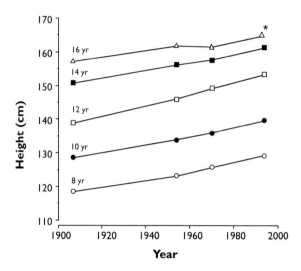

Figure 22 Heights for 8 – 16-year-old females since 1906.
    * Mean height for 16-year-old females from DASET (1992).

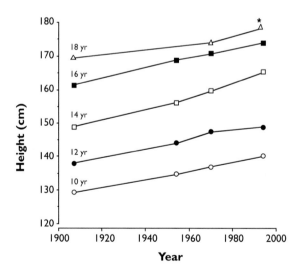

Figure 23 Heights for 10 – 18-year-old males since 1906. *Mean height for 18-year-old males from DASET (1992).

Figures 22 and 23 have been produced using summaries of data collected on Sydney school (or school-aged) children throughout this century: (Gard, 1995; Meredith, 1976; NSW Department of Public Health, 1955; Roth & Harris, 1908). * Mean height for 18-year-old males from DASET (1992).

3.1 Evolution of body size of athletes

Athlete body size has been of great interest within the general population (e.g. Johnson, 1974; Sachare, 1994). It is common to find statistics on players' sizes in weekly game magazines at most sporting events. Players' heights and masses are critical elements used in recruitment and selection, are routinely discussed by supporters and the media, and ultimately influence achievement. However, in the scientific discussion of the evolution of sporting records there has only occasionally been mention of the alteration in size, shape and composition of athletes participating in the sports (Ackland et al., 1994; Cox et al., 1995; Wang, Downey, Perko, Yesalis, 1993). There is little question that equipment design, training strategies, greater opportunities for competition and technological developments have been important in contributing to record performances. Equally, however, we suggest that the evolution of body types has too often been overlooked and has been instrumental in the establishment of most of the current records.

It should be pointed out that many events do not have world records as such, for example, team sports, racquet sports and other non-Olympic sports. In these cases it is not easy to determine the extent of the evolution of performers' bodies. The task is even more difficult to quantify since there is a scarcity of information on players' size beyond the last 30 to 40 years. When historical data on athletes are available they are important since they not only reflect the status of player size at specific points in time but can be used to assess the evolving requirements of body size in particular sports and predict future player sizes. Data on athletes are also useful since they may, with some assumptions, be used as a basis for estimating secular trends in the general population where data are absent or lean. These comparisons both within and between athletic and non-athletic groups may reveal distinct patterns of alterations in body size over time which may be related to other aspects of sporting life such as training, dietary manipulation, rule modifications and other interventions such as drug use. We suggest a model to classify sports according to the player types they are likely to select in the future. This is based on theoretical considerations of the sports today, together with data available from the literature on athletes over a number of generations.

There are four broad groups of athletic events which we have used to describe our model, combining morphological optimisation and the evolution of humans (athletes and non-athletes). These are open upper-end optimisation, relative optimisation, absolute optimisation and open lower-end optimisation. These models of classification are illustrated in Figure 24. Each of these models will be discussed individually using examples from several sports.

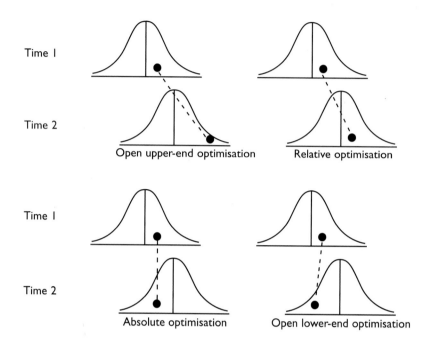

Time 1

Time 2

Open upper-end optimisation   Relative optimisation

Time 1

Time 2

Absolute optimisation   Open lower-end optimisation

Figure 24 Models of morphological optimisation with reference to time. See text for details.

3.2 Open upper-end optimisation

Sports in this category are those where athletes with a larger absolute or relative size or proportion will have an advantage in competition. That is, the bigger the better, all other things being equal. There are only a few sports that will be found within this category and they include those which generally do not require moving large distances or for extended periods of time (without rest). Also sports requiring athletes to overcome external, non-human resistance will be included in this group. Open upper-end optimisation includes sports such as super-heavyweight lifting, sumo wrestling and American football for attributes such as body mass; netball, basketball and heavyweight rowing for height; boxing and weightlifting at the two extremes for upper limb length to stature ratio and Ap in cycling. Figure 25 illustrates the consequence of one example of upper open-end optimisation. In this case super-heavyweight lifting performances since 1948 are shown relative to those within lower (closed) weight categories.

The effect of this open upper-end optimisation is the appearance of athletes in excess of 160 kg such as the Russian Alexyev (Jokl, 1976). World records for the super-heavyweights have increased at a rate approximately twice that found with the other classes of lifters.

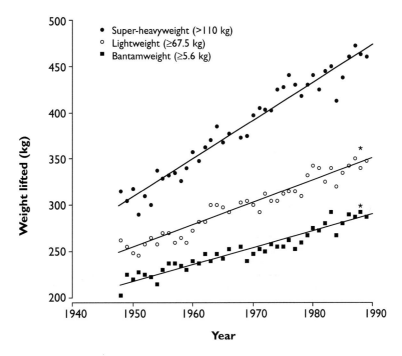

Figure 25 The relationship between the weight lifted during world record lifts and the year of achievement for three weight classes.

Data are from Jokl, 1976; Mathews & Morrison, 1990. Equations are: Superheavyweight y' = −7739.3 + 4.127x; Lightweight y' = −4572.1 + 2.474x; Bantamweight y' = −3260 + 1.784x. * records subsequently denied due to a positive drug test.

A further example can be found by careful analysis of the data collected on Australian rules footballers (Olive, Norton & Olds, 1994). Despite the fact that there is little information on the body size of the general population of adult Australians prior to the last two or three decades, there is considerable data available on athletes in three of the main football codes played in Australia (Australian rules, rugby league and rugby union). Data on body size (height and mass) of footballers were obtained from a number of sources, primarily archival records usually held by the sporting organisations. The analysis for Australian rules ruckmen is shown in Figure 26.

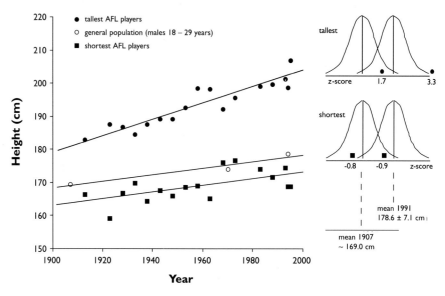

Figure 26 The relationship between the mean heights of Australian football players and the year of playing.

These data are shown relative to the general population of young adult males. The 3 tallest and 3 shortest AFL players were combined for each data point in the respective groups. Data are from AFL records (1994); DASET (1992); Meredith (1976); Roth & Harris (1908). The right panel shows the z-scores for the football groups relative to the changing general population at two time points this century. The exaggerated rate of height increase of the tallest players is represented by a greater z-score in the more recent comparison with the general population (z = 3.3 vs 1.7).

These data highlight the change in height of the ruckmen relative to both the young adult male population and the smallest players over nearly 100 years of the game's history. The ruckmen are increasing at a rate over two times faster than either of the other groups. For example, the tallest player in the 1913 grand final (182 cm), would be ranked below the 30th percentile against his contemporary peers when the *whole* team is considered. A player of 182 cm would be almost 25 cm shorter than the mean height of the three tallest ruckmen today. This perhaps reflects the specialist nature of the position, the fact these athletes can now be rested more frequently during the game and selective recruitment for tall players. It also means that the potential pool of ruckmen is much smaller now than ever before. Predictions for future players indicate by the year 2050 the mean of the three tallest ruckmen will be about 221 cm (Olive et al., 1994), heights achieved presently only in male basketball centres.

Figure 27 illustrates the BMI (mass × height^{-2}) changes over the course of this century across the three football codes. Data for high school All-American football players are also presented for reference.

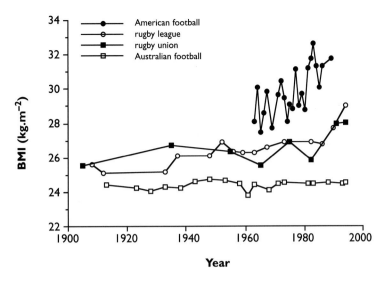

Figure 27 The relationship between mean BMI and year of playing for players in four football codes.

Data for Australian rules football players are from VFL and AFL official records of grand final teams over 5-year intervals (AFL records, 1994); rugby league data are from the NSWRL statistician (ARL records, 1994). These data are from Australian Kangaroo representatives in 4-year intervals. Rugby union data are from Pollard (1984) and the Australian rugby union official records post 1984 (ARU records, 1994). American football data are from Wang et al. (1993).

Two features stand out. Firstly, mean BMI in the two rugby codes has increased throughout the century indicating proportionally greater increases in mass (presumably mainly muscle) relative to changes in height. Secondly, there has been a dramatic acceleration in BMI among the rugby players since the early 1980s. It is probable that much of this increase is due to longer and more intense resistance training throughout their careers as players have adopted a more professional level. It is also possible that there are more players who are using size (and performance) enhancing drugs such as anabolic steroids and human growth hormone.

Basketball

Figure 28 shows another example of open upper-end optimisation. In this case the height of every NBA player since 1945 (and a few from earlier seasons) is presented. The regression equation indicates the rate of change in mean height of all players (2.25 cm × decade^{-1}) is significantly greater than that of the general population [about 1 cm × decade^{-1} in North Americans (Tanner, 1978)]. Furthermore, the rate of height increase for the tallest players joining the NBA each year (4.38 cm × decade^{-1}) is almost twice that of the mean height increase and about 4 times that of the general population. At this rate of rise in height it is predicted that the first player standing 244 cm (8'0") will be seen in the NBA by about 2030.

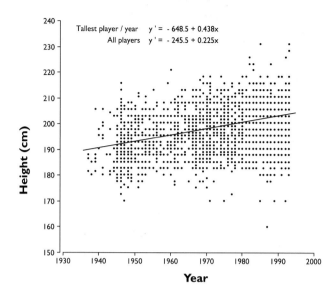

Figure 28 The relationship between the height of NBA basketball players and the first year of their professional careers. Data are from Sachare (1994), n=2826.

As pointed out earlier, there are implications associated with this progression of larger players. Already a number of changes have been introduced to the game for safety reasons and to reduce congested play and excessive body collisions. For example, as DuPree (1994) points out, hydraulic mount systems and collapsible rims were installed to support large players hanging on the rims and to avoid shattering backboards. Also 15 cm was shaved from the bottom of the backboards to prevent players from hitting their heads while dunking and blocking. Other changes are also being suggested such as using larger courts and balls, smaller rims and even a restriction of players on the field.

Ackland et al. (1994) reported that the mean height for international female players had increased by 3.1 cm and their mass by 3.2 kg during the last decade. Despite their increased body mass the athletes were also less endomorphic indicating a lower sum of skinfolds used in the somatotype calculations. Thus the rate of change relative to that of the general population supports the placement of both male and female basketball in the open upper-end optimisation category.

A precise explanation for the seemingly endless trend toward open upper-end optimisation in several sports is not possible at present, but in addition to the secular trend influences, it may be related to any one or more of the following factors:

- greater selectivity in recruitment (i.e. specifically targeting taller and/or heavier players, for example in the NBA)
- the influence of other external factors such as improved weight-training techniques
- possible drug use
- the generation of a genetic pool of big athletes who result from athletes breeding with other athletes
- internationalisation versus regionalisation of sport where the potential populations are far greater for sports.

3.3 Relative optimisation

Relative optimisation refers to sports where optimal player size increases at about the same rate as that of the general population. Since the general population are increasing in size and athletes, on average, remain the same number of SDs away from the mean, the absolute size of athletes must increase. Most sports which do not have restrictions of weight classes fall into this category. Several examples are presented.

Football

In Figure 26 above it was shown that Australian rules ruckmen were increasing out of proportion to the general population but the smaller players were increasing proportionally to this change. Thus, the smaller players are exhibiting relative optimisation. This indicates that, assuming the variances are the same, the same relative proportion of the population have the opportunity to play the game today as has been the case in previous generations. Other examples can be found by reviewing the data on the two other football codes, rugby union and rugby league. For example, mean height for rugby union players has been relatively constant with reference to the general population secular trend. This is illustrated in Figure 29.

Heavyweight boxers

Ford (1984), analysed data originally obtained from McCallum (1974) on the body size of world heavyweight boxing champions from 1889 to 1978. Despite the "naive expectation that larger and stronger athletes make better boxers" he concluded that the advantages derived from increased absolute muscle power in larger boxers are not as great as the disadvantages of decreased speed and agility. Using McCallum's data Ford concluded that only three heavyweight boxers in history were taller than 189.2 cm, with all three holding the title for no more than one title defence. However, we re-analysed the complete data set from 1882 to 1994 (Ballarati, 1994; Goldman, 1986; Ford, 1984;

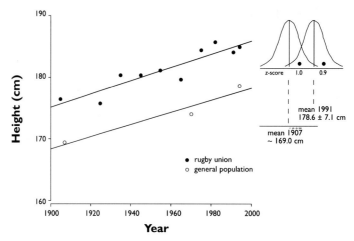

Figure 29 The relationship between the mean height of rugby union players and the year of playing relative to the general population height over the same period. Rugby union data are from sources outlined in the text. For reference data see Figure 26.

Mullan, 1995) to reveal that, on average, the modern champion is indeed taller and heavier than their early twentieth century predecessors. The difference between the mean height of the boxers and that of the adult male in the general population is about 2 standard deviations (178.6 versus 191 cm). The fact that the rate of change of boxing champions is not different from the rate of change in the general population (95% CI for the lower slope of the boxing line is +0.029 cm × decade^{-1}) results in the secular trend of body size in the general population presenting a relatively constant potential pool of heavyweight boxers. These data also suggest that size alone is not necessarily an advantage in boxing. Perhaps the trade-off of size for speed and acceleration may be particularly important in this sport.

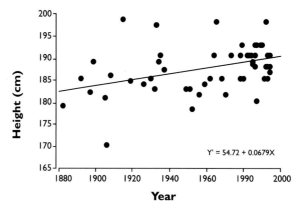

Figure 30 The relationship between the height of boxing heavyweight champions (undisputed, IBF, WBC and WBF champions have been included) and the year of winning the title. Data are from Ballarati (1994), Ford (1984), Goldman (1986) and Mullan (1995).

3.4 Absolute optimisation

Jockeys

The average jockey size has not changed much over the major part of this century. The mean ± SD body mass in 1933 (n = 138) was 49.9 ± 3.3, in 1964 (n = 77) it was 48.9 ± 2.3, and in 1995 (n = 103) it is 51.0 ± 1.4 kg (AJC records, 1933, 1964; Jenkins, 1995). The frequency distributions of the licensed jockeys used in these analyses are shown in Figure 31.

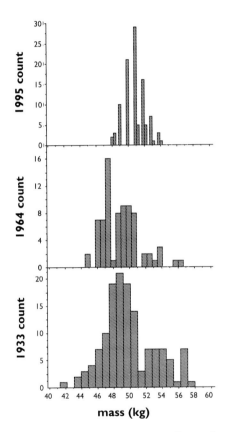

Figure 31 Frequency distributions of the mass of licensed professional jockeys at three periods during this century.

Data are from AJC records, (1933, 1964); Jenkins, (1995)

This figure illustrates a number of important points. Absolute optimisation is apparent over this period where the mean mass is unchanged (and the variability of body masses narrows). That is, the mean mass of jockeys is constrained while that of the general population increases. The means are therefore drifting apart, reducing the OZ value. This variability or range of jockey size is influenced by the range of weights the horses typically carry in races. This currently varies between a minimal weight of 51 kg, including jockey, saddle and equipment, to top weights of around 70 kg. In 1964 it was 49 kg. The figure for 1933 is unknown. Thus, minimal weights have risen due to both the difficulties the jockeys encountered in order to maintain a low mass (this was the primary reason the minimal mass carried by the horses was increased from 49 to 51 kg), and to the decreased number of small people owing to secular trends. Over time, the lower portion of the distribution has been eroded. The lowest mass in 1995 was 48.0 kg compared to 41.3 kg in 1933. One explanation for the decreased upper levels for the jockey mass may be that heavier jockeys receive less opportunity to ride, that is, they reduce their potential number of rides. Finally, races where horses are allocated heavier loads, such as highweights and hurdles, are becoming less popular. Hurdle events are no longer held at Sydney metropolitan race meetings. Since hurdlers, in general, carried greater weights than flat runners, a considerable potential jockey population has been removed from the sport.

Since the potential pool of jockeys is getting smaller each generation (OZ currently = 3.23% for males), supply and demand today makes horse riding a lucrative professional sport. This has undoubtedly led to many athletes, who are barely within the range of desirable jockey size, finding it increasingly difficult to make weight. This may, in part, also explain the increase in licensed female jockeys, who now represent about 5% of jockeys compared to no representation in the previous surveys (Jenkins, 1995).

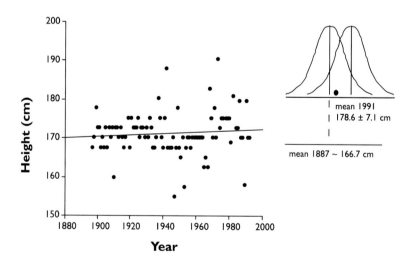

Figure 32 The relationship between the height of male Boston marathon winners and year of winning. Data are from Jenkins (1995).

Data are from Falls (1977) and Fox (1979 – 1993).

Football

Figure 27 above illustrates that the mean BMI of the Australian rules football players has deviated by less than one BMI unit over the past 81 years (Olive et al., 1994). This fact together with the concomitant body mass increases suggests that the Australian rules football players have maintained similar linear body shapes throughout the sports evolution.

Marathon runners

The Boston marathon is the world's oldest still existing annual race. Data were re-analysed on the body size of winners of the Boston marathon from 1897 to 1992 (Falls, 1977; Fox, 1979 – 1993). The mean height of the male marathon winners is 171.3 ± 5.4 cm (range 154.9 – 190.5 cm) with height remaining constant over nearly 100 years as illustrated in Figure 32.

The mean height of the winners in Boston has not changed despite the secular trend in the general population (about $1 \text{ cm} \times \text{decade}^{-1}$ in North Americans; Tanner, 1978). This trend suggests that an optimum body size for the event exists. The notion that an optimum body size exists, is further supported by the Boston marathon runners' mass and body mass index (mass × height^{-2}) over time. The mean mass of the runners has remained relatively constant over time (61.6 ± 5.1 kg). BMI has also remained unchanged over the same period as illustrated in Figure 33.

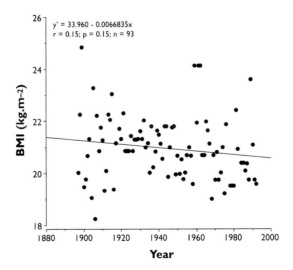

Figure 33 The relationship between the BMI of male Boston marathon winners and year of winning.

Data are from Falls (1977) and Fox (1979 – 1993).

Data for female winners from 1979 to 1992 were available (Fox, 1979). Although more scattered over this short time period, the regression equations for height, mass and BMI remain not significantly different from zero (Figure 34). The mean height of the female runners is 164.2 ± 7.2 cm.

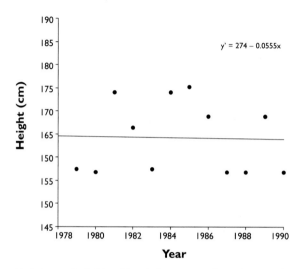

Figure 34 The relationship between the height of female Boston marathon winners and year of winning.

Data are from Fox (1979 – 1993).

Optimum body size for the marathon will be dependent upon other factors including the type of course (flat courses where larger runners will be at a relative advantage or undulating courses where smaller runners will be at a relative advantage), and the benefits of body size to thermoregulation (BSA/mass ratio) in the Boston climate.

3.5 Open lower-end optimisation

There are only a few events which fit into this category. One of the sports placed in this group is women's gymnastics. Nodeny (1994) reports the average size of USA national female representatives has decreased during the past 30 years. This is illustrated in Figure 35.

Over this period height and mass have steadily deceased from 1.6 m, 47.7 kg in 1976 to 1.45 m, 40 kg in 1992. BMI in women has declined from 21.1 in the 1964 Olympics to 19.2 kg × m^{-2} in the 1987 World Championships (Claessens et al., 1991). In concert with these trends the mean age of the female gymnasts competing at Olympic and World Championships has decreased from 22.7 yr in 1964 to 16.5 yr in 1987. In essence, because of the demands of the sport (for smaller size), the potential pool of optimally proportioned female gymnasts has been reduced among the adult population. In response to this, younger girls have progressively become suited to the sport and, as a product of this age and high volume of training, they have developed characteristic patterns of delayed menarche and the maintenance of child-like growth features (such as low body fat levels). This has influenced the recent rule change to international women's gymnastics where there is now a lower age limit of 15 years. No doubt this rule change will result in an alteration in the morphology of the very best international level female competitors in ways that, at this stage, are unpredictable.

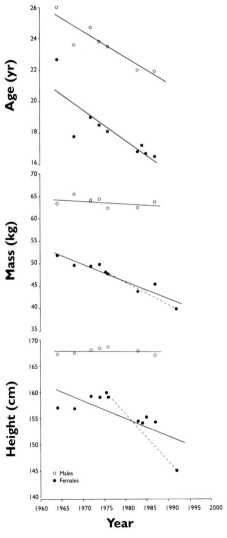

Figure 35 The relationship between the age, mass and height of male and female gymnasts competing at Olympic and World Championship events since 1964. Data are from Claessens et al., 1991 (Table 6); and Nodeny, 1994 (dotted line).

4 Summary

This chapter has reviewed the concept of morphological optimisation. This is the process whereby the physical demands of a sport lead to the selection of body types (structure and composition) best suited to that sport. This is most obvious at the professional level of sport. The anatomical features apparent among the elite level performers are not fixed within the athletic population. Rather, they are continually undergoing refinement within each generation as a response to training and along generations as humans evolve, rules and technologies are altered, and the status of sports changes. All of these characteristics impact upon the sport to modify the potential population from which athletes are selected. We present a model for statistically determining the probability of an anthropometric variable being found within the general (or potential) population. This enables analysis of selection pressures for any anthropometric variable and quantification of how these may vary across gender, competitive levels and over time. An analysis of the (recent) evolution of human size and shape has also enabled estimates of future body dimension requirements in a number of sports.

5 References

AADBase (1995).
Australian Anthropometric Database. School of Sport and Leisure Studies, The University of New South Wales, Sydney, Australia.

Ackland, T., Schreiner A., & Kerr, D. (1994).
Anthropometric profiles of world championship female basketball players.
International conference of science and medicine in sport, Brisbane, **Sports Medicine Australia** (Abstract).

AFL records (1994).
Col Hutchinson, Statistician,
Australian Football League, Melbourne, Australia

AJC records (1933-1964)
The Australian Jockey Club Racing Calendar (September 1, 1933; September 1, 1964).
Australian Jockey Club, Alison Road, Randwick, New South Wales, Australia.

ARL records (1994).
David Middleton, Statistician
League Information Services, 31 Morton Street, Wollstonecraft, New South Wales, Australia.

ARU records (1994)
Rob Bradley, Statistician,
Australian Rugby Union, 353 Anzac Parade, Kingsford, New South Wales, Australia

Åstrand, P.O., & Rodahl, K. (1986).
Textbook of Work Physiology, 3rd Ed. (p. 595).
New York: McGraw-Hill.

ATP Tour (1995).
ATP 1995 player guide.
Ponte Vedra Beach, Florida: ATP Tour.

Bale, J. (1998).
Sport Geography.
New York: E & F.N. Spon.

Ballarati, G. (1994).
Pugilato.
Rome: Ballerati Publishing.

Bartlett, R.M., & Best, R.J. (1988).
The biomechanics of javelin throwing: a review.
Journal of Sports Science, 6, 1-38.

Bouchard, C., & Lortie, G. (1984).
Heredity and endurance performance.
Sports Medicine, 1, 38-64.

Bouchard, C., & Perusse, L. (1994).
Heredity, activity level, fitness, and health. In C. Bouchard, R.J. Shepherd, & T. Stephens (Eds.), **Physical activity, fitness and health** (pp. 106-118).
Champaign, Illinois: Human Kinetics.

Brownell, K.D., Nelson Steen, S., & Wilmore, J.H. (1987).
Weight regulation practices in athletes; analysis of metabolic and health effects.
Medicine and Science in Sports and Exercise, 19, 546-556.

Burke, E.R., Faria, I.E., & White, J.A. (1990).
Cycling. In T. Reilly, N. Secher, P. Snell, & C. Williams (Eds.), **Physiology of Sports** (pp. 175-213).
London: E & F. N. Spon.

Burke, L.M., & Read, R.S.D. (1987).
Diet patterns of elite male triathletes.
Physician and Sports Medicine, 15, 140-155.

Burke, L.M., Read, R.S.D., & Gollan, R.A. (1985).
Australian Rules football: an anthropometric study of participants.
British Journal of Sports Medicine, 19, 100-102.

Carlson, B.R., Carter, J.E.L., Patterson, P., Petti, K., Orfanos, S.M., & Noffal, G.J. (1994).
Physique and motor performance characteristics of US national rugby players.
Journal of Sports Sciences, 12, 403-412.

Carter, J.E.L., Ross, W.D., Aubry, S.P., Hebbelinck, M., & Borms, J. (1982).
Anthropometry of Montreal Olympic athletes.
Medicine Sport 16 (pp. 25-52).
Karger: Basel.

Carter, J.E.L. (Ed.). (1984).
Physical Structure of Olympic Athletes. Part II:
Kinanthropometry of Olympic Athletes.
Karger: Basel.

Chilibeck, P.D., Sale, D.G., & Webber, C.E. (1995).
Exercise and bone mineral density.
Sports Medicine, 19, 103-122.

Claessens, A.L., Veer, F.M., Stijnen, V., Lefeure, J., Maes, H., Steens, G., & Beunen, G. (1991).
Anthropometric characteristics of outstanding male and female gymnasts.
Journal of Sports Sciences, 9, 53-74.

Claessens, A.L., Hlatky, S., Lefevre, J., & Holdhaus, H. (1994).
The role of anthropometric characteristics in modern pentathlon performance in female athletes.
Journal of Sports Science, 12, 391-401.

Claremont, A.D., Costill, D.L., Fink, W., & Van Handel, P. (1976).
Heat tolerance following diuretic induced dehydration.
Medicine and Science in Sports, 8, 239-243.

Clark, P.J. (1956).
The heritability of certain anthropometric characters as ascertained from measurements of twins.
American Journal of Human Genetics, 8, 49-54.

Clarys, J.P., Martin, A.D., & Drinkwater, D.T. (1984).
Gross tissue weights in the human body by cadaver dissection.
Human Biology, 56, 459-473.

Conners, M., Dupuis, D.L., & Morgan, B. (1992).
The Olympic Factbook.
London: Visible Ink Press.

Cox, M.H., Miles, D.S., Verde, T.J., & Rhodes, E.C. (1995).
Applied physiology of ice hockey.
Sports Medicine, 19, 184-201.

Craig, N.P. (1984).
South Australian state representative sportsmen: relative body fat, somatotype and anthropometric prediction of body density. Unpublished master's thesis, The Flinders University of South Australia, Adelaide, South Australia, Australia.

Cureton, K.J., & Sparling, P.B. (1980).
Distance running performance and metabolic responses to running in men and women with excess weight experimentally equated.
Medicine and Science in Sports and Exercise, 12, 288-294.

Cureton, K.J., Sparling, P.B., Evans, B.W., Johnson, S.M., Kong, U.D., & Purvis, J.W. (1978).
Effect of experimental alterations in excess weight on aerobic capacity and distance running performance.
Medicine and Science in Sports, 10, 194-199.

DASET (1992).
>Department of the Arts, Sport, the Environment and Territories.
>**Pilot survey of the fitness of Australians.**
>Canberra: Australian Government Printing Service.

Dupree, D. (1994).
>Shaq, 'Zo and beyond: A peek into the future. In A. Sachare (Ed.), **The official NBA basketball encyclopedia** (pp. 164-173).
>New York: Villard Books.

Dyson, G.H.G. (1975).
>**The mechanics of athletics** (pp. 146-163).
>London: Hodder and Stoughton.

Eveleth, P.B., & Tanner, J.M. (1976).
>**Worldwide variation in human growth** (pp. 276-433).
>Cambridge: Cambridge University Press.

Falls, J. (1977).
>**The Boston Marathon** (pp. 163-165).
>New York: Macmillan.

Faulkner, R.A. (1976).
>**Physique characteristics of Canadian figure skaters.**
>Unpublished Master's thesis, Simon Fraser University, Vancouver.

Fleck, S.J., Case, S., Puhl, J., & Van Handle, P. (1985).
>Physical and physiological characteristics of elite women volleyball players.
>**Canadian Journal of Applied Sport Sciences, 10**, 122-126.

Fogelholm, M. (1994).
>Effects of bodyweight reduction on sports performance.
>**Sports Medicine, 18**, 249-267.

Foley, J.P., Bird, S.R., & White, J.A. (1989).
>Anthropometric comparison of cyclists from different events
>**British Journal of Sports Medicine, 23**, 30-33.

Ford, L.E. (1984).
>Some consequences of body size.
>**American Journal of Physiology, 247**, H495-H507.

Fox, E. (Ed.) (1979 - 1993).
>**Track and Field News**, (Vols. 32,#11 - 46#1).
>Mt View, California: Track and Field Publications

Floud, R., Wachter, K.W., & Gregory, A. (1990).
>**Height, health and history: Nutritional status in the United Kingdom, 1750-1980.**
>Cambridge: Cambridge University Press.

Fry, A.C., Ryan, A.J., Schwab, R.J., Powell, D.R., & Kraemer, W.J. (1991).
Anthropometric characteristics as discriminators of body-building success.
Journal of Sports Sciences, 9, 23-32.

Gard, M. (1995).
Anthropometric survey of Sydney school children. Unpublished
Master's thesis, The University of New South Wales, Sydney, Australia.

Goldberg, K.E. (1984).
The skeleton: Fantastic framework (p. 57).
Washington: U.S. News Books.

Goldman, H. G. (Ed.). (1986).
Ring Record Book.
New York: Ring Publishing Corporation.

Goldman, A., & Dill, D. B. (1977).
A physiological profile of a jogging class young and old, male and female. In P. Milvy (Ed.), The marathon,
physiological, medical, epidemiological and psychological studies.
Annals of the New York Academy of Sciences, 301, 550-560.

Hagerman, F., Hagerman, G., & Meckelson, T. (1979).
Physiological profiles of elite rowers.
The Physician and Sports Medicine, 7, 74-83.

Hahn, A. (1990).
Identification and selection of talent in Australian rowing.
Excel, 6, 5-11.

Hahn, A., & Bourdon, P. (1995).
Protocols for the physiological assessment of rowers.
In J. Draper, B. Minikin, & R, Telford (Eds.). **Test methods manual**, section III.
Canberra: Australian Sports Commission.

Hanson, J.S. (1973).
Exercise responses following production of experimental obesity.
Journal of Applied Physiology, 35, 587-591.

Hartland, M. (1981).
The anthropometric prediction of body density and relative body fat in South Australian males.
Unpublished Honours thesis, The Flinders University of South Australia, Adelaide, South Australia, Australia.

Holly, R.G., Barnard, R.J., Rosenthal, M., Applegate, E., & Pritikin, N. (1986).
Triathlete characterisation and response to prolonged strenuous competition.
Medicine and Science in Sports and Exercise, 18, 123-127.

Holmer, I., & Bergh, U. (1974).
Metabolic and thermal responses to swimming in water at varying temperature.
Journal of Applied Physiology, 37, 702-705.

Horstman, D.H., & Horvath, S.M. (1973).
Cardiovascular adjustments to progressive dehydration.
Journal of Applied Physiology, 35, 501-504.

Horswill, C.A., Hickner, R.C., Scott, J.R., Costill, D.L., & Gould, D. (1990).
Weight loss, dietary carbohydrate modifications and high intensity physical performance.
Medicine and Science in Sports and Exercise, 22, 470-477.

Ireland, M.L., & Micheli, L.J. (1987).
Triathletes: biographic data, training, and injury patterns.
Annals of Sports Medicine, 3, 117-120.

Ingen Shenau, G.J., & de Groot, G. (1983).
On the origin of differences in performance level between elite male and female speed skaters.
Human Movement Science, 2, 151-159.

Jacobs, I. (1980).
The effects of thermal dehydration on performance of the Wingate anaerobic test.
International Journal of Sports Medicine, 1, 21-24.

Jenkins, P.H. (Ed.). (1995).
Australian Jockey Club Racing Calender (Vols. 72 #9; April, 1995)
Sydney: Australian Jockey Club, Alison Road, Randwick, New South Wales, Australia.

Johnson, W.O. (1974).
From here to 2000.
Sports Illustrated, 41, 80.

Jokl, E. (1976).
Record physiology.
In E. Jokl (Ed.), **Advances in exercise physiology** (pp. 3-22).
Basel: Karger.

Katch, F.I., & Katch, V.L. (1984).
The body composition profile.
In J.A. Nicholas, & E.B. Hershman (Eds.), **Clinics in Sports Medicine 3** (pp. 31-42).
London: W.B. Saunders.

Klinzing, J.E., & Karpowicz, W. (1986).
The effects of rapid weight loss and rehydration on a wrestling performance test.
Journal of Sports Medicine, 26, 149-156.

Khosla, T. (1968).
Unfairness of certain events in the Olympic games.
British Medical Journal, 4, 111-113.

Khosla, T. (1983).
Sport for tall.
British Medical Journal, 287, 736-738.

Khosla, T., & McBroom, V.C. (1988).
Age, height and weight of female Olympic finalists.
British Journal of Sports Medicine, 19, 96-99.

Kunitz, S.J. (1987).
Making a long story short: a note on men's height and mortality in England from the first through the nineteenth centuries.
Medical History, 31, 269-280.

Leake, C.N., & Carter, J.E.L. (1991).
Comparison of body composition and somatotype of trained female triathletes.
Journal of Sports Sciences, 9, 125-138.

LeVeau, B., Ward, T., & Nelson, R.C. (1974).
Body dimensions of Japanese and American gymnasts.
Medicine and Science in Sports, 6, 146-150.

MacLaren, D. (1990).
Court games: volleyball and basketball.
In T. Reilly, N. Secher, P. Snell, & C. Williams, (Eds.), **Physiology of Sports** (pp. 427-464).
London: E & F. N. Spon.

Maffulli, N. (1992).
Making weight: a case study of two elite wrestlers.
British Journal of Sports Medicine, 26, 107-110.

Malina, R.M. (1982).
Menarche in athletes: A synthesis and hypothesis.
Annals of Human Biology, 10, 1-24.

Malina, R.M. (1994).
Physical activity: relationship to growth, maturation, and physical fitness. In C. Bouchard, R.J. Shepherd, & T. Stephens (Eds.), **Physical activity, fitness and health** (pp. 918-930).
Champaign, Illinois: Human Kinetics.

Mathews, P., & Morrison, I. (1990).
The Guinness encyclopedia of international sports records and results.
Middlesex: Guinness Publishing.

Mazza, J.C., Ackland, T.R., Bach, T.M., & Cosolito, P. (1994).
Absolute body size. In J.E.L. Carter, & T.R. Ackland (Eds.), **Kinanthropometry in Aquatic Sports** (pp. 15-54).
Champaign, Illinois: Human Kinetics.

McCallum, J.D. (1974).
The world heavyweight boxing championship, a history.
Radnor, PA: Chilton.

McLean B.D. & Parker, A.W. (1989).
An anthropometric analysis of the elite Australian track cyclist.
Journal of Sports Science, 7, 247-255.

Meredith, H.V. (1976).
  Findings from Asia, Australia, Europe and North America on secular change in mean height of children, youths and young adults.
  American Journal of Physical Anthropology, 44, 315 - 326.

Micheli, L.J., Gillespie, W.J., & Walaszek, R.P.T. (1984).
  Physiologic profiles of female professional ballerinas. In J.A. Nicholas & E.B. Hershman (Eds.). **Clinics in Sports Medicine 3** (pp. 199-213).
  London: W.B. Saunders.

Mikkelsen, F. (1979).
  Physical demands and muscle adaptation in elite badminton players. In J. Terauds (Ed.), **Science in Racquet Sports** (pp. 55-67).
  Del Mar, California: Academic.

Miller, F.R., & Manfredi, T.G. (1987).
  Physiological and anthropometrical predictors of 15-kilometre time trial cycling performance.
  Research Quarterly for Exercise and Sport, 25, 250-254.

Minard, D. (1970).
  Body heat content. In: J.D. Hardy, A.P. Gagge, & J.A.L. Stolwijk (Eds.). **Physiological and Behavioural Temperature Regulation** (pp. 345-357).
  Illinois: Charles C. Thomas Publishers.

Montgomery, D.L. (1982).
  The effect of added weight on ice hockey performance.
  Physician and Sports Medicine, 10 (11), 91-99.

Mullan, H. (1995).
  Boxing News.
  London: Boxing News Ltd.

Nadel, E.R., Holmer, I., Bergh, U., Astrand, P-O., & Stolwijk, J.A.J. (1974).
  Energy exchanges of swimming man.
  Journal of Applied Physiology, 36, 465-471.

Nicholas, C.W., & Baker, J.S. (1995).
  Anthropometric and physiological characteristics of first- and second-class rugby players.
  Journal of Sports Sciences, 13, 15.

Niinimaa,V., Wright, G., Shepherd, R.J., & Clarke, J. (1977).
  Characteristics of the successful dingy sailor.
  Journal of Sports Medicine and Physical Fitness, 17, 83-96.

Nodeny, M. (Aug. 8, 1994).
  Dying to win.
  Who Weekly, 130, 50-57.

Norton, K.I. (1984).
  South Australian females: Body fat, somatotype, body density and anthropometric fractionation of body mass.
  Unpublished Master's thesis, The Flinders University of South Australia, Adelaide, South Australia, Australia.

NSW Department of Public Health, School Medical Service. (1955).
Height and weight tables.
Sydney: New South Wales Government Printer (Australia).

Olds, T.S., Norton, K.I., & Craig, N.P. (1993).
Mathematical model of cycling performance.
Journal of Applied Physiology, 75, 730-737.

Olds, T.S., Norton, K.I., Lowe, E.L.A., Olive, S., Reay, F., & Ly, S. (1995).
Modeling road cycling performance.
Journal of Applied Physiology, 78, 1596-1611.

Olive, S.C., Norton, K.I., & Olds, T.S. (1994).
The evolution of body size in Australian male athletes. **Proceedings of the Australian Sports Medicine National Scientific Conference**, Brisbane.

O'Toole, M.L., & Douglas, P.S. (1995).
Applied physiology of triathlon.
Sports Medicine, 19, 251-267.

O'Toole, M.L., Douglas, P.S., & Hiller, W.D. (1989).
Applied physiology of a triathlon.
Sports Medicine 8, 201-225.

Parnell, R.W. (1958).
Behaviour and physique.
London: Arnold.

Parr, R.B., Wimore, J.H., Hoover, R., Bachman, D., & Kerlan, R. (1978).
Professional basketball players: athletic profiles.
Physician and Sportsmedicine, 6, 77-84.

Pavicic, L. (1986).
Anthropometrical characteristics in relation to activity in sports. In T. Reilly, J., Watkins, J., & Borms, J. (Eds.),
Kinanthropometry III (pp. 221-226).
London: E & F. N. Spon.

Pendergast, D.R., Di Prampero, P.E., Craig, A.B. Jr, Wilson, D.R., & Rennie, D.W. (1977).
Quantitative analysis of the front crawl in men and women.
Journal of Applied Physiology, 43, 475-479.

Pheasant, S. (1988).
Bodyspace. Anthropometry, ergonomics and design.
London: Taylor and Francis.

Pollard, J. (1984).
Australian rugby union: The game and the players.
Sydney: Angus and Robertson.

Pugh, L.G.C.E., Edholm, O.G., Fox, R.H., Wolff, H.S., Hervey, G.R., Hammond, W.H., Tanner, J.M., & Whitehouse, R.H. (1960).
Physiological study of channel swimming.
Clinical Science, 19, 257-273.

Pyke, F.S. (1981).
    Physiological considerations during exercise in hot climates.
    Transactions of the Menzies Foundation, 2, 213-220.

Quinney, H.A. (1990).
    Sport on ice. In T. Reilly, N. Secher, P. Snell, & C. Williams (Eds.), **Physiology of Sports** (pp. 311-334).
    London: E & F. N. Spon.

Radford, P.F. (1990).
    Sprinting. In T. Reilly, N. Secher, P. Snell, & C. Williams (Eds.), **Physiology of Sports** (pp. 71-99).
    London: E & F. N. Spon.

Reilly, T. (1990a).
    Football. In T. Reilly, N. Secher, P. Snell, & C. Williams (Eds.), **Physiology of Sports** (pp. 371-425).
    London: E & F. N. Spon.

Reilly, T. (1990b).
    Swimming. In T. Reilly, N. Secher, P. Snell, & C. Williams (Eds.), **Physiology of Sports** (pp. 217-257).
    London: E & F. N. Spon.

Reilly, T. (1990c).
    The racquet sports. In T. Reilly, N.Secher, P. Snell, & C. Williams (Eds.), **Physiology of Sports** (pp. 337-369).
    London: E & F.N. Spon.

Rodriguez, F.A. (1986).
    Physical structure of international lightweight rowers. In T. Reilly, J. Watkins, & J. Borms (Eds.),
    Kinanthropometry III (pp. 255-261).
    London: E & F. N. Spon.

Ross, W.D., Brown, S.R., Faulkner, R.A., & Savage, M.V. (1976).
    Age of menarche of elite Canadian skaters and skiers.
    Canadian Journal of Applied Sports Sciences, 1, 288.

Ross, W.D., Leahy, R.M., Mazza, J.C., & Drinkwater, D.T. (1994).
    Relative body size. In J.E.L. Carter, & T.R. Ackland (Eds.),
    Kinanthropometry in Aquatic Sports (pp. 83-101).
    Champaign, Illinois: Human Kinetics.

Ross, W.D., Ward, R., Leah, R., & Day, J. (1982).
    Proportionality of Montreal athletes. In J. Carter (Ed.). **Physical structure of Olympic Athletes. Part 1: The Montreal Olympic Games Anthropological Project** (pp. 81-106).
    Basel: Karger.

Ross, W.D., & Marfell-Jones, M.T. (1991).
    Kinanthropometry. In J.D. MacDougall, H.A. Wenger, & H.J. Green (Eds.),
    Physiological Testing of the High-Performance Athlete, 2nd Ed. (pp. 223-308).
    Champaign, Illinois: Human Kinetics.

Roth, R.E., & Harris, M. (1908).
    The physical condition of children attending public schools in New South Wales.
    Sydney: Department of Public Instruction.

Sachare, A. (Ed.). (1994).
The official NBA basketball encyclopedia.
New York: Villard Books.

Sawka, M.N., Toner, M.M., Francesconi, R.P., & Pandolf, K.B. (1983).
Hypohydration and exercise: effects of heat acclimation, gender and environment.
Journal of Applied Physiology, 55, 1147-1153.

Secher, N. (1983).
The physiology of rowing.
Journal of Sports Sciences 1, 23-53.

Secher, N. (1990).
Rowing. In T. Reilly, N. Secher, P. Snell, & C. Williams (Eds.), **Physiology of Sports** (pp. 259-285).
London: E & F. N. Spon.

Shephard, R.J. (1990).
Sailing. In T. Reilly, N. Secher, P. Snell, & C. Williams (Eds.),
Physiology of Sports (pp. 287-309).
London: E & F. N. Spon.

Sinning, W.E. (1985).
Body Composition and Athletic Performance. Proceedings of the 56th Annual Meeting of the American Academy
of Physical Education, 18: 45-56.
Champaign, Illinois: Human Kinetics.

Smith, D.M., Nance, W.E., Kang, K.W., Christian, J.C., & Johnston, C.C. (1973).
Genetic factors in determining bone mass.
Journal of Clinical Investigations, 52, 2800-2808.

Smith, J.R. (1982).
**The relationship of selected biomechanical and anthropometric measures to accuracy in netball
shooting.** Unpublished Honours thesis,
University of Western Australia, Perth, Australia.

Sobral, F., Paula Brito, A., Alves, J., Fragoso, M.I., & Rodriguez, M.A. (1986).
Physique, personality and strength as related with menarcheal age in college women. In T. Reilly, J. Watkins, & J.
Borms (Eds.), **Kinanthropometry III** (pp. 181-184).
London: E & F. N. Spon.

Soares, J., De Castro Mendes, O., Neto, C.B., & Matsudo, V.K.R. (1986).
Player fitness characteristics of Brazilian national basketball team as related to game function. In J.A.P. Day (Ed.),
Perspectives in Kinanthropometry (pp. 127-133).
Champaign, Illinois: Human Kinetics.

Sovac, D., & M.R. Hawes. (1987).
Anthropological states of international calibre speed skaters.
Journal of Sports Sciences, 5, 287-304.

Spence, D.W., Disch, J.G., Fred, H.L., & Coleman, A.E. (1980).
Descriptive profiles of highly skilled women volleyball players.
Medicine and Science in Sport and Exercise, 12, 299-302.

Steele, J.R. (1987).
The relationship of selected anthropometric and lower extremity characteristics to the mechanics of landing in netball.
Technical Report 1, Part B.
Canberra: Australian Sports Commission.

Stepnicka, J. (1986).
Somatotype in relation to physical performance, sports and body posture. In T. Reilly, J. Watkins, & J. Borms (Eds.), **Kinanthropometry III** (pp. 39-52).
London: E & F. N. Spon.

Swain, D.P. (1994).
The influence of body mass in endurance bicycling.
Medicine and Science in Sports and Exercise, 26, 58-63.

Tanner, J.M. (1978).
Foetus into man (p. 143).
London: Open Books.

Telford, R. Egerton, W. Hahn, A., & Pang, P. (1988).
Skinfold measures and weight controls in elite athletes.
Excel 5, 21 - 26.

Telford, R., Tumilty, D., & Damm, G. (1984).
Skinfold measurements in well-performed Australian Athletes.
Sports Science and Medicine Quarterly, 1 (2), 13-16.

Tittel, K., & Wutscherk, H. (1992).
Anatomical and anthropometric fundamentals of endurance. In R.J. Shepherd, & P.-O. Astrand (Eds.), **Endurance in Sports** (pp. 35-45).
London: Blackwell Scientific.

Vujovic, D., Lozovina, V., & Pavicic, L. (1986).
Some differences in anthropometric measurements between elite athlete in waterpolo and rowing. In T. Reilly, J. Watkins, & J. Borms, (Eds.), **Kinanthropometry III** (pp. 27-32).
London: E & F. N. Spon.

Wang, M.Q., Downey, G.S., Perko, M.A., & Yesalis, C.E. (1993).
Changes in body size of elite high school football players: 1963-1989.
Perceptual and Motor Skills, 76, 379-383.

Watman, M. (1986).
World records in Europe.
Athletics weekly, September 27, 5-10.

Webster, S., Rutt, R., & Weltman, A. (1990).
Physiological effects of a weight loss regimen practiced by college wrestlers.
Medicine and Science in Sports and Exercise, 22, 229-234.

Wilmore, J.H. (1983).
Appetite and body composition consequent to physical activity.
Research Quarterly for Exercise and Sport, 54, 415-425.

Wilmore, J.H., & Costill, D.L. (1987).
   Training for Sport and Activity: The Physiological Basis of the Conditioning Process, 3rd Ed.
   Boston: Allyn and Baun.

Wilmore, J.H., & Haskell, W.L. (1972).
   Body composition and endurance capacity of professional football players.
   Journal of Applied Physiology, 33, 564-567.

Withers, R.T., Craig, N.P., Bourdon, P.C., & Norton, K.I. (1987).
   Relative body fat and anthropometric prediction of body density of male athletes.
   European Journal of Applied Physiology, 56, 191-200.

Withers, R.T., Norton, K.I., Craig, N.P., Hartland, M.C., & Venables, W. (1987).
   The relative body fat and anthropometric prediction of body density of South Australian females aged 17-35 years.
   European Journal of Applied Physiology, 56, 181-190.

Withers, R.T., Whittingham, N.O., Norton, K.I., La Forgia, J., Ellis, M.W., & Crockett, A. (1987).
   Relative body fat and anthropometric prediction of body density of female athletes.
   European Journal of Applied Physiology, 56, 169-180.

Zupp, A. (1994).
   A gutful of Sumo.
   Inside Sport, 34, October, 108-116.

Acknowledgments

The authors wish to thank the following people who have helped with data presented in this chapter:

Dr Tim Ackland, The University of Western Australia, Perth
Rob Bradley, Australian Rugby Union, Sydney
Pitre Bourdon, The South Australian Sports Institute, Adelaide
Dr Enid Ginn, Performance Edge Health & Fitness Services, Queensland
Dr Alan Hahn, The Australian Institute of Sports, Canberra
John Hogg, Boxing Historian, Brisbane, Queensland
Col Hutchinson, Australian Football League, Melbourne, Victoria
David Middleton, Rugby League Information Services, Sydney
Mauri Aho, Chief Handicapper, Australian Jockey Club, Sydney
Julie Steele, Wollongong University, Wollongong, NSW

Chapter 11

Chapter 12
Anthropometry, Health and Body Composition

Peter Abernethy, Tim Olds, Barbara Eden, Michelle Neill and Linda Baines

1   The relationship between health, body composition and anthropometry

In this chapter we will discuss how mass, fatness and the distribution of adipose tissue, as determined by surface anthropometry, may be involved in various pathologies and syndromes, and whether anthropometric profiling can be used in the risk management of these pathologies and syndromes.

Anthropometric techniques may potentially be used in several distinct ways in relation to risk management. Anthropometric profiling may be used to

- identify those **at risk** of developing a pathology;
- identify those who are **suffering** from a pathology;
- provide insights into the **mechanisms** underpinning a particular pathology;
- **direct** health interventions, and
- **monitor** the effects of interventions.

For the most part, this chapter will focus on the "metabolic syndrome", a constellation of symptoms which frequently co-occur: obesity, high blood pressure, high blood triglyceride levels, glucose intolerance, high cholesterol levels, and type II (non-insulin-dependent) diabetes mellitus. One study found that only 36% of people in a population were free of all six symptoms (reported in Barnard & Wen, 1994). However, we will also touch upon the relationship between various forms of cancer, all-cause mortality and anthropometric indicators.

2   Surface anthropometric indices of health status

Central to understanding the relationship between anthropometry and health are the overlapping issues of levels of mass, variability of mass, levels of fatness, and the location of fatness (see Figure 1). It is likely that the major cardiovascular and metabolic health risks associated with body composition are most closely related to the distribution of body fat (particularly the size of deep abdominal fat depots), rather than to high levels of body fat *per se*, or excess mass. Mass, relative weight and body mass index (BMI, $kg.m^{-2}$) are all indicators of heaviness, and are largely valuable to the extent to which they reflect overall fatness.

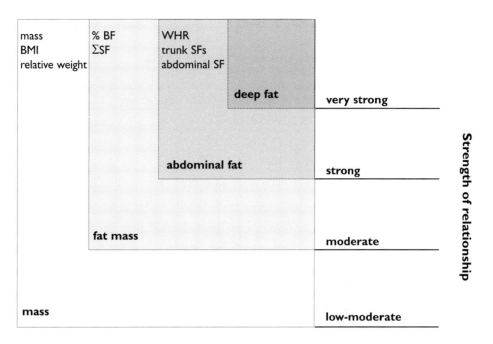

Figure 1 Relationship of anthropometric measures to risk factors for major pathologies. BF = body fat; SF = skinfold; WHR = waist-hip ratio.

Body fatness has been quantified using skinfold and/or girth measures, though these procedures have usually been viewed less favourably than hydrostatic weighing, [40]K counting or total body water measurement (Martin & Drinkwater, 1991). Measures of body fatness are valuable not only as a measure of overall fatness, but also to the extent to which they reflect increases in specific fat deposits (particularly, levels of deep abdominal fat).

Anthropometric measures such as skinfold ratios and the waist-to-hip ratio (WHR) have been used extensively to profile the distribution of fat. Surface anthropometry alone cannot quantify deep fat deposits. Computed tomography (CT) and magnetic resonance imaging (MRI) have greater validity (Bouchard, 1994; Després et al., 1991; Ferland et al., 1989). However, the cost of MRI and CT, and in the case of CT its associated irradiation, precludes their use in most clinical contexts. Surface anthropometric techniques often represent the only tools available to most clinicians. Consequently, optimising their use is fundamental to good health management.

2.1 Measures of heaviness

2.1.1 Body mass and variability in mass

Total body mass and change in body mass are relatively blunt anthropometric instruments as far as health status is concerned. They fail to distinguish between fat and non-fat mass, and there is ample evidence that the former is more closely implicated in disease processes (Sjöstrom, 1992a). The proportion of weight gain which is fat, and the proportion which is fat-free mass ("nutrient partitioning") shows great inter-individual variability. Overfeeding studies using identical twins (Bouchard, 1991) have shown that genetic constitution influences nutrient partitioning. The ratio of fat to fat-free mass gained may vary between 1:2 and 4:1. Subjects who gained more total mass also usually gained a greater proportion of fat mass. This may be due to the fact that overweight subjects may have reduced fat oxidation rates, which are further suppressed by overfeeding (Diaz, Prentice, Goldberg, Murgatroyd & Coward, 1992). Similarly, significant weight reduction usually involves the loss of both fat mass and lean body mass (Young, Garza & Steinke, 1984). Because the energy value of fat is 37 kJ.g^{-1}, and that of lean tissue (~20% protein) is 5 kJ.g^{-1}, a fat person (who loses proportionally more fat) will show a smaller decline in body mass for a given energy deficit than a lean person. For these reasons, changes in body mass are not reliable indices of changes in fat mass.

Nonetheless, body mass should be a routine measurement in any health-related anthropometric profile, as excessive mass and excessive variability in body mass are associated with a range of pathologies (Sjöstrom, 1992a, b), including

- **Angina pectoris and coronary heart disease (CHD)**. In one study, women between the ages of 35 and 55 who had increased their weight by more than 10 kg after the age of 18 were found to be at greater risk of angina pectoris and CHD than women who increased their mass by less than 3 kg (Goldstein, 1992).
- **Type II diabetes**. It has been estimated that a 10 kg weight loss would negate about one third of the loss in longevity normally associated with Type II diabetes (Goldstein, 1992).
- **Hypertension**. Prevention of weight gain in normotensive individuals reduces the likelihood of hypertension, while modest reductions in the mass of many hypertensives reduces their blood pressure (Goldstein, 1992). Furthermore, reducing mass following the withdrawal from five years of successful hypertensive drug therapy was effective in sustaining acceptable blood pressure in many individuals (Goldstein, 1992).

- **Abnormal blood lipid profiles**. Modest reductions in mass have been shown to increase HDL levels and decrease LDL and triglyceride concentrations (Goldstein, 1992).

Both a gain in body mass and cyclic increments and decrements in mass can influence health. Cycles of weight loss followed by the re-attainment of the original mass ("yo-yo dieting") appear to exacerbate glucose intolerance, insulin resistance and hypertension (Ashley & Kannel, 1974; Drenick, Brickman & Gold, 1972), and increase total and CHD mortality, particularly in men (Lissner, et al, 1991). Data are scarce on what constitutes normal and excessive fluctuations in weight. Lissner et al. (1991) quantified body mass variability as the coefficient of variation (CV) of mass (standard deviation/mean × 100) measured over a period of 16 years. For men, the mean CV was 5.7% (range 1% to 18.7%). For females, the mean CV was 6.7% (range 1.1% to 21.4%). However, shorter periods of time may be associated with smaller CVs.

2.1.2 Relative weight

Relative body weight (i.e. the ratio of current body mass to predicted normal mass for a given height) has been used extensively for insurance purposes, and in epidemiological investigations [e.g. the Garfinkel (1985) investigation involved 750,000 subjects]. The "normal" mass for a given height is usually defined statistically from large population surveys. The Metropolitan Life Insurance Company data have often been used in the United States. These data date from the 1940s, and have since been updated (Society of Actuaries and Association of Life Insurance Medical Directors of America, 1979). In Australia, weight-for-height data are available from the Commonwealth Department of Health from 1957 (reprinted in Schell & Leelarthaepin, 1994, p. 48.)

Optimal relative body weight appears to be between 90 and 109% for males and 80 and 109% for females (Garfinkel, 1985). Individuals with relative weights of >110% or <90% are deemed to be over- and underweight respectively. Relative weights falling outside this range have been associated with increased specific and all-cause mortality. The all-cause mortality ratios for men and women with relative weights of ≥140% are 1.87 and 1.89 respectively (Garfinkel, 1985).

Approximately 50% of diabetic men and women (for the most part, Type II diabetics) have a mass more than 110% of normal weight (Bray 1992a). Garfinkel (1985) found that endometrial, uterine, cervical and gall bladder carcinoma morbidity was significantly greater in women whose mass was 120% greater than their nominal ideal weight. Furthermore, the risk of these cancers increased with increments in relative weight up to at least 140% of their ideal weight. At this level of overweight there was also a significant increase in the risk of ovarian and breast cancer. For men the risk of prostate cancer became significant at 120% of the nominal ideal body weight, but did not increase with further increments in mass, while the risk of colon and rectal carcinoma became significant, and increased with increments in relative weight beyond 130%. In summary, men and women are at greater risk of some forms of cancer when their relative weight is more than 120% normal.

Relative weight probably represents a satisfactory measure of risk for whole populations, but it is doubtful that it is satisfactory measure of individual risk. This is because relative weight does not take into account inter-individual differences in fat mass and distribution. Thus, relative weight probably should not be used in isolation to identify an unhealthy body conformation or monitor the effects of dietary, exercise and/or pharmacological interventions.

2.1.3 Body Mass Index (BMI)

Like body mass and relative weight, BMI ($kg.m^{-2}$) does not differentiate between the non-fat and fat masses (Sjöstrom, 1992a). It is not uncommon for lean, healthy athletes to present elevated BMIs (>30). The correlations between percentage body fat scores (determined hydrostatically and anthropometrically) and BMI are only moderate (r = 0.5–0.8) (Bouchard, 1991; Ducimetière, Richard & Cambien, 1986; Sedgwick & Haby, 1991). Consequently, BMI is best viewed as a measure of heaviness. Furthermore, BMI is of questionable value during periods of growth when height is continually changing, and can be distorted by the proportionality of sitting height and leg length (Garn, 1986). Relatively long legs will decrease BMI scores.

Nonetheless, BMI has been related to total mortality and specific morbidities. For example, Bray (1992b) indicated that mortality was very low for individuals with BMIs between 20 and 25, low for BMIs between 25 and 30, moderate for BMIs between 30 and 35, high for BMIs between 35 and 40 and very high where BMIs exceeded 40. CHD sufferers have been shown to have greater BMIs than non-sufferers (Ducimetière et al., 1986). Waaler (1983) reported that the lowest risk of CHD was at a BMI of 23 $kg.m^{-2}$, and that each digit increment in BMI above this nadir increased CHD mortality by 2%. BMIs have a significant and positive correlation with insulin resistance (Bray, 1992b; Donahue, Orchard, Becker, Culler & Drash, 1987). A high BMI is also associated with gall bladder disease and elevated triglyceride levels (Bray, 1992b; Seidell et al., 1992).

BMIs of less than 20 are correlated with digestive and pulmonary illness (Bray, 1992b). BMI (r = 0.26) and sum of trunk skinfolds (r = 0.26) are similarly correlated with systolic blood pressure (Ducimetière et al., 1986). However, the relationship between BMI and HDL levels appears to be equivocal (Hodgson, Wahlqvist, Balazs & Boxall, 1994; Seidell et al., 1992). Furthermore, BMI was not significantly correlated with the degree of coronary atherosclerosis, nor the area of myocardium under threat from lesion in Australian men and women (Hodgson et al., 1994).

In summary, BMI is a measure of heaviness (i.e. both fat and non-fat compartments) and not fatness. While increments in heaviness at a population level are most often associated with increments in fat (Garrow & Webster, 1985), this assumption cannot be made at an individual level (i.e. increments in BMI may be due to increments in muscle mass). Thus, BMI should not be used exclusively to quantify an individual's fatness.

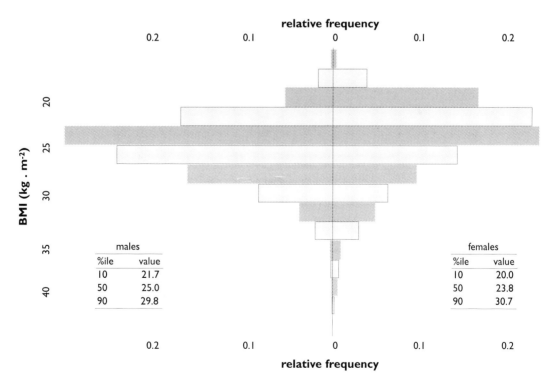

Figure 2 Distribution of BMI values (kg.m⁻²) in the Australian population (from the survey of the Department of the Arts, Sports, Environment and Territories, 1991). The insets show the 10th, 50th and 90th percentiles.

2.2 Measures of body fat

The major problem with measures of heaviness (total body mass, relative weight and BMI) is that they do not distinguish between fat mass and non-fat mass. Fat mass (and particularly the distribution of fat mass) are generally better indices of disorders associated with body composition than body mass alone. Buskirk (1987) reported that hypertension, atherosclerosis and CHD, congestive heart failure, Type II diabetes, osteoarthritis, some forms of cancer, and ailments affecting the gall bladder, liver and kidney were all associated with obesity. It has been estimated that 4.3% of all mortality between 30 and 79 years can be attributed to obesity (i.e. excessive levels of body fat) (Waaler, 1983).

Non-site-specific reductions in fat mass appear to be positively correlated with changes in total cholesterol and LDL scores ($r \approx 0.6 - 0.7$) in obese women following a 12 month exercise intervention (Després et al., 1991). That is, changes in these lipids were similarly correlated with reductions in subcutaneous fat from the abdomen, trunk and thigh and also deep abdominal fat. Moreover, changes in fat mass are significantly correlated with changes in glucose function ($r = 0.64$), cholesterol ($r = 0.67$), LDL ($r = 0.61$) and the HDL:LDL ratio ($r = -0.60$) (Després et al., 1991). A further consideration is that changes in overall fatness may be a surface anthropometric indicator of changes in regional fat masses (such as deep abdominal fat) more directly implicated in health status (see below).

An overall measure of fatness (such as a sum of skinfolds, percentage body fat, or absolute fat mass) may therefore be desirable since this provides information which total body mass, relative weight or BMI do not provide. Various interventions differentially affect fat and non-fat masses, and such information may provide insights into whether the intervention is working. For example, it is necessary to know whether increments in BMI are the result of increments in fat or lean body mass. The former situation may be negative to health, while the latter may enhance health.

Sums of skinfolds are often used as estimates of total body fatness. Body density, and hence percentage body fat and absolute fat mass, may be estimated from surface anthropometric measurements (usually girths and skinfolds). However, regression equations are population-specific and usually involve sizeable standard errors of estimate. Differences in fat distribution among subcutaneous depots, and between subcutaneous and visceral depots, mean that skinfold measurements are an imperfect index of overall fatness. Subcutaneous fat distribution differs between males and females (Karatsu et al., 1987; Krotkiewski, Björntorp, Sjöstrom & Smith 1983; Leibel, Edens & Fried, 1989), with skinfold values at all sites tending to be greater in females than in males. The thickest folds tend to be located in the lumbar-abdominal region for both sexes (Karatsu et al., 1987).

2.2.1 Nutrient composition and changes in body composition

Although fat contains 37 kJ.g^{-1}, protein 17 kJ.g^{-1} and carbohyrdate 16 kJ.g^{-1}, not all kilojoules are "treated equally" by the body. Dietary fat is converted more efficiently to body fat (a net cost of approximately 3% of the energy value of the ingested fat). Carbohydrate, on the other hand, requires 23% of the energy value of the ingested food to be stored as body fat. There is therefore an evolutionary advantage (from a thermodynamic perspective) in storing dietary fat in adipocytes. Population studies (Miller, 1991) show significant positive correlations ($r = 0.37 - 0.38$) between dietary fat intake and percentage body fat. These data suggest that a change in the composition of the diet, even without a change in total energy intake, may affect body composition.

2.3 Measures of body shape and body fat distribution

It is becoming increasingly clear that obesity has many phenotypes (Bouchard, 1991) characterised by different fat distributions. Some obesities appear to adversely affect health more than other obesities (Seidell et al., 1992). Bouchard (1991) has identified four major types of obesity:
- Type I (excessive fat and/or mass which is distributed across all body regions);
- Type II (excessive subcutaneous fat in the abdominal region or android fatness);
- Type III (excessive deep abdominal fat), and
- Type IV (excess fat in the gluteal and femoral regions or gynoid fatness).

Usually an overfat person will have Type I obesity in combination with another form of obesity. For example, it is not uncommon for overfat women to have Type I and Type IV obesities. The health implications do not appear to be uniform for each form of obesity or combination of obesities.

Android obesity (Types II and III) has been associated with metabolic dysfunctions and morbidities (e.g. hypertension, increased very low density lipoprotein [VLDL] and low density lipoprotein [LDL] levels, decrements in HDL concentrations, hyperlipidæmia, Type II diabetes and CHD) (Bouchard, 1994; Goldstein, 1992; Larsson, 1991; Larsson et al., 1984; Schmidt, Duncan, Canani, Karohl & Chambless, 1992). In fact, the correlation between Type II obesity and CHD is of a similar magnitude to the correlations between CHD and smoking, hypertension and hyperlipidemia (Larsson, 1991).

Subcutaneous abdominal and deep abdominal fat appear to be particularly dangerous in increasing the risk of CHD, hypertension, gallstones and Type II diabetes (Bray, 1992b; Larsson et al., 1984). High levels of deep abdominal fat have been correlated with glucose intolerance, hyperinsulinæmia, hypertension, increases in plasma triglyceride level and decrements in high density lipoprotein (HDL) levels (Després et al., 1991; Kissebah et al., 1982; Zamboni et al., 1992). This metabolic profile is consistent with CHD, Type II diabetes and stroke morbidity. Bergstrom et al. (1990) reported that even when the effects of glucose tolerance and BMI were accounted for, males with clinical CHD had more deep abdominal fat than their subclinical counterparts. Reductions in Type III adiposity (i.e. deep abdominal fat) are also correlated with positive changes in triglyceride levels (r = 0.67) and the HDL:LDL ratio (r = −0.66) (Després et al., 1991). These data suggest that persons suffering from Type III obesity have an increased risk of CHD. These relationships are thought to be due to a sequence of metabolic events which Bouchard (1994) has labelled the "metabolic syndrome".

There is disagreement as to how Types II and III obesity are related to the metabolic syndrome. One school of thought argues that these obesities trigger the metabolic syndrome. Specifically, elevated cortisol levels promote fat deposition in the subcutaneous and visceral regions of the abdomen (Bray, 1992b). This is in contrast to low cortisol levels which in combination with a high estradiol to testosterone ratio apparently promote fat deposition around the gluteal and thigh regions (Bray, 1992b). Fat cells located in the abdominal region are more sensitive to lipolysis (i.e. the breakdown of storage fat into plasma FFAs and plasma glycerol) than those found in the gluteo-femoral region (Gerber, Madhaven & Alderman, 1987). FFAs from abdominal sites are released directly into the portal circulation (Larsson et al., 1984). Increased portal plasma FFAs lead to decreased insulin uptake by the liver (Ohlson et al., 1985). Abdominal obesity is associated with increased lipolysis and thus, greater plasma FFA levels within the portal circulation, which in turn increases the potential for insulin uptake to be inhibited, leading to peripheral high blood insulin levels and increased insulin resistance (Figure 3; Ohlson et al., 1985). Alternatively, Barnard and Wen (1994) argue that the metabolic syndrome is a phenomenon of the Western life style (i.e. sedentary behaviour and the consumption of a high fat, refined sugar diet). Specifically, this lifetyle causes insulin resistance in susceptible individuals. The development of

Types II and III obesity follows the development of this insulin resistance. In summary, the metabolic syndrome appears to have a strong potential to compromise health by increasing the probability of type II diabetes, CHD and cerebrovascular disease. It remains unclear as to whether types II and III obesity are instigators or indicators of the associated insulin resistance.

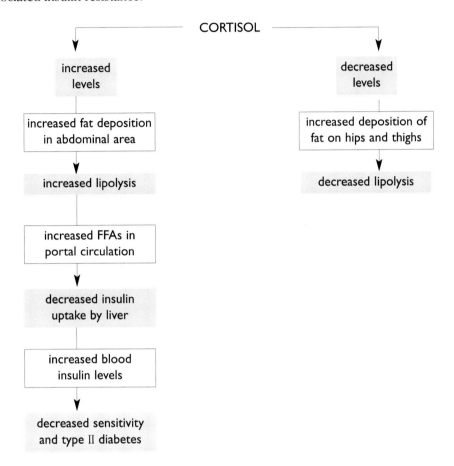

Figure 3 One possible chain of events relating to the "metabolic syndrome".

Reducing abdominal fatness through health interventions (e.g. regular aerobic exercise) may attenuate the insulin resistance associated with the metabolic syndrome (Goldstein, 1992). Decreasing abdominal fatness reduces the level of FFAs being deposited into the portal circulation, which in turn would enhances hepatic uptake of insulin. Increased insulin clearance appears to be the initial mechanism for increased insulin sensitivity (Després et al., 1991). Reductions in deep abdominal fat appear to be necessary for positive changes in glucose metabolism (i.e. glucose area), triglyceride levels and the HDL:LDL ratio (Després et al., 1991). Ferland et al. (1989) reported that BMI and WHR were moderately correlated with deep abdominal fat and the deep abdominal to total abdominal fat ratio. Clearly, more work is required to determine whether any anthropometric indices can provide insights into Type III obesity for the general population or specific groups.

Types II and III obesities acting via the metabolic syndrome are potentially strong antagonists to good health. Consequently, the practitioner is confronted with a dilemma: on the one hand Type III obesity is difficult to assess in most clinical contexts, on the other the identification and management of Type III obesity may be critical to positive health outcomes.

2.3.1 Specific skinfolds and skinfold ratios

While sums of skinfolds may be used as estimates of overall fatness, specific skinfolds, and ratios between skinfolds, can be used to map subcutaneous fat distribution. Often, two broad classes of fat distribution are distinguished. Many women present a gynoid subcutaneous fat distribution (i.e. subcutaneous fat preferentially distributed about the gluteal and thigh regions), while males tend to present an android distribution (i.e. subcutaneous fat preferentially distributed about the abdominal region). Certain skinfolds may yield more reliable information about health risks than others. There are data to suggest that trunk skinfolds (e.g. subscapular and abdominal) provide more information in relation to health outcomes than appendicular skinfolds (e.g. front thigh and triceps) (Ducimetière et al, 1986; Ferland et al., 1989). Trunk skinfold thickness is positively correlated with high blood pressure, high triglyceride levels, BMI, angina pectoris and CHD morbidity and mortality (Ducimetière et al, 1986; Ferland et al., 1989; Haffner, Stern, Hazuda, Pugh & Patterson, 1987; Higgins, Kannel, Garrison, Pinsky & Stokes, 1988; Seidell et al., 1992). The correlation coefficients for the sum of trunk skinfolds and systolic blood pressure ($r = 0.26$), total cholesterol ($r = 0.24$) and triglyceride levels ($r = 0.35$) are greater than for the sum of limb skinfolds (0.08, 0.08 and 0.15 respectively) (Ducimetière et al, 1986). In addition, changes in subcutaneous abdominal obesity have been correlated with changes in cholesterol ($r = 0.71$) and LDL ($r = 0.63$) levels (Després et al., 1991).

Haffner et al. (1987) reported that for Mexican men and women the subscapular-to-triceps ratio (STR) was correlated with Type II diabetes, and triglyceride ($r = 0.20$) and HDL ($r = -0.16$) levels. Furthermore, STR and WHR were thought to be indicative of different metabolic events. Consequently Haffner et al. (1987) urged clinicians to measure STR in addition to other anthropometric indices when profiling fatness. Similarly, Karatsu et al. (1987) reported correlations between the triceps-to-subscapular ratio (i.e. the inverse of the STR) and triglyceride (r = –0.38), total cholesterol (r = –0.27), LDL (r = –0.27) and HDL (r = 0.26) levels in regularly exercising Japanese. However, Seidell et al. (1992) only reported a significant correlation between STR and serum triglyceride levels (r = 0.12) when adjusted for BMI in European males. Correlations were not significant between STR and diastolic blood presure, total cholesterol, HDL nor insulin levels. These equivocal outcomes of research into STR may be a function of racial, sex and age factors within considered samples and/or limitations in the statistical methods used.

Of particular interest is subcutaneous abdominal fat, which is an independent predictor of cardiovascular risk. An important question is the extent to which this depot reflects deep abdominal adiposity, which appears to have a greater capacity to compromise health than other obesity phenotypes (Bouchard, 1991). The correlations between the sum of seven truncal (subscapular, suprailiac and abdominal) and appendicular (biceps, triceps, front thigh and medial calf) skinfolds with total abdominal fat, deep abdominal fat and subcutaneous abdominal fat are modest but significant (r ≈ 0.60; Ferland et al., 1989). These intercorrelations suggest that about one third of the variation in deep abdominal adiposity could be accounted for by the skinfolds.

There is no fixed ratio of subcutaneous to deep abdominal fat. Leibel et al. (1989) reported that in men and women deep abdominal fat accounted for 20.9 ± 7.1% and 8.1 ± 3.1% of total abdominal adiposity respectively. This percentage is greater in obese individuals. For example, Ferland et al. (1989) reported that in obese premenopausal women deep abdominal fat accounted for 19.0% (± 5; range: 9-33) of total abdominal adiposity. The wide range in deep abdominal fatness found in obese women could be a function of age and/or menstrual status (Zamboni et al., 1992).

Nor do surface and deep abdominal fat components respond similarly to dietary/ exercise interventions (Després et al., 1991; Ferland et al., 1989). Specifically, reductions in subcutaneous abdominal fat precede those of the deep abdominal compartment. Prolonged aerobic exercise has been shown to significantly reduce subcutaneous abdominal fat, but not deep abdominal fat (Després et al., 1991).

2.3.2 Waist-to-hip ratio (WHR)

Another way of describing fat distribution is to use girth ratios such as the waist-to-hip ratio. This simple ratio is characterised by good reliability (r = 0.92), though there appears to be greater error in the WHR measurement of females than males (Wing et al., 1992). However, a review of the literature of WHR showed that there is a great deal of confusion about the exact location of the waist and hip girth sites (Alexander & Dugdale, 1990; Jakicic et al., 1993). For one group of obese women, measured WHRs ranged from 0.76 to 0.95 according to the sites chosen, placing either 23% or 100% of the sample in the "at-risk" category. Cut-off scores for increased risk have ranged from 0.91 to 1.00 for men, and from 0.80 to 0.91 for women. Consequently, recommendations about cut-off scores should be interpreted in relation to measurement sites. In the anthropometric profile, WHR is defined as the ratio of the waist girth (item 17 of the full anthropometric profile) to the gluteal (hip) girth (item 18 of the full profile). The precise locations of these sites are described in Chapter 2.

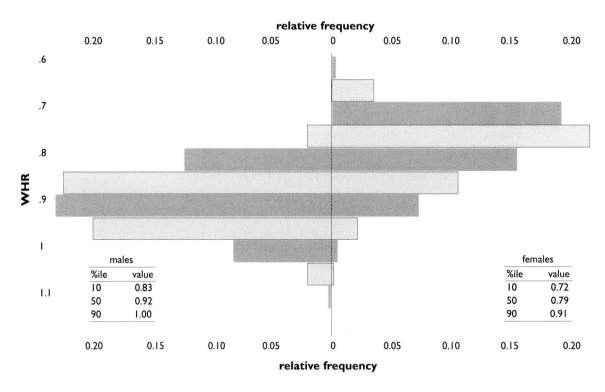

Figure 4 Distribution of waist-to-hip ratio (WHR) values (kg.m^{-2}) in the Australian adult population (from the survey of the Department of the Arts, Sports, Environment and Territories, 1991). The insets show the 10th, 50th and 90th percentiles.

The WHR has been extensively used to discriminate between android (Type II) and gynoid (Type IV) fat distributions (Bray, 1992b; Larsson et al., 1984; Sedgwick & Haby, 1991). Higher and lower WHRs respectively indicate greater android and gynoid fat distributions. Male and female WHRs in excess of 0.95 and 0.80 for males and females respectively have a high risk of illness (Bray, 1992b). As has been indicated above, these thresholds will be modified by procedural and a number of other factors, including: age, race and current level of obesity (Seidell, 1992). Larsson (1991) estimated that 20% of the CHD within the USA could be attributed to excessive android fat (i.e. WHR > 0.901). In contrast, excessive gynoid fat is not correlated with CHD risk factors (Terry, Stefanick, Haskell & Wood, 1991). Figure 4 shows the distribution of WHRs in the Australian community.

Significant correlations between WHR and CHD (or indicators of increased CHD risk) have often been reported (e.g. Hodgson et al., 1994; Jakicic et al., 1993) but are not universally found, particularly for men (Hubinger, 1994; Wing et al., 1992). This inconsistency in correlation may partially be due to the dissociation of deep and subcutaneous compartments of abdominal fat (Busetto et al., 1992; Ferland et al., 1989). The clinical value of the WHR may also be modified by sex, ethnicity, level of obesity and geographic factors (Busetto et al., 1992; Valdez, Seidell, Ahn & Weiss, 1993).

WHR appears to be sensitive to training. In obese populations, the change in WHR occurs as a result of preferential loss of subcutaneous abdominal fat. Després et al. (1991) reported that 14 months of regular aerobic activity by obese women (BMI = 34.5 ± 4.3 kg.m^{-2}) reduced subcutaneous abdominal fat more than femoral fat. Interventions appear to reduce subcutaneous fat prior to deep abdominal fat (Després et al., 1991). Prolonged (14 months) aerobic exercise led to an 11% reduction in subcutaneous abdominal fat, but only a 2.5% reduction in deep abdominal adiposity. However, this preferential reduction of waist over hip fatness may be dependent upon factors like the duration of the intervention, initial BMI and/or level of activity. Sedgwick and Haby (1991) reported that women with initial BMIs of 25.0 (± 4.6) kg.m^{-2} who expended approximately 21.7 MJ during exercise in a ten week exercise program had greater reductions in hip than waist girth.

2.3.3 Conicity index (CI)

Valdez, Seidell, Ahn and Weiss, (1993) recently developed the conicity index (CI) which may have clinical value when endeavouring to measure fat distribution. The CI models the human body as a cylinder at its leanest extreme (CI score of 1.00) to two perfect cones with a common base at the waist for its fattest extreme about the abdomen (CI score of 1.73). It is calculated by the following formula:

$$CI = \frac{girth}{0.109\sqrt{\dfrac{Mass}{Ht}}}$$

where *girth* is the abdominal girth (m) measured at the level of the umbilicus, *Mass* is mass (kg), and *Ht* is height (m).

The correlation between CI and WHR is moderate to large for most populations ($r = 0.64$–0.86) (Valdez et al., 1993). The correlation coefficents between CI and WHR and blood lipids were similar for 2240 North Americans and Europeans (Valdez et al., 1993). These data suggest that both these anthropometric indices may have similar clinical value. Valdez et al. (1993) nominate three advantages of the CI:

- there is a theoretical range (1.00-1.73);
- it can be used to make inter-individual comparisons as waist girth is adjusted for height and mass within the formula; and
- there is no need to measure hip girths.

More research is required to establish the clinical potential of the CI.

2.3.4 Somatotype

The study of the relationship between body morphology and disease is called "constitutional medicine". Carter and Heath (1990, pp. 292-311) have reviewed a number of studies which have examined the relationships between somatotype and a range of disease states. These are summarised in Table 1 below.

In addition to the studies summarised in Table 1, associations have been found between somatotype and the incidence of injury. Individuals with high endomorphy and mesomorphy are more susceptible to sprains and strains, while those with high ectomorphy are more susceptible to chronic injuries. Some studies have also found correlations between somatotype components and posture, with mesomorphs showing better posture than either endomorphs or ectomorphs.

Table 1 Relationships between somatotype components and developed disease states (summarised from Carter and Heath, 1990, pp. 292-311). A plus sign (+) indicates a positive association between the somatotype component and the developed disease state. A minus sign (−) indicates a negative association.

disease state	endomorphy	mesomorphy	ectomorphy
cervical cancer		−	
endometrial cancer	+		
cardiovascular disease	+	+	
obesity	+		
diabetes (esp. females)	+	+	
Down's syndrome	+	+	−
achondroplasia[a]		+	−
Marfan's syndrome[b]		−	+
Klinefelter's syndrome[c]		−	+
dyslipidæmia (males)	+	+	
Legge-Calvé-Perthes syndrome[d]		+	

[a] dwarfism
[b] disease characterised by very long, drawn-out limbs and "spider-like" fingers
[c] feminisation in males due to a chromosomal disorder
[d] osteochondritis of the hip joint

3   Recommendations: a multi-step profiling system

The approach outlined here proposes a multi-step profiling system which clinicians may use to assess health status and health risk for pathologies associated with body composition. The need fo a multi-step system was accurately stated by Seidell et al. (1992, p. 21): "different indicators of fat distribution are related to different aspects of ... disease". When using this profiling approach, several points should be considered.

*   Fatness, fat distribution and mass should be assessed serially over a lifetime. By way of illustration it has been shown that increasing levels of obesity increase the risk of CHD more than stable obesity (Bray, 1992b).
*   There is a need to take into account the age and medical history of the client. For example, the association between CHD and obesity increases the longer someone is excessively fat. In the Framingham study obesity and CHD were strongly

correlated after 26, but not 12 years follow up (Ducimetière et al., 1986).

- There is also a need to take into account gender differences, as obesity appears to have less of an effect on women than men (Bray, 1992b). Bray (1992b) reported that women needed to gain approximately 20 kg more fat than their male counterparts to produce similar deteriorations in glucose function and blood pressure.

- For those whose anthropometric profiles suggest a risk of developing the metabolic syndrome, blood pressure, glucose tolerance and/or blood lipid profiles should be monitored regularly.

Step 1 – WHR

WHR is the first anthropometric measurement we use to identify whether health is at risk due to heaviness and/or fatness. WHR has been shown to be an excellent anthropometric predictor of CHD morbidity and mortality, stroke and diabetes mellitus in men and women (Ducimetière et al., 1986; Ohlson et al., 1985) especially in individuals less than 70 years old, and not already obese (Gerber et al., 1987; Larsson, 1991; Larsson et al., 1984; Seidell, 1992). Men and women with WHRs of ≥ 0.95 and ≥ 0.80 respectively can be classified as having Type II (i.e. subcutaneous abdominal obesity; Bray, 1992b). Clearly, such a classification is seen as an indicator of potential health problems, and intervention recommended.

Fairly large changes in mass are required before significant changes occur in WHR. Wing et al. (1992) reported that in males a 9.8 kg reduction in mass as a result of exercise produced a reduction in WHR (0.035 ± 0.03), while a 6.4 kg loss in women did not (0.006 ± 0.005). Furthermore, changes in WHR for women were not correlated with changes in cholesterol, HDL or triglyceride levels; systolic or diastolic blood pressure; and glucose tolerance. In males, the change in WHR was correlated with cholesterol ($r = 0.35$) and triglyceride ($r = 0.32$), and systolic ($r = 0.21$) and diastolic ($r = 0.25$) blood pressures. However, none of these correlations were significant when adjustments were made for BMI. The reason that WHR appears to be of little value in monitoring the effects of health interventions is that fat appears to be reduced differentially at two levels. First, in some cases there is preferential reduction in gynoid fat, and in others android fat; and second, reductions in subcutaneous and deep fat are not necessarily linked (Després et al., 1991; Ferland et al., 1989; Sedgwick & Haby, 1992).

According to this system anyone presenting an elevated WHR should be noted as a potential candidate for health interventions.

Step 2 – BMI

The ability to identify persons at risk is enhanced when BMI and WHR information are combined. BMI and WHR are fundamentally measuring different qualities (commonality between the two indices ranges between 9 and 36% in males, and is thought to be less than 1% in females) (Hodgson et al., 1994; Laws, Terry & Barrett-Connor, 1990; Haffner et al., 1987; Ohlson et al., 1985; Wing et al., 1992). A combination of android obesity and high BMI increases the chances of CHD and diabetes mellitus (Lapidus et al., 1984; Larsson et al., 1984; Ohlson et al., 1985). While the correlations between WHR and most blood lipids is moderate ($r = 0.27 - 0.39$) in individuals presenting a high BMI (≥ 29.6 kg.m^{-2}), they are nonethless higher than those in individuals with smaller BMIs (Jackicic et al., 1993). Nevertheless, a low BMI in combination with a high WHR apparently elevates the risk of CHD and all cause death in males and females (Lapidus et al., 1984; Larsson et al., 1984; Table 2). The relative probability of CHD was 20.8 for males in the highest WHR and lowest BMI tertiles (thirds), and only 12.4 for men with the highest WHR and BMI tertiles (Larsson et al., 1984). It was also reported that the risk of all cause death was least in men who were in the lowest and highest tertiles for WHR and BMI respectively (Larsson et al., 1984). This body conformation is not unlike that of physically active (mesomorphic) individuals.

Table 2 Percentage probability of all cause mortality relative to BMI and WHR tertiles of European men (54–68 years) and women (38–60 years). (Data adapted from Larsson et al., 1984 and Lapidus et al., 1984).

Males		WHR		
		lowest tertile	middle tertile	highest tertile
BMI	lowest tertile	13.1	13.1	29.2
	middle tertile	13.1	13.1	19.0
	highest tertile	5.3	8.8	18.2

Females				
		lowest tertile	middle tertile	highest tertile
BMI	lowest tertile	7.6	4.7	7.0
	middle tertile	2.5	4.7	5.2
	highest tertile	1.0	4.7	6.3

Wing et al. (1992) found that BMI was superior to WHR in terms of monitoring changes as a result of an exercise intervention in overweight men and women. Changes in BMI were significantly correlated, even when adjusted for WHR, with changes in plasma cholesterol (males $r = 0.35$; females $r = 0.29$) and triglyceride (males $r = 0.35$; females $r = 0.29$) levels (Wing et al., 1992). In the case of males the inter-correlations were also significant for systolic ($r = 0.37$) and diastolic ($r = 0.45$) blood pressure. Clearly however, it is yet to be determined how effective BMI, and for that matter WHR are in monitoring intervention effectiveness in individuals with low BMIs and high WHRs prior to intervention.

It is our recommendation that individuals presenting an elevated WHR in combination with either a high or low BMI should enter health interventions.

Step 3 – Trunk skinfolds

A series of trunk skinfold measurements (e.g. subscapular, abdominal, supraspinale) are desirable for several reasons. First, as has been discussed earlier, trunk skinfolds are better correlated with ill-health than skinfold measurements made at the limbs (Ducimetière et al., 1986; Higgins et al., 1988). Second, it is desirable to have an estimate of absolute subcutaneous abdominal fatness. This will become important when monitoring the effects of fat reduction interventions, as the WHR may not detect changes in fat from the abdominal region (see above). One would expect interventions to reduce subcutaneous abdominal adiposity, though it should not be assumed that such reductions, particularly early within an intervention, would also reduce type III obesity (see above) (Després et al., 1991). Third, subcutaneous abdominal fat is implicated in the metabolic syndrome (see above), consequently, reducing type II obesity may enhance health indices (Després et al., 1991).

Population norms: the OzScale

The anthropometrist wishing to give advice on health issues faces the problem of determining where his or her client lies in relation to population norms. The OzScale (see Chapter 5) is a system which relates individual anthropometric values to Australian population norms. The OzScale uses geometrical similarity to normalise skinfolds, girths, corrected girths and mass. Individual values are height-corrected. Data have been collected in a large-scale study (n = 1263) of Australians (Department of the Arts, Sport, the Environment, and Territories, 1992). Height-corrected values have been calculated and grouped into gender and age-specific slices (age bands of 18–29, 30–39,

40–49, 50–59, 60–69, and 70+ have been used). The distributions of some measures (notably skinfolds) are markedly skewed. For this reason, percentiles have been calculated for each measure and each gender- and age-specific group, rather than using means and standard deviations. In this way, an individual's values can be assigned a percentile ranking specific to his or her gender and age.

These reference values can be considered as descriptive norms to the extent that the major determinants of size and shape (that is, age and gender) have been accounted for. For example, a percentile ranking of 20% for height-corrected triceps skinfold means that the individual's height-corrected triceps skinfold is larger than the height-corrected triceps skinfolds of 20% of Australians of the same gender and age. This is important as it provides the clinician an opportunity to place an individual within a population context. Tables 3a and 3b show the percentile ratings for BMI, WHR and sum of height-adjusted trunk skinfolds (supraspinale + subscapular + abdominal) for 10-year age slices in the Australian population. Details on how to calculate OzScale values are shown in Chapter 5.

4 Conclusion

The metabolic syndrome offers a plausible explanation as to why fat distribution rather than fat levels per se can negatively affect health. Excessive subcutaneous and/or deep abdominal adiposity is of particular concern. Unfortunately, it is not possible to anthropometrically quantify or directly monitor deep abdominal fatness. Furthermore, the dissociation of the subcutaneous and deep fat compartments makes estimation of deep fatness from anthropmetric measures problematic. Equally however, cost precludes the extensive use of MRI. However, regular anthropometric measurements (i.e. WHR, BMI and trunk skinfolds) in conjunction with standard clinical tests (i.e. blood pressure, blood lipids and glucose tolerance) may enhance the quality of health intervention that clinicians can render to their clients in relation to adiposity.

Table 3a Scores corresponding to various percentiles for BMI, WHR and the height-adjusted sum of three "central" skinfolds (subscapular, supraspinale, abdominal; Σ3SF) in Australian males.

percentiles for males 18-29

	1	2	5	10	20	30	40	50	60	70	80	90	95	98	99
BMI	17.5	18.1	18.8	19.9	21.2	22.2	23.2	23.6	24.7	25.2	26.3	27.5	29.2	31.2	36.6
WHR	0.77	0.78	0.78	0.80	0.81	0.82	0.83	0.85	0.86	0.88	0.89	0.93	0.96	0.99	1.00
Σ3SF	14.4	15.0	16.6	18.3	20.4	25.1	31.6	35.5	43.0	51.8	57.6	76.8	91.1	95.6	111.3

percentiles for males 30-39

	1	2	5	10	20	30	40	50	60	70	80	90	95	98	99
BMI	18.2	18.7	20.3	21.2	22.3	23.4	24.1	24.9	25.1	26.0	27.0	29.5	30.6	33.2	33.8
WHR	0.80	0.81	0.82	0.84	0.86	0.87	0.88	0.90	0.91	0.92	0.94	0.97	1.00	1.07	1.08
Σ3SF	15.9	16.5	18.9	25.8	34.3	41.6	45.3	50.6	57.0	62.0	69.2	77.3	94.6	99.0	116.0

percentiles for males 40-49

	1	2	5	10	20	30	40	50	60	70	80	90	95	98	99
BMI	19.7	20.1	20.9	22.0	22.6	23.7	24.2	25.2	26.1	27.4	28.4	30.4	32.3	33.8	34.2
WHR	0.79	0.80	0.82	0.84	0.86	0.88	0.90	0.91	0.94	0.95	0.98	0.99	1.02	1.05	1.06
Σ3SF	17.8	18.1	27.0	29.9	38.8	44.8	49.0	55.5	62.2	66.7	71.1	85.4	96.4	108.3	110.9

percentiles for males 50-59

	1	2	5	10	20	30	40	50	60	70	80	90	95	98	99
BMI	20.4	21.1	21.8	22.6	23.4	23.9	24.9	25.9	26.4	28.0	28.7	30.6	31.8	34.7	36.2
WHR	0.81	0.82	0.84	0.86	0.89	0.91	0.92	0.94	0.95	0.96	0.99	1.02	1.05	1.08	1.09
Σ3SF	20.9	21.9	25.2	31.5	39.8	44.4	49.1	54.1	59.8	66.2	72.6	85.1	95.4	101.5	110.2

percentiles for males 60-69

	1	2	5	10	20	30	40	50	60	70	80	90	95	98	99
BMI	18.1	20.4	22.4	23.1	24.0	24.6	25.0	26.1	27.1	27.9	28.8	29.9	31.4	31.9	32.6
WHR	0.81	0.83	0.87	0.88	0.92	0.93	0.95	0.96	0.98	0.99	1.00	1.02	1.03	1.05	1.06
Σ3SF	19.6	23.2	27.5	36.8	43.5	46.6	50.5	55.0	59.7	62.9	70.3	83.1	87.3	94.1	97.0

percentiles for males 70+

	1	2	5	10	20	30	40	50	60	70	80	90	95	98	99
BMI	18.4	19.5	21.0	22.1	22.7	24.5	25.0	25.5	26.0	26.6	27.2	28.9	31.2	35.4	36.8
WHR	0.86	0.86	0.88	0.90	0.91	0.93	0.94	0.96	0.98	1.00	1.00	1.02	1.03	1.05	1.06
Σ3SF	21.1	21.6	24.0	27.9	33.4	39.3	44.7	47.3	50.3	56.5	59.0	66.1	70.0	92.0	107.8

Table 3b Scores corresponding to various percentiles for BMI, WHR and the height-adjusted sum of three "central" skinfolds (subscapular, supraspinale, abdominal; Σ3SF) in Australian females.

percentiles for females 18-29

	1	2	5	10	20	30	40	50	60	70	80	90	95	98	99
BMI	17.4	17.6	19.3	20.0	20.6	21.2	21.8	22.2	22.8	23.4	24.5	27.1	30.3	32.2	33.8
WHR	0.65	0.68	0.68	0.70	0.71	0.72	0.74	0.75	0.76	0.77	0.80	0.83	0.86	0.88	0.96
Σ3SF	19.9	23.5	25.9	30.6	35.5	42.0	45.7	51.6	57.2	67.9	77.4	90.6	98.0	110.1	112.8

percentiles for females 30-39

	1	2	5	10	20	30	40	50	60	70	80	90	95	98	99
BMI	17.9	17.9	18.7	19.1	20.1	21.0	21.9	22.4	23.5	24.7	26.1	30.5	31.9	35.3	36.3
WHR	0.68	0.68	0.70	0.71	0.73	0.74	0.75	0.77	0.78	0.79	0.82	0.87	0.91	0.92	0.93
Σ3SF	17.5	20.5	23.6	26.7	34.2	40.5	46.8	52.4	59.4	66.7	82.9	99.1	109.2	113.7	115.4

percentiles for females 40-49

	1	2	5	10	20	30	40	50	60	70	80	90	95	98	399
BMI	17.9	18.3	19.4	20.3	21.3	22.5	23.3	24.2	25.1	26.7	28.5	31.1	34.6	38.6	39.8
WHR	0.67	0.69	0.71	0.72	0.74	0.75	0.77	0.78	0.81	0.83	0.86	0.88	0.91	0.92	0.95
Σ3SF	20.7	21.3	29.2	33.1	43.7	53.0	67.6	74.9	81.8	87.9	96.3	109.6	116.3	122.0	124.1

percentiles for females 50-59

	1	2	5	10	20	30	40	50	60	70	80	90	95	98	99
BMI	18.2	18.7	19.5	20.2	21.6	22.8	23.7	24.3	25.0	26.6	28.5	31.8	33.5	34.8	38.0
WHR	0.70	0.70	0.71	0.73	0.74	0.77	0.78	0.80	0.81	0.84	0.87	0.91	0.94	0.98	1.00
Σ3SF	21.2	24.1	27.8	36.5	51.0	60.3	73.3	77.7	83.5	92.4	104.9	115.4	118.7	121.2	125.3

percentiles for females 60-69

	1	2	5	10	20	30	40	50	60	70	80	90	95	98	99
BMI	17.4	18.8	19.8	21.1	22.3	23.2	24.4	25.0	25.9	27.4	28.7	30.5	32.9	35.3	37.1
WHR	0.69	0.70	0.72	0.75	0.77	0.81	0.82	0.84	0.86	0.89	0.91	0.95	0.99	1.01	1.05
Σ3SF	23.4	27.6	34.7	48.6	56.3	65.8	72.4	76.1	82.6	91.3	96.8	107.7	115.8	127.6	132.1

percentiles for females 70+

	1	2	5	10	20	30	40	50	60	70	80	90	95	98	99
BMI	19.4	19.7	20.9	21.9	22.6	23.9	25.4	26.4	28.2	29.0	29.6	31.2	31.6	33.8	34.5
WHR	0.76	0.76	0.77	0.79	0.84	0.85	0.86	0.89	0.91	0.92	0.94	0.96	0.98	0.99	0.99
Σ3SF	27.6	29.3	36.1	51.0	59.7	64.5	67.2	79.7	85.2	91.8	99.2	103.8	107.3	109.2	109.5

5 References

Alexander, H., & Dugdale, A. (1990).
Which waist-hip ratio?
The Medical Journal of Australia, 153, 367.

Ashley, F.W., & Kannel, W.B. (1974).
Relation of weight change to changes in atherogenic traits.
Journal of Chronic Disorders,7, 103-114.

Barnard, R.J., & Wen, S.J. (1994).
Exercise and diet in the prevention and control of the metabolic syndrome.
Sports Medicine, 18, 218-228.

Bergstrom, R.W., Leonetti, D.L., Newell-Morris, L.L., Shuman, W.P., Wahl, P.W., & Fujimoto, W.Y. (1990).
Association of plasma triglyceride and C-peptide with coronary heart disease in Japanese-American men with a high prevalence of glucose intolerance.
Diabetologia, 33, 489-496.

Bouchard, C. (1991).
Heredity and the path to overweight and obesity.
Medicine and Science in Sports and Exercise, 23, 285-291.

Bouchard, C. (1994).
Positive and negative effects of exercise: biological perspectives.
In **Proceedings of the International Conference of Science and Medicine in Sport, 5-8 October, 1994.**
Brisbane: Sports Medicine Australia.

Bray, G.A. (1992a).
Obesity increases risk for diabetes.
International Journal of Obesity, 16 (Suppl. 4), S13-S17.

Bray, G.A. (1992b).
Pathophysiology of obesity.
American Journal of Clinical Nutrition, 55, 488S-494S.

Busetto, L., Baggio, M.B., Zurlo, F., Carraro, R., Digito, M., & Enzi, G. (1992).
Assessment of abdominal fat distribution in obese patients: anthropometry versus computerized tomography.
International Journal of Obesity, 16, 731-736.

Buskirk, E.R. (1987).
Obesity.
In J.S. Skinner (Ed.) **Testing and exercise prescription for special cases: theoretical bases and clinical applications** (1st ed.). Philadelphia: Lea & Febiger.

Cater, J.E.L., & Heath, B.H. (1990).
Somatotyping – development and applications.
Cambridge: Cambridge University Press.

Department of the Arts, Sport, the Environment and Territories (1992).
Pilot survey of the fitness of Australians.
Canberra: Australian Government Publishing Service.

Després, J.-P., Pouliot, M.-C., Moorjani, S., Nadeau, A., Tremblay, A., Lupien, P.J., Thériault, G., & Bouchard, C. (1991). Loss of abdominal fat and metabolic response to exercise training in obese women. **American Journal of Physiology, 261**, E159-E167.

Diaz, E.O., Prentice, A.M., Goldberg, G.R., Murgatroyd, P.R., & Coward, W.A. (1992). Metabolic response to experimental overfeeding in lean and overweight healthy volunteers. **American Journal of Clinical Nutrition, 56**, 641-655.

Donahue, R.P., Orchard, T.J., Becker, D.J., Kuller, L.H., & Drash, A.L. (1987). Sex differences in the coronary heart diease risk profile: a possible role for insulin. **American Journal of Epidemiology, 125**, 650-657.

Drenick, E.J., Brickman, A.S., & Gold, E.M. (1972). Dissociation of the obesity-hyperinsulinism relationship following dietary restriction and hyperalimentation. **American Journal of Clinical Nutrition, 25**, 746-755.

Ducimetière, P., Richard, J., & Cambien, F. (1986). The pattern of subcutaneous fat distribution in middle-aged men and the risk of coronary heart disease: the Paris prospective study. **International Journal of Obesity, 10**, 229-240.

Ferland, M., Després, J.-P., Tremblay, A., Pinault, S., Nadeau, A., Moorjani, S., Lupien, P.J., Thériault, G., & Bouchard, C. (1989). Assessment of adipose tissue distribution by computed axial tomography in obese women: association with body density and anthropometric measurements. **British Journal of Nutrition, 61**, 139-148.

Garfinkel, L. (1985) Overweight and cancer. **Annals of Internal Medicine, 103(6.2)**,1034-1036.

Garn, S.M., Leonard, W.R., & Hawthorne, V.M. (1986). Three limitations of the body mass index. **American Journal of Clinical Nutrition, 44**, 996-997.

Garrow, J.S., & Webster, J. (1985). Quetelet's Index (W/H^2) as a measure of fatness. **International Journal of Obesity, 9**, 147-153.

Gerber, L.M., Madhaven, S., & Alderman, M.H. (1987). Waist-to-hip ratio as an index of risk for hyperglycemia among hypertensive patients. **American Journal of Preventive Medicine, 3**, 64-68.

Goldstein, D.J. (1992). Beneficial health effects of modest weight loss. **International Journal of Obesity, 16**, 397-415.

Haffner, S.M., Stern, M.P., Hazuda, H.P., Pugh, J., & Patterson, J.K. (1987). Do upper-body and centralised adiposity measure different aspects of regional body-fat distribution? Relationship to non-insulin-dependent diabetes mellitus, lipids, and lipoproteins. **Diabetes, 36**, 43-51.

Higgins, M., Kannel,W., Garrison, R., Pinsky, J., & Stokes, I. (1988).
Hazards of obesity – the Framingham experience.
Acta Medica Scandinavica (Suppl. 723), 23-36.

Hodgson, J.M., Wahlqvist, M.L., Balazs, N.D.H., & Boxall, J.A. (1994).
Coronary athero-sclerosis in relation to body fatness and its distribution.
International Journal of Obesity, 18, 41-46.

Hubinger L. (1994).
Lipoprotein [a] (LPa) levels and physical activity in middle-aged males.
Unpublished Doctoral Thesis, The University of Queensland.

Jakicic, J.M., Donnelly, J.E., Jaward, A.F., Jacobsen, D.J., Gunderson, S.C., & Pascale R. (1993).
Association between blood lipids and different measures of body fat distribution: effects of BMI and age.
International Journal of Obesity, 17, 131-137.

Karatsu, K., Nagao, N., Arie, J., Inomoto, T., Imai, Y., & Sawada, Y. (1987).
Classification of subcutaneous skinfold thickness in the middle-aged by cluster analysis, and the relationship between its distribution pattern and serum cholesterol.
Journal of Sports Medicine, 27, 453-460.

Kissebah, A.H., Vydelingum, N., Murray, R., Evans, D.J., Hartz, A.J., Kalkhoff, R.K., & Adams, P.W. (1982).
Relation of body fat distribution to metabolic complications of obesity.
Journal of Clinical Endocrinology and Metabolism, 54 (2), 254-260.

Krotkiewski, M., Björntorp, P., Sjöstrom, L., & Smith, U. (1983).
Impact of obesity on metabolism in men and women: importance of regional adipose tissue distribution.
Journal of Clinical Investigation, 72:, 1150-1162.

Lapidus, L., Bengtsson, C., Larsson, B., Pennert, K., Rybo, E., & Sjöstrom, L. (1984).
Distribution of adipose tissue and risk of cardiovascular disease and death: a 12 year follow up of participants in the population study of women in Gothenburg, Sweden.
British Medical Journal, 289, 1257-1260.

Larsson, B., Svärdsudd, K., Welin, L., Eriksson, H., Wilhelmsen, P., Björntorp, P., & Tibblin, G. (1984).
Abdominal adipose tissue distribution, obesity, and risk of cardiovascular disease and death: 13 year follow up of participants in the study of men born in 1913.
British Medical Journal, 288, 1401-1404.

Larsson, B. (1991).
Obesity, fat distribution and cardiovascular disease.
International Journal of Obesity, 15, 53-57.

Laws, A., Terry, R.B., & Barrett-Connor, E. (1990).
Behavioral covariates of waist-to-hip ratio in Rancho Bernardo.
American Journal of Public Health, 80, 1358-1362.

Leibel, R., Edens, N.K., & Freid, S.K. (1989).
Physiological basis for the control of body fat distribution in humans.
Annual Review of Nutrition, 9, 417-443.

Lissner, L., Odell, P.M., D'Agostino, R.B., Stokes, J., Kreger, B.E., Belanger, A.J., & Brownell, K. (1991).
   Variability of body weight and health outcomes in the Framingham population.
   The New England Journal of Medicine, 324, 1839-1844.

Martin, A.D., & Drinkwater, D.T. (1991).
   Variability in the measures of fat: assumptions or technique?
   Sports Medicine, 11, 277-288.

Miller, W. C. (1991).
   Diet composition, energy intake, and nutritional status in relation to obesity in men and women.
   Medicine and Science in Sports and Exercise, 23, 280-284.

Ohlson, L.O., Larsson, B., Svärdsudd, K., Welin, L., Eriksson, H., Wilhelmsen, P., Björntorp, P., & Tibblin G. (1985).
   The influence of body fat distribution on the incidence of diabetes mellitus: 13.5 years follow-up of the participants in
   the study of men born in 1913.
   Diabetes, 34, 1055- 1058.

Schell, J., & Leelarthaepin, B. (1994).
   Physical fitness assessment in exercise and sport science.
   Matraville, NSW: Leelar Biomediscience.

Schmidt, M.I., Duncan, B.B., Canani, L.H., Karohl, C., Chambless, L. (1992).
   Association of waist-hip ratio with diabetes mellitus.
   Diabetes Care, 15(7), 912-914.

Sedgwick, A..W., & Haby, M. (1991).
   Effects of exercise on female body shape.
   The Australian Journal of Science and Medicine in Sport, 23(3), 75-80.

Seidell, J.C. (1992).
   Regional obesity and health.
   International Journal of Obesity, 16 (Suppl. 2), S31-S34.

Seidell, J.C., Cigolini, M., Charzwska, J., Ellsinger, B.-M., Deslypere, J.P., & Cruz, A. (1992).
   Fat distribution in European men: a comparison of anthropometric measurements in relation to cardiovascular
   risk factors.
   International Journal of Obesity, 16, 17-22.

Sjöstrom, L.V. (1992a).
   Morbidity of severely obese subjects.
   American Journal of Clinical Nutrition, 55, 508S-515S.

Sjöstrom, L.V. (1992b).
   Mortality of severely obese subjects.
   American Journal of Clinical Nutrition, 55, 516S-523S.

Society of Actuaries and Association of Life Insurance Medical Directors of America (1979).
   Build study.
   Chicago.

Terry, R.B., Stefanick, M.L., Haskell, W.L., & Wood, P.D. (1991).
Contributions of regional adipose tissue depots to plasma lipoprotein concentrations in overweight men and women: possible protective effects of thigh fat.
Metabolism, 40, 733-740.

Valdez, R., Seidell, J.C., Ahn, Y.I., & Weiss, K.M. (1993).
A new index of abdominal adiposity as an indicator of risk for cardiovascular disease: a cross-population study.
International Journal of Obesity, 17, 77-82.

Waaler, H.T. (1983).
Height, weight and mortality: the Norwegian experience.
Acta Medica Scandinavica (Suppl. 3), 679.

Wing, R.R., Jeffery, R.W., Burton, L.R., Thorson, C., Kuller, L.H., & Folsom, A.R. (1992).
Change in waist-hip ratio with weight loss and its association with change in cardiovascular risk factors.
American Journal of Clinical Nutrition, 55, 1086-1092.

Zamboni M., Armellini, F., Milani, M.P., De Marchi, M., Todesco, T., Robbi, R., Bergamo-Andreis, I.A., & Bosello, O. (1992).
Body fat distribution in pre- and post-menopausal women: metabolic and anthropometric variables and their inter-relationships.
International Journal of Obesity, 16, 495-504.

accreditation in anthropometry

Chapter 13
Accreditation in Anthropometry: an Australian Model

Christopher Gore, Kevin Norton, Tim Olds, Nancy Whittingham, Kim Birchall, Melissa Clough, Briony Dickerson and Loretta Downie

1 Introduction

In 1993, the Australian Sports Commission's (ASC) Laboratory Standards Assistance Scheme (LSAS) focused on improving the quality of anthropometry conducted at the state sports institutes and sports academies that routinely assess élite athletes. The LSAS began working with members of the International Society for the Advancement of Kinanthropometry (ISAK) to develop training courses and an accreditation scheme for anthropometry. At the same time a number of Australian universities were teaching anthropometry to their students and were also conducting training courses for health and fitness professionals. Although many teachers were using the guidelines for anthropometry proposed by ISAK, there was still considerable variability in anthropometric techniques being practised throughout Australia. With this background as a starting point, attempts were made for a consensus on anthropometry within Australia. ISAK has now been accepted by several Australian professional groups as the governing body for matters related to the practice and theory of anthropometry.

While the initial courses (1993-1994) were aimed at practising sport scientists they were subsequently generalised to include academics working in universities, university students across a number of areas including sports science, nutrition, nursing, psychology and ergonomics, and health and fitness professionals. The development of the national courses and accreditation system described in this chapter is one of the first attempts to standardise anthropometry on a nation-wide basis across a broad spectrum of disciplines. A feature of this national standardisation is the estbalishment of a centralised anthropometric database, the Australian Anthropometric DataBase (AADBase), which will collate measurements taken by accredited anthropometrists across Australia. It is hoped that similar accreditation systems will be adopted in other countries so that uniformity in anthropometric techniques and training will become commonplace. This would allow data taken in many different countries to be cumulated in a global anthropometric database, perhaps under the direction of ISAK. In this regard, the Australian courses may provide a model for other countries to use.

The concept of a four level hierarchy was based on the Australian Coaching Council courses for training coaches. The first three levels of anthropometry are awarded on the basis of formal theoretical and practical training. This may be followed by a Level 4 ("criterion" anthropometrist) which is awarded by ISAK, which has determined its own requirements for this level of accreditation.

One of the key elements of the Australian accreditation scheme is that all levels have to submit technical error of measurement (TEM) data on 20 subjects to indicate satisfactory precision of measures. This is an objective method of maintaining quality control of all persons who are accredited. Furthermore, only Levels 3 and 4 are accredited to conduct anthropometry training courses where certificates will be issued by the LSAS.

A direct outcome of the first training courses in 1993-1994 was the development of curriculum guidelines to standardise courses throughout Australia. The following pages outline the core requirements for Level 1, 2 and 3 courses and give some examples of ways in which the materials might be presented.

2   Accreditation guidelines

In general terms, the four accreditation levels of anthropometry are:
- Level 1 (Technician – Restricted Profile): a person who can demonstrate adequate technical precision in measuring stretch stature, mass, the nine skinfolds, five girths and two breadths of the "Restricted" anthropometric dimensions.
- Level 2 (Technician – Full Profile): a person who can demonstrate adequate technical precision in all of the 40 anthropometric dimensions.
- Level 3 (Instructor): in addition to technical competence, a Level 3 person has adequate theoretical knowledge about anthropometry to be able to instruct and accredit Level 1 and 2 anthropometrists.
- Level 4 (Criterion Anthropometrist): a criterion anthropometrist has many years of experience in taking measurements, a high level of theoretical knowledge, has been involved in several large anthropometric projects and has a publication record in anthropometry.

2.1   Level 1 Anthropometrist (Technician – Restricted Profile)

This person will be instructed for assessment of a Restricted anthropometric profile. In addition to stretch stature and body mass, the Restricted Profile consists of the following sites:

Skinfolds	Girths	Bone breadths
1 triceps	1 arm (relaxed)	1 humerus
2 subscapular	2 arm (flexed and tensed)	2 femur
3 biceps	3 waist (minimum)	
4 iliac crest	4 gluteal (hips)	
5 supraspinale	5 calf (maximum)	
6 abdominal		
7 front thigh		
8 medial calf		
9 mid-axilla		

Pre-requisites (minimum):

* Registration with the Australian Fitness Accreditation Council (AFAC) or equivalent state authority, or other qualifications that may be deemed appropriate by the ASC Laboratory Standards Coordinator in association with ISAK-recognised Criterion Anthropometrists in Australia.

Certification will be issued after:

* Successful completion of an anthropometry course (at Level 1) containing theory and practical components in accordance with those shown in the course outline (see Table 1).
* Successful demonstration of the stretch stature procedure, landmarking and equipment manipulation (skinfold calipers, girth tape and small sliding calipers) in front of a Level 3 or Level 4 anthropometrist. Landmarks for *acromiale, radiale, mid-acromiale-radiale, xiphoidale, iliospinale, iliocristale*; marked skinfold sites for *triceps, subscapular, biceps, iliac crest, supraspinale, abdominal, front thigh, medial calf* and *mid-axilla*.
* Successful completion of at least two Restricted Profiles in the presence of a Level 3 (Instructor) of Level 4 (Criterion) anthropometrist, and successful completion of repeated tests on 20 subjects. Inter- and intra-tester TEMs must be within the prescribed limits (see Table 9 below).

Table 1 Curriculum structure for the Australian accreditation scheme.

	Level 1	Level 2	Level 3
Prerequisites	AFAC or equivalent registration.	Level 1 or Bachelor's student.	Level 2 plus University degree, 2 yrs and ≥100 profiles.

Practical	Time	6 hrs theory 10 hrs practical ~20 hrs own time (20 repeated Restricted Profiles)	10 hrs theory 14 hrs practical ~20 hrs own time (20 repeated Full Profiles)	18 hrs theory 22 hrs practical ~20 hrs own time (20 repeated Full Profiles)
	Landmarking Equipment handling	Restricted Profile Skinfold calipers, measuring tape, small sliding calipers, stadiometer.	Full Profile Revision of Level 1 plus segmometer, large calipers and wide-spreading calipers.	Full Profile Revision of Level 2.
	Measurement	Restricted Profile, repeated measures in correct order.	Full Profile, repeated measures in correct order.	As for Level 2.
	TEMs	Use data to calculate intra-and inter-tester %TEMs.	Use data to calculate TEMs, ICCs and TEMs for >2 measures.	As for Level 2.
	Application within course	Repeated measures on minimum of 10 subjects (Restricted Profile).	Repeated measures on minimum of 10 subjects (Full Profile).	Simulated large-scale survey. Teaching skills. Repeated measures on minimum of 10 subjects.
	Exam	Practical exam. %TEMs within prescribed limits (see Table 9).	Practical exam. %TEMs within prescribed limits (see Table 9).	Theory and practical exam. %TEMs within prescribed limits (see Table 9).
Theory	Anatomy Body composition	Restricted Profile. Predicting total body fat from skinfolds. Assumptions and errors.	Full Profile. As for Level 1 plus quantitative assessment of errors.	Full Profile. As for Level 2.
	Health	Mass, BMI, WHR, fat distribution.	As for Level 1 plus changes with diet and exercise.	As for Level 2 plus physiological mechanisms/genetics.
	Scaling	General notion. Geometric similarity.	Level 1 plus fractionation and reference humans (e.g. the Phantom).	Level 2 plus other similarity systems, scaling functional variables, growth.

	Somatotype	General notion. The somatochart.	As for Level 1 plus calculation using rating form, equations and computer. Frequency distributions of somatotypes.	As for Level 2, plus photoscopic method, history, changes in somatotype with growth, age, exercise and diet.
	Calibration	Vernier calibration of skinfold caliper jaw gap. Foam block calibration of jaw pressure. Caliper maintenance.	As for Level 1 plus use of rods and spacers. Effect of calibration errors on estimated % BF.	As for Level 2, plus upscale vs downscale, static vs dynamic calibration.
	Computer labs	Use of specific anthropometric software (e.g. LifeSize).	As for Level 1.	As for Level 1.
	TEMs	Intra- vs inter-tester %TEMs (2 measures only). Use of TEMs to interpret real changes, determine confidence intervals and reduce error.	As for Level 1 plus 3 measures per subject and ICC.	As for Level 2 plus establishing TEMs for large surveys.
	Anthropometry and sports performance	Notion of morphological optimisation. Body fat, height, mass and performance.	As for Level 1 plus proportionality. Evolution of body size in athletes.	As for Level 2, plus physiological and biomechanical aspects of anthropometry.
Other theory areas (optional)	Body image		Introduction to body image.	As for Level 2, plus recent research into body image.
	Ergonomics		Workspace design, application of anthropometry in ergonomics.	As for Level 2 plus body envelopes.
	Multi-compartment models			Models using ≥2 compartments. Recent high-tech methods.

2.2 Level 2 Anthropometrist (Technician – Full Profile)

This person will be instructed for assessment of a full anthropometric profile. In addition to stretch stature and body mass, the full profile consists of the following sites (9 skinfolds, 13 girths, 16 bone breadths/segment lengths):

Skinfolds
1 triceps
2 subscapular
3 biceps
4 iliac crest
5 supraspinale
6 abdominal
7 front thigh
8 medial calf
9 mid-axilla

Girths
1 head
2 neck
3 arm (relaxed)
4 arm (flexed and tensed)
5 forearm (maximum)
6 wrist (distal styloids)
7 chest (mesosternale)
8 waist (minimum)
9 gluteal (hips)
10 thigh (1 cm below gluteal)
11 thigh (mid–trochanterion tibiale laterale)
12 calf (maximum)
13 ankle (minimum)

Lengths
1 acromiale–radiale
2 radiale–stylion
3 midstylion–dactylion
4 iliospinale–box height
5 trochanterion–box height
6 trochanterion–tibiale laterale
7 tibiale laterale
8 tibiale mediale–sphyrion tibiale

Breadths / Lengths
1 biacromial
2 biiliocristal
3 foot length
4 sitting height
5 transverse chest
6 AP chest
7 humerus
8 femur

Pre-requisites (minimum):
- Successful completion of a Level 1 course or currently completing a university bachelor's degree or other qualifications that may be deemed appropriate by the ASC Laboratory Standards Coordinator in association with ISAK-recognised Criterion Anthropometrists in Australia.

Certification will be issued after:
- Successful completion of an anthropometry course (at Level 2) containing theory and practical components in accordance with those suggested in the course outline (see Table 1).

- Successful demonstration of the stretch stature procedure, landmarking and equipment manipulation (skinfold calipers, girth tape, small sliding calipers, segmometer, large sliding caliper and widespreading caliper) in front of a Level 3 or Level 4 anthropometrist. Selected landmarks from *acromiale, radiale, mid-acromiale-radiale, stylion, mid-stylion, dactylion, mesosternale, xiphoidale, iliospinale, trochanterion, iliocristale, tibiale laterale, tibiale mediale, sphyrion;* marked skinfold sites for *triceps, subscapular, biceps, iliac crest, supraspinale, abdominal, front thigh, medial calf* and *mid-axilla.*
- Successful completion of two full profiles in the presence of a Level 3 (Instructor) of Level 4 (Criterion) anthropometrist, and successful completion of repeated tests on 20 subjects. Inter- and intra-tester TEMs must be within the prescribed limits (see Table 9 below).

2.3 Level 3 Anthropometrist (Instructor)

This person will be instructed for assessment of a full anthropometric profile (stretch stature, body mass, 9 skinfolds, 13 girths, 16 bone breadths/segment lengths) consisting of the sites listed for Level 2. The Level 3 candidate will also be certified to teach Level 1 and 2 courses using guidelines and materials issued by the ASC Laboratory Standards Coordinator.

Pre-requisites (minimum):
- Bachelor's degree in a relevant area (e.g. human movement, anatomy, physical education, nutrition, physiotherapy), and
- Completion of a Level 2 course or equivalent course, and
- Significant experience (>2 years) in anthropometry (e.g. at least 100 Full Profiles) or other qualifications that may be deemed appropriate by the ASC Laboratory Standards Coordinator in association with ISAK-recognised criterion anthropometrists in Australia.

Certification will be issued after:
- Successful completion of an anthropometry course (at Level 3) containing theory and practical components in accordance with those suggested in the course outline (see Table 1).
- Successful completion of both theory and practical examinations, including;
- Successful demonstration of the stretch stature procedure, landmarking and equipment manipulation (skinfold calipers, girth tape, small sliding calipers, segmometer, large sliding caliper and widespreading caliper) in front of a Level 3

or Level 4 anthropometrist. Selected landmarks from *acromiale, radiale, mid-acromiale-radiale, stylion, mid-stylion, dactylion, mesosternale, xiphoidale, iliospinale, trochanterion, iliocristale, tibiale laterale, tibiale mediale, sphyrion*; marked skinfold sites for *triceps, subscapular, biceps, iliac crest, supraspinale, abdominal, front thigh, medial calf* and *mid-axilla*.

- Successful completion of two full profiles in the presence of a Level 4 (Criterion) anthropometrist, and successful completion of repeated tests on 20 subjects. Inter- and intra-tester TEMs must be within the prescribed limits (Table 9).

2.4   Level 4 Anthropometrist (Criterion)

A criterion anthropometrist has many years of experience in taking measurements, a high level of theoretical knowledge, has been involved in several large anthropometric projects and has a publication record in anthropometry.

Level 4 can only be acquired by making a submission directly to ISAK at the following address: Dr Alan Martin,

President,
International Society for the Advancement of Kinanthropometry,
School of Physical Education,
University of British Columbia,
6081 University Blvd, Vancouver, BC, Canada V6T 1Z1.
email: Alan_martin@mtsg.ubc.ca)

3   Target TEMs: requirements and rationale

TEMs represent the quality control dimension of the accreditation scheme. At each level, anthropometrists are required to demonstrate intra-tester and inter-tester TEMs within prescribed limits. Inter-tester TEMs are determined by comparing measurements made by the student with measurements made by a Level 3 or Level 4 Anthropometrist (for Levels 1 and 2) or by a Level 4 Anthropometrist (for Level 3) on a number of subjects. The student and the Criterion/Instructor anthropometrist should use the same equipment and measure the subject on the same day. Intra-tester TEMs are determined by the student making repeated measurements on a number of individuals.

A number of studies have been conducted in an attempt to quantify the inter- and intra-tester technical error involved in taking anthropometric measurements (e.g. Johnston, Hamill & Lemeshow, 1972; Keys & Brozek, 1953; Lohman, 1981; Sloan & Shapiro, 1972; Wilmore & Behnke, 1969; Womersley & Durnin, 1973). While recognising the implications of testers having large technical errors, many authors fail to provide recommendations for target TEMs, and when they do, a clear rationale supported by empirical evidence is often lacking. Ross and Marfell-Jones (1991) suggest a 5% intra-tester tolerance limit for skinfolds and 1–2 mm (or 1–3%) for girths. An accreditation system was developed in 1984 by the Canadian Association of Sport Sciences, in conjunction with Sport Canada, for laboratories associated with physiological testing of élite athletes (Quinney, Petersen, Gledhill & Jamnik, 1984). This scheme recommended the following tolerances:

- standing height and mass: 0.5%
- biacromial breadth: 1.0%
- biepicondylar femur breadth: 3.5%
- sum of eight skinfolds: 10%

It is clear that technical error limits should be set so as to maximise precision and reliability. In theory, the smaller the TEMs the better. However, there are constraints on the size of target TEMs:

- TEMs should ideally be commensurate with the magnitude of the physiological differences they aim to measure.
- We should be aware of how the size of TEMs will affect variables derived from raw anthropometric measures (such as somatotype, fractionated masses and estimated percentage body fat).
- TEMs must be achievable by the majority of trainee testers, given their level of skill and experience.

3.1   How small must TEMs be to detect real changes?

Ideally, TEMs should be small enough to be sensitive to the changes they will be used to detect. Often, changes in anthropometric variables following exercise and/or dietary interventions are quite small. Using weighted measures of central tendency, we have reviewed 55 studies which have used aerobic exercise as an intervention, where skinfolds and other anthropometric measurements were taken before, during and after training programmes. These training programmes were fairly typical of those undertaken by young recreational exercisers (see Tables 2 and 3).

Table 2 Mean values of characteristics of subjects involved in aerobic training programmes where changes in skinfolds were measured, programme characteristics, median absolute percentage changes in the sum of skinfolds ($|\Sigma SF\%|$) and intra-tester %TEMs required to detect these changes.

	males	females
n	1503	335
age	38.9	28.2
mass (kg)	78.7	65.0
% body fat	18.4	29.2
weeks	20.9	12.2
minutes/session	34.1	35.4
sessions/week	2.4	5.4
median $|\Delta\Sigma SF\ (\%)|$	10.9	5.7
%TEM required for 68% confidence	7.7	4.0
%TEM required for 95% confidence	3.9	2.0

Table 3 Mean values of characteristics of subjects involved in aerobic training programmes where changes in girths were measured, programme characteristics, median absolute percentage changes in the sum of girths ($|\Sigma G\%|$) and intra–tester %TEMs required to detect these changes.

	males	females
n	1007	288
age	24.3	28.3
mass (kg)	79.7	66.0
% body fat	21.4	30.3
weeks	19.1	12.3
minutes/session	32.0	30.7
sessions/week	2.2	5.4
median $|\Delta\Sigma G\ (\%)|$	1.7	1.5
%TEM required for 68% confidence	1.2	1.1
%TEM required for 95% confidence	0.6	0.5

The median absolute change in the sum of skinfolds (ΣSF) expressed as a percentage of the original values was 10.9% for males (n = 1503) and 5.7% for females (n = 335). To detect these changes in any one individual with 68% confidence would require intra-tester TEMs of 7.7% for male subjects and 4.0% for female subjects. For 95% confidence, the required TEMs would be 3.9% for males and 2.0% for females. These figures suggest that such changes may not be able to be detected with confidence by some anthropometrists on an individual basis unless multiple measures are taken to reduce error. The median absolute change in the sum of girths in these studies, expressed as a percentage of initial values, was 1.7% for males (n = 1007) and 1.5% for females (n = 288). To detect these changes in any one individual with 68% confidence would require intra-tester TEMs of 1.2% for male subjects and 1.1% for female subjects. For 95% confidence, the required TEMs would be 0.6% for males and 0.5% for females.

We have also reviewed 25 studies of resistance training programmes where anthropometric measures were made throughout the programmes. Details of the training programmes are shown in Tables 4 and 5.

Table 4 Mean values of characteristics of subjects involved in resistance training programmes where changes in skinfolds were measured, programme characteristics, median absolute percentage changes in the sum of skinfolds ($|\Sigma SF\%|$) and intra-tester %TEMs required to detect these changes.

	males	females
n	80	122
age	26.9	24.5
mass (kg)	78.9	59.9
% body fat	16.5	26.5
weeks	11.0	12.3
minutes/session	38.3	36.9
sessions/week	2.7	2.6
median $|\Delta\Sigma SF\ (\%)|$	9.3	9.3
%TEM required for 68% confidence	6.6	6.6
%TEM required for 95% confidence	3.3	3.3

Table 5 Mean values of characteristics of subjects involved in resistance training programmes where changes in girths were measured, programme characteristics, median absolute percentage changes in the sum of girths ($|\Sigma G\%|$) and intra-tester %TEMs required to detect these changes.

	males	females
n	190	61
age	23.7	20.6
mass (kg)	83.6	60.7
% body fat	14.6	24.5
weeks	6.5	11.7
minutes/session	37.5	44.5
sessions/week	3.0	2.2
median $|\Delta\Sigma G\ (\%)|$	2.0	0.4
%TEM required for 68% confidence	1.4	0.3
%TEM required for 95% confidence	0.7	0.1

The median absolute change in the sum of skinfolds, expressed as a percentage of initial values, was 9.3% for both males (n = 80) and females (n = 122). To detect these changes in any one individual with 68% confidence would require an intra-tester TEM of 6.6%. For 95% confidence, the required TEM would be 3.3%. In these studies, the median absolute change in the sum of girths, expressed as a percentage of initial values, was 2.0% for males (n = 190) and 0.4% for females (n = 61). To detect these changes in any one individual with 68% confidence would require intra-tester TEMs of 1.4% for male subjects and 0.3% for female subjects. For 95% confidence, the required TEMs would be 0.7% for males and 0.1% for females.

In élite athletes, anthropometric measures often follow a cyclical pattern based on seasonal training patterns. Very few data are available on intra-season variability in surface anthropometric measures in athletes. Table 6 shows data on the sum of six skinfolds for an Olympic gold medal winning cyclist who was measured 12 times over a seven month period (N. Craig, personal communication). The overall variability of skinfold thicknesses is quite large (CV = 20.7%). The table shows the TEMs that would be required to detect, with 95% confidence, the change from baseline (16 Nov 1987) to each of the measurement occasions (3rd column), and from each measurement occasion to the next (4th column).

Table 6 Sum of six skinfolds (triceps, subscapular, biceps, iliac crest, front thigh, medial calf) in an Olympic gold medal winning cyclist over a six-month period, and the intra-tester %TEMs required to be 95% sure of a real change (a) from the baseline measurement on 16 Nov 87 and (b) from the previous measurement.

date	Σskinfolds	required TEM (a) baseline	(b) previous
16 Nov 87	54.8		
25 Nov 87	48.5	4.3	4.3
2 Dec 87	45.8	6.4	2.1
9 Dec 87	44.0	7.9	1.4
13 Jan 88	38.7	12.3	4.5
27 Jan 88	32.9	17.5	5.7
2 Feb 88	34.7	16.6	1.9
17 Feb 88	32.7	18.8	2.1
2 Mar 88	30.6	21.2	2.3
16 Mar 88	30.3	22.1	0.4
18 May 88	34.7	18.2	4.8
2 Jun 88	33.7	19.4	1.1

Skinfold measurements spaced approximately 2 weeks apart for this individual would require a very high level of skill to be 95% sure of a real change. The alternatives available to the anthropometrist with a lower skill level are to use multiple measures, or to space measurements further apart.

3.2   Implications of the magnitude of TEMs for derived variables

Raw anthropometric data are often used to estimate derived variables, such as body density, percentage body fat, somatotypes and fractionated masses. In some of these derived variables, there is only one input variable for which a TEM has been determined. For example, body density is calculated using the Durnin and Womersley (1974) equation using a sum of skinfolds as the only input variable. In situations such as these, it is easy to calculate the effect of the magnitude of the TEM on the derived variable (in this case, body density and hence percentage body fat). For example, using average skinfold data from the DASET (1992) survey, a 20–29 year old Australian female has a four-site skinfold total of 61.4 mm. This equates to a predicted percentage body fat of 31.1% using the Durnin and Womersley (1974) equation. The 95% confidence limits for this predicted percentage body fat for a tester with a 5% TEM would be 29.1% to 33.2%. For a tester with a 10% TEM, the confidence interval would be 26.5% to 34.9% – limits which are perhaps narrower than might be expected.

When the derived variable uses input variables for which TEMs must be determined separately (for example, the calculation of a mesomorphy index requires both girths and skinfolds), it is much more problematical modelling the effect of the magnitude of TEMs on the magnitude of the derived variable. This is because the magnitudes of TEMs and the signs of measurement differences are probably not independent. Testers may consistently err in one direction, or, when a tester shows a large measurement error in one area, they might also systematically show a large error in another area.

3.3 Proposed target TEMs

These considerations and experience from a number of training courses allow us to make some tentative suggestions regarding target TEMs for different levels. The proposed limits are shown in Table 7. While it is clear that anthropometrists with TEMs of this magnitude would not, in many cases, be able to detect with confidence changes in an individual following typical recreational programmes, or in competitive athletes on whom repeated measures are performed within short time-intervals, it is probably unrealistic to set more stringent TEM standards. In these cases, alternative strategies of multiple measurements and/or longer periods between tests should be employed.

Some latitude in the application of these target TEMs should be allowed for non-skinfold sites, particularly for bony breadths and for sites which are affected by respiratory movements (see Ross, Kerr, Carter, Ackland & Bach, 1994, Table B.1).

Table 7 Proposed target inter- and intra-tester TEMs for the three accreditation levels (a) following the training course and (b) following performance of 20 repeated profiles. Note that the target TEMs are the same for Levels 2 and 3.

		Level 1		Level 2		Level 3	
		a post-course	b post-profiling	a post-course	b post-profiling	a post-course	b post-profiling
Inter-tester	skinfolds	12.5	10.0	10.0	7.5	10.0	7.5
	other	2.5	2.0	2.0	1.5	2.0	1.5
Intra-tester	skinfolds	10.0	7.5	7.5	5.0	7.5	5.0
	other	2.0	1.5	1.5	1.0	1.5	1.0

4   Guidelines for determining TEMs

TEMs will vary according to the nature of sites measured, the target population, and equipment and testing conditions. It is important, therefore, to standardise the determination of TEMs.

4.1   The specificity of the test population

TEMs are usually expressed as percentages of mean values because one would expect larger absolute errors in larger subjects. However, this may not entirely create a "level playing field" across subjects of different skinfold thicknesses, perhaps because fatter subjects pose additional problems of site location, variable compressibility, etc. When determining TEMs, therefore, testers should use subjects with skinfold thicknesses similar to those they will be testing.

It seems likely that TEMs will vary with other subject characteristics (e.g. gender). The general rule, therefore, is that TEMs should be determined on subjects as similar to the target population as possible. For those involved in athlete testing, this will probably entail sport-specific TEMs to be established. Those involved in testing a wide range of subjects (such as in fitness centres) should determine their TEMs on widely variable populations.

4.2 Procedural aspects

Various procedural aspects of determining TEMs can affect the magnitude of the TEM. These include the time between repeated measures and whether landmarks are erased and relocated between measurements. Often, the intra-tester TEMs are calculated without remarking the subject (e.g. during an examination situation). This would be expected to reduce the TEM, so that the values reported here may represent lower TEMs than would be encountered in situations where measurements were taken a day apart.

When measurements are made on different occasions on the same person, a degree of biological variation comes into play. Smaller skinfolds will be recorded if one is well-hydrated one day, as opposed to being dehydrated another day. This is because dehydration increases the turgidity or tension in the skin, making it tauter, and likely to "pull apart" the caliper faces (Consolazio, Johnson & Pecora, 1963, p. 303). Height is usually about 1–2 cm less in the afternoon than in the morning, as the intervertebral discs become compressed during the course of the day. Saunas, showers, weight-bearing exercise and menstrual phase can also affect anthropometric measurements. It is important therefore when establishing TEMs to replicate environmental conditions so as to minimise sources of biological variability.

5 References

Consolazio, C.F., Johnson, R.E., & Pecora, L.J. (1963).
Physiological measurements of metabolic function in man.
London: McGraw-Hill.

Department of the Arts, Sport, the Environment and Territories (1992).
Pilot survey of the fitness of Australians.
Canberra: Australian Government Publishing Service.

Durnin, J.V.G.A., & Womerseley, J. (1974).
Body fat assessed from total body density and its estimation from skinfold thickness: measurements on 481 men and women aged 16 to 72 years.
Brtitish Journal of Nutrition, **32**, 77-97.

Johnston, F.E., Hamill, P.V.V., & Lemeshow, J. (1972).
Skinfold thickness of children 6-11 years. (United States National Health Survey, Series 11, Number 120, 1-60).
Washington, DC: U.S. Department of Health, Education and Welfare.

Keys, A., & Brozek, J. (1953).
Body fat in adult man.
Physiological Reviews, 33, 245-325.

Lohman, T.G. (1981).
  Skinfolds and body density and their relation to body fatness: a review.
  Human Biology, 53, 181-225.

Quinney, H.A, Petersen, S.R., Gledhill, N., & Jamnik, V. (1984).
  Accreditation of élite athlete testing laboratories in Canada.
  In: T. Reilly, J. Watkins, & J. Borms (Eds.), **Kinanthropometry III** (pp. 233-238). London: E. & F.N. Spon.

Ross, W.D., Kerr, D.A., Carter, J.E.L., Ackland, T.R., & Bach, T.M. (1994).
  Appendix B: Anthropometric techniques: precision and accuracy.
  In J.E.L. Carter & T.R. Ackland (Eds.), **Kinanthropometry in aquatic sports** (pp. 158-169). Champaign, Illinois:
  Human Kinetics.

Ross, W.D., & Marfell-Jones, M.T. (1991).
  Kinanthropometry.
  In: J.D. Macdougall, H.A. Wenger, & H.J. Green (Eds.), **Physiological testing of the high performance athlete**
  (2nd ed., pp. 223-308). Champaign, Illinois: Human Kinetics.

Sloan, A.W., & Shapiro, H. (1972).
  A comparison of skinfold measurements with three standard calipers.
  Human Biology, 44, 29-36.

Wilmore, J.H., & Behnke, A.R. (1969).
  An anthropometric estimation of body density and lean body weight in young men.
  Journal of Applied Physiology, 27, 25-31.

Womersley, J., & Durnin, J.V.G.A. (1973).
  An experimental study on variability of measurement of skinfold thickness on young adults.
  Human Biology, 45, 281-292.

411

Index

415

417

Index